HAROLD EDGERTON

# HAROLD EDGERTON

# SEEING THE UNSEEN

Edited by

Ron Kurtz
Deborah G. Douglas
Gus Kayafas

With essays by

Deborah G. Douglas, Gus Kayafas,
J. Kim Vandiver, Gary Van Zante

Steidl

Published in collaboration with the MIT Museum

# CONTENTS

**Introduction**  7
*Ron Kurtz*

**Biography**  11
*Deborah G. Douglas*

**Personal Memories of Studying and Working with Edgerton**

"Doc" as Teacher  17
*J. Kim Vandiver*

"Doc" in the Darkroom  21
*Gus Kayafas*

**Historical Essays**

Harold Edgerton's Milk Splashes in the History of Photography  25
*Gary Van Zante*

Speed, Efficiency, and the Sublime  35
*Deborah G. Douglas*

**Plates**  43

**Pages from Edgerton's Notebooks**  171

**Notebook Captions**  204
**Recommended Reading**  205
**Acknowledgements**  207

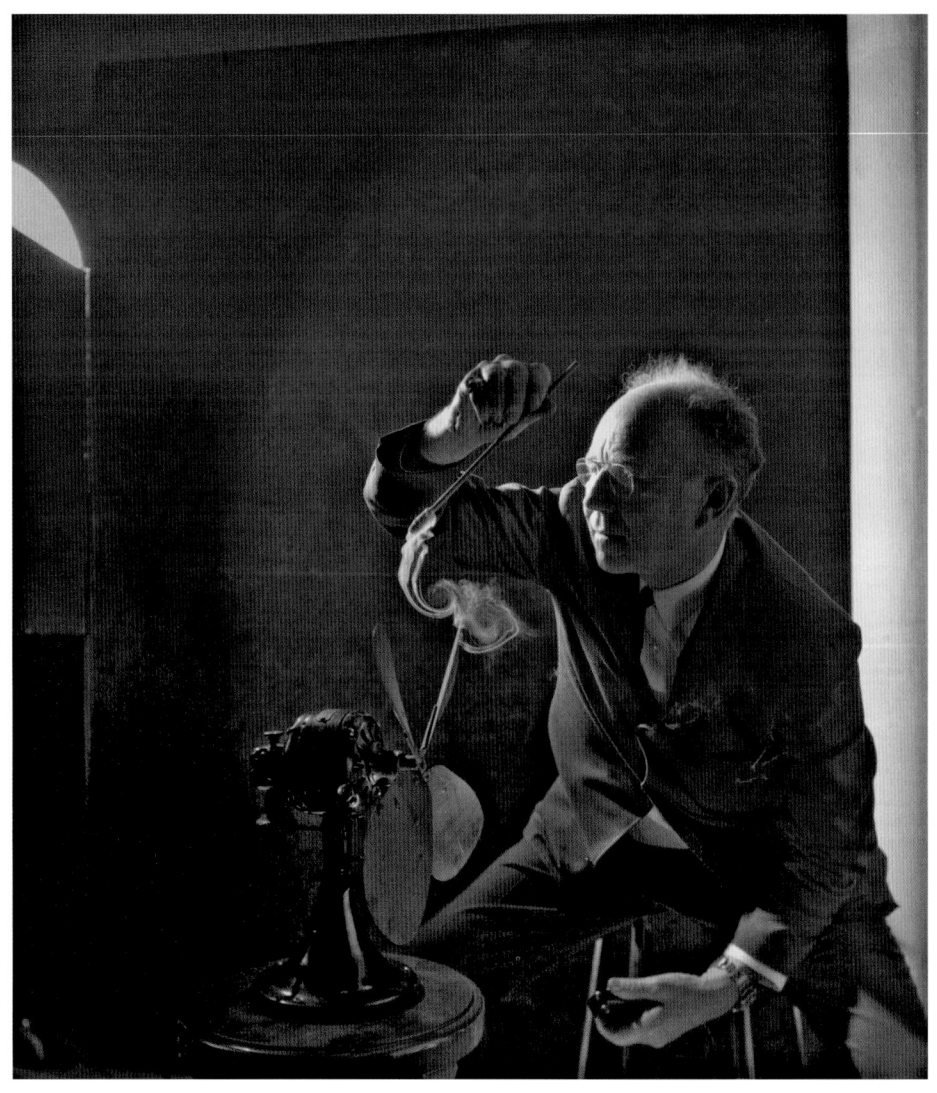

Harold E. Edgerton, photographed by Arnold Newman, 1958.
© Arnold Newman Properties/Getty Images

# INTRODUCTION

*Ron Kurtz*

This book is very personal. There is no fine line between my love of science and photography. My fascination with the physics and chemistry of photography would lead me first to MIT and then to a career in technology, and a lifelong involvement in photography. I made my first trip to the Massachusetts Institute of Technology (MIT) with my father who was working on materials that the famous professor Harold Edgerton wanted to use in his strobe lights. I could not believe my good fortune in meeting this remarkable man who I knew only from his photographs in magazines and books. My admiration for Edgerton and his work has never diminished. This book is about the work of a giant in the history of photography, but it is also a tribute to MIT, the place where Edgerton spent his entire adult life and which has deeply enriched my own.

Recently, *Time* magazine declared Edgerton's color "Milk Drop Coronet" to be one of the 100 most influential photographs of all time. The editors of the volume accompanying *Time's* "100 Photographs" project noted in a caption: "The picture proved that photography could advance human understanding of the physical world, and the technology Edgerton used to take it laid the foundation for the modern electronic flash."[1]

The magazine's accolades are hardly the first for Edgerton. As the memoirs and essays in the volume attest, Harold Edgerton enjoyed exceptional acclaim throughout his career. From the very beginning, his photographs astonished people. Curators immediately sought to collect and exhibit them. (No museum today would be considered to have a serious photography collection without a reasonable representation of Edgerton images.) They appeared in both popular and scholarly publications. Edgerton won countless awards from an Oscar to the National Medal of Technology and Innovation.

For all the acclaim, it has been more than 30 years since the last serious book of Edgerton photographs was published. It is time to reintroduce these path-breaking images. This beautiful volume includes more than 100 of Edgerton's most breathtaking photographs. Whether this is the first time you have seen these images or they are among your most beloved visual treasures, I know that this book will captivate you. Edgerton's photographs are not only illuminating (in the sense of teaching us to see what we otherwise could not) but also are aesthetically compelling. His curiosity, inventive genius, and aesthetic vision resonate in these unforgettable images.

I am delighted that the book also includes memoirs and essays from four individuals at MIT who know and love Edgerton's work. The two personal memoirs by J. Kim Vandiver and Gus Kayafas reveal fascinating insights about Edgerton (or "Doc" as they called him). Edgerton was a deeply generous man, beloved by generations of MIT students and faculty alike. Vandiver and Kayafas went from being Doc's students to treasured colleagues. In their accounts, you will be reminded of Edgerton's immense dedication to teaching, his collaborative style of research, and the extent to which he transformed lives.

Gary Van Zante and Deborah G. Douglas are curators at the MIT Museum and are the keepers of Edgerton's photographs, films, and artifacts collection. Their essays represent their understanding of Edgerton's contributions to photography and history. In short, these essays will help the reader better understand the significance of Edgerton's technical and artistic contributions and his place in history.

Distinct among all Edgerton books is the inclusion of a rich selection of reproductions from Edgerton's amazing research notebooks. These pages provide a unique perspective into the fundamental science and the experiments that resulted in some of the images presented. As I have found in my own life, it is impossible to separate the strands of science, technology, and art. These pages confirm the truth of that for Edgerton.

I believe Edgerton helped define a novel and important relationship between science and art in our times. His inventions changed the world of photography. Edgerton's photographs have unveiled aspects of the unseen world, providing insights, answering questions, and always arousing our visual appetites. I have been honored to help create this elegant volume, and hope that it excites and teaches the reader as much as it has me.

1   Ben Goldberger, Paul Moakley, and Kira Pollack, *100 Photographs: The Most Influential Images of All Time* (New York: Time Inc. Books, 2015), p. 200.

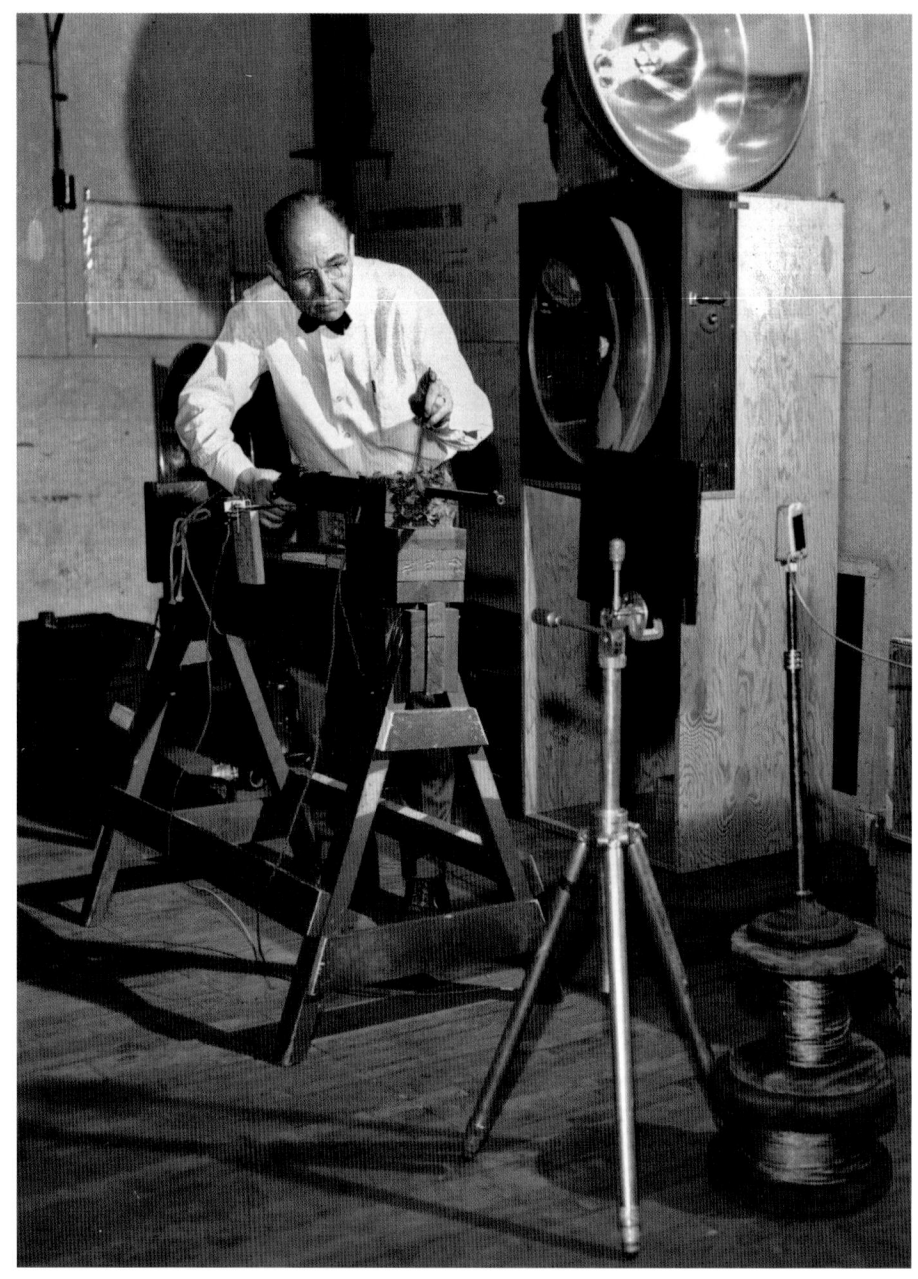

Edgerton sets up a rifle for one of his famous "Bullet through a ..." photographs.

# HAROLD EUGENE EDGERTON
## APRIL 6, 1903 – JANUARY 4, 1990

*Deborah G. Douglas*

Harold Eugene Edgerton was an engineer, educator, explorer, and entrepreneur as well as a revolutionary photographer. An internationally eminent electrical engineer, Edgerton is sometimes called the "father of electronic strobe flash photography," for his pioneering research and inventions that transformed an obscure 19th-century device into a key technology of the 20th century. Edgerton gained an equal measure of fame as a deep-sea explorer and for his applications of sonar technology to the field of maritime archaeology. Always, however, Edgerton could be found with a camera—still and moving—for research, for documentation, and for the creation of some of the most compelling and iconic images of all time. He is perhaps most famous, then, as the photographer of the "unseen," able to freeze motion and reveal the wonders of the natural and human-built worlds.

Harold Edgerton was born in Freemont, Nebraska, on April 6, 1903, to Mary and Frank Edgerton. His father was a lawyer and journalist who worked for state and federal governments and ran a farm, so Edgerton moved with his family from Fremont to Lincoln, Nebraska; Washington, DC; and Winnebago, Nebraska, before finally setting in Aurora, Nebraska, in 1915. He graduated from the University of Nebraska with a degree in electrical engineering in 1925. Nebraska Light and Power Company, where Edgerton had worked summers in high school and college, offered him a job, but his father urged him to take a position at General Electric and then again a year later to attend graduate school at the Massachusetts Institute of Technology (MIT). Edgerton would earn a master's of science (SM, 1927) degree and a doctor of science (ScD, 1931) degree in electrical engineering from MIT.

In 1927, the MIT Department of Electrical Engineering appointed Edgerton to a research assistant position. He was promoted to instructor in 1928, assistant professor in 1932, associate professor in 1938, and full professor in 1948. In 1966, MIT named him Institute Professor, its highest faculty honor. Required to retire at age 65 in 1968, Edgerton continued his teaching and research until the day he died in 1990.[1]

Edgerton was an exceptionally able and creative instructor. He had a particular talent for involving his students in substantial research projects. There are countless stories of students coming to meet with "Doc" for help figuring out an undergraduate or graduate thesis project. Edgerton's love of teaching and working with students would be a key factor in turning down a lucrative job offer from General Electric when he finished his doctorate.[2]

Edgerton married Esther May Garrett, also of Aurora, Nebraska, in 1928. Together they had three children: Mary Louise (1931), William (1933), and Robert (1935). The Edgerton home was an especially welcoming place. Photographs and movies document the numerous gatherings filled with food, songs (Edgerton played guitar and banjo), and skits. One 1946 class assignment read: "Appear at 205 School Street, Belmont, about 6:30 p.m. equipped with appetite. No textbooks, slide rules or class notes will be allowed. ... Try to memorize words of these Tech songs. Penalty for non-perfection may be an opportunity to help with the dishes!"[3] Esther, it should be noted, was an important partner in her husband's early entrepreneurial efforts, accompanying him on his sales calls to companies en route from Massachusetts to Nebraska each summer. She also kept the books for Edgerton's first commercial endeavor, Edgerton, Germeshausen, and Grier.

That partnership began accidentally. Among Edgerton's very first students was Kenneth Germeshausen. Edgerton supervised the joint bachelor's thesis of Germeshausen and Gordon Brown (who would later chair the MIT Department of Electrical Engineering and become dean of the School of Engineering). His approach was to get his students involved in real-world problems. In 1931, that meant he had Brown and Germeshausen help him with his work on synchronous induction motors. He was very impressed with the improvements that Germeshausen made to his stroboscope.

Graduating in the depths of the Great Depression, Germeshausen could not find work so Edgerton proposed an unconventional arrangement to his department chair, Dugald C. Jackson, to support his talented student. If Jackson would approve Germeshausen's appointment as a research assistant, Edgerton would pay his salary from the proceeds from industrial consulting projects.

Two years later in 1933, Edgerton made the same arrangement with Herbert Grier, another student whose technical abilities he admired. This was the start of the creative and lifelong consulting partnership of Edgerton, Germeshausen, and Grier. It was a very active enterprise, supporting a growing laboratory and staff as well as providing considerable aid to the Department of Electrical Engineering.

During World War II, Edgerton's "Strobe Lab," as it was formally designated in 1931, became involved in military projects, most notably, aerial nighttime photography. While still aiding Edgerton, Germeshausen and Grier also began working in other wartime labs at MIT. Both men became especially involved in partnerships with Raytheon. Raytheon gave a special contract to MIT to help develop new firing sets, devices that timed and triggered nuclear bomb tests.

At war's end, MIT wanted to eliminate classified research on campus, which led to the incorporation of Edgerton, Germeshausen, and Grier (EG & G) in 1947. Edgerton was named chairman of the board of directors (a post he held until 1965). A high-tech conglomerate, EG & G worked on a broad range of sensing, detection, and imaging products for the automotive, medical, aerospace, and photography industries; as well as instrumentation, technical services, and facilities management.

At EG&G's peak, it employed more than 20,000 people worldwide. In both official and unofficial capacities, Edgerton, who mainly preferred to stay in the lab, would be a key source of inspiration and innovation for EG&G employees and executives throughout his life.

Edgerton's personal research agenda shifted after World War II as he became increasingly fascinated by another unseen world. In the 1930s, Edgerton had developed a camera with the advice of researchers at the Woods Hole Oceanographic Institute; but in April 1952, he met the French underwater explorer Jacques-Yves Cousteau, co-inventor of SCUBA (self-contained underwater breathing apparatus) through an introduction by the National Geographic Society. That summer, Edgerton's experiments began in earnest with research trips to the Woods Hole Oceanographic Institute in August and Hawaii in October. MIT's Alumni Pool became a site of frequent experimentation.

Edgerton's initial investigations focused on improving lighting and then equipment that would work in deep water. During his first expedition with Cousteau, he noticed something intriguing. Edgerton had used sonar to make key depth measurements. Incidentally, he noticed that the acoustic waves were penetrating through surface sediments and reflecting off of layers that were below the bottom of the sea floor. This initial observation led to several decades of research developing sub-bottom profilers and side-scan sonar devices (what Edgerton usually called "pingers," "boomers," and "thumpers"). As with the stroboscope, Edgerton did not "invent" these technologies, but his sustained experiments did have a significant impact.

Beginning in the 1960s, Edgerton became a fixture on numerous underwater archaeology expeditions, including the discovery of the *Mary Rose* (King Henry VIII's flagship which sank in 1545) and the famous Civil War ironclad USS *Monitor*. (One highly reported project, albeit with indeterminate results, was Edgerton's joining of the search for the mythical Loch Ness monster in the 1970s and 1980s.) Edgerton's sonar technologies offered archaeologists new ways to see, and they also had profound commercial implications. Two of Edgerton's students, Samuel Raymond and Martin Klein, both founded their own companies, which became leaders in this field.

While Edgerton loved black-and-white photography best, he fully embraced color film in the postwar period. Taking pictures underwater, he learned how to compensate for the filtering of red light through the use of flashes. On land, he began to take new versions of photographs shot in the 1930s. His 1957 color "Milk Drop Coronet" is now considered to be among the most important photographs of all time. The 1964 picture of a .30 caliber bullet piercing an apple became the centerpiece of a popular lecture entitled, "How to Make Applesauce at MIT." Elsewhere in this volume, J. Kim Vandiver describes how Edgerton challenged and then helped him figure out how to take spectacular color Schlieren photographs capturing the supersonic shock waves of bullets in flight.

In the 1930s, Edgerton's photographs had begun to be featured in exhibitions and magazines from *Technology Review* to *Life* magazine. He won prizes at the Royal Photographic Society's annual exhibition in London. Edgerton collaborated with Hollywood producer Pete Smith and MGM Studios to make *Quicker'n a Wink*, a short documentary that won an Academy Award in 1940. After World War II, these exhibitions became even more frequent. At the suggestion of his darkroom collaborator and former student Gus Kayafas, Edgerton began to create limited-edition portfolios that are cherished by collectors and museums around the world. Edgerton was featured on television from documentaries to an appearance on "Late Night with David Letterman" in 1985.

Edgerton received hundreds of awards, citations, and honorary degrees throughout his career. The Secretary of War awarded Edgerton the Medal of Freedom in 1946 for his contributions to World War II intelligence gathering efforts. He received the National Medal of Science in 1973 from President Richard Nixon and the National Medal of Technology and Innovation from President Ronald Reagan in 1988. The New England Aquarium named a research vessel in his honor in 1977. He was elected to the American Philosophical Society, National Academy of Sciences, the National Academy of Engineering, and was a fellow of numerous other societies. Edgerton authored or contributed to nearly 200 articles, papers, and books. He had 47 patents and was inducted into the National Inventors Hall of Fame in 1986.

The honorific that Edgerton treasured most of all, however, was the appellation "Doc." He was tremendously proud of his achievements, but the goal was always to be useful, to solve problems, and to make things work. The nickname reflected Edgerton's supremely collegial approach to work and life. MIT's 11th president, Julius Stratton, put it this way: "Of his many talents, perhaps the most enviable was his unfailing ability to infuse every task with a heightened sense of interest and excitement and to derive from it so much fun."[4]

A stroke and heart problems slowed (slightly) Edgerton in the 1980s, but he mostly ignored the condition. "If you don't wake up at three in the morning and want to do something, you're wasting your time," is an expression Edgerton often used. He died in the MIT faculty dining hall on January 4, 1990, at age 86. In a 1983 feature in the *Boston Globe*, Edgerton observed: "A lot of kids come here [to MIT] thinking everything's been done. That it's all in the textbooks. Well, the most important things haven't even been thought of yet. Nobody's going to tell you something original."[5]

It is not surprising that Edgerton's family, friends, and colleagues quickly determined after his death that the most meaningful way to honor Edgerton's legacy as an educator was to establish hands-on learning centers. For more than a quarter-century, the Edgerton Explorit Center in Aurora, Nebraska, and the MIT Edgerton Center, through exhibitions, programs, courses, workshops, and more, have enabled several million people to go beyond the textbooks and share in the joy of discovery and exploration.

Edgerton's photographs and strobes remain the most important legacy of his personal technical and artistic accomplishments. "Every professional photographer, particularly the news cameraman, shall long remember the inventor of the strobelight," wrote Gil Friedberg, camera editor of the *Boston Globe*, in 1959. John Szarkowski, director of photography at the Museum of Modern Art (MoMA), who exhibited Edgerton's photographs in at least a dozen exhibitions, commented that his work was "as familiar to many of our visitors as the *Guernica*." At MIT, Edgerton's work exerted considerable influence on the thinking of artist, photographer, and MIT colleague, György Kepes, and he contributed significantly to the MIT Center for Advanced Visual Studies' hallmark installation, *Centerbeam*.[6]

For much of the 20th century, Harold Edgerton's brilliant images were ubiquitous, compelling to everyone. His tools and techniques transformed entire professions from sports photography to maritime archaeology. In a review of a 1999 Australian exhibition of Edgerton's photographs, Myra McIntyre wrote: "The gift of American scientist, writer, and artist, Dr. Harold E. Edgerton, to humanity was the ability to witness a world lost to the perception of the naked eye." Edgerton's work, she observed simply, "radically altered our view of time and space."[7] In his appreciation of Edgerton's life, *Boston Globe* writer Stan Grossfeld said it best: "The beloved professor emeritus at the Massachusetts Institute of Technology made the whole world see better with his revolutionary techniques in both high-speed strobe and underwater photography. … Edgerton's lamps retain their magic—and so do the photographs, a combination of art and science unparalleled in the history of photography."[8]

1   MIT's News Office produced several biographical sketches of Harold Edgerton during his 64-year association with the Institute. This account draws on news releases prepared in 1944, 1966, and 1980. Copies may be found in the Harold E. Edgerton biographical file at the MIT Museum, Cambridge, MA.

2   Karl L. Wildes and Nilo A. Lindgren, *A Century of Electrical Engineering and Computer Science at MIT, 1882–1982* (Cambridge: MIT Press, 1985), p. 147.

3   Harold Edgerton, "Fundamentals of Electrical Engineering," assignment sheet for May 3, 1946, Papers of Harold E. Edgerton (MC.0025), Institute Archives and Special Collections, MIT Libraries, Cambridge, MA quoted in J. Kim Vandiver and Pagan Kennedy, "Harold Eugene Edgerton, 1903–1990," *Biographical Memoirs* 86 (Washington: National Academies Press, 2005), p. 15.

4   Julius A. Stratton, "Harold Eugene Edgerton (April 6, 1902–January 4, 1990)," *Proceedings of the American Philosophical Society 135* (1991), p. 450.

5   Michael B. McPhee, "At MIT, they call it the Edgerton Factor," *Boston Globe* (September 20, 1983), p. 69.

6   Gil Friedberg, "Dr. Harold E. Edgerton stops a bullet in flight," *Boston Globe* (February 22, 1959), p. 65; Szarkowski quoted in Harold E. Edgerton and James R. Killian, Jr., *Moments of Vision: The Stroboscopic Revolution in Photography,* (Cambridge: MIT Press, 1979), p. 13.

7   Myra McIntyre, "Pictures that altered our perceptions," *Canberra Times* (January 16, 1999), p. 16.

8   Stan Grossfeld, "Edgerton: Maestro of Strobe," *The Boston Globe* (January 5, 1990), p. 78.

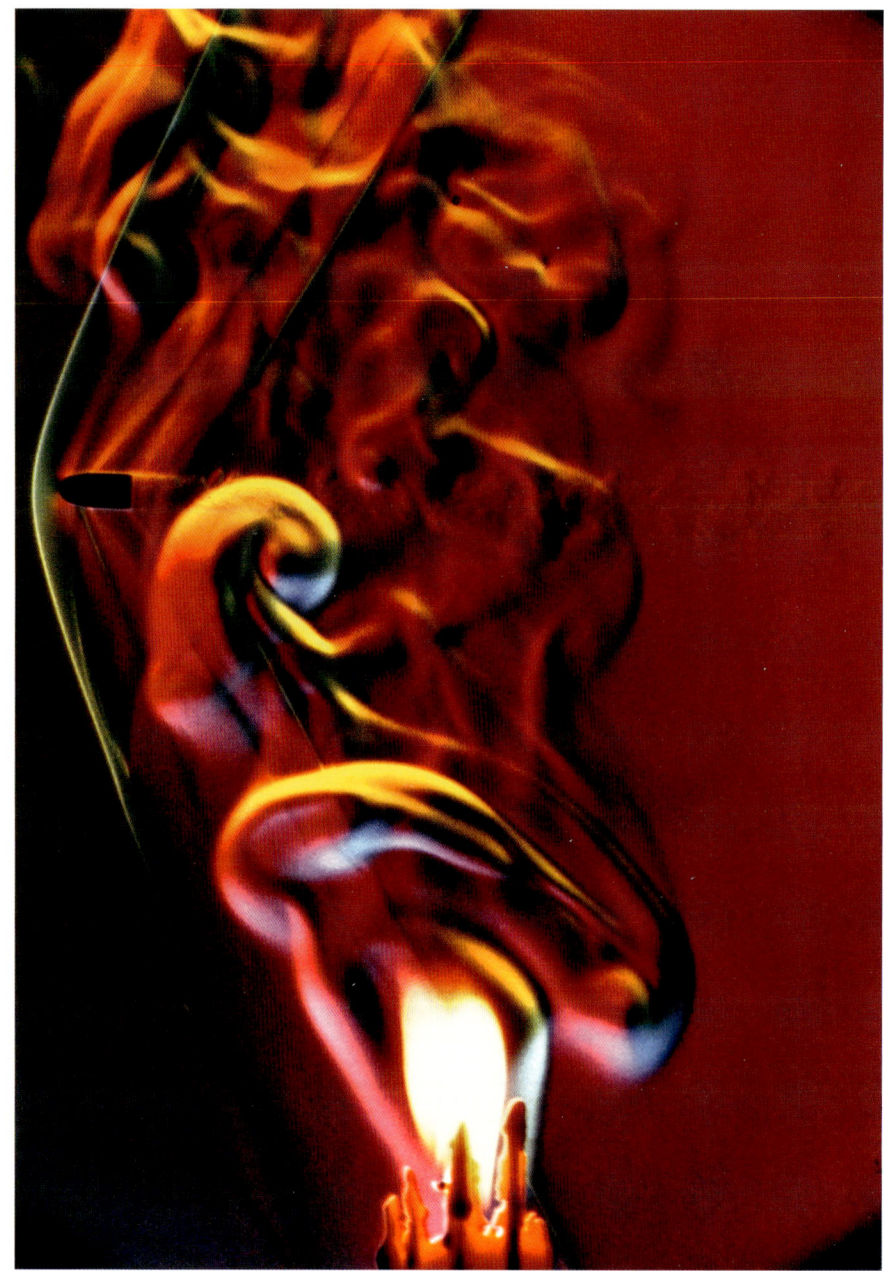

Edgerton challenged Kim Vandiver to make a color Schlieren photograph. He then gave an extraordinary boost to Vandiver's career by helping him get this striking image published on the cover of *Nature* in November 1974.

# "DOC" AS TEACHER

*J. Kim Vandiver*

In January 1972, after serving two years in the U.S. Army Corps of Engineers, I returned to graduate school in ocean engineering at MIT. One of my first stops was to knock on Professor Harold "Doc" Edgerton's office door and ask him if I could learn about high-speed photography by taking his undergraduate course "Strobe Project Lab." After learning that I had taken up photography as a hobby while in the army and taught myself how to develop color film, he agreed. The course was pure pleasure and included a personal term project on the high-speed photography of cavitating marine propellers. During the summer of 1972, Doc offered me the job of teaching assistant (TA) for the 1972–73 academic year. This gave me time to find a suitable PhD thesis topic in ocean engineering while working at Strobe Alley.

Doc suggested that I do a research project while being the TA and mentioned that he had never done color Schlieren photography.[1] Thus began a mentoring relationship that would change my life and deeply ingrain in me Doc's philosophy of "try it and see" experiential learning. To do Schlieren required high-quality concave mirrors. Doc knew that Professor Jack Kerrebrock, the department head in Aeronautical Engineering, had a pair of 10-inch telescope mirrors, which we borrowed on a very longterm loan. Doc seemed to know just about everyone and had done so many good deeds for people that no one could say 'no' when he asked for a favor. For me, another life lesson learned. He was known to say: "Tell everyone everything you know, seal a deal with a handshake, work like hell, and have fun."

Between September 1972 and January 1973, I tried four different color Schlieren methods described in the supersonic wind tunnel literature. With each new trial, Doc would review the film with his 10X loop magnifier and make cryptic comments like, "Looks out of focus to me," or "I don't like the color," but always encouraging me to keep trying. In December, I read about a new technique developed by a grad student in Tennessee, Gary Settles. It was in an article in the "Amateur Scientist" section of *Scientific American*.

After seeing my first color transparencies of a bullet in flight, using the new method, Doc finally said, "Van, I think you've got it." He encouraged me to write up my work and present it at the 11th International Congress on High Speed Photography in London in the summer of 1973. He was, after all, the father of modern high-speed photography, and attending the conference with him was a privilege. Within a few months, my photographs were published in the same "Amateur Scientist" section of the August 1974 issue of *Scientific American*[2] as well as on the cover of the November 1974 issue of *Nature*.[3]

Doc was generous in other ways as well. Anytime an unusual visitor dropped by, he would walk into my laboratory office and say, "Come over to my office, there is someone you should meet." Edwin Land, the founder of Polaroid, and Jacques Cousteau were among the many. He regularly invited students to go out to test his latest sonar in his small boat on the Charles River or come over to his home for Thanksgiving dinner with him and his lifelong partner, Esther. He helped people start companies: Sam Raymond founded Benthos, and Marty Klein founded Klein Associates, a pioneering firm in the side scan sonar field, both with Doc's help. He seemed to touch everyone in some good way.

People like to tell me how they met Doc. Their stories almost always mention a postcard, which Doc would hand out to everyone he met. On one occasion in the fall of 1972, I was standing by the classroom door with Doc, greeting students arriving for our weekly freshman seminar, which often featured showings of movies and photographs and the stories to go with them. One student stopped to ask if it would be okay if his girlfriend, who was visiting MIT, could attend the class. With a twinkle in his eye and a stern expression, he said to the young woman, "You can't come to class without a pass." He whipped out a postcard and said to the startled young woman, "Here's a pass."

After finishing my dissertation in late 1974, I joined the faculty of the MIT's Department of Ocean Engineering in 1975. My very first graduate student research assistant was Charles Mazel. Much to my surprise, I learned that he had already worked with Doc, having gone to sea with him in Greece on a marine archaeology expedition in the early 1970s. Doc was a great storyteller, and both Charlie and I picked up presentation skills just watching him charm an audience. To this day, I use techniques acquired from Doc. For the next 15 years, we crossed paths often.

With Doc's passing in January of 1990, it was time to find ways to honor his legacy at MIT. Everyone knew the importance of his contributions to photography. But I knew his importance as a teacher and mentor. He had guided students for 60 years at MIT and had shown by example the power of experiential learning. When asked by a small group of experts, mostly from the museum world, what I recommended as a fitting tribute, I told them of his influence on students and that a wonderful way to honor him would be to turn Strobe Alley into the Edgerton Center, a place where MIT students could pursue personal projects and inventions. The idea found traction and was supported by Paul Penfield, the head of Electrical Engineering and Computer Science; Paul Gray, the chair of MIT's Corporation and formerly MIT's 14th president; and, most importantly, Esther Edgerton, Doc's wife.

The Edgerton Center officially opened in August 1992. Esther and the Edgerton Family Foundation supported it financially for many years, including a complete renovation of the physical space. Now 25 years after its founding, the Center operates three student shops and supports a dozen or so student teams who compete worldwide with robots, underwater vehicles, and solar and electric vehicles. The

Center carries on Doc's belief in hands-on experiential learning by inspiring the next generation of youth to engage in science, engineering, and art. We do this with after-school programs and summer camps, with our own hands-on curriculum, and through workshops for teachers. We motivate students by making the experience so satisfying that they can't wait to do more. Doc was fond of saying, "The trick to education is to not let them know they are learning until it's too late." Our work is supported by an endowment left by Harold and Esther, and also by gifts from alumni and alumnae who were also touched by his generosity. When asked to present to alumni club audiences around the world, my favorite topic is to share with them the life, legacy, and photography of Harold "Doc" Edgerton.

1   Schlieren photography is a flow visualization technique, invented in the mid-19th century to study supersonic motion. It uses photography to capture the flow of fluids of different densities. For example, this technology made it possible to photograph the shockwaves produced by a bullet in flight or the thermal plume from a burning candle. The word comes from German and means "streak."

2   C. L. Stong, ed., "The Amateur Scientist: An air flash lamp advances color schlieren photography," *Scientific American*, 231 (August 1974), pp. 104–09.

3   J. K. Vandiver, "High Speed Color Schlieren Photography," *Nature* 252 (November 29, 1974, No. 5482), cover photo and pp. 346–47.

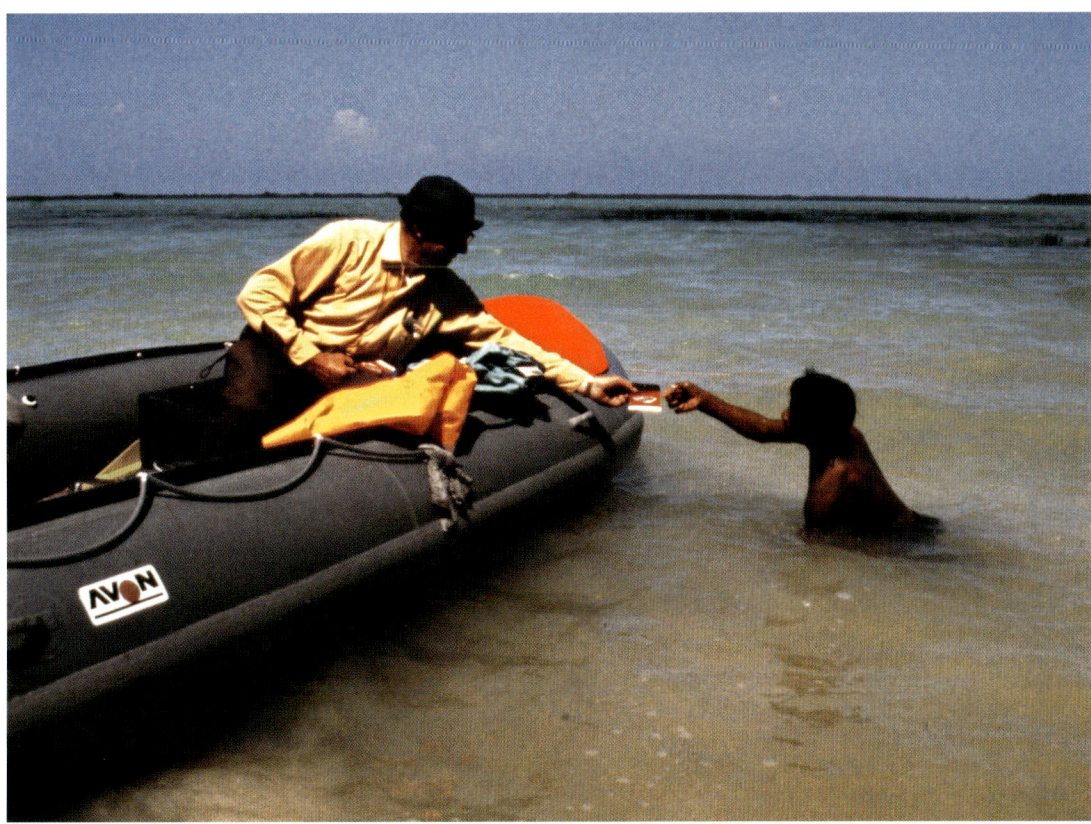

Edgerton handed out postcards to everyone he met. This snapshot captures him giving away the famous "Milk Drop Coronet" while on a 1975 archeological sonar survey near the Yucatan in Mexico.

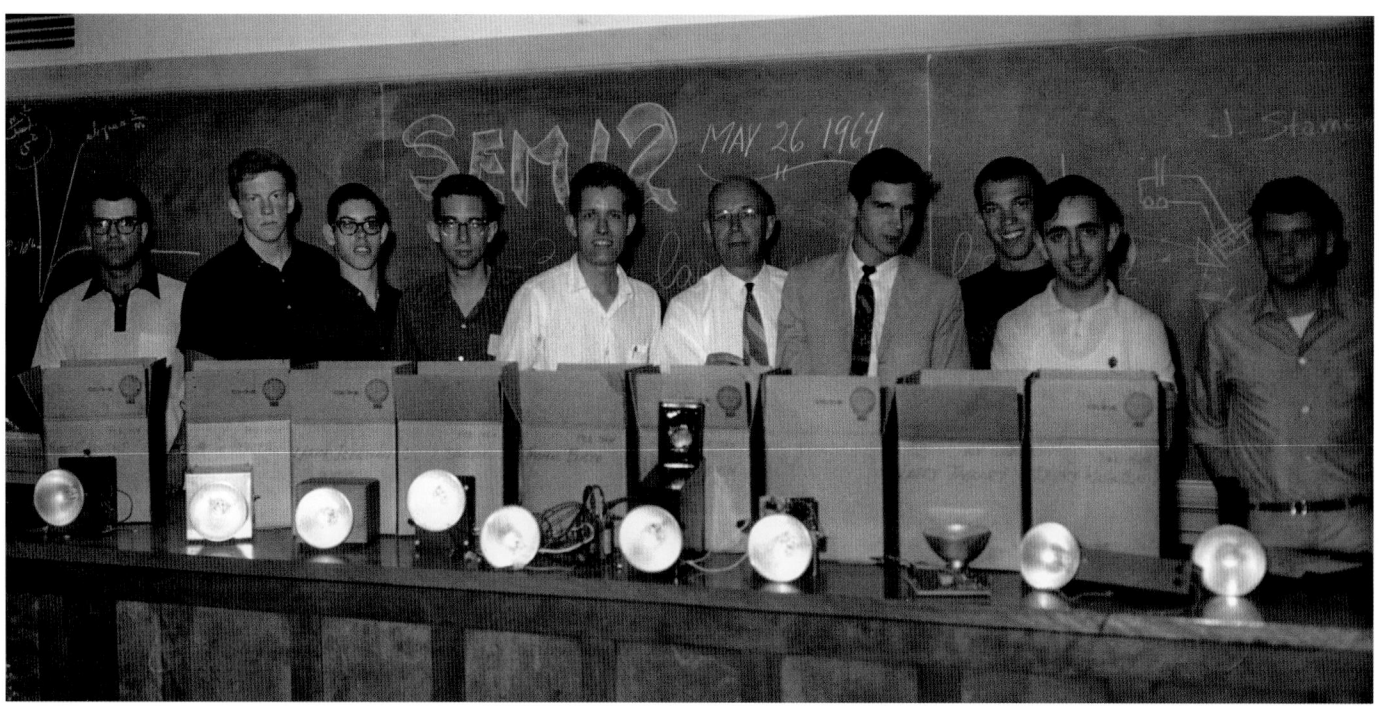

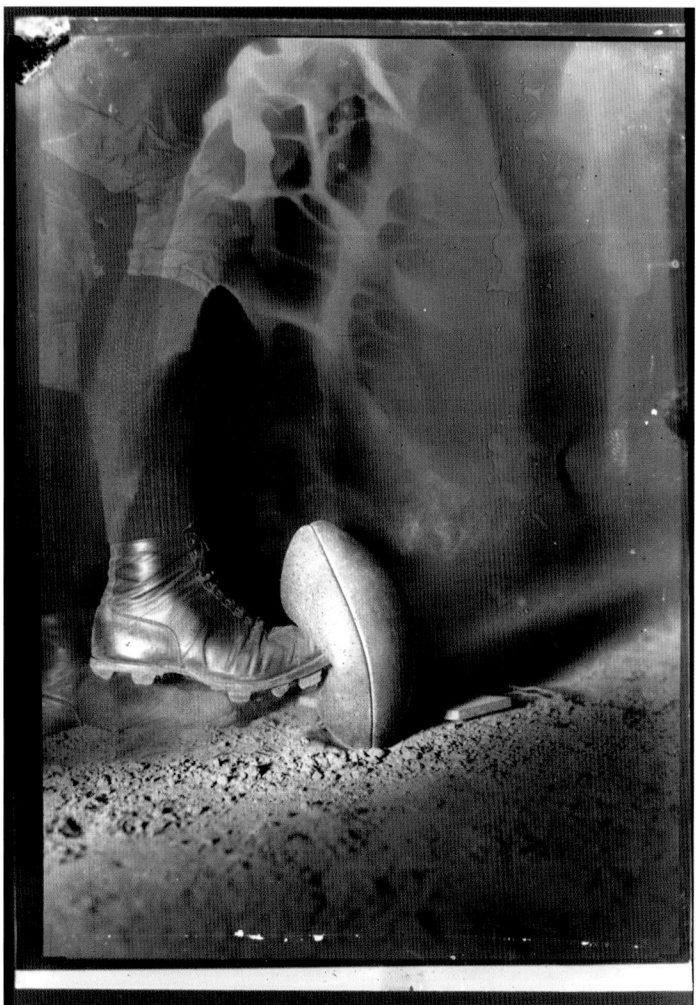

*(top)* Edgerton taught an extremely popular freshman seminar each year. Here the students from the 1963–64 seminar line up with "Doc" to show off their hand-made strobes.

*(left)* Gus Kayafas' discovery of Edgerton's "rejects" led to important insights about his methods and aesthetic sensibilities. This blotchy negative of Wesley Fesler was unusable. Only one picture out of the half dozen they took turned out right.

# "DOC" IN THE DARKROOM

*Gus Kayafas*

I first met "Doc" (Professor Harold Edgerton) while I was wandering the halls of MIT (Massachusetts Institute of Technology) in late August 1965. I was an incoming freshman physics major and had arrived two weeks early to visit friends and explore. I discovered "Strobe Alley," Doc's fourth floor, "24/7" museum at around 6:30 a.m. one morning. Doc came out of his office pushing an equipment-laden cart, startling us both, and then asked if I "had a strong back"? My reply—"Yes, I'm 18…"—made him laugh and I helped him transport what I discovered to be sonar equipment down to his launch on the Charles River. He was testing it before loaning it to Jacques Cousteau for an "expedition." At the end of our first conversation, I knew that I was going to sign up for his freshman seminar. (I heeded his recommendation and arrived very early because it was so popular.) Doc knew that I was eager and curious, and already had nine years of darkroom experience (thanks to my Dad). Doc was an enabler of experiences and expeditions, large and small, always seeking to explore the unseen and include all who were willing to work to share the journey. It did not take long for me to become a fellow traveler.

One of the benefits of taking a strobe course was ongoing access to the darkroom and the lab; but even more importantly, Doc's seminar was an antidote for the MIT grind. Whether one was watching Italian glassblowers at work or visiting a lab full of bats flying in the dark, the connection between exploring problems—research—and solving them was thrilling. Blowing and making our own flash tubes, creating the circuit to fire them, or working in the darkroom to make visible and measurable what could not be seen by the eye alone was an adventure. It rewarded hard work. It made clear Doc's commitment to "experiences" and not simply experiments. One of his observations was that MIT students were so smart that they thought they knew the answers before they began the exploration. He wanted them to learn that the great pitfall that this attitude engendered was that it denied learning from the unexpected and limited true innovation.

It became apparent to me that fall that my MIT experience was evolving in ways for which I could have no intimation. During that first semester, I became Doc's "go-to" guy for photographic assistance, teaching fellow students and, finally, making some prints for him to exhibit. Doc's technical mastery of the photographic process was complete. I was amazed when he even hand processed 16mm color movie film so that he might get results of his explorations as quickly as possible.

His emphasis on speedy results was sometimes a problem. Often the subtleties of darkroom processing were lost to the need to immediately review the results. Doc certainly knew what a good print looked like, and he had a highly developed sense of composition. He had an amazing "eye" for framing and capturing the right moment as evidenced by nearly 60 years of making great photographs and the fact that his prints are in most major art and science museums worldwide. The Museum of Modern Art collected and published his work in 1937. Doc's idea of a great print was this: It should be clear, in focus, well exposed, and interesting. (It's that last quality that is the most significant but also the hardest to define.)

It is important to remember that early on, strobe exposures were challenging. They were always on the edge of underexposure since the motion-stopping duration was so short, and it was difficult to get enough light on the subject. In the early days, every advance of film speed, reflector efficiency, and power represented a door for new (and probably difficult) challenges. Doc loved the revealing surface of a glossy print, and I knew that I had passed muster when I was allowed to use the only piece of darkroom equipment that was off-limits to students: his rotary ferrotyping print dryer.

There was a large, old, wooden cabinet in the darkroom for which only Doc had the key. It contained negatives and some cameras. In the late 1970s (by which time I was making prints, had produced a portfolio, and was arranging exhibits and gallery representations for Doc), I earned regular access to the cabinet. I came across a couple boxes of negatives that were marked "Rejects" and I started exploring them. It is through this collection that I discovered many important insights about Doc's work methods and editing process. Doc liked to quote the scientist Louis Pasteur saying: "Chance favors the prepared mind." (He used to also claim that Blaise Pascal and Ansel Adams said it, too.) Looking through the rejects, I realized how Doc's photographs regularly proved its truth.

For example, I found an envelope full of outtakes from his famous "Wes Fesler Kicks the Football, 1934" (see p. 71), I learned that the kicker, Harvard's new football coach (and one of the most famous Ohio State players) had missed the ball in the total darkness required by the low output of the argon flash; that a couple negatives had stuck together during the initial stages of development, permanently marking them; and that the only really good negative was also the perfect one.

I also discovered the problem of Doc's inconsistent dating of images. His training regarding the protection of his ideas and patents had taught him to date and sign his sketches and lab notebook entries. He wrote the current date (not the date the image was taken) on his negative sleeves whenever he replaced a worn or damaged envelope. And Doc was not careful dating prints. In the 1970s, he could not remember exactly when he had taken one of his most famous photographs of Gussie Moran serving a tennis ball. It was only because of that discovery of an envelope full of rejects from his 1949 session at Longwood Cricket Club that he and I were able to properly date this famous image (see p. 119).

Doc was always amazed at the obsession collectors had for "vintage" prints. He wondered why some people would pay much more money for "old, yellow, cracked" prints when they could have a perfect print made just for them. Over the years, I became responsible for making many of those prints. When I started, Doc and I would discuss the variations he wanted me to make including cropping issues, proper contrast, and density. Initially, he was insistent that I follow his requirements exactly. He would select and approve from among the finished proofs. Later on, he left that to me as we embarked on the project of printing editions of his most important images in varying sizes. As we completed editions, I always set aside a group from each image as "family prints" and would proudly deliver them to his wife, Esther, to put aside. She wasn't sure that the family members would really want them (they did), and she would sometimes complain about the size telling me there was "no more room under the beds."

A story I really like occurred one day when Doc was signing dye transfer prints of "Cutting the Card Quickly, 1964"(see p. 134). A young man knocked on the office door. As he entered, the student very nervously explained he wanted to talk to Professor Edgerton about a thesis project. Quickly, Doc said he was retired but that he'd discuss it with the student. Doc asked him if he could handle a rifle and showed him the print he was signing. "Could he split a card like this ... in the dark?" Doc inquired. Dejected and somewhat overwhelmed, the student began to excuse himself and back out of the office but Doc insisted he come in. We ended up discussing the picture, what a dye transfer was, how you synchronized the flash, the delight of unknown results revealed, and that you could line up the card's edge through the rifle barrel before the lights went out. That young man ended up completing his thesis with Doc as the advisor. Doc changed his life just like he had mine years earlier.

One of Doc's greatest delights as he got older was visiting the exhibitions we created and giving talks. He never lost his passion for sharing the "importance of strobe!" and revealing to others how they too could see the unseen. Everywhere we went he asked for volunteers, usually a "ten-year old." When I asked "Why ten?" Doc explained that when you are ten you still believe that you can do all the things you dream of. I think Doc was a ten-year-old his entire life, except even better because he really did accomplish the things he dreamed about.

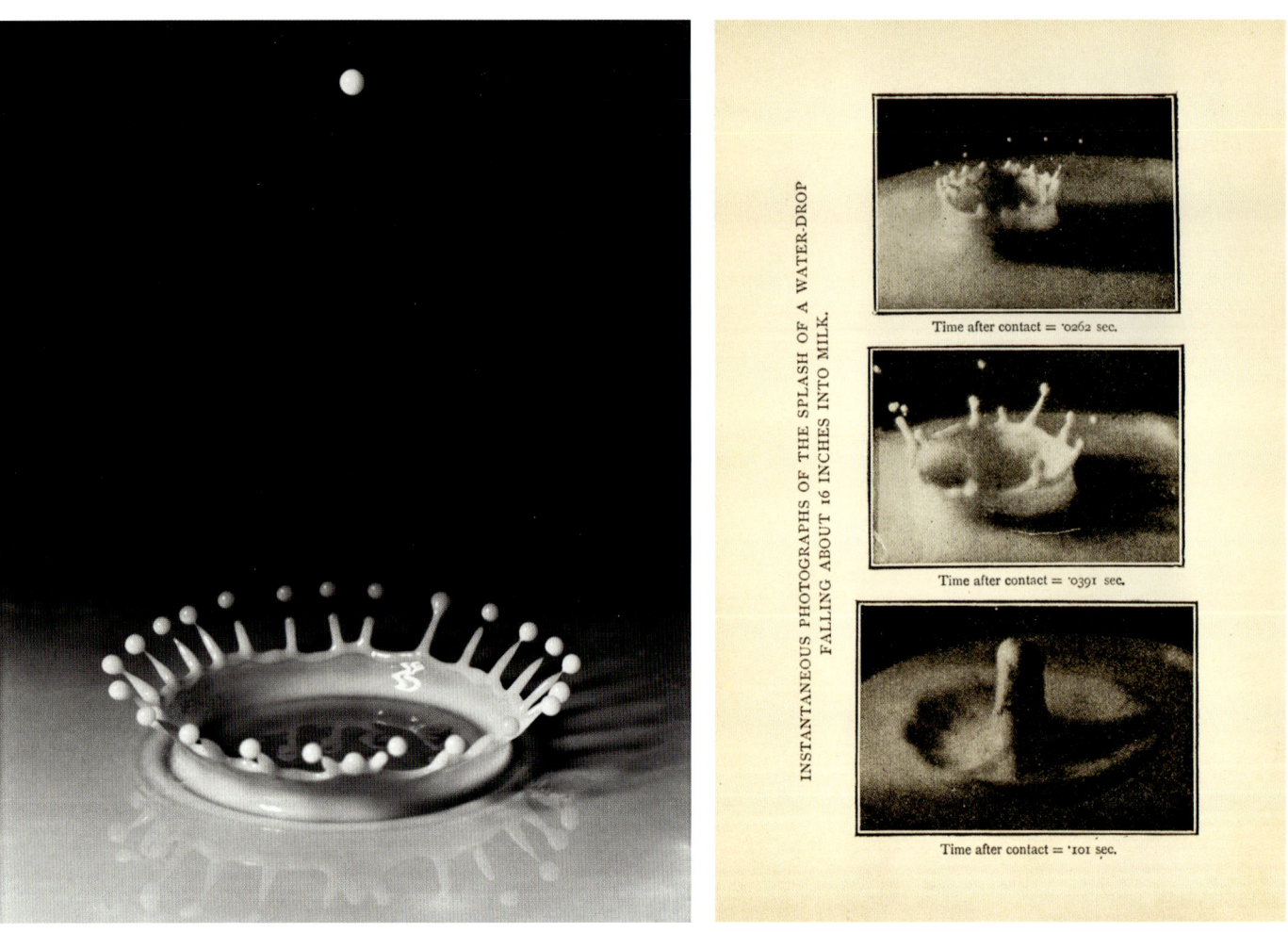

INSTANTANEOUS PHOTOGRAPHS OF THE SPLASH OF A WATER-DROP
FALLING ABOUT 16 INCHES INTO MILK.

Time after contact = ·0262 sec.

Time after contact = ·0391 sec.

Time after contact = ·101 sec.

Edgerton was not the first to photograph drops and splashes as the frontispiece (right) from Arthur M. Worthington's *The Splash of a Drop*, published in 1895 makes clear. Still his famous black-and-white *Coronet* (left) taken in 1936 was considered a masterpiece by scientists and photographers alike.

# HAROLD EDGERTON'S MILK SPLASHES
## IN THE HISTORY OF PHOTOGRAPHY

*Gary Van Zante*

In 1942, the Scottish polymath D'Arcy Wentworth Thompson added a photographic frontispiece to a new edition of *On Growth and Form*, his influential text on the mathematical basis of natural form first published in 1917.[1] The photograph that opened the book was Harold Edgerton's milk splash coronet—a drop of milk forming a crown of splattered droplets—that was among the most widely published and exhibited images in scientific photography. Selected to illustrate one of the most important scientific books of the century, Edgerton's milk splash gained not only credibility as documentation but also confirmation that it was a highly effective photograph, and a beautiful one.[2] Thompson commented that Edgerton's photograph showed the milk splash "still more beautifully" than the earlier work of physicist Arthur M. Worthington, whose milk splash photographs, made in the 1890s, also illustrated Thompson's text (see p. 24).[3]

Thompson's recognition of Edgerton's photograph is less significant in itself than in the way it encapsulates Edgerton's ascendancy as a photographer only ten years after he began to publish and exhibit his high-speed images. Edgerton's position straddling the worlds of scientific research and art practice, and his revelatory images, have an unusual place in the history of photography.[4] Acknowledged as one of the masters of the medium, Edgerton often denied any artistic intention in his work. "I am no artist," he claimed in an interview in the 1980s. "I am an engineer after the facts."[5] If as an engineer he put application before art, it does not change the fact that Edgerton was an astute image-maker who exceeded the conventions of scientific photography of his day. Although his work followed a long line of experimentation and innovation in photography and in the study of time and motion in the laboratory, which he did not fail to recognize, his photographs appeared to supplant all precedents to become fixed in the popular imagination. They remain so even today, decades after they were made.

Worthington's work is today far less known than Edgerton's, and it is useful to examine why. Worthington presented his splash photographs to London's Royal Institution in 1894, published them in *Pearson's Magazine* and *Scientific American*, and later in book form in *The Splash of a Drop* and *A Study of Splashes* (see p. 24, right)[6] His images were astonishingly beautiful, but in translating them into print their photographic qualities were much diminished, as Worthington himself noted in the preface to *A Study of Splashes*: "Much of the beauty of the original photographs was lost in the reproduction, or was sacrificed in a selection of which the only object was the elucidation of points of technical scientific interest." [7] While he lamented the fact that his publisher seemed only to see his very accomplished photographs as mere records of laboratory data, he was also confronting an issue of reproducibility following the transition from interpretive wood engraving to the half-tone process as the dominant form of photographic reproduction in print. The results of this graphic shift were images that were poorly resolved in many print forms where Worthington's work circulated.

Other early pioneers of high-speed photography faced similar issues in the reproduction, circulation, and reception of their images, and exposure to their work was by and large confined to scientific periodicals that gave scant attention to the visual qualities of images or their graphic context. The Harvard/MIT astronomer William Henry Pickering, who also photographed splashes; John William Strutt, who punctured a soap bubble and pictured its collapse; or Ernst Mach and Charles V. Boys, who produced striking photographs of bullets in flight—all phenomena that Edgerton himself later photographed—did not have access to high-quality print reproductions of their work, or even to satisfactory public display of original photographs. [8]

Edgerton's case is different. Working and publishing decades later, he benefitted not only from the continuous development of photographic technology (apart from his own highly significant contributions) but also from reproductive technology. Advances in printing and graphic techniques resulted in the superior reproducibility of Edgerton's images and in their widespread distribution in print. A comparison of Edgerton's illustrations in Thompson's book (a second milk splash illustrated the text) with Worthington's earlier reproductions, either half-tone or wood engravings, is immediately illuminating.

Worthington's images, like laboratory data, had a raw, unmediated beauty, specificity, and proximity; Edgerton's appeared carefully composed and the natural world orderly but enigmatic, remote and inaccessible. Technical qualities of reproduction that gave Edgerton's images superior clarity and legibility were essential to his photographic vision, as was his meticulous attention to composition: He selected an exposure (hard-won in the laboratory) that resulted in a nearly symmetrical crown of milk and a suspended droplet centered above it, the graphic impact enhanced by the brilliant white splash piercing a deep black, featureless background. Characteristically, the documentary record says nothing about Edgerton's engagement with contemporary art photography, although the blackness and ambiguous pictorial space of Edgerton's images were similar to the effects modernist photographers of the 1930s obtained in their work, most influentially László Moholy-Nagy, who rejected conventional pictorial perspective and adopted unmodulated backgrounds that suggested infinite space. [9]

Edgerton's ongoing research brought improvements to his early strobes and images produced at 1/50,000 or 1/100,000 of a second were soon surpassed by exposures of over one millionth of a second, allowing him to picture the unseen world more powerfully than ever. His laboratory success documented in scientific journals was the outcome of restless experimentation but most remarkable was Edgerton's trajectory of public recognition that began with the publication of his milk splashes and other images in the early 1930s. MIT's *Technology Review* reproduced an Edgerton milk splash in 1932 and moved his splashes to a cover illustration in 1934.[10] Editor James R. Killian, Jr. recognized in Edgerton's photographs visual qualities that complemented his own modernist sensibility and his design ambitions for the magazine; Edgerton's work, Killian claimed, "gave the magazine pioneering photographic distinction."[11] Under Killian's direction, *Technology Review* published Edgerton's photographs 32 times during the decade, so often that his work could be reproduced with only brief captions or commentary, isolated from editorial matter as stand-alone illustrations or "singles."

*Technology Review*, with high production values but limited circulation, was a springboard. An average readership in the millions could have seen Edgerton's work in the weekly pictorial magazine *Life*, which published Edgerton's photographs, including the milk drop series, ten times in eight years, beginning in the fourth issue of November 1936.[12] Edgerton's work epitomized publisher Henry R. Luce's use of photography "to see and be amazed, to see and be instructed," and the magazine proclaimed that Edgerton's pictures "show science as true and beautiful."[13] Features in the *New York Times*, beginning in 1932, and other newspapers expanded Edgerton's audience even more, and luxurious rotogravure newspaper supplements with a long tonal range registered the beauty, particularly the deep blacks, of Edgerton's prints.[14] In the short span of about four years during the 1930s, the reception of Edgerton's photographs as media objects had grown from a specialized academic audience to a broad general public.[15] Photographic reproductions flooding the popular press during the decade provided a context for public acceptance of the veracity and credibility of photography, an important aspect of Edgerton's rising prominence.

The early reception in the art community of Edgerton's work was similarly auspicious, at a time when photography was struggling to be recognized as an art form, and development of institutional and private collections of photography was in its infancy. In 1933, Edgerton's milk splashes appeared in the Royal Photographic Society's annual exhibition, and he continued to show work there regularly into the next decade.[16] It was probably at the R. P. S. that the great collector and pioneering historian of photography, Helmut Gernsheim, became aware of Edgerton's work, which he came to regard as "of great historical importance." Edgerton's milk drop later received a full-page illustration in Gernsheim's *Creative Photography*, facing Albert Renger-Patzsch's powerfully conceived close-up of a locomotive drive shaft. The association suggested a relationship between Edgerton and the esteemed German photographer, trained as a chemist, whose work exemplified scientific precision and an experimental approach to observation of the natural world that Edgerton shared.[17]

# flash!

## SEEING THE UNSEEN BY
## ULTRA HIGH-SPEED PHOTOGRAPHY

---

BY

HAROLD E. EDGERTON

AND

JAMES R. KILLIAN, Jr.

---

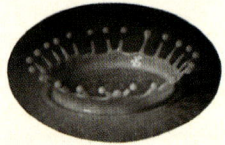

HALE, CUSHMAN & FLINT
Boston

The title page from Edgerton's first photobook, published in 1939.

It was, above all, exhibition at the Museum of Modern Art that brought recognition of Edgerton's work in the art world. For MoMA's highly successful inaugural photography exhibition in 1937, curator Beaumont Newhall (assisted by Ansel Adams) chose six Edgerton photographs – a remarkable number by one artist even in a very large exhibition.[18] Newhall selected an Edgerton milk splash to illustrate the exhibition catalogue, *Photography 1839–1937*, which would become a foundational text in the history of photography.[19] "No eye has ever seen the form of a drop of milk splashing," Newhall wrote of the photograph he found of "spectacular interest." For an image to capture Newhall's exceptional interest meant it would be admitted into a nascent canon of photographic art that would establish the rationale by which 20th-century photography would be judged for decades. Newhall's exhibition, a groundbreaking international survey, examined the medium's technological and artistic evolution, and included a variety of utilitarian applications such as X-ray images.[20] Edgerton's photographs, opening up hidden worlds of motion, exemplified "experiments in abstraction" in Newhall's thematic treatment of the first century of photographic history.

Another example of Edgerton's growing acclaim as a photographer was the inclusion of two of his photographs in Lucia Moholy's pioneering history of photography, published in 1939.[21] That same year, Edgerton's work reappeared at the Museum of Modern Art in the tenth anniversary exhibition, *Art in Our Time*.[22] Newhall selected only seven living photographers for exhibition, including Ansel Adams, Walker Evans, Berenice Abbott, Man Ray, Brett Weston, Ralph Steiner and Edgerton, from whom he acquired a milk splash and five other pictures. All of the selections represented work that demonstrated, according to Newhall, the "direct use of the camera … as opposed to the abstract desire to produce Fine Art." Edgerton and the other "straight" photographers exhibited sought to produce an "accurate visual record" in their work, which Newhall endorsed as the "basis for the most genuinely creative aspect of photography … brilliant technically and highly artistic."[23]

Edgerton's work appeared again in MoMA's *Sixty Photographs: Camera Aesthetics*, the Department of Photography's inaugural exhibition in 1940–41, and over the next 27 years Newhall and his successors Edward Steichen and John Szarkowski exhibited Edgerton's work in at least ten more exhibitions, an exposure that Szarkowski remarked made Edgerton's work "as familiar to many of our visitors as the *Guernica*."[24] The MoMA exhibitions and high-speed photography demonstrations there in the 1940s brought Edgerton's work into contemporary art practice; Jackson Pollock, for example, who was creating his own transformative splashes on canvas, became aware of Edgerton's work in New York in the 1940s.[25]

Edgerton's first decade of publications and exhibitions culminated in his first book, *flash! Seeing the Unseen by Ultra High Speed Photography* (1939; see p. 28).[26] His collaborating writer and contextualizer was former *Technology Review* editor James Killian, who can probably be credited with bringing the work to press.[27]

Publisher Hale, Cushman & Flint's catalogue included primarily illustrated books, notably not science or academic titles, which Killian (if not also Edgerton himself) must have felt appropriate to Edgerton's public aspirations. Always bridging the scientific and art audience for Edgerton's work, Killian claimed that the photographs published in *flash!* were "not only facts, but new aesthetic experiences" which he boldly compared to the work of the acknowledged contemporary masters Edward Steichen, Edward Weston, and Alfred Steiglitz.[28]

*flash!* was indeed a milestone of artistic autonomy for Edgerton. It was a photobook, not a scientific text, firmly in the convention of photobooks that reached back to the beginnings of photography, and for which modern photographic history has made a claim as a virtually independent art form. In book design, *flash!* was a step up from the illustrated press and far removed from conventional scientific texts, as signaled by the vignetted milk splash cleverly positioned on the title page. The photo spreads in *flash!* make a telling comparison to one of Edgerton's earliest published photographs in the *Science Newsletter* of 1932.[29] Context was everything, and Edgerton must have seen the evidential power of his photographs enhanced by their impactful presentation. It is with this recognition that Edgerton's rhetorically charged photographs become, with their publication in *flash!*, fully developed media objects.

*flash!* was not itself innovative in design, but its visual grammar reflected changes that had taken hold in modernist book design in the 1930s, characterized by bleed photography, bold use of black-and-white space, asymmetrical layouts and incisive typography. Technical data that created a credible context for the photography was confined to (a dreary) un-illustrated appendix, where presumably few readers ventured. The choice of typeface – a sturdy, heavily inked, uppercase slab serif was simple and direct. The overall effect of the book design was crisp and bold, creating for Edgerton's images a context of contemporaneity, broadly enhancing their impact. Edgerton was working here within a new visual language of design practice, and with the book's success his photography was increasingly shaped by the destination of his images on the printed page. Already in 1939, in the first decade of a nearly 60-year career as a scientist photographer, he created for himself a genre of publication to present his research that was more visually compelling than the scientific press and in subject matter for which there was no recognized artistic convention.

Celebrated as a public image-maker and credentialed as a photographic artist, Edgerton brought his photographs to an even larger public audience in the coming decades, through exhibitions and in print. A second edition of *flash!* in 1954 led eventually to a new photobook, *Moments of Vision*, published in 1979, again in collaboration with Killian and repurposing many of the same images as *flash!*, with his milk drop coronet as a frontispiece.[30]

Confidence as an experimenter and photographer gave Edgerton opportunities for more subjective expression, often witty and humorous, which is evident in his captioning. The remarks reveal a side of his personality as a showman and entrepreneur that contributed to his public image. He produced many breathtaking images showing speeding projectiles, but a bullet slicing a Jack of Diamonds playing card in half had something of the spunk of county fair chicanery (see page 134). The photograph demonstrated Edgerton's sense of wit and theater (and his ties to his Nebraska roots), as well as his instinct for an appealing and entertaining, yet meaningful image. He also produced a large number of self-referential images that include himself as orchestrator of the action, as if he were a conjurer of the magical image he created.[31]

Always keenly aware of context, Edgerton, despite his disclaimers, understood art practice and the artistic quest for perfect form that ultimately made his milk splashes so visually articulate and communicative – more successful, as Thompson had observed, than Worthington's pictures, and surpassing all, or nearly all, other scientific imagery of the century in public recognition.[32] For Edgerton the scientist and experimenter, it was a quest that was doubly challenging: ultimately, a search for perfect pictorial form as well as perfect data. He advised students that there was "no such thing as a 'perfect' result" in scientific experimentation, yet he appeared to believe that artistic exactitude was attainable if only he kept on trying[33] He photographed milk splashes for over 25 years before finally reaching, in 1957, a *merely acceptable* resolution of symmetry, balance, orderliness, and arrested motion (see p. 55). Executed in color, the image was also Edgerton's response to the rapidly growing public interest in color photography. A photograph "of intensity and subtlety, of show and substance, of beauty and precision," according to an award citation, the color milk splash was a media object of wide circulation in magazines and books, and in postcard and poster reproductions, and remains Edgerton's most-recognized image.[34]

Behind that famous result were thousands of attempts in the laboratory; but as good as it was, it was not Edgerton's perfect image. "Although I have tried for years to photograph a drop of milk splashing on a plate with all the coronet's points spaced equally apart," Edgerton recounted, "I have never succeeded."[35] "Many times, as in his studies of splashes," Killian observed in *flash!*, Edgerton made "definitive pictures only to discard them because he sought a description that was eloquent as well as lucid … [and] the best possible correlation between meaning and expression."[36]

This relentless quest for photographic exactitude and perfection of form separates Edgerton from most other scientist photographers who preceded him. He cared deeply about the quality and reception of his images, and about his ability to communicate science to a public who were astonished by what Szarkowski called "wondrous and beautiful images" that expand "our sense of the visually possible."[37] Through convincing and compelling photographic form, Edgerton made the natural world comprehensible. He "changed most fundamentally the way in which we come to know the world through photography," the photographer Richard Benson observed.[38] His ability to communicate his achievements, and the wonder and beauty of science, was his greatest success as a photographer, as well as, arguably, as a scientist.

1   D'Arcy Wentworth Thompson, *On Growth and Form* (Cambridge: University Press, 1942), frontispiece. I would like to thank Deborah Douglas, Jon Duval, Gus Kayafas, Daryl McCurdy, Julie Van Haaften and Dietmar Winkler for their assistance with this essay.

2   Stephen Jay Gould called Thompson's book "the greatest work of prose in twentieth century science," in "Foreward: This Was a Man", *id., On Growth and Form*, (Cambridge: University Press, 1992).

3   Thompson, *op cit.*, 1942, p. 390.

4   See Richard L. Kremer, "Educating the High-Speed Eye: Harold E. Edgerton's Early Visual Conventions," in Nancy Anderson and Michael R. Dietrich, eds., *The Educated Eye: Visual Culture and Pedagogy in the Life Sciences* (Hanover, N. H.: Dartmouth University Press, 2012, pp. 186–212; Ben Burbridge, ed., *Revelations: Experiments in Photography* (London: MACK; Media Space, Science Museum, 2015), pp. 116–68, esp. 148–57.

5   Harold E. Edgerton, interviewed by James Sheldon, Aurora, Nebraska, April 12, 1983. Transcript in the "Harold E. Edgerton folder," Biographical Files, General Collection, MIT Museum. Hereafter abbreviated: "Edgerton Biographical Files."

6   Worthington's photographs were made in collaboration with the experimenter R. S. Cole. The Royal Institution lecture was reprinted in Arthur M. Worthington, *A Study of Splashes* (New York: Macmillan, 1963), pp. 133–62. Later publication of the splashes was in *Scientific American*, Supplement No. 1026 (August 31, 1895), pp. 16,402–04; *Pearson's Magazine*, 6 (July–Dec. 1898), pp. 10–16, 130–35; Arthur M. Worthington, *The Splash of a Drop* (London: Society for Promoting Christian Knowledge, 1895); and *id., A Study of Splashes* (London: Longmans Green, 1908). Worthington's original photomontages of splashes are in the National Science and Media Museum, Bradford, UK. See Keith Gordon Irwin, "A. M. Worthington and His Study of Natural Phenomena," in A. M. Worthington, *A Study of Splashes*, 1963, *op. cit.*, pp. ix–xviii; Marta Braun, "The Expanded Present: Photographing Movement," in Ann Thomas, *Beauty of Another Order: Photography in Science* (New Haven: Yale University Press, 1997), pp. 150–250; Martin Kemp, *Visualizations: The Nature Book of Art and Science* (Berkeley: University of California Press, 2000), pp. 78–79; Peter Geimer, "Fotografie als Wissenschaft," in *Berichte zur Wissenschaftsgeschichte*, 28, 2005, pp. 114–22; *Revelations, op. cit.*, pp. 18–19.

7   Arthur M. Worthington, *A Study of Splashes*, 1908, *op. cit.*, "Preface."

8   On Mach and Boys, see Braun, *op. cit.*, pp. 178–80.

9   Notably, in his widely published photograms; see *Moholy-Nagy: the Photograms, Catalogue Raisonné*, Renate Heyne, *et al.*, Ostfildern: Hatje Cantz, 2009.

10  "A Falling Drop of Milk Caught in the Act by a New Method of High Speed Photography," *Technology Review* 34 (April 1932), p. 278; "Successive Portraits of a Falling Drop of Milk…," *Technology Review* 34 (July 1932), pp. 376–77. Publication was timely; several of Edgerton's early milk drop experiments are recorded in his *Notebooks* for January 31 and February 14, 1932. The cover illustrations appeared in July and October, 1934.

11  James R. Killian, Jr., *The Education of a College President: A Memoir* (Cambridge, MA: MIT Press, 1985), p. 14. Killian was highly attuned to *Technology Review*'s visual impact; he hired the innovative book designers and typographers William Addison Dwiggins and Daniel Berkeley Updike to redesign the magazine.

12  *Life*'s circulation was 1.5 million for the early issues, four million by 1946, with a total readership far higher; See John di Folco, "*Life* Magazine," *History of Photography*, 29, 2, (2005), pp. 207–08.

13  *Ibid*, p. 207; "Speaking of Pictures…," *Life* (July 29, 1941), p. 9

14  Waldemar Kaempffert, "The Week in Science," *New York Times*, October 23, 1932. An example of a rotogravure supplement featuring Edgerton's work is "Super-Speed Photography," *New York Times*, November 19, 1939. For more on photomechanical processes and turn of the 20ᵗʰ-century mass media, see Gerry Beegan, *The Mass Image: A Social History of Photomechanical Reproduction in Victorian London, England* (London: Palgrave Macmillan, 2008).

15  Edgerton's photographs also figured more prominently in public exhibitions. In 1939, some number of the 44 million visitors to the New York World's Fair saw the milk splashes and other Edgerton photographs on display in the Eastman Kodak exhibition.

16  Kremer, *op. cit*, p. 191.

17  Helmut Gernsheim, *Creative Photography: Aesthetic Trends 1839–1960* (Boston: Boston Book & Art Shop. 1962), pp. 170–71; See Roy Flukinger, *The Gernsheim Collection* (Austin: University of Texas Press, 2010), p. 286.

18  "Press Release, March 13, 1937", MoMA Archives; *Photography 1839–1937*, New York: Museum of Modern Art, 1937; Allison Bertrand, "Beaumont Newhall's 'Photography 1839–1937': Making History," *History of Photography*, 21, 2 (1997), pp. 137–46; Christine Y. Hahn, "Exhibition as Archive: Beaumont Newhall, *Photography 1839–1937* and the Museum of Modern Art," *Visual Resources* 18, (2002), pp. 145–52; Alessandra Mauro, ed., *Photoshow: Landmark Exhibitions that Defined the History of Photography* (Rome: Contrasto, 2014), pp. 149–58.

19  *Photography 1839–1937, op. cit.*, p. 88, and for the following quote.

20 Alessia Tagliaventi, "Photography at MoMA: Four Landmark Exhibitions" in *Photoshow, op. cit.*, pp. 148–59; Hahn, *op. cit.*, p. 147; Maria Morris Hambourg and Christopher Phillips, *The New Vision: Photography During the World Wars* (New York: Abrams, 1989), pp. 60–61.

21 Lucia Moholy, *A Hundred Years of Photography, 1839–1939* (Harmondsworth: Penguin, 1939), np. In the 1920s, Moholy had been instructor of photography at the Bauhaus and was married to László Moholy-Nagy, who also taught there; see Rolf Sachsse, *Lucia Moholy* (Düsseldorf: Marzona, 1985).

22 "Press Release, April 3, 1939," Museum of Modern Art Archives (and for the quotes that follow); *Beaumont Newhall, Focus: Memoirs of a Life in Photography* (Boston: Bulfinch Press, Little Brown and Co., 1993), p. 56.

23 "Press Release," *op. cit.*, pp. 3–5.

24 Harold E. Edgerton and James R. Killian, *Moments of Vision: The Stroboscopic Revolution in Photography* (Cambridge, MA: MIT Press, 1979), p. 13.

25 Yvonne Szafran, *et al.*, *Jackson Pollock's Mural: The Transitional Moment* (Los Angeles: The J. Paul Getty Museum, 2014), p. 22; Martin Kemp, *Structural Intuitions: Seeing Shapes in Art and Science* (Charlottesville: University of Virginia Press, 2016), pp. 154–56.

26 Harold E. Edgerton and James R. Killian, *flash! Seeing the Unseen by Ultra High-Speed Photography* (Boston: Hale, Cushman & Flint, 1939).

27 Jimena Canales, "Harold E. Edgerton, 'Doc' and His Laboratory Notebooks," *Aperture*, 211 (Summer 2013), pp. 72–73.

28 Killian, *flash!, op. cit.*, 1954, p. 22.

29 "Knocking It Sideways," *Science Newsletter* (December 3, 1932), cover.

30 Harold E. Edgerton and James R. Killian, *flash! Seeing the Unseen by Ultra High-Speed Photography*, (Boston: C. T. Branford, 1954).

31 Kremer, *op. cit.*, pp. 193–96.

32 Thompson, *op cit.*, 1942, p. 390; Helmut Gernsheim, *Concise History of Photography* (New York: Grosset & Dunlap. 1965), p. 160.

33 Edgerton cited in Joyce Bedi, "Drops and Splashes," Edgerton Digital Collections Website, *http://edgerton-digital-collections.org/stories/features/drop-of-water*, accessed July 10, 2017.

34 Citation for the Eugene McDermott Award of the MIT Council for the Arts, quoted in Gus Kayafas, ed., *Stopping Time: the Photographs of Harold E. Edgerton* (New York: Harry N. Abrams, 1987), p. 126.

35 Quoted by Canales, *op. cit.*, p. 73.

36 Killian, *flash!*, 1954, *op. cit.*

37 Szarkowski in "Press Release" for *Once Invisible*, June 20, 1967, Museum of Modern Art Archives.

38 Richard Benson, "A Flash of Inspiration," *New York Times*, March 19, 1995.

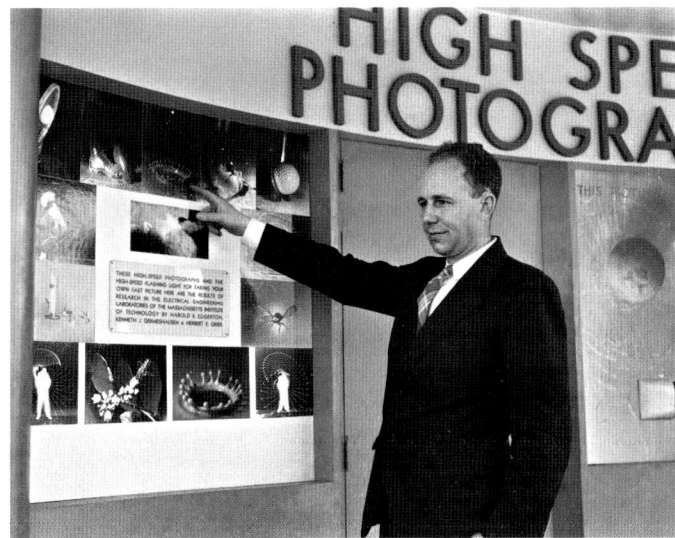

Edgerton stands outside his high-speed photography display at the Eastman Kodak exhibit at the 1939 New York World's Fair.

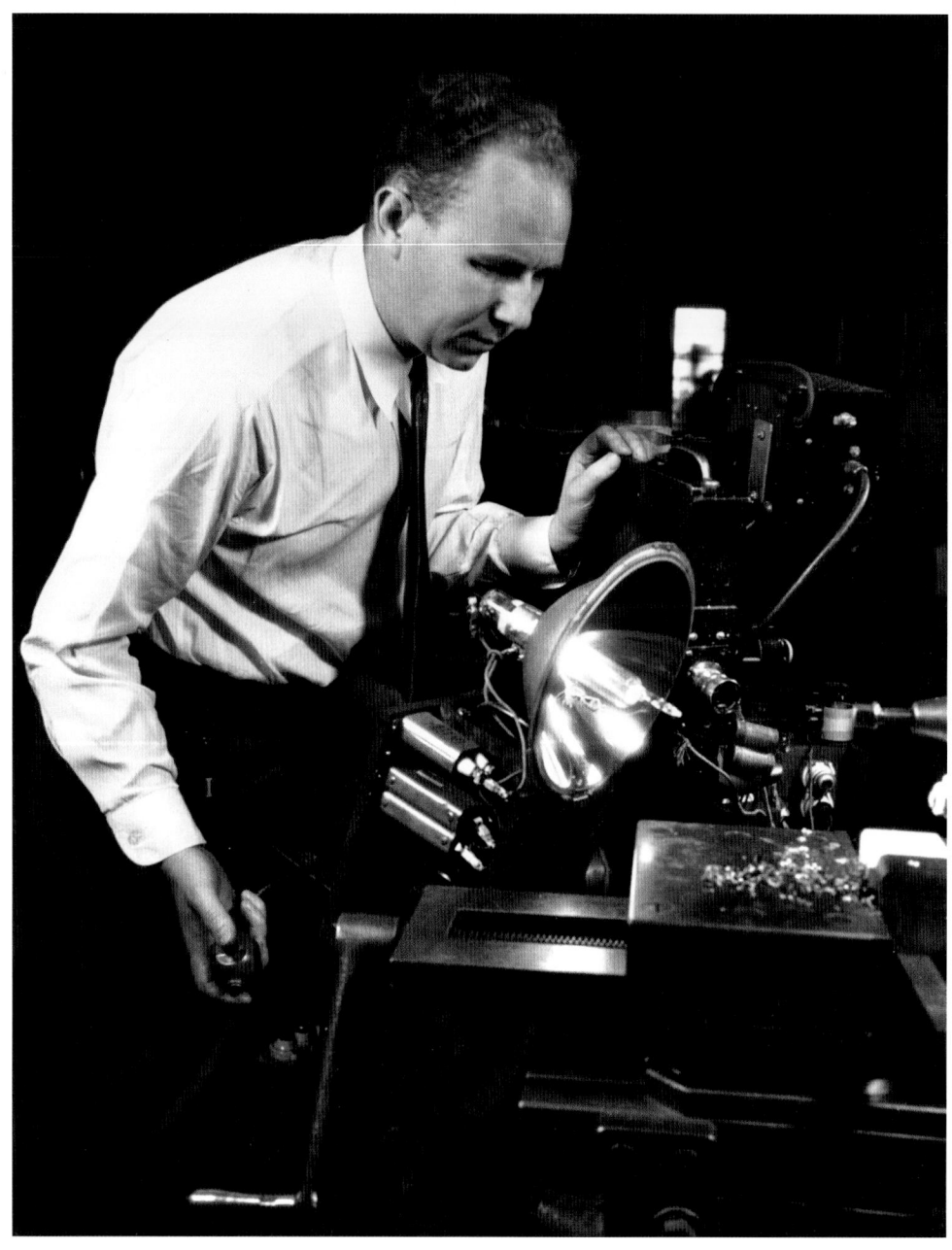

In this 1937 portrait Edgerton trains his stroboscope on a machine tool in operation.

# SPEED, EFFICIENCY, AND THE SUBLIME: SOME THOUGHTS ON THE HISTORIC SIGNIFICANCE OF HAROLD EDGERTON AND HIS ICONIC IMAGES

*Deborah G. Douglas*

Asked if he found his work exciting in a 1983 interview, Harold Edgerton replied enthusiastically: "Oh yes! Every time I touch the cameras, it is like going to the moon and back. It is real full of aura; lots of excitement. You always find out something that you didn't know, [and] that is what really makes the difference."[1] The ebullient, plainspoken Midwesterner, then age 80, was one of MIT's most iconic and beloved professors, but Edgerton was much more than an outstanding educator and engineer. His former student and longtime *Life* magazine photographer Gjon Mili called Edgerton "an American original."[2] Whether one thinks of Edgerton as an engineer or artist, educator or entrepreneur, the description fits.

Edgerton was born in 1903, the year the Wright Brothers made their famous "first" flight at Kitty Hawk. A few years later in 1909 at age six, his father took him to Fort Myer in Virginia to witness some of the early demonstration flights the Wrights made for the U.S. Army. As a boy, he developed an insatiable curiosity about how the world worked but especially the machines on his family farm and the wonders of photography. He worked summers in high school for Nebraska Power and Light Company, as a janitor, meter reader, coal handler, and lineman. This, Edgerton thought, would be his life's work.[3] Exceptionally bright, he went off to the University of Nebraska to study electrical engineering in the fall of 1921. Following graduation in 1925, Edgerton took a job at the famous General Electric research laboratory in Schenectady, New York. After a year, his father urged him to go on to graduate school at the Massachusetts Institute of Technology.[4]

Edgerton arrived at MIT in the fall of 1926 with a passion for electrical machinery and a spark of an idea. By chance when he was working at GE, Edgerton encountered an intriguing new apparatus called a Stroborama, invented by Laurent and Augustin Seguin to observe and photograph propellers and motors. Inspired (but frustrated) by the flashing strobe, it became Edgerton's passion. Being able to adjust the rate of the flash meant it was possible to study machines in motion. But both Edgerton and later scholars would observe that the Stroborama "produced weak, long flashes that were not suitable for photography."[5]

Edgerton loved studying generators and engines using what he would later characterize as "primitive" stroboscopes. He finished his master's degree in 1927 but was quickly hired as a research assistant and then instructor while he continued his studies toward a doctorate. A consummate experimentalist, Edgerton began keeping detailed laboratory notebooks documenting his daily investigations and observations. On September 16, 1930, Edgerton wrote: "I constructed a stroboscope to be used for observation of the electrical angle of displacement of the generators of the 15 mile falls development of the New England Power Company, located near St. Johnsbury and East Barnet, Vermont."[6] This would be a major milestone in his career. Edgerton made a public announcement of his invention in the May 1931 issue of *Electrical Engineering*.[7]

At the time, Edgerton was studying the cutting-edge electrical engineering challenge of power system stability (how to keep the synchronous electric motors that generate electricity to stay "in step" after disturbances such as lightning strikes).[8] Edgerton's doctoral research focused on the development of new tools for precision measurement so that he might help solve the problem of "pulling into step" a synchronous motor.[9] His thesis had involved using Vannevar Bush's famous Integraph[10] to investigate this problem mathematically, but his real passion derived from experimenting with stroboscopic technology. The goal was to use the stroboscope to study high-speed motion of mechanical objects. But Edgerton wanted to do more than simply illuminate movement; he wanted to make precision measurements. To that end, Edgerton wanted to use photography—both still and motion picture technologies—to create a record that could be scrutinized by researchers.

Edgerton's work completely transformed the 19th-century stroboscope. In two papers for the *Journal of the Society of Motion Picture Engineers*, Edgerton revealed: "that mercury-arc lamps when excited by quick violent electrical transients make a practical source of intermittent light which is very actinic and has a short duration flash." Further, he noted, "the timing of the flashes is easily controlled."[11] The technical description offered by Edgerton simply meant that he had found a way to make very fast and very controllable flashes of a type of light that would work well with photographic film. While Edgerton had applied this technology to study electric motors, he had already recognized its value (as his 1930 notebook entry indicates) for a myriad of industrial applications, from the study of printing presses to spinning airplane propellers.[12]

While Edgerton had once thought he would be the manager of an electric power plant, he had become enthralled with research. He loved finding practical solutions. Asked if he preferred to "work on theories" or "trial and error" experimentation, he replied: "Both. You exploit both systems as fully as you can." But then he went on to say: "I personally am an addict to experimentation. My argument is that, that the way to get to the real world is to go out and work with it. Other people like to be able to form matter in mathematical terms, formulas, theories … the whole thing is in the formula. Formulas are fine but they usually do not include all the factors. If you have one factor that isn't included, why, your theory is good for nothing."[13]

Edgerton's approach to research was not uniformly appreciated. Instead of writing scholarly papers, he went out hawking his stroboscope like a traveling salesman during the summer drives he and his wife Esther made to visit their families in Nebraska. He scrounged funds to employ two of his favorite students, Kenneth Germeshausen and Herbert Grier, during the height of the Great Depression (and later started a business with them: Edgerton, Germeshausen, and Grier) and took them everywhere to find the consulting jobs that would fill the pages of his notebooks with countless annotations, notes, sketches, and comments. Some have suggested that but for MIT president Karl Compton's personal appreciation for Edgerton, he might have been asked to leave the Institute.[14]

Compton appreciated the avuncular young instructor, but he also recognized the genius of Edgerton was not formulas but photographs. Compton was manifestly committed to the visual. James Killian, the man who would ultimately be Compton's successor in the MIT presidency, recalls Compton's introduction of an ambitious public relations program (from brochures to films and even an exhibit at the Chicago World's Fair) soon after taking office in 1930.[15] Working across the Institute to gather compelling images, Killian "discovered" Edgerton. The images that captured Killian's attention were not the ones Edgerton was taking for research, but rather Edgerton's stunning new collection of photographs taken of more ordinary subjects. This work began in 1932, when Edgerton turned his camera and strobe to take a picture of water flowing from the faucet in the laboratory sink (see p. 45). The cropped image looked like a piece of crystal. Encouraged by his family and colleagues, Edgerton began to take more images, which he in turn shared with Killian.

It was Killian, the new young editor of MIT's alumni publication *Technology Review*, who would be the first to publish Edgerton's photographs. The MIT News Service began to make regular releases of Edgerton's images throughout the 1930s. In 1933, Edgerton was invited to submit three images in the Royal Photographic Society's annual exhibition in London. He showed a short reel—"The Demonstration of High-Speed Photography of Motions of Animals and Insects"—at the autumn meeting of the National Academy of Sciences. MIT included action shots in Edgerton's laboratory in a 1934 film made to recruit promising high-school students to come to MIT. *Life* magazine began to feature Edgerton's images beginning in 1936. Killian and Edgerton began collaborating on a book project—*flash! Seeing the Unseen by Ultra High-Speed Photography*—that would be published in 1939. And even Hollywood came calling. The resultant documentary short, *Quicker'n a Wink*, made by Pete Smith at MGM Studios, won an Oscar in 1940.

Edgerton's images, whether for research or the pleasure of discovery, were wholly original but so too was Edgerton's way of understanding the world. On the surface, Edgerton seemed an anachronism, the embodiment of the truism "science discovers; engineering applies." His folksiness and hustle belied a more sophisticated sensibility. Richard Kremer in his essay in *The Educated Eye: Visual Culture and Pedagogy in the Life Sciences* perceptively wrote that Edgerton did not promulgate his philosophy "by writing prose on aesthetics but by making and publishing high-speed photographs of commonplace events."[16] To understand Edgerton the engineer, one really does have to look at the pictures.

Edgerton's images were deeply appealing to the artists and photographers (most especially Alfred Stieglitz) of the 1930s. To them, Edgerton's images effortlessly exuded the modern 20th-century engineering ideals of power, speed, and form.[17] Art historian Wanda Corn observed these machine-age modernists were busy "discarding older definitions that linked America to nature, wilderness, democracy, and a 'new Adam,' and focusing instead on "industrialized America, replacing the iconography of Niagara Falls and the Rocky Mountains with that of skyscrapers, billboards, brand-name products, factories, and plumbing fixtures."[18] Lewis Mumford put it this way in *Technics and Civilization*: "Expression through the machine implies the recognition of relatively new esthetic terms: precision, calculation, flawlessness, simplicity, economy."[19] Simply put, Edgerton's images – whether still or moving – were perfect illustrations of the new American technological sublime.[20]

Edgerton, when asked if he considered himself an artist, consistently responded this way: "I am an electrical engineer, and I work with strobe lights and circuits and make useful things."[21] Edgerton had an exceptional ability to use the tool of "visual surprise" to render comprehensible the most fundamental American industrial and cultural virtue: speed.[22] Personally, Edgerton hated "wasting time." His notebooks reveal a life of constant motion that only seemed to get faster and more complex, a characterization apropos of the 20th century. Edgerton's research resulted in tools and techniques that increased efficiency for his factory owner clients. His photographs represent a more complex commentary on the forces of industrialization. These frozen moments are not simply precise, efficient renderings of machines in motion. Edgerton's images are also full of life, joy, humor, kindness, and intrigue. They reveal the wonders of the natural world as much as the human-built one. They invite extended contemplation.

Edgerton explored this paradox when asked why he called his strobe, "the magic lamp." "It does so many things that are seemingly impossible," he said in an interview. "If a person comes along and has never seen one before, the eyes open up and they can't understand it. You try to explain it in nice physical, practical, terms [but] they are so awed by what they see, [that] they don't even listen to you. Just tell them it's magic."[23] This then is the unique gift of Harold Edgerton: Through his photographs, this American original displayed an alchemist's ability to turn the straw of industrialization's relentless, systemic demand for efficiency for the ends of power and wealth into the gold of sublime awe and appreciation of human creativity in service to the common good.

1   Harold E. Edgerton, interview by James Sheldon, Aurora, Nebraska, 12 April 1983. Transcript in the "Harold E. Edgerton folder," Biographical Files, General Collection, MIT Museum. Hereafter abbreviated: "Edgerton Biographical Files."

2   James R. Killian, Jr., "Papa Flash and His Magic Lamp," in *Moments of Vision: The Stroboscopic Revolution in Photography* by Harold E. Edgerton and James R. Killian, Jr. (Cambridge: MIT Press, 1979), p. 1.

3   In a later interview, Edgerton was asked why was he interested in electricity, to which he responded: "Well, electricity is the most important thing in the world, except maybe for religion … but everything is electricity. You think with electricity. … Every civilized person has got to know everything about electricity." Harold E. Edgerton, interview by James Sheldon. *op. cit.*

4   Massachusetts Institute of Technology, "Biographical Sketch: Dr. Harold E. Edgerton, Institute Professor, Emeritus; Professor of Electrical Measurements, Emeritus, Massachusetts Institute of Technology," press release, March 1980. Edgerton Biographical Files.

5   *Encyclopedia of 20th-Century Technology*, "Strobe Flash," by Joyce Bedi, p. 765.

6   Harold E. Edgerton, Notebook T-I, September 16, 1930, p. 44. Harold E. Edgerton Papers, MC-0025, Box 50, Institute Archives and Special Collections, Massachusetts Institute of Technology, Cambridge, MA.

7   H. E. Edgerton, "Stroboscopic Moving Pictures," *Electrical Engineering* (May 1931), pp. 327–29.

8   James R. Killian, Jr., *The Education of a College President: A Memoir* (Cambridge: MIT Press, 1985), p. 451.

9   Harold E. Edgerton, "Benefits of Angularly-Controlled Field Switching on the Pulling-into-Step Ability of Salient-Pole Synchronous Motors" (Sc.D. dissertation, Massachusetts Institute of Technology, 1931).

10  More commonly known today as a differential analyzer.

11  H. E. Edgerton, "Stroboscopic and Slow-Motion Moving Pictures by Means of Intermittent Light," *Journal of the Society of Motion Picture Engineers* 18 (1932), p. 356. Edgerton's first paper on this subject published in the Journal was: "The Mercury Arc as a Source of Intermittent Light," 16 (June 1931), p. 735.

12  Julius A. Stratton, "Harold Eugene Edgerton (April 6, 1903–January 4, 1990)," *Proceedings of the American Philosophical Society* 35 (1991), p. 446.

13  Harold E. Edgerton, interview by James Sheldon. Edgerton Biographical Files.

14  Louis Rosenblum made this observation in a taped conversation about Edgerton's teaching style with Gus Kayafas and Charles Wyckoff. The conversation was intended to be incorporated into a volume honoring Edgerton. It was inspired by the Edgerton Imaging Symposium held during the Society of Photographic Scientists and Engineers (SPSE) in May 1989. Copies of the transcript and draft manuscript are available in the Edgerton Biographical Files.

15  Killian, pp. 15–16.

16  Richard L. Kremer, "Educating the High-Speed Eye: Harold E. Edgerton's Early Visual Conventions," in Nancy Anderson and Michael R. Dietrich, eds., *The Educated Eye: Visual Culture and Pedagogy in the Life Sciences* (Lebanon, NH: Dartmouth University Press, 2012), p. 189.

17  David P. Billington and David P. Billington Jr., *Power, Speed, and Form: Engineers and the Making of the Twentieth Century* (Princeton: Princeton University Press, 2006), p. xv.

18  Wanda M. Corn, *The Great American Thing: Modern Art and National Identity, 1915–1935* (Berkeley: University of California Press, 1999), p. xv.

19  Lewis Mumford, *Technics and Civilization* (New York: Harcourt Brace Jovanovich, 1934), p. 350.

20  See David E. Nye, *American Technological Sublime* (Cambridge: MIT Press, 1994).

21  Harold E. Edgerton, interview by James Sheldon. Edgerton Biographical Files.

22  See Christian Gelzer, "The Quest for Speed: An American Virtue, 1825–1930" (Ph.D. dissertation, Auburn University, 1998).

23  Harold E. Edgerton, interview by James Sheldon. Edgerton Biographical Files.

Sept 16 1930        Stroboscope.

H. E. Edgerton.

     I constructed a strob...
be used for observation...
electrical angle of dis...
of the generators of the 15...
development of the New Ea...
company, located near...
and East Vern Barnet Ve...

     Previously I had go...
a G.E. single phase tube...
and measured the angle of a
5 kw induction machine. Mr.
Spencer brought Mr. L. Thurston
(movie camera man) over and he
took some shots with a 1.9 lens
and 12 frames a second. He said that
the light was sufficient for photographic
purposes. (Panchromat...
used)

     On thursday the 4th of...
went to the 15 mile falls...
was constructed so that...
rotor of #2 generator...
Upon this was mounte...
Below it was a sheet...
was part of the fan in...
the rotor. Upon this were accurately
located 52 white lines...
52 poles) adhesive take...
stuck to the lines in ord...
photographs have mor...

     the windage was te...
with a cold spell wa...
conditions for the thyr...
circuit that I was u...
transformer could not...
voltage to trip the circuit. After ypenm
some I got a 110-440 volt transformer and
pot

1 SEC.   F. 4.5.

found that it gave much better operation.
I returned to Boston on the 8th of Sept.

On the 12 Spencer again called and
wished me to bring up the oscillograph
and an assistant to watch the stroboscope.
Mr. Sullivan went with me.

I took a 1000 volt plate transformer
which had a mid tap. Thus I could use
both tubes in opposition. 15000 ohms was
put in the grid circuits where I used
5000 before. This was increased because
the 5000 ohm resistors could not
stand the current.

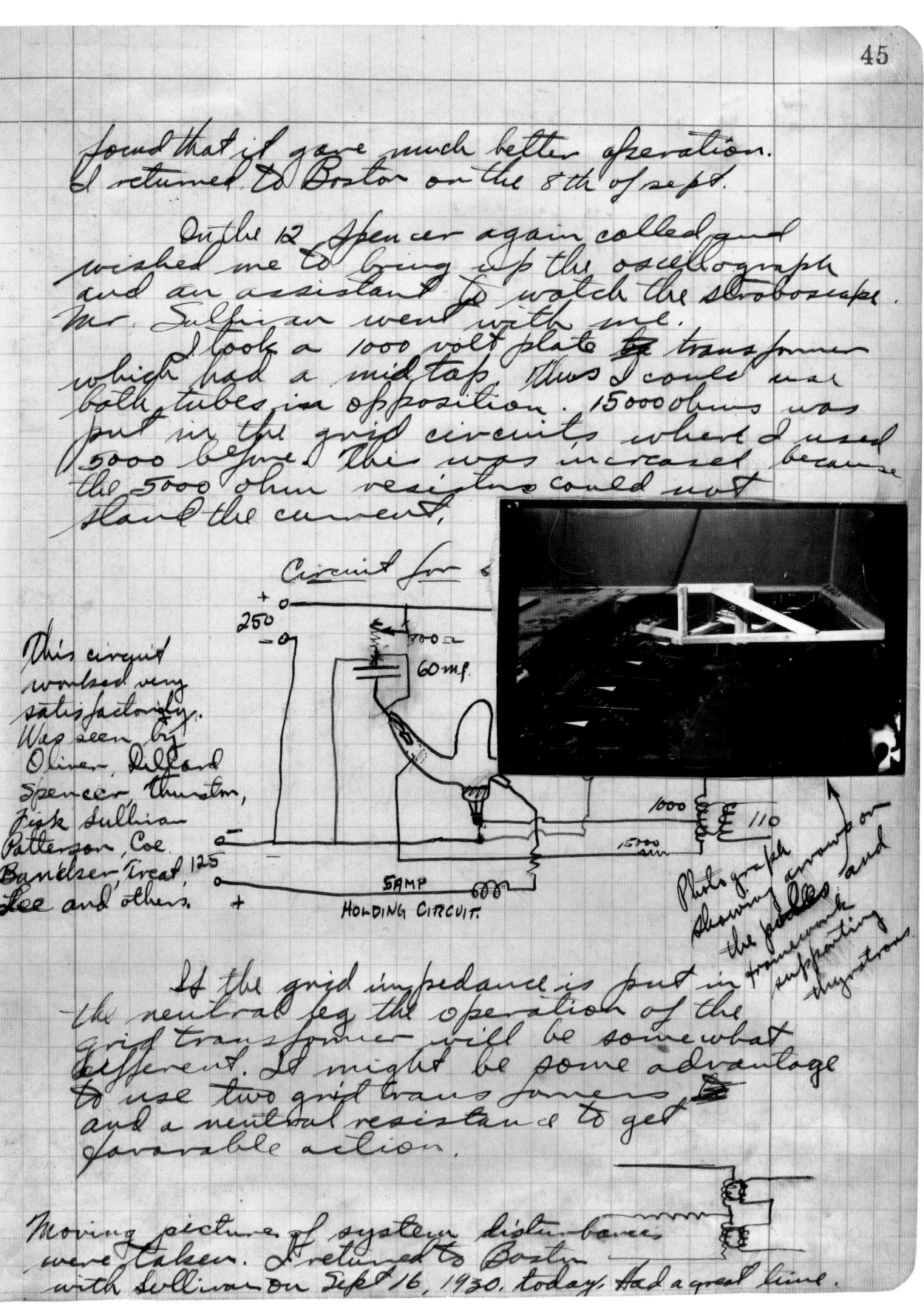

Circuit for

This circuit
worked very
satisfactorily.
Was seen by
Oliver, Dillard
Spencer, Thurston,
Fisk Sullivan
Patterson, Coe.
Banelser Treat
Lee and others.

HOLDING CIRCUIT.

Photograph showing arrangement on
the poles and framework supporting
thyratrons.

If the grid impedance is put in
the neutral leg the operation of the
grid transformer will be somewhat
different. It might be some advantage
to use two grid transformers
and a neutral resistance to get
favorable action.

Moving pictures of system disturbance
were taken. I returned to Boston
with Sullivan on Sept 16, 1930. today. Had a great time.

Edgerton's description of his first stroboscope. Notebook Number T-I, September 16, 1930, pp. 44–45.

PLATES

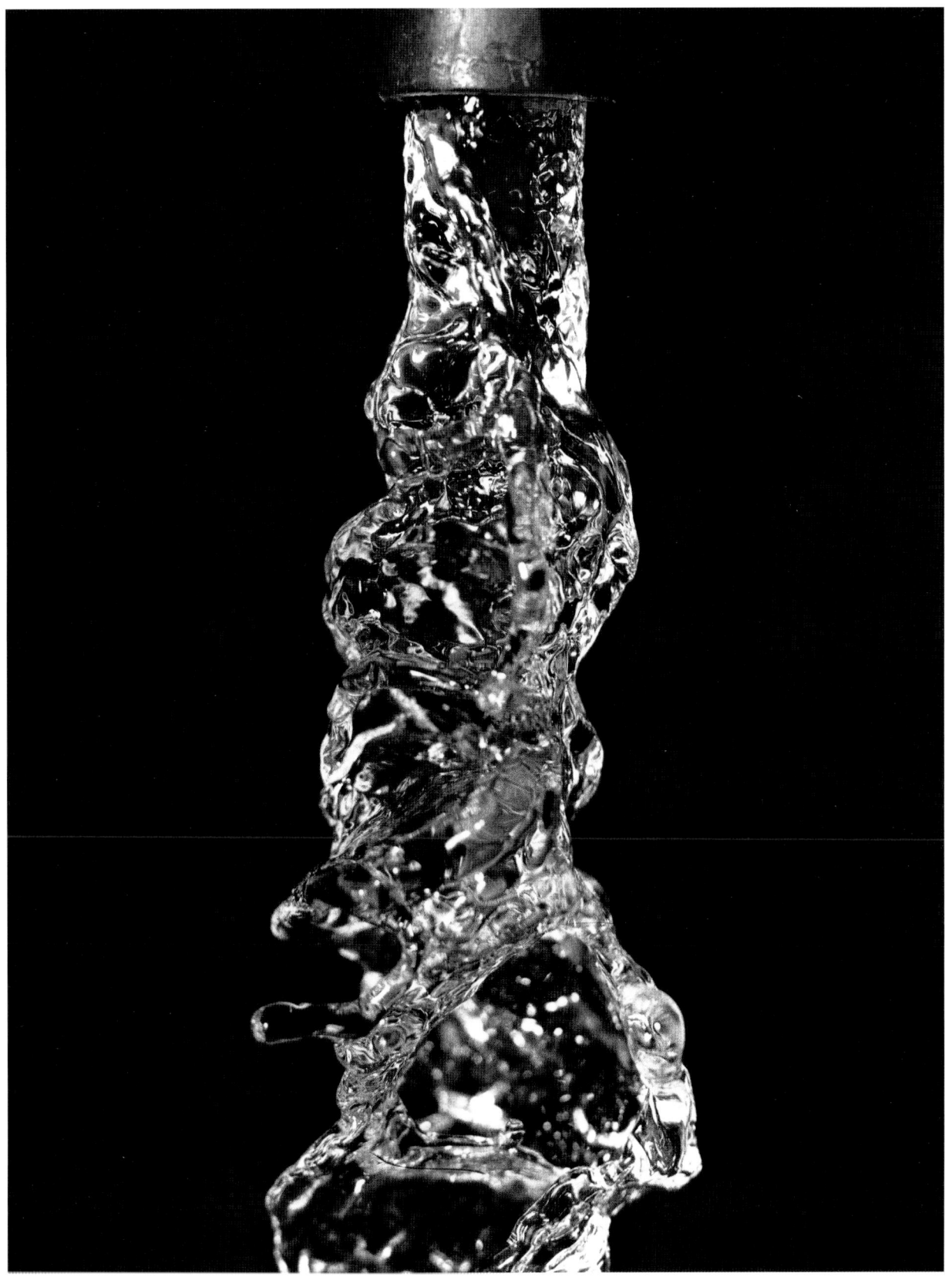

**Water flowing from a faucet, 1932**

Edgerton turned his camera and flash to capture water flowing from the tap in his laboratory, one of his earliest "non-research" images. Later he wrote: "In 1/50,000 of a second even this turbulence poses with glassy immobility." From *flash! Seeing the Unseen by Ultra High-Speed Photography.*

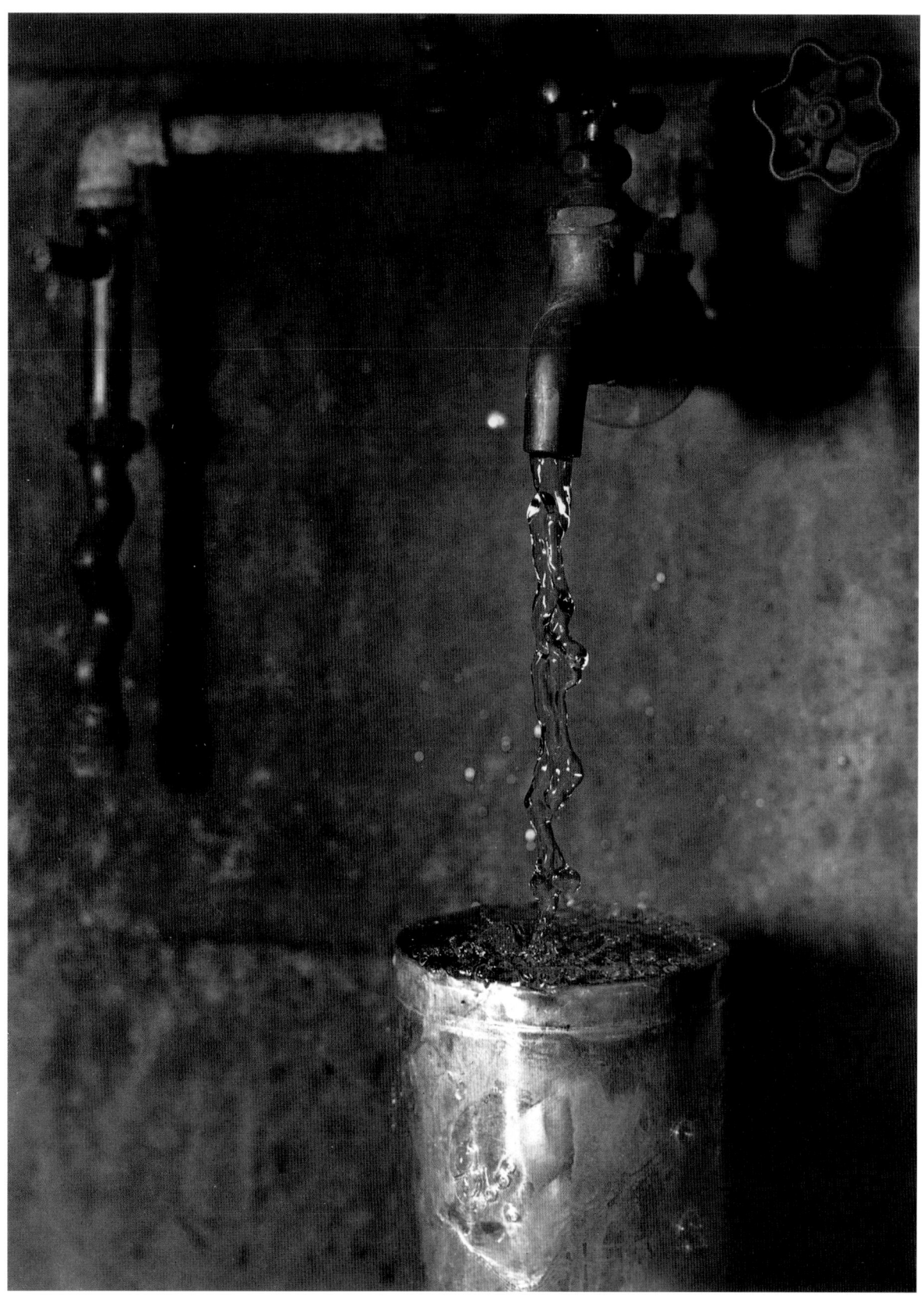

Water flowing into a can, c. 1932

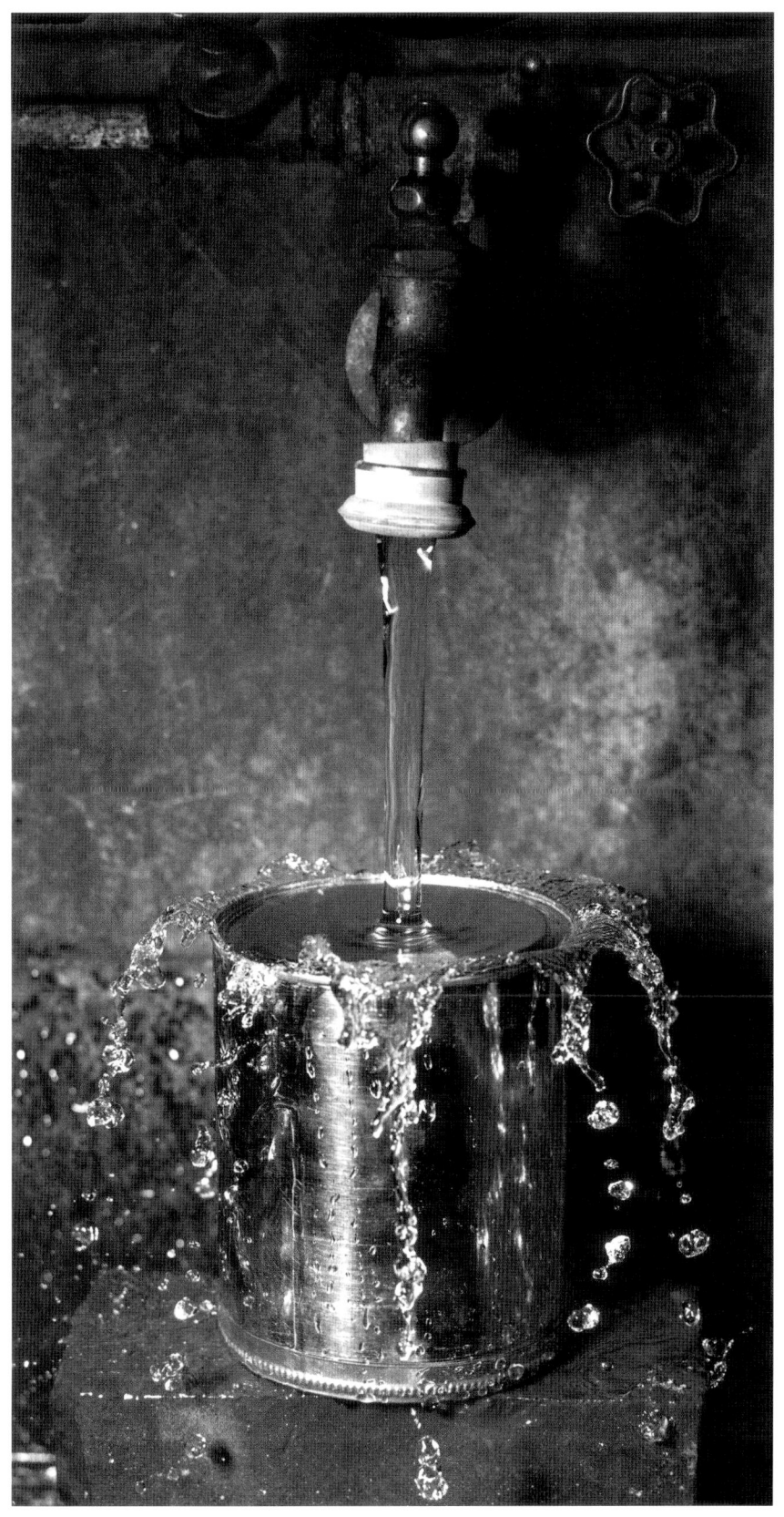

**Water flowing onto a paint can, 1934**

Edgerton captured the beauty of laminar flow, the smooth column of water, hitting the bottom of an overturned paint can.

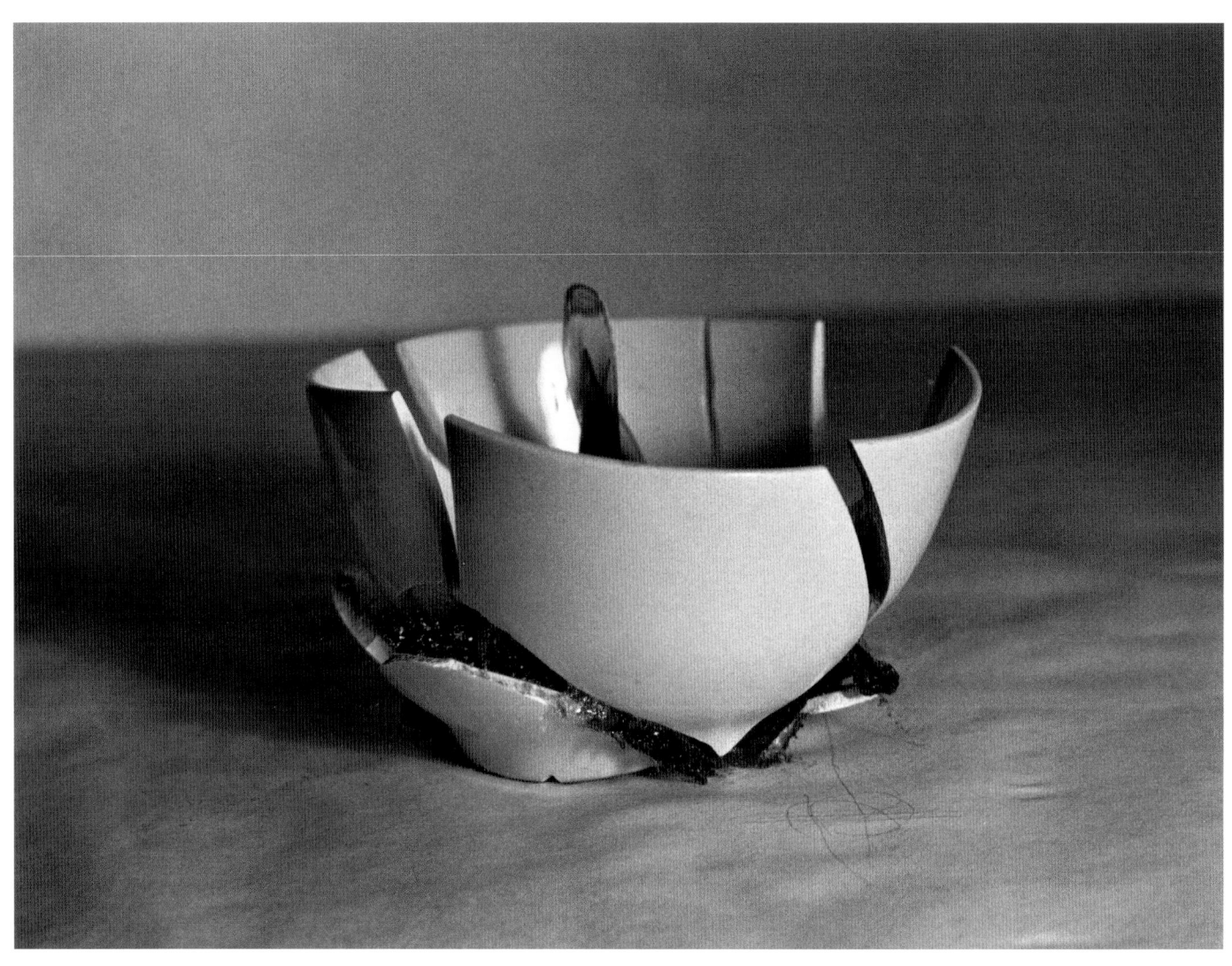

**This is coffee, 1933**

"As the dropped cup hits the floor, a delicate spout leaps upward and coffee slowly oozes through the cracks. The concussion of the cup tripped the contact mechanism which set off the flash."
From *flash! Seeing the Unseen by Ultra High-Speed Photography*.

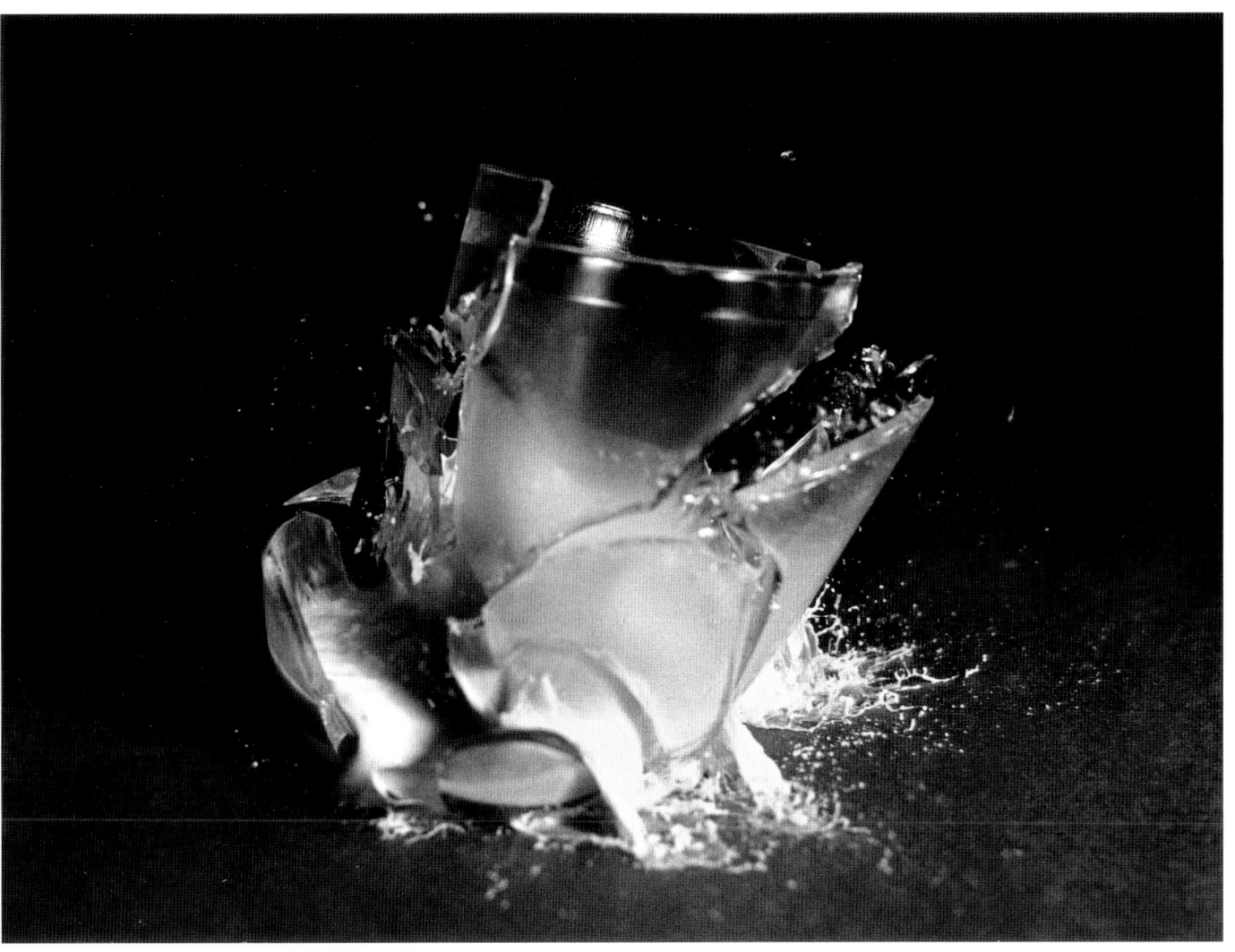

**This is milk, 1933**

"When the glass of milk strikes the floor after falling five feet, pieces of glass fly upward and the milk seems to flow out with molasses-like deliberation." From *flash! Seeing the Unseen by Ultra High-Speed Photography*.

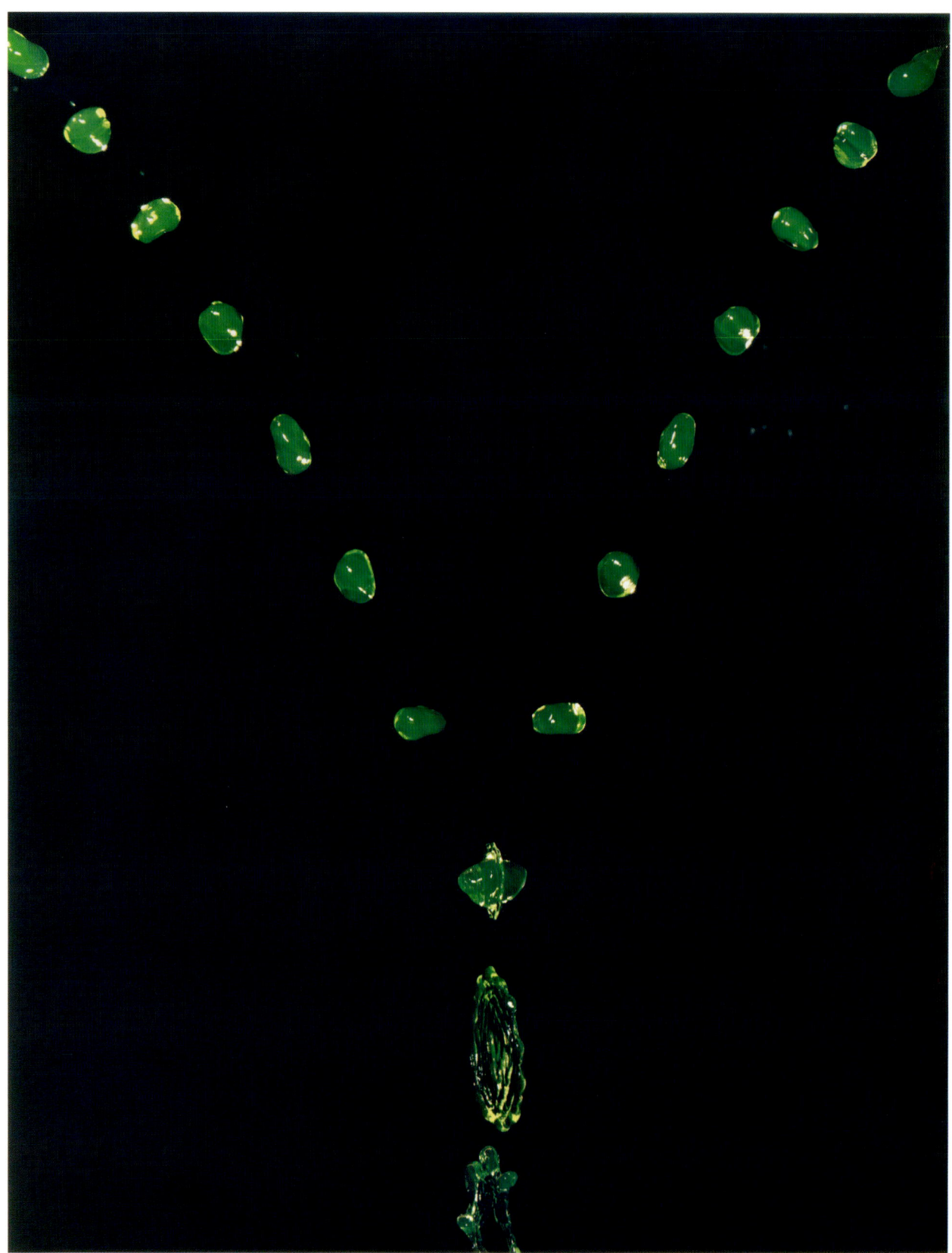

**Falling drops, 1971**

Edgerton built a wonderful hydraulic strobe demonstration device called a "Piddler," which featured a flashing strobe and pump that would draw water dyed with fluorescein from a small basin. Popular with students and museum visitors, the Piddler allows visitors to control the flash frequency to make the droplets appear to stand still or move backwards or forwards.

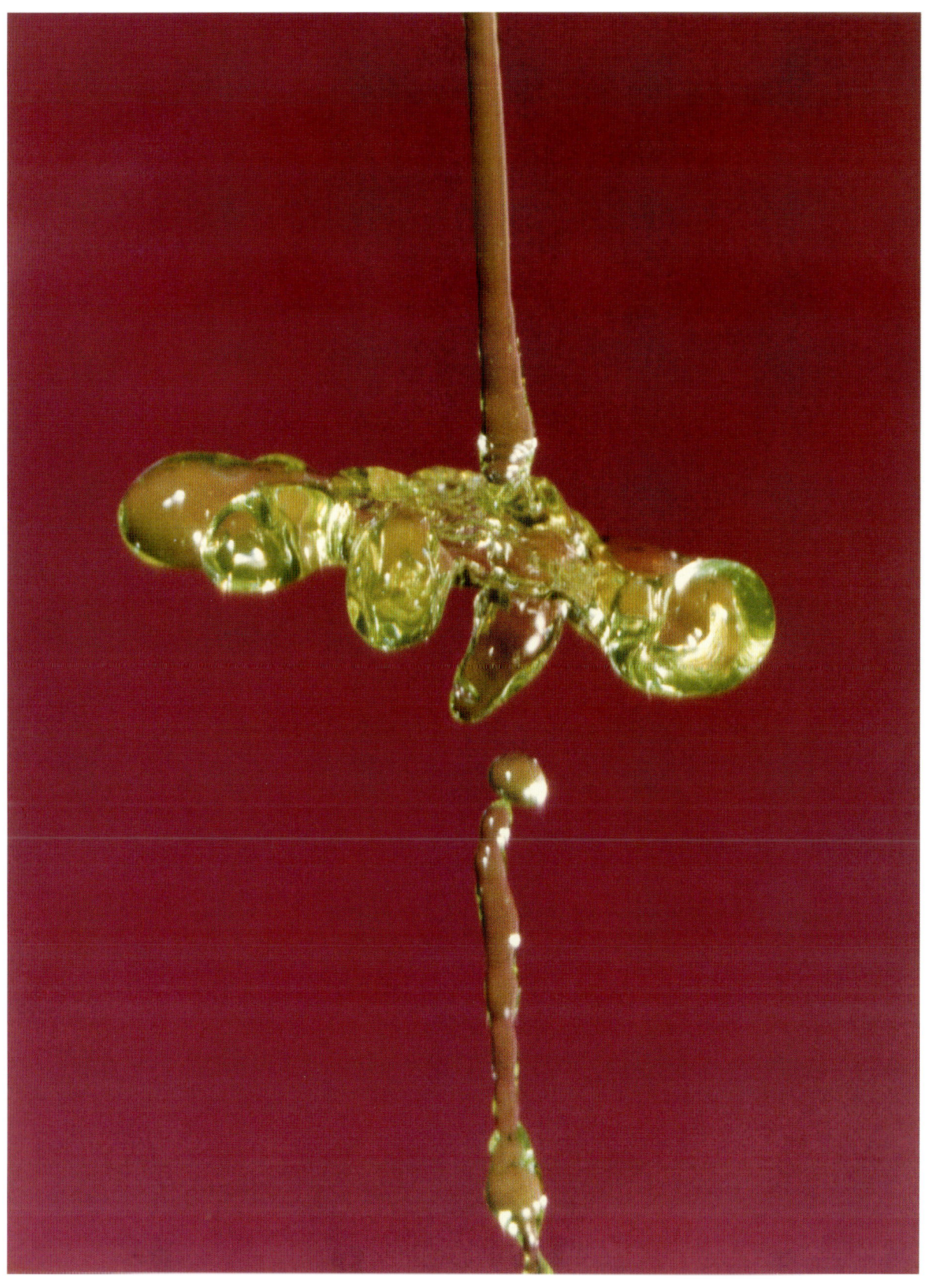

Water "flower," 1981

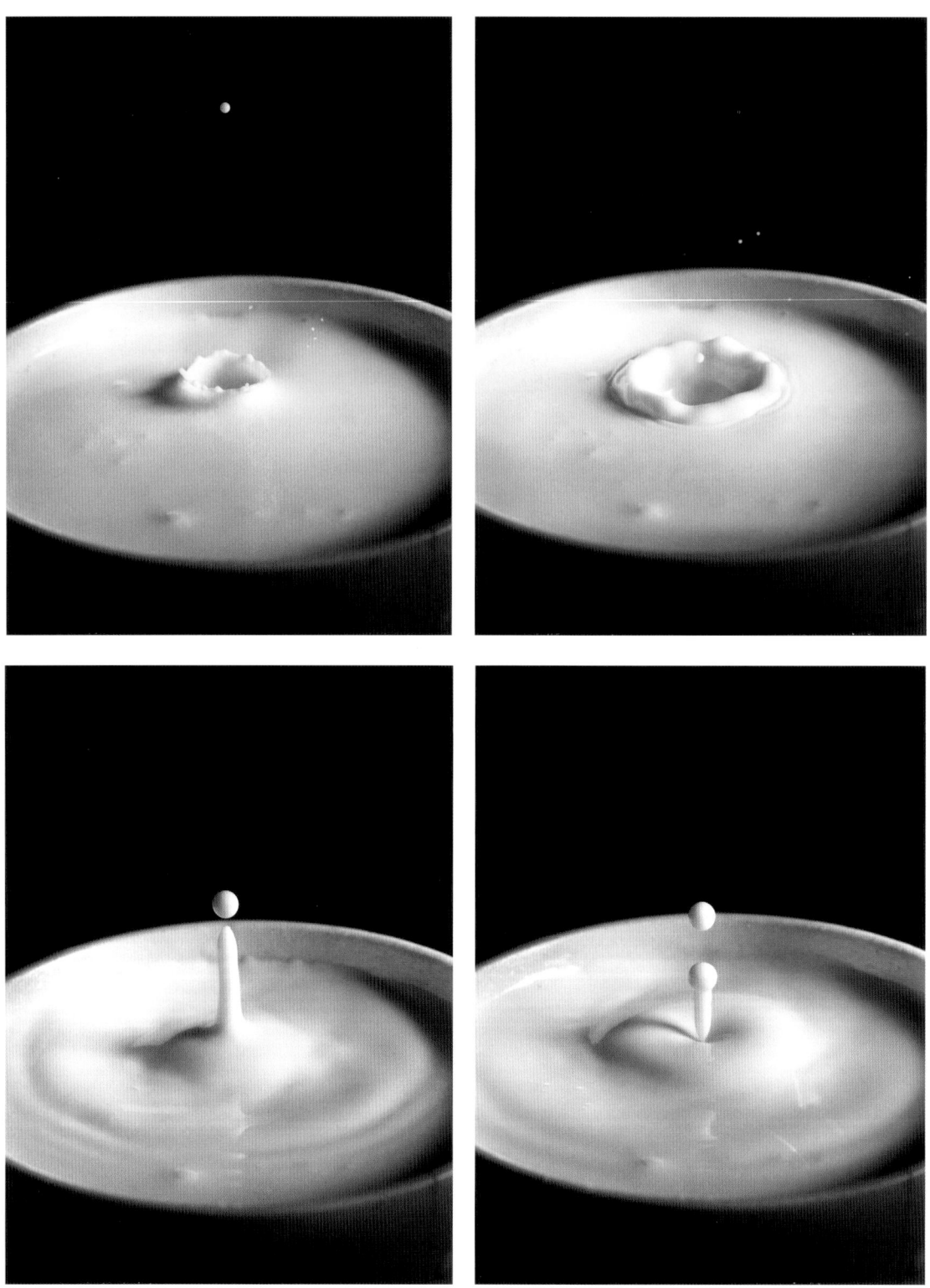

**Drop falling into reservoir of milk, 1935**

Four images from a series of nine capture the formation of a splash and subsequent segmentation of the spout or column of liquid. Edgerton's work on splashes continued what he called the "pioneer investigation" of A. M. Worthington, a professor of physics at England's Royal Naval Engineering College, begun in the 1890s and published in 1908.

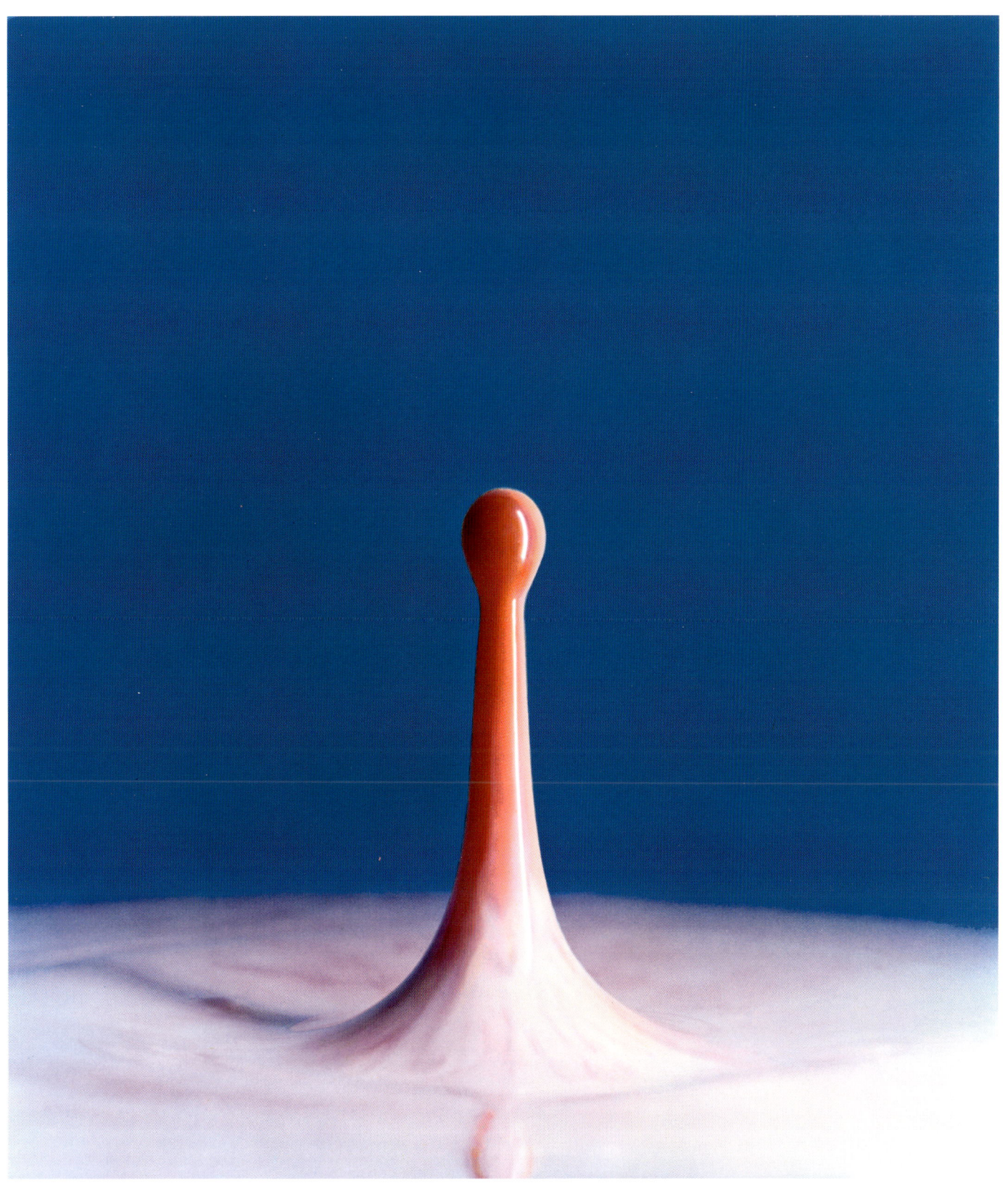

**Cranberry juice dropping into milk, 1960**

Microsecond exposure of a drop of cranberry juice falling into a glass of milk.

54

12    Jan 10 1957
      H.E. Edgerton

      Dynamite photos were terrific. The
scheme is all set to try on the roof in
sun light now.

      Ice Capades photos made yesterday
at garden with Red Elmendorf
obs Wycroft, Roy Swansen.

18" Spot                    Spot 8"
        25 mfd        25 mfd
        4000 v        4000 v.

                    f9  8x10

Camera
light - subject about 17 feet.
4 flashes - 3, - etc to catch.
Ronnie Robertson
Bobbie Spec.
Rose marie Henderson.

      Milk Drop exposure tonight.

            7½ or 8"    Background Dark bright Rey,

                        Green Pitcher upside down

                        Lamp FX-1 in cyl reflector
                          25 mfd 4000 volts.
Photo trip
Delay to            Camera 8x10  f 64
catch crown.        Panchromatic atomic  x ⎫
                    Ekta color.          ⎭

Edgerton describes plans for photographing his famous color milk drop coronet.
Notebook Number 24, January 10, 1957, p. 12.

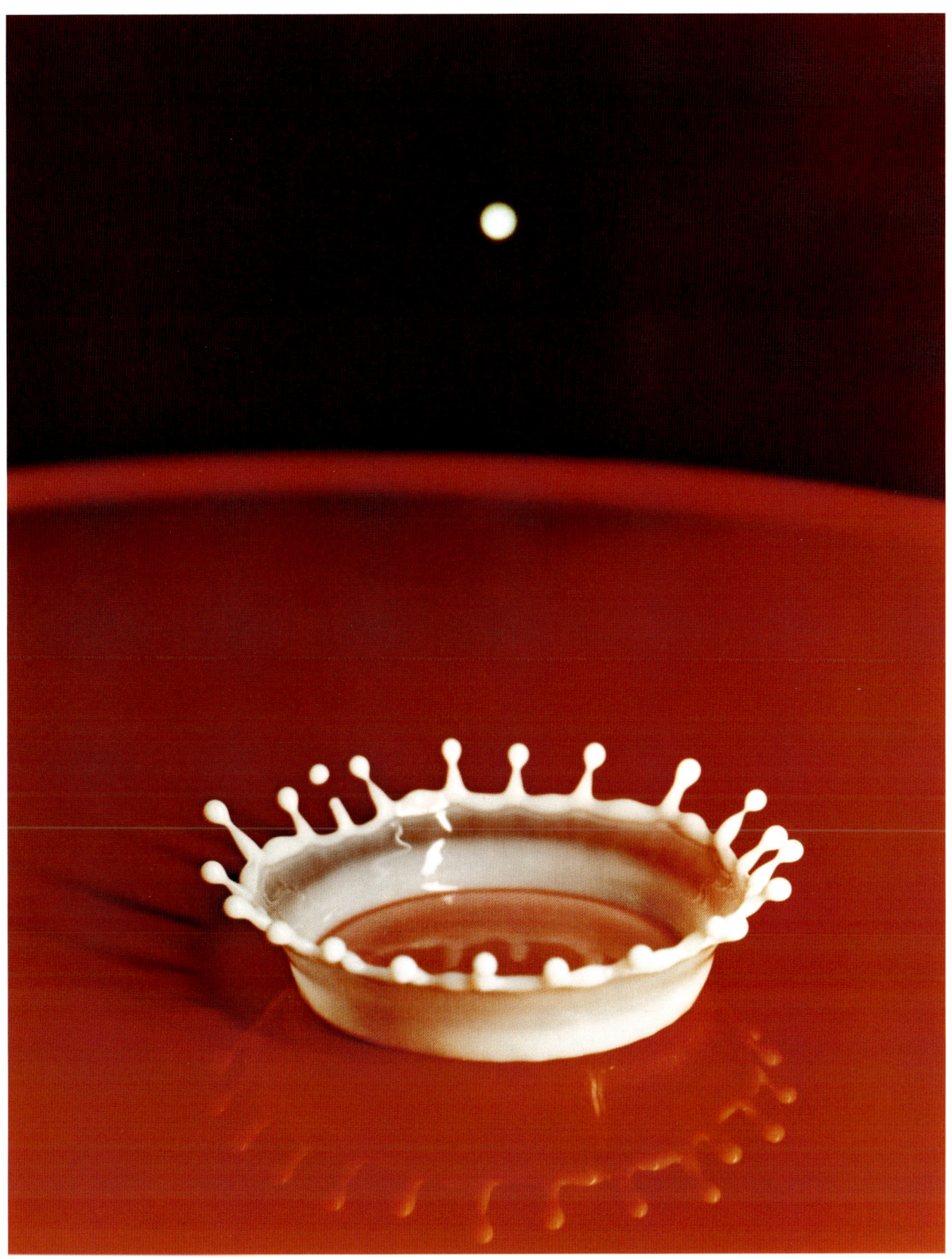

**Milk drop coronet, 1957**

Considered one of the most important photographs of all time, Edgerton saw this image as just one of many in a lifelong quest for the perfect coronet. Doc's lab notebook entry for January 10, 1957, describes the details of how he conceptualized this particular image. What goes unstated is that it was Edgerton's development of electronic flash technology and triggering mechanisms that made such extraordinary images possible.

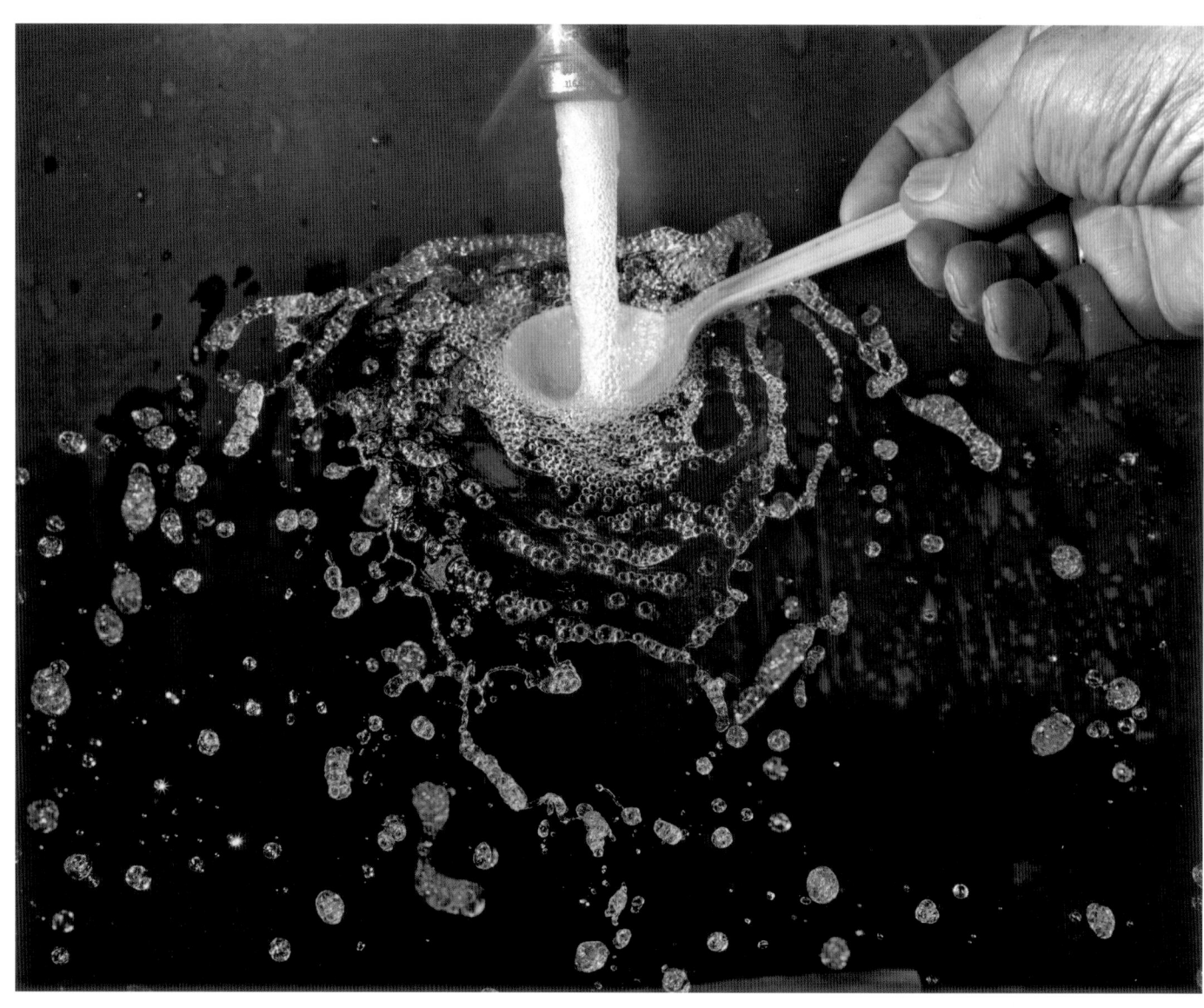

Spoon in water flow, 1987

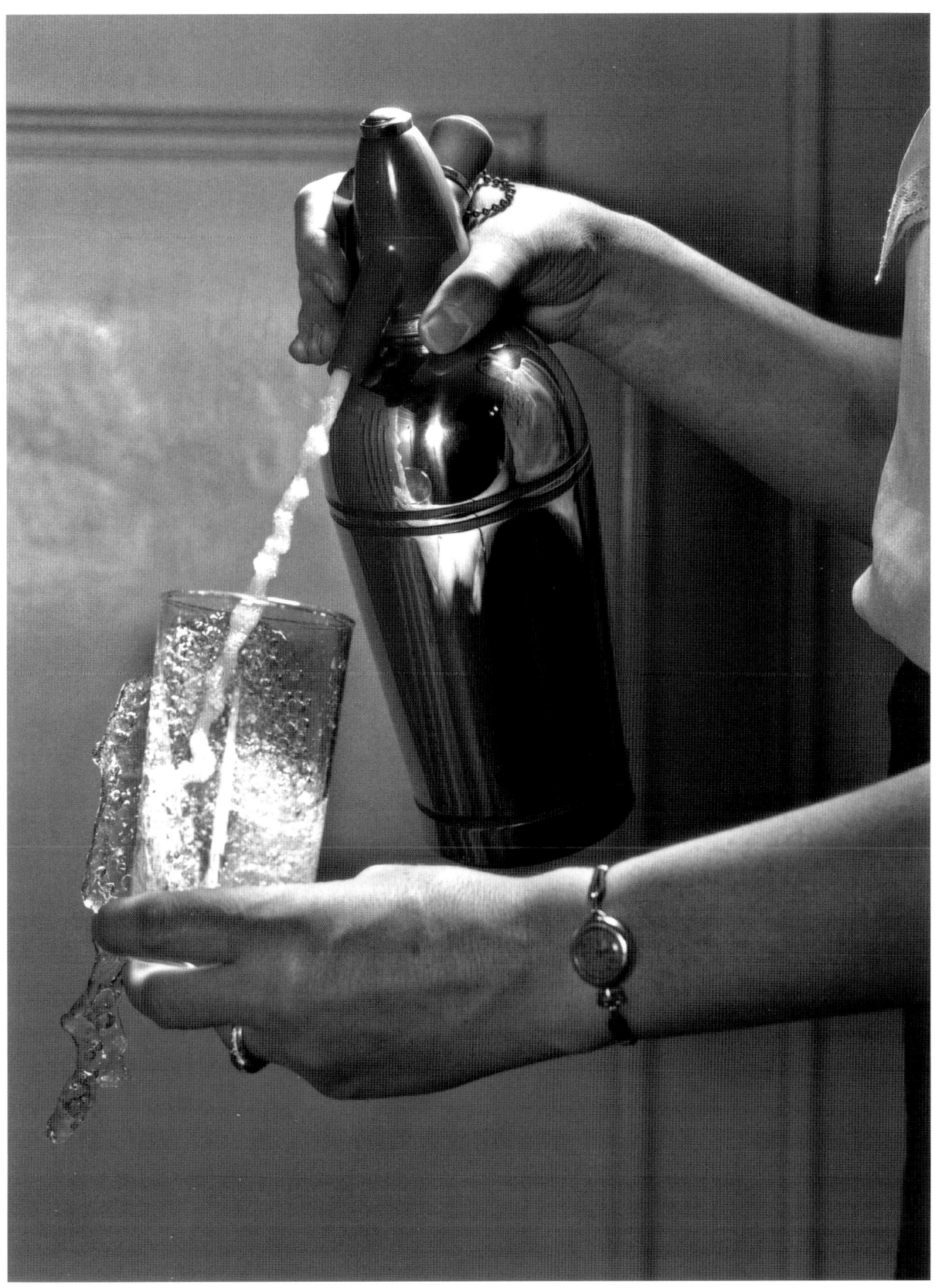

**Soda water, 1933**

Esther Edgerton attempts to fill a highball glass from a soda siphon.
Mrs. Edgerton and Doc's flash can be seen reflected on the stainless bottle.

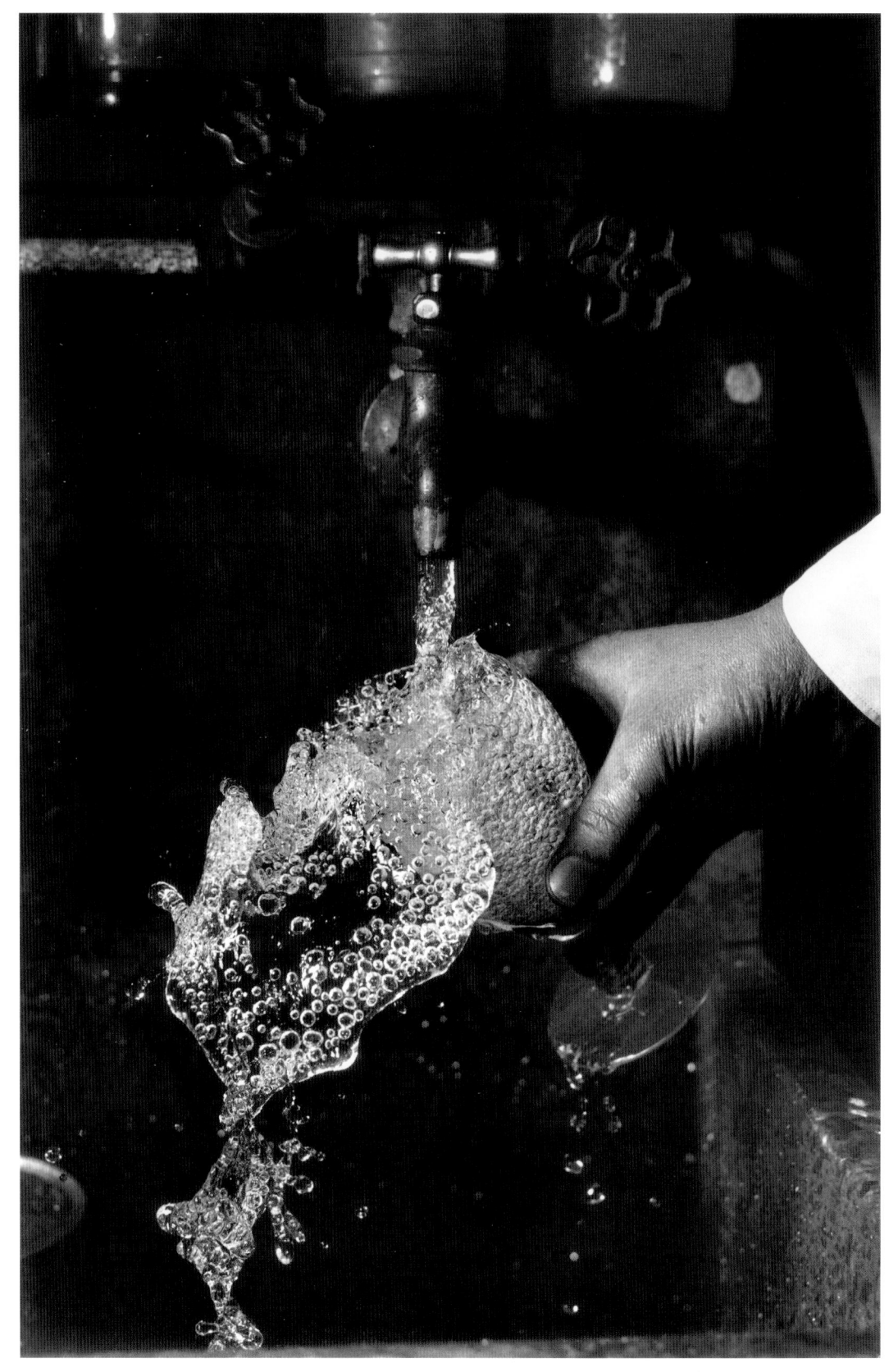

Water flowing into a goblet, 1934

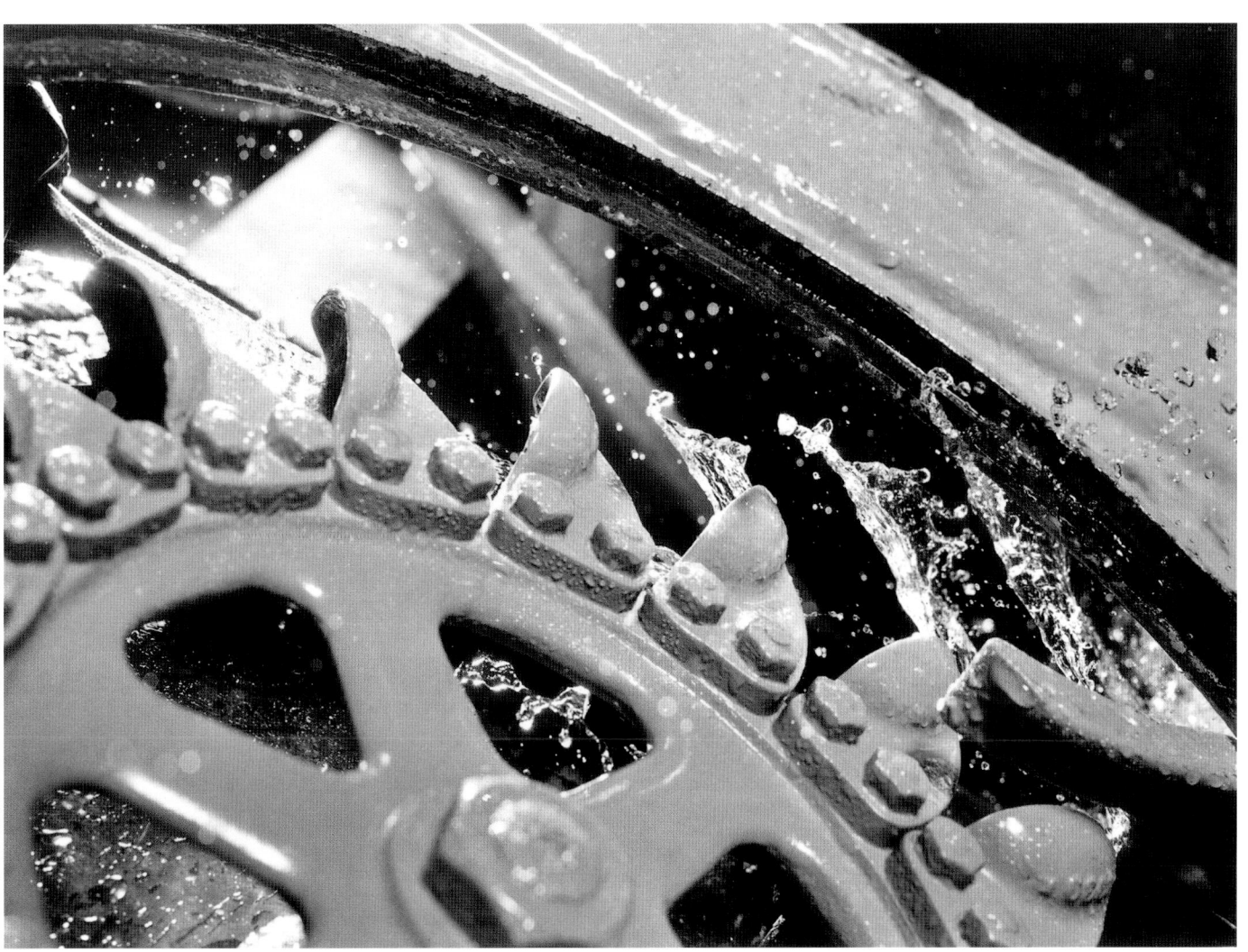

**Pelton wheel, 1939**

From a series of images showing "the action of a jet of water impinging on the buckets of a Pelton wheel."
From *flash! Seeing the Unseen by Ultra High-Speed Photography*.

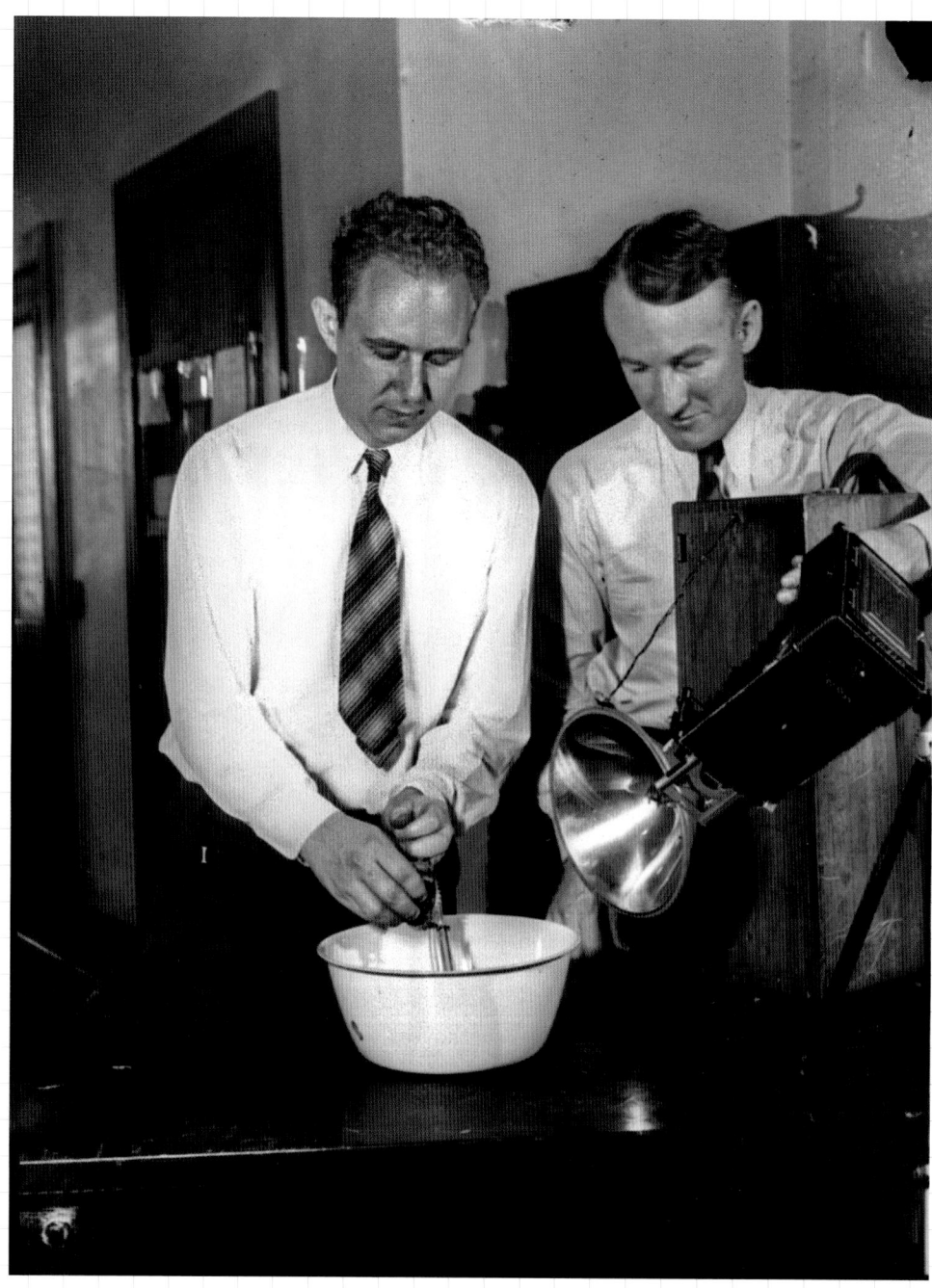

Edgerton (left) and Kenneth Germeshausen demonstrating the setup to capture an egg beater in motion in 1933.

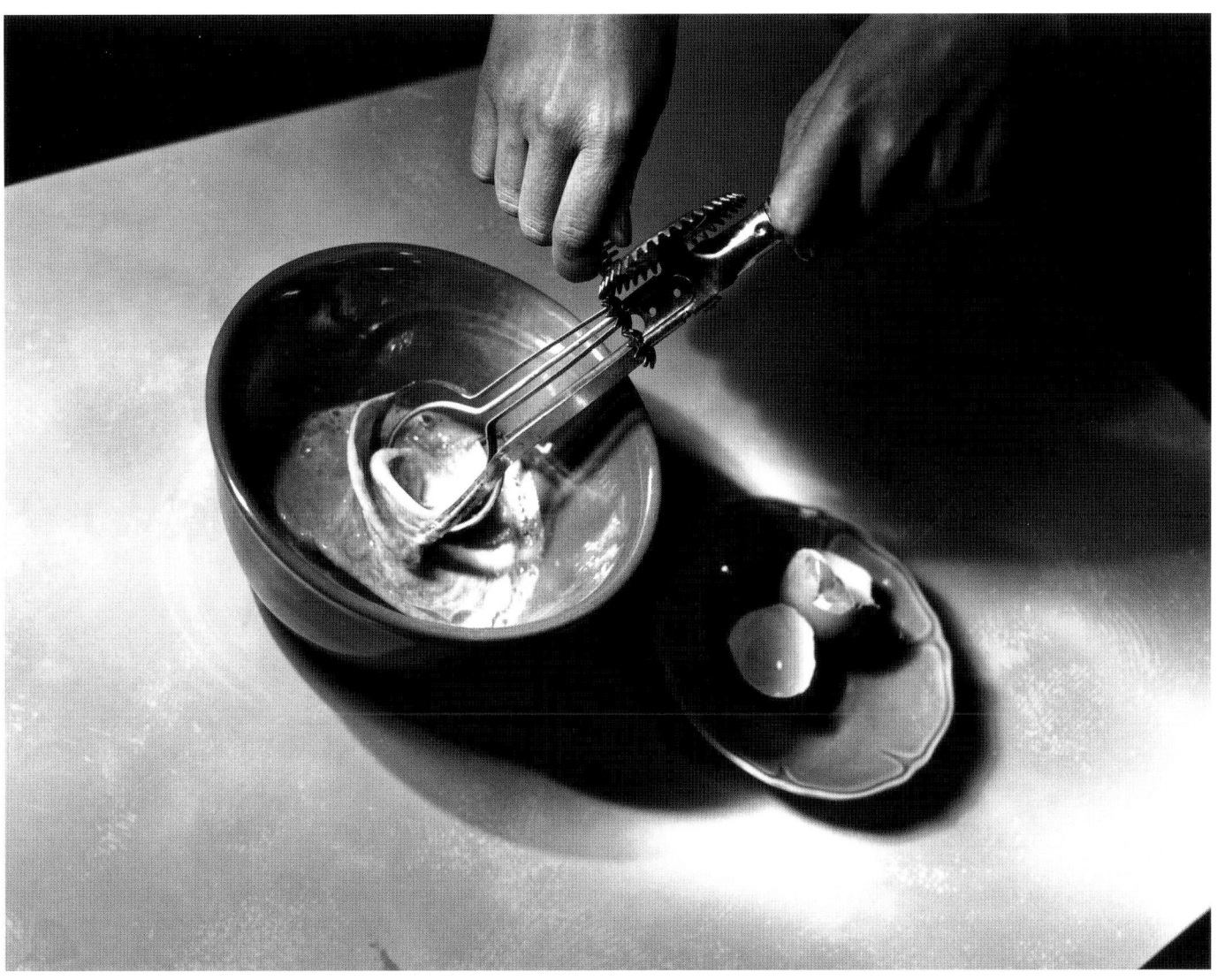

Egg beater, 1933

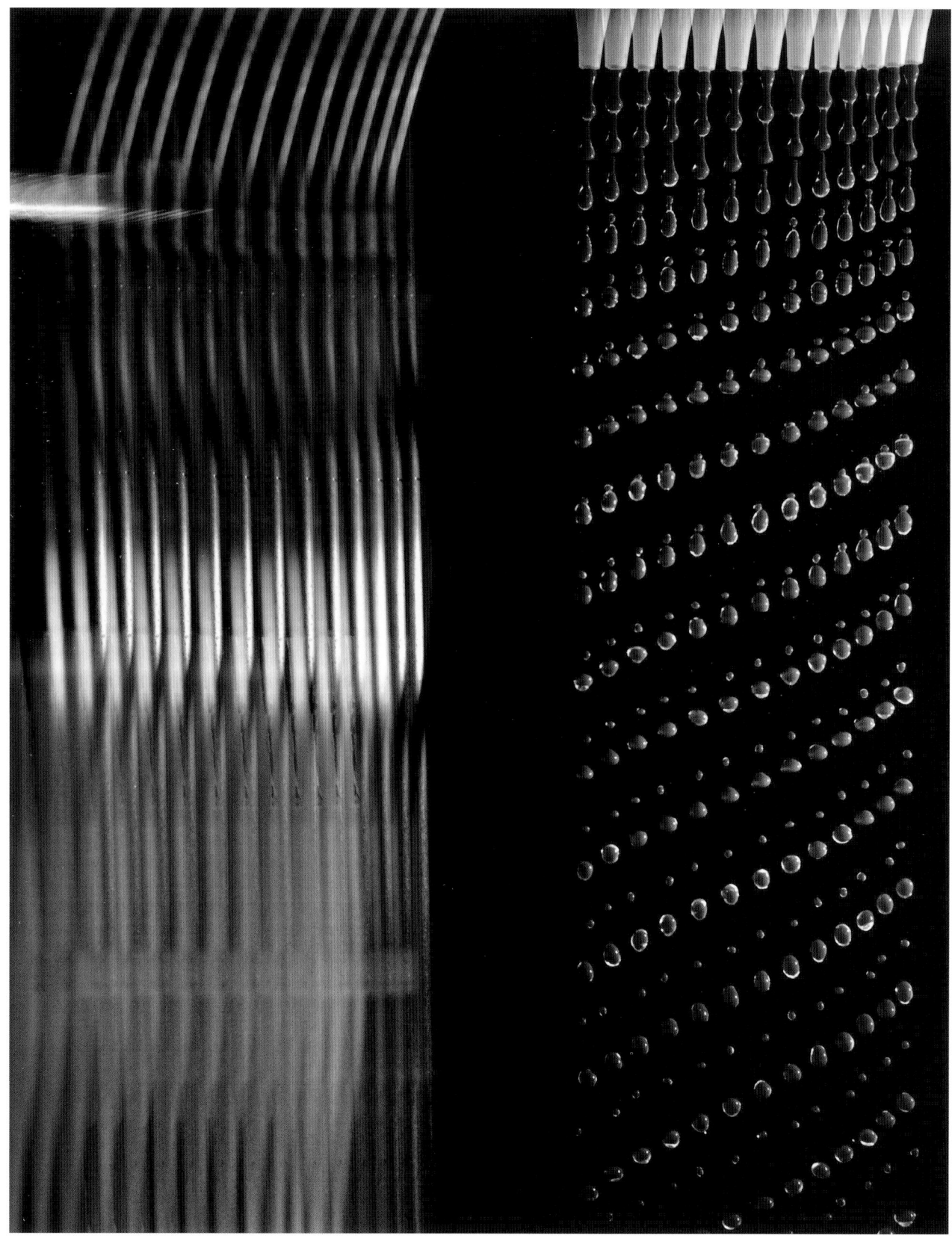

**Water droplets, 1983**

This unique image of falling water droplets illustrates the difference
between conventional (left) and multiflash (right) photographs.

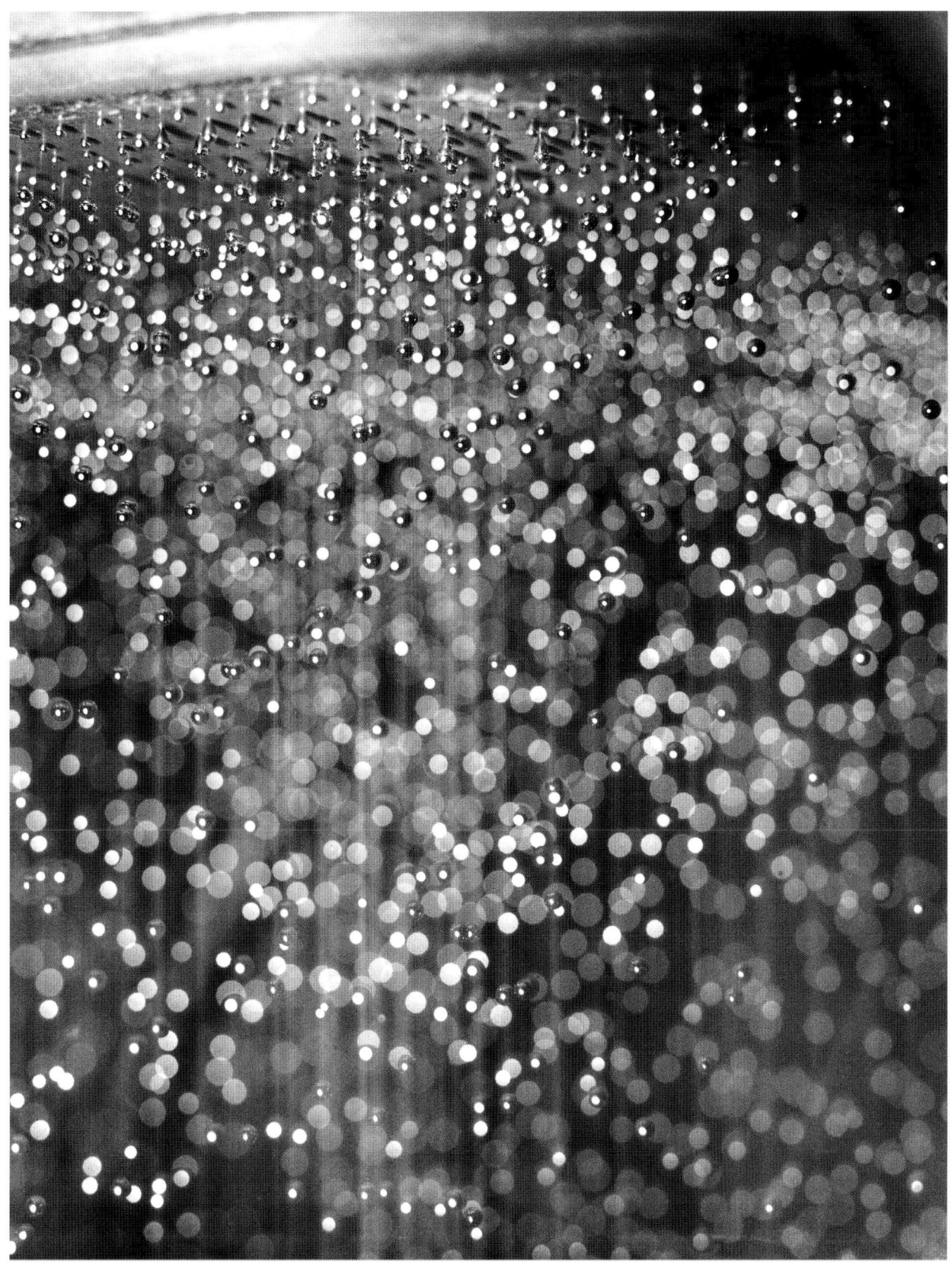

**In a shot tower, 1936**

This picture was taken as part of a manufacturing process study Edgerton conducted for the Winchester Repeating Arms Company, New Haven, Connecticut. Edgerton captioned this image: "Molten lead congealing into shot as it falls. Out-of-focus reflections of the light source on the drops produce the array of halos." From *flash! Seeing the Unseen by Ultra High-Speed Photography*.

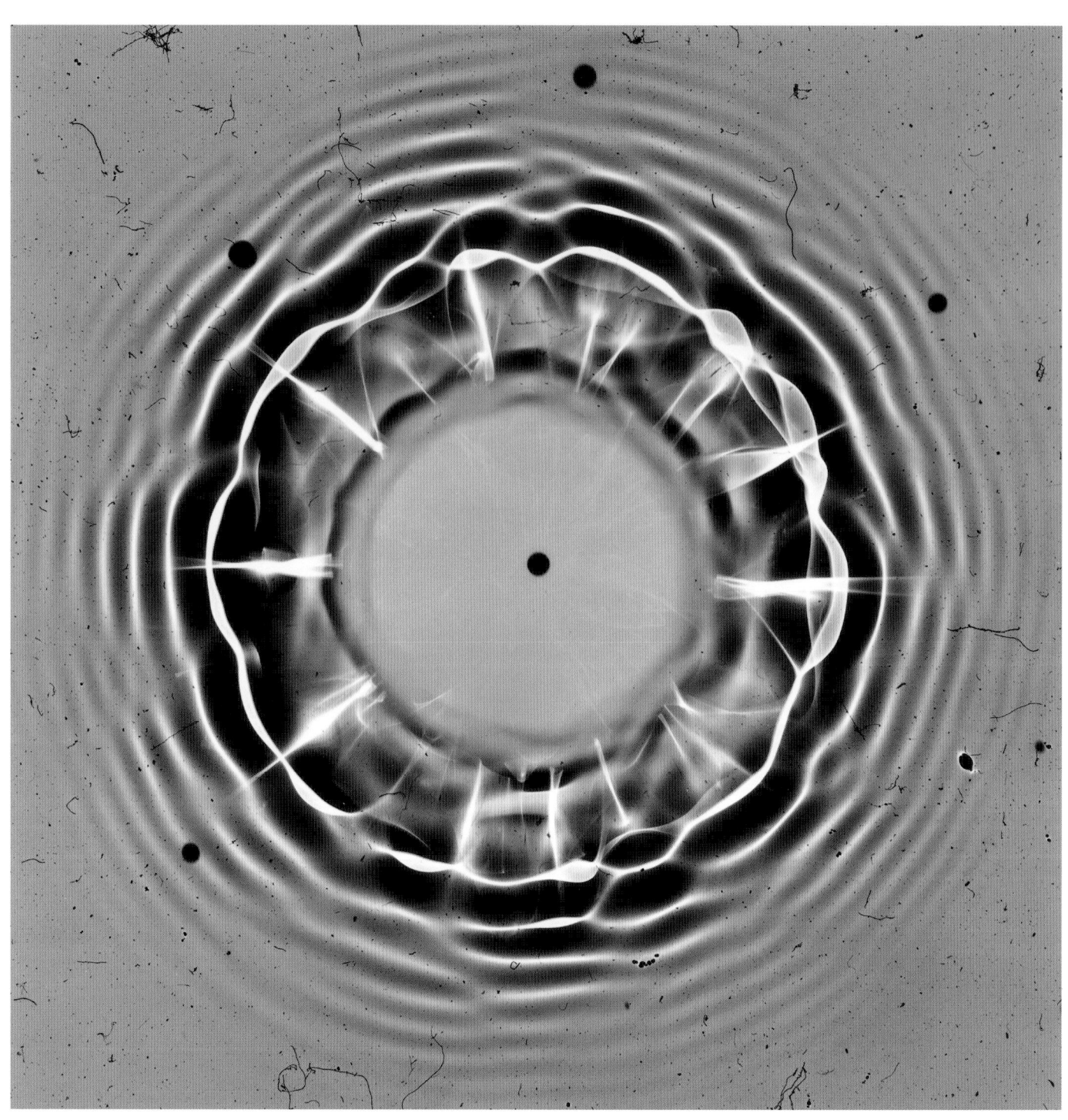

**Water drop splash, 1986**

Edgerton created this unusual image without using a camera. Instead, a drop of water passing through a photoelectric beam triggered a point-source flash just as the drop hit the thin layer of water atop the emulsion of the fine-grain film.

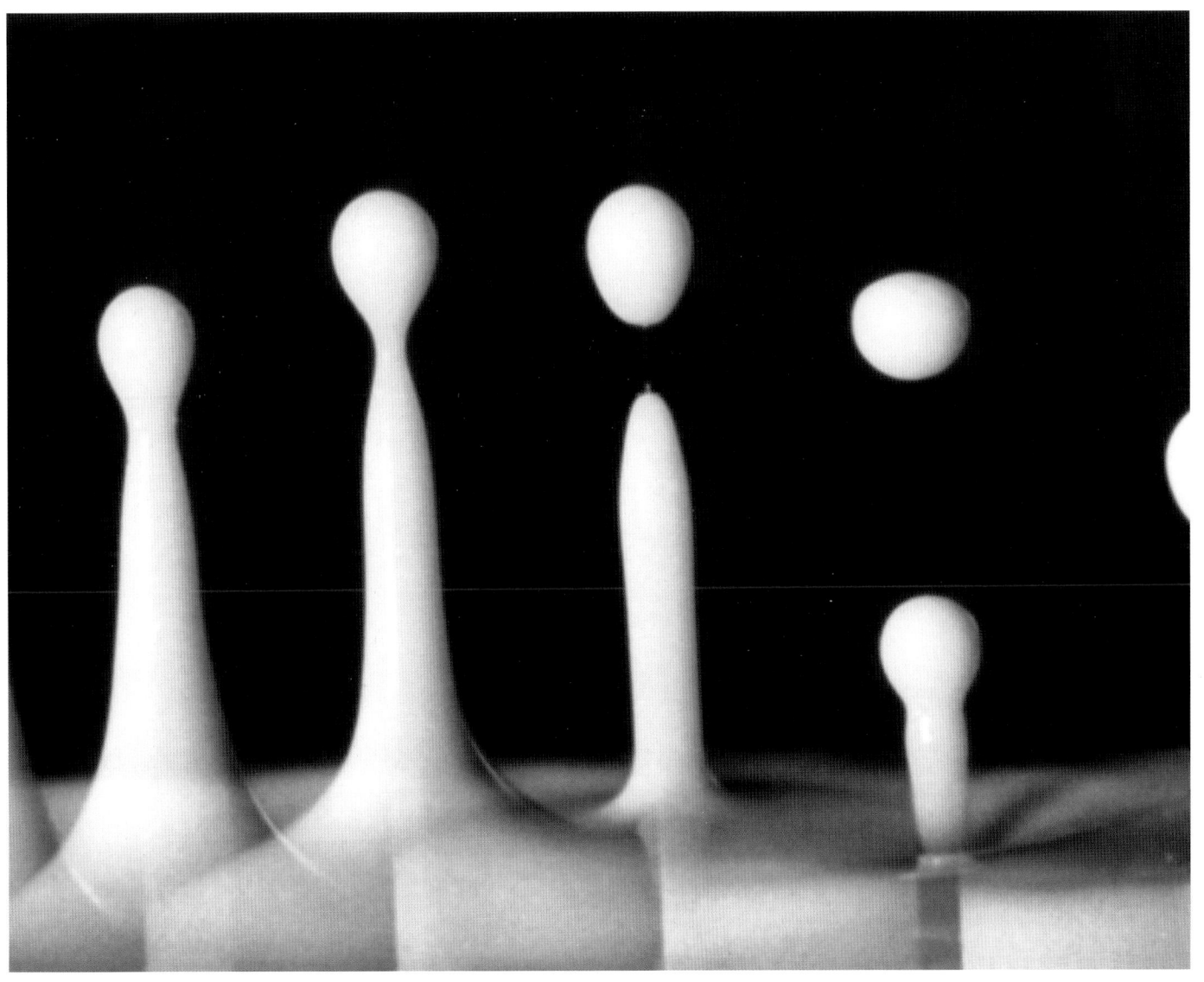

Milk drops, 1983

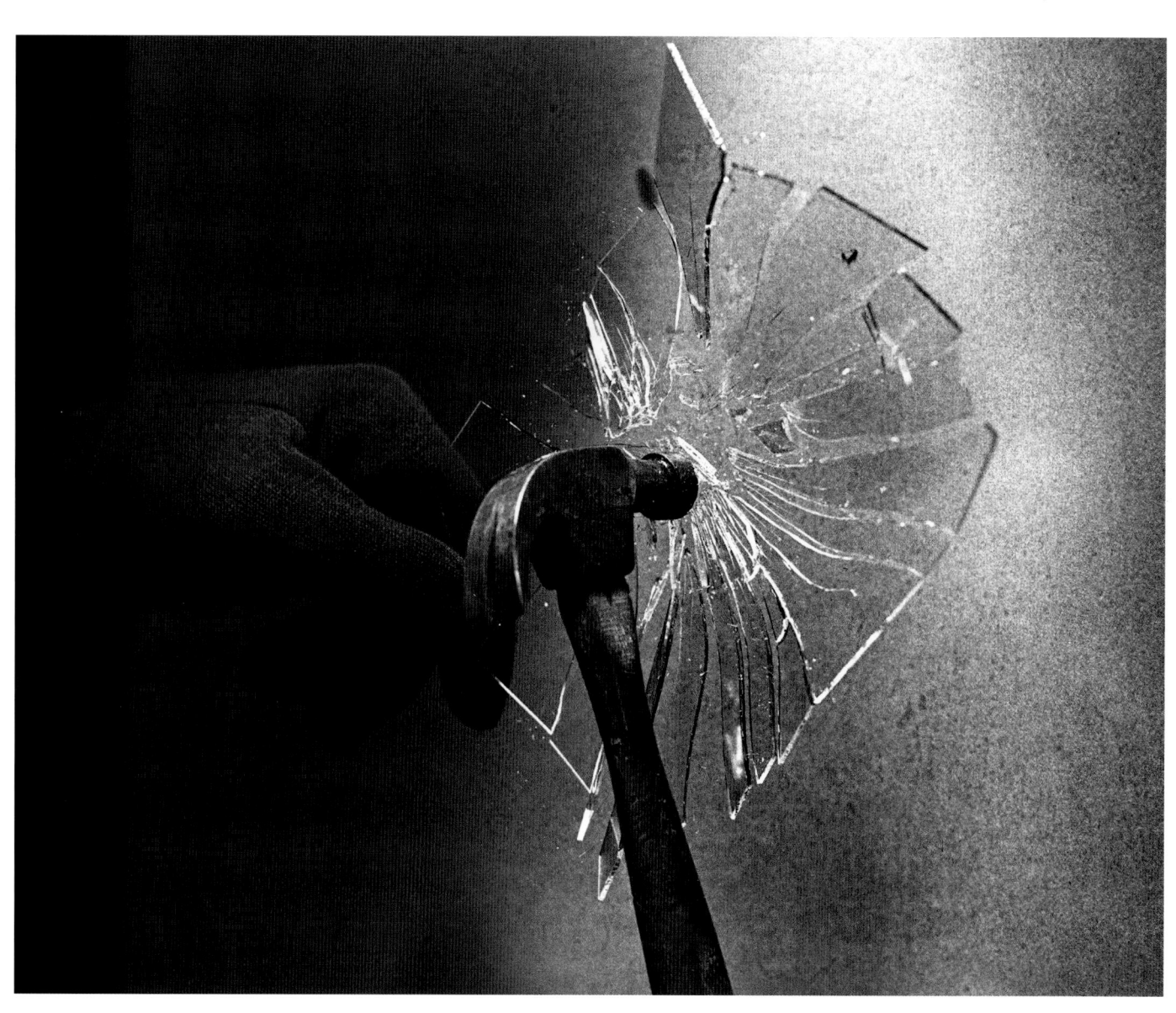

Hammer breaks glass plate, 1933

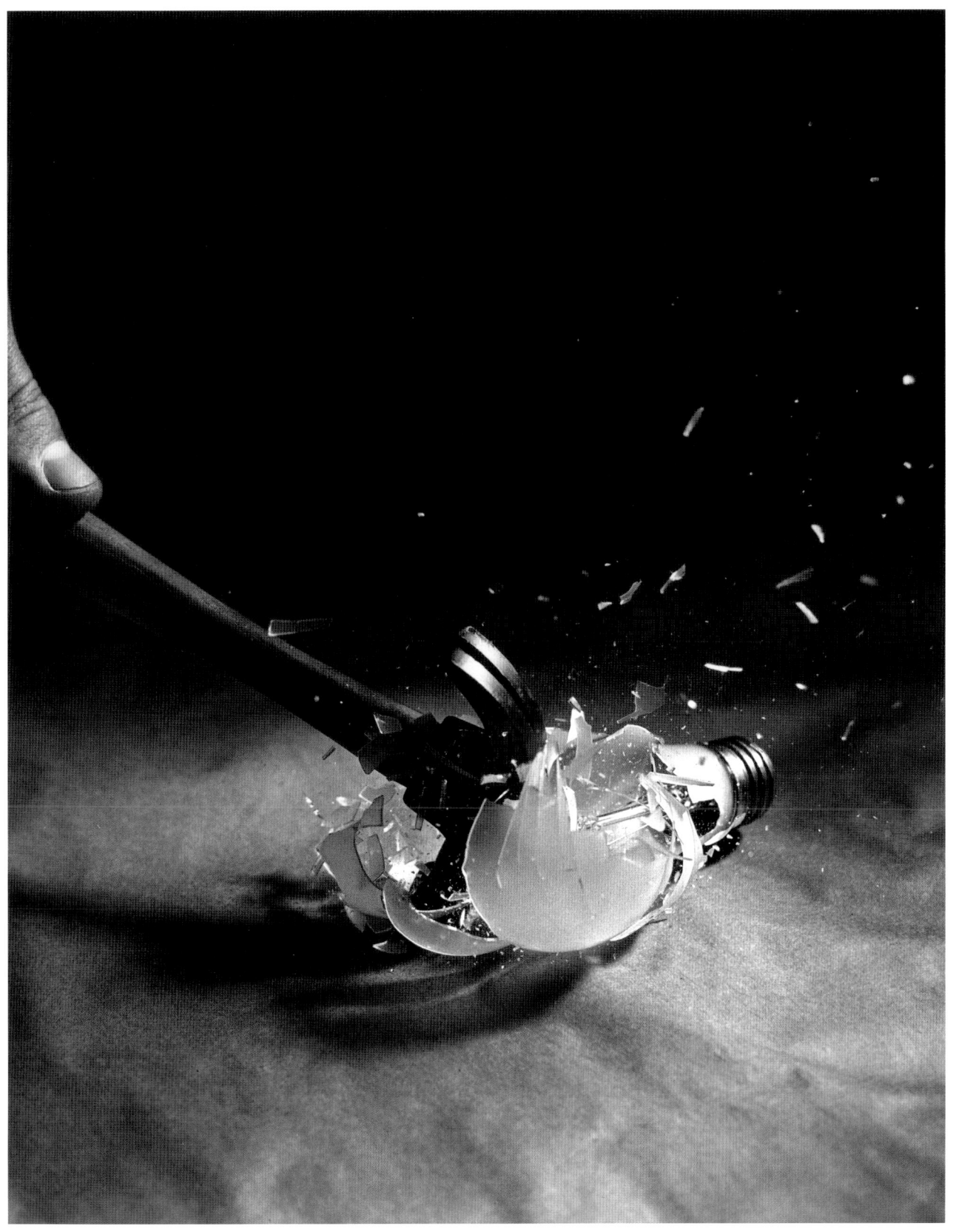

Smash!, 1933

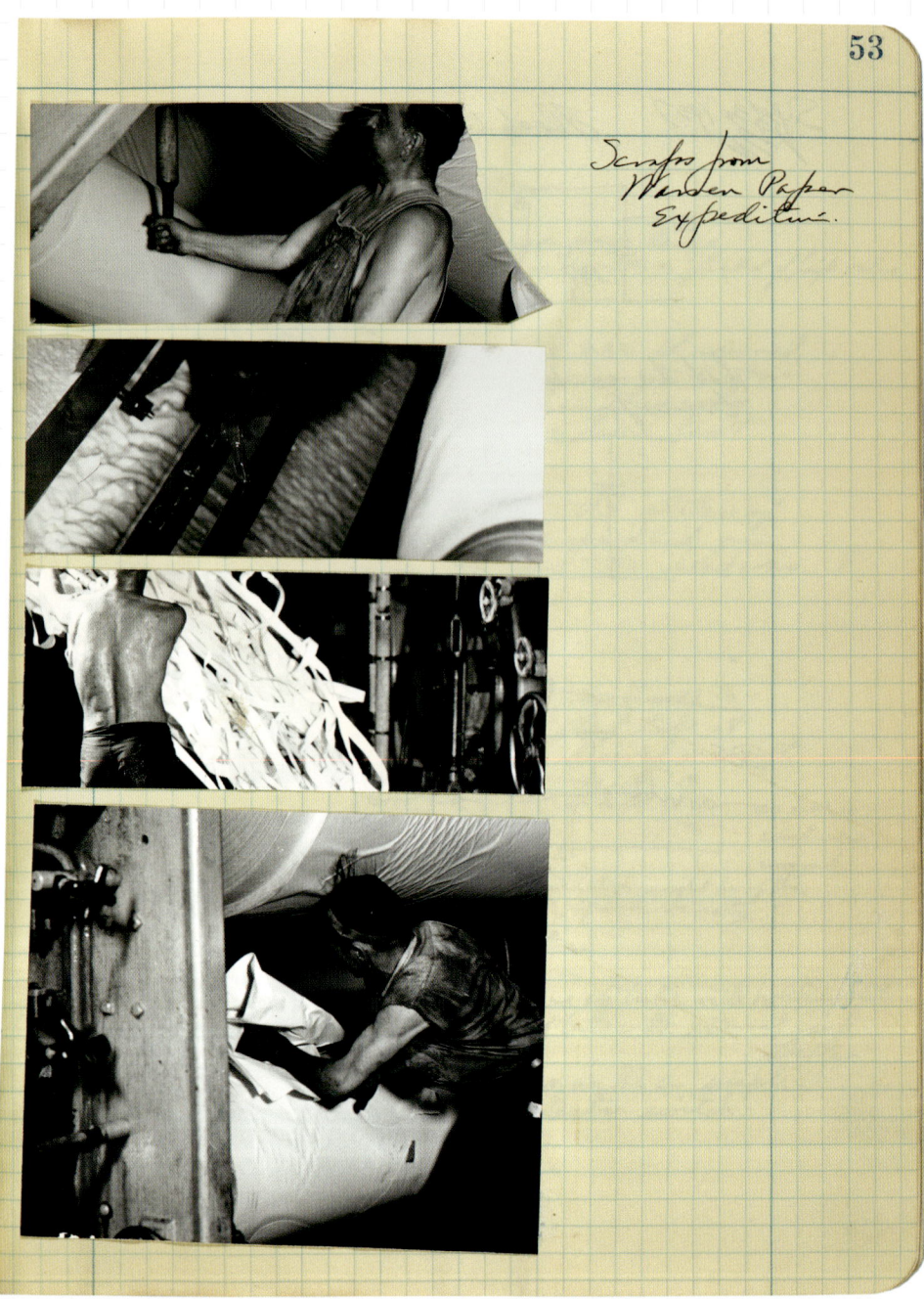

In August 1937, Edgerton and Kenneth Germeshausen visited the S.D. Warren Paper Company to take pictures at the mill for *Fortune* magazine. In September, he pasted several examples of his work into his notebook. Notebook Number 8, after September 27, 1937, p. 53.

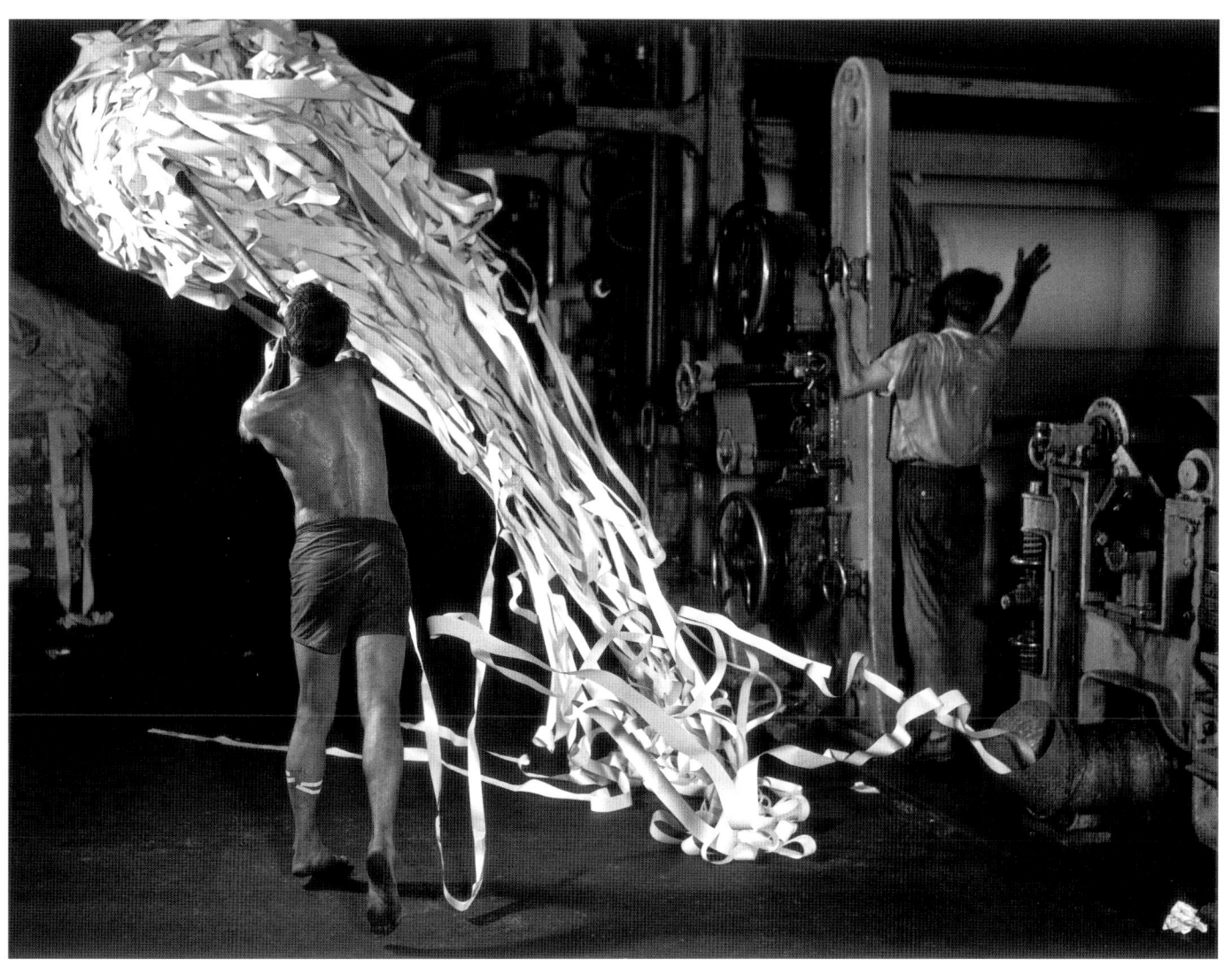

**Paper mill worker, 1937**

Edgerton and Kenneth Germeshausen captured this famous photograph of a mill worker at the
S.D. Warren Company plant in Westbrook, Maine.

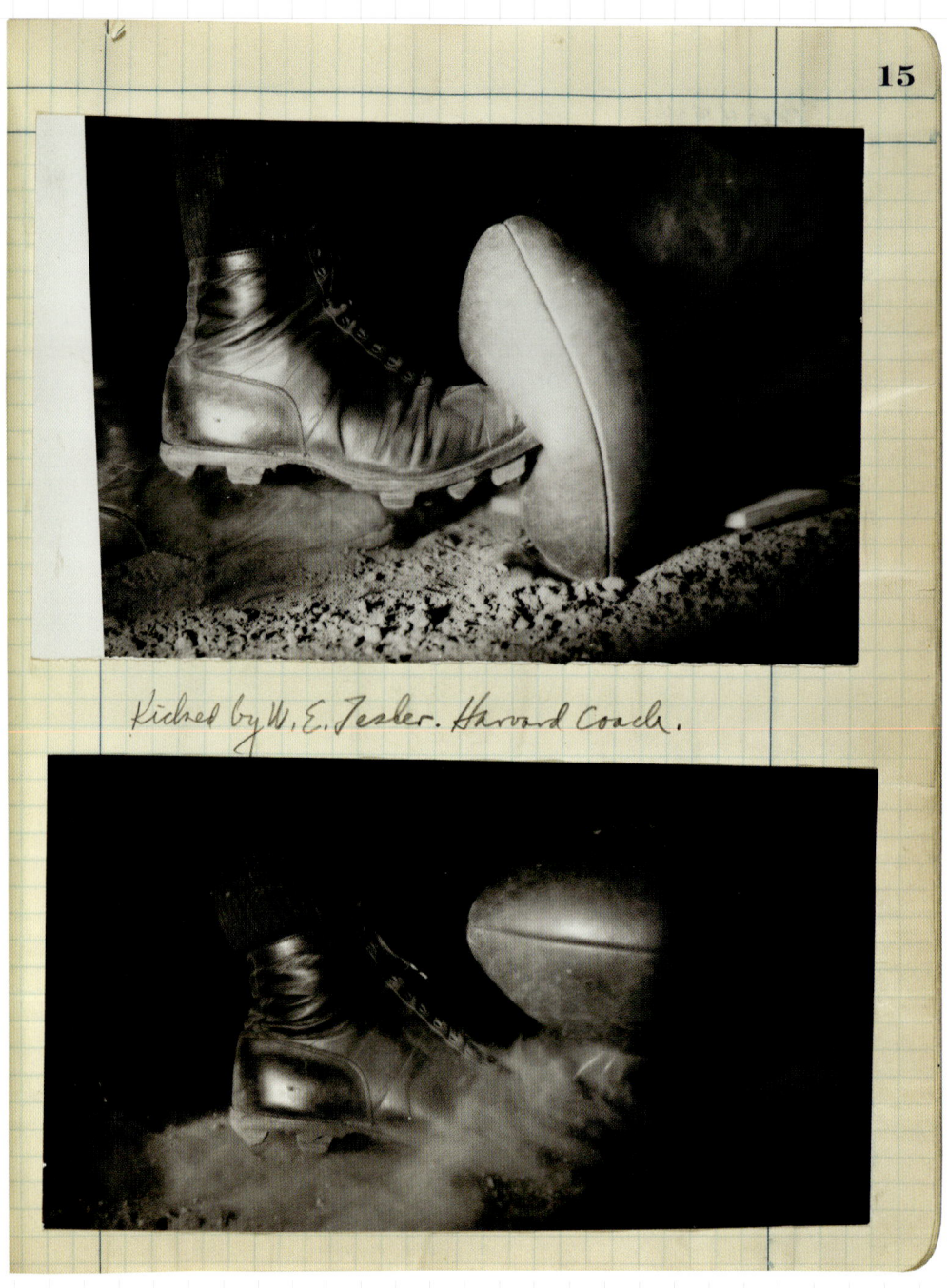

Kicked by W. E. Fesler. Harvard Coach.

"Herb Grier and I went up to Harvard and took some spark photos of a football being kicked," wrote Edgerton in his journal. "The kicker was a fellow from Ohio State (last year's team)." Harvard had hired the all-star Wesley Fesler to coach football and basketball beginning in 1933. Notebook Number T-5, November 22, 1934, p. 15.

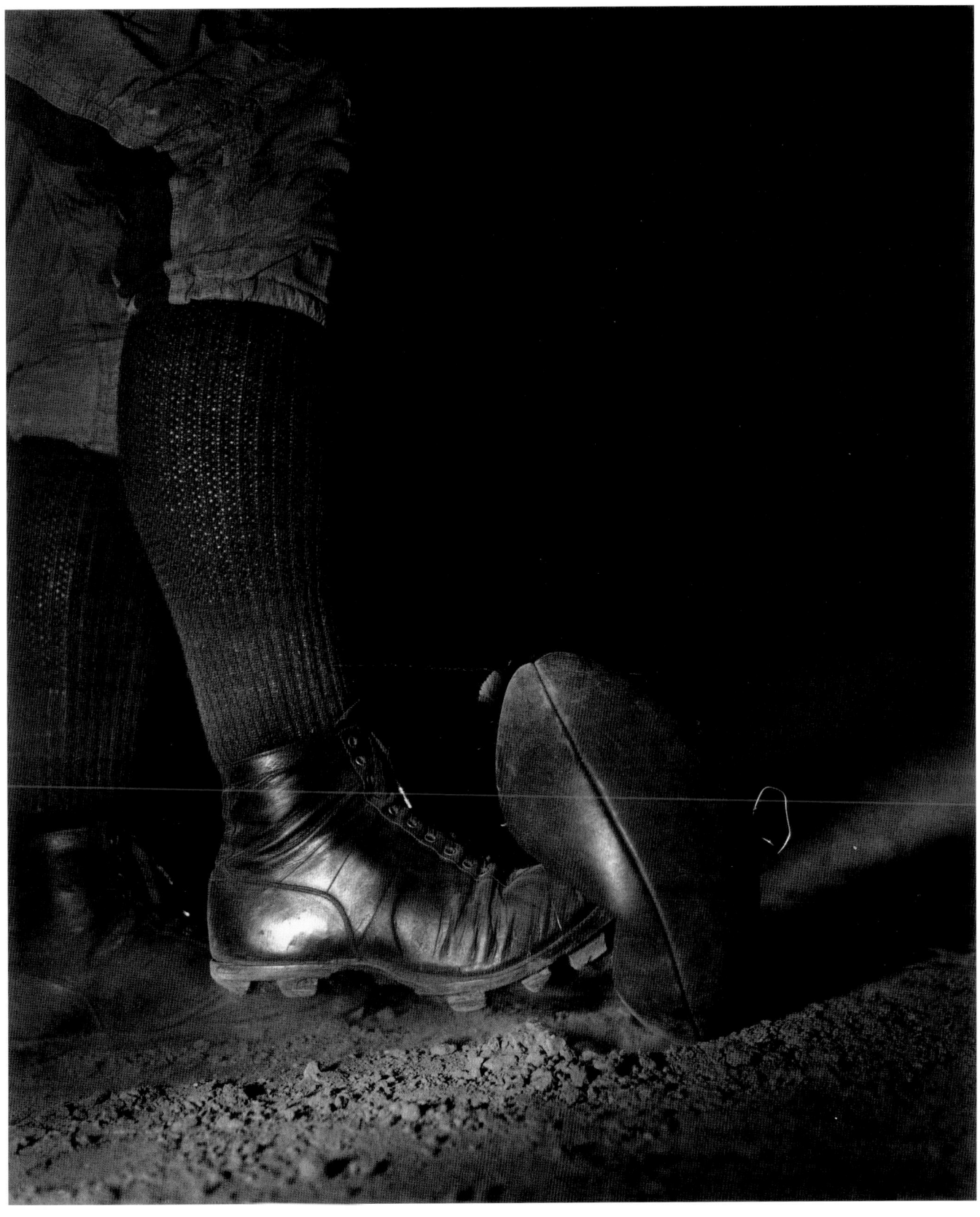

Placement kick, 1934

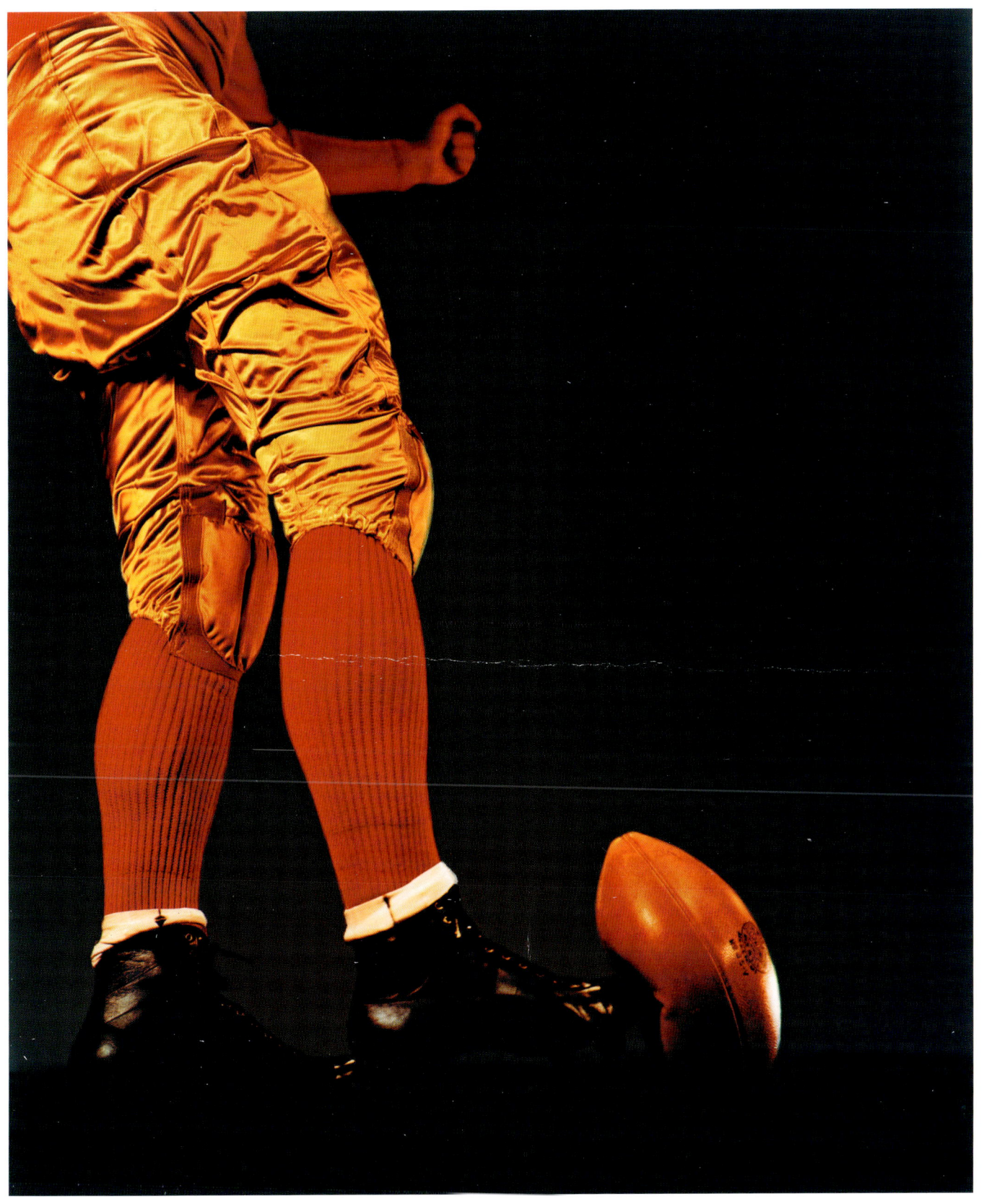

**Kick-off, 1938**

Chicago Bears running back Joe Maniaci kicks the football for a *Life* magazine photo shoot.
This was one of the first color electronic flash sports photographs taken.

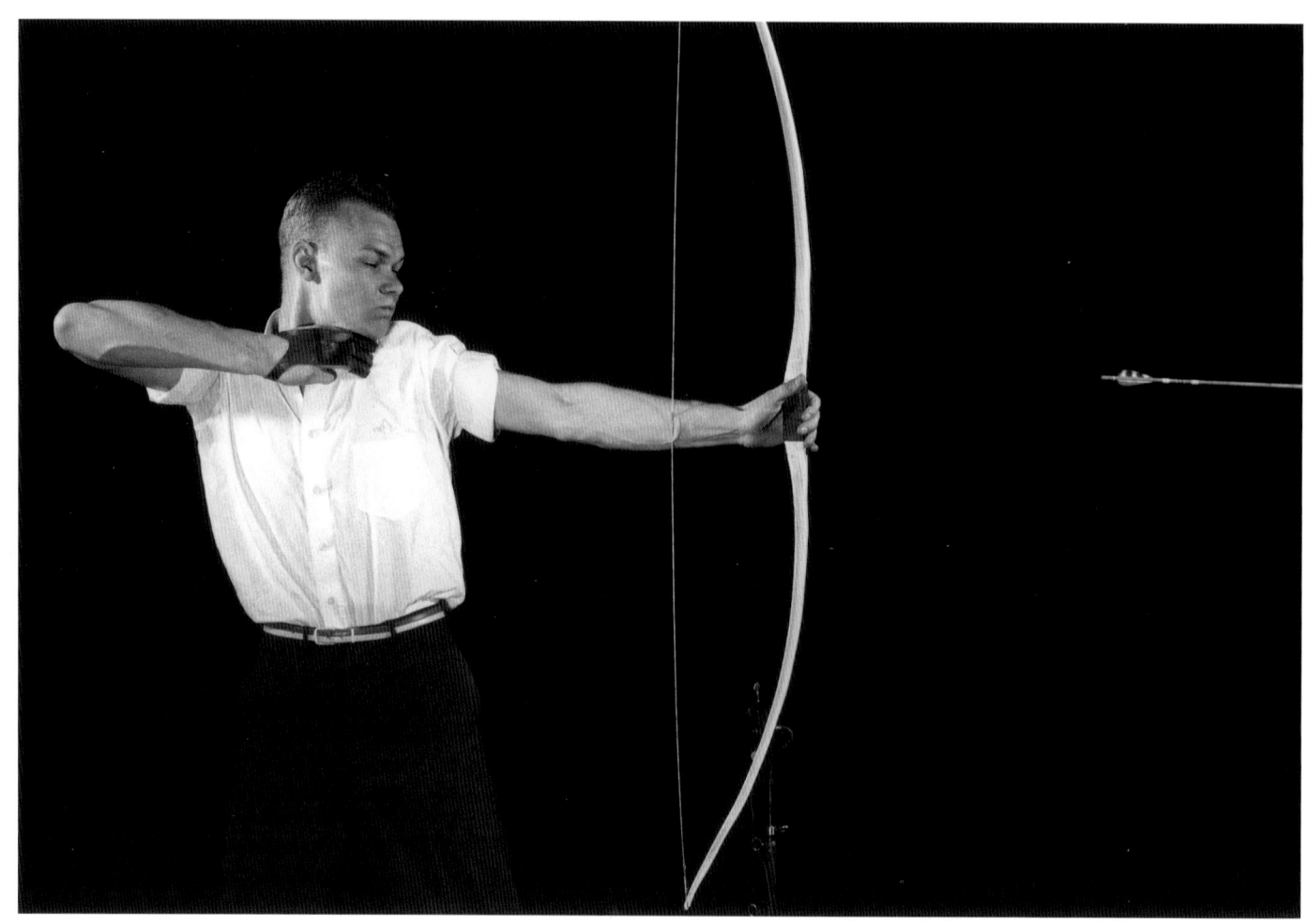

**Ouch!, 1939**

"The arrow has been in flight 1/30 of a second, the eyes of the archer are closed, the string painfully rolls up the skin on his unprotected arm." From *flash! Seeing the Unseen by Ultra High-Speed Photography*.

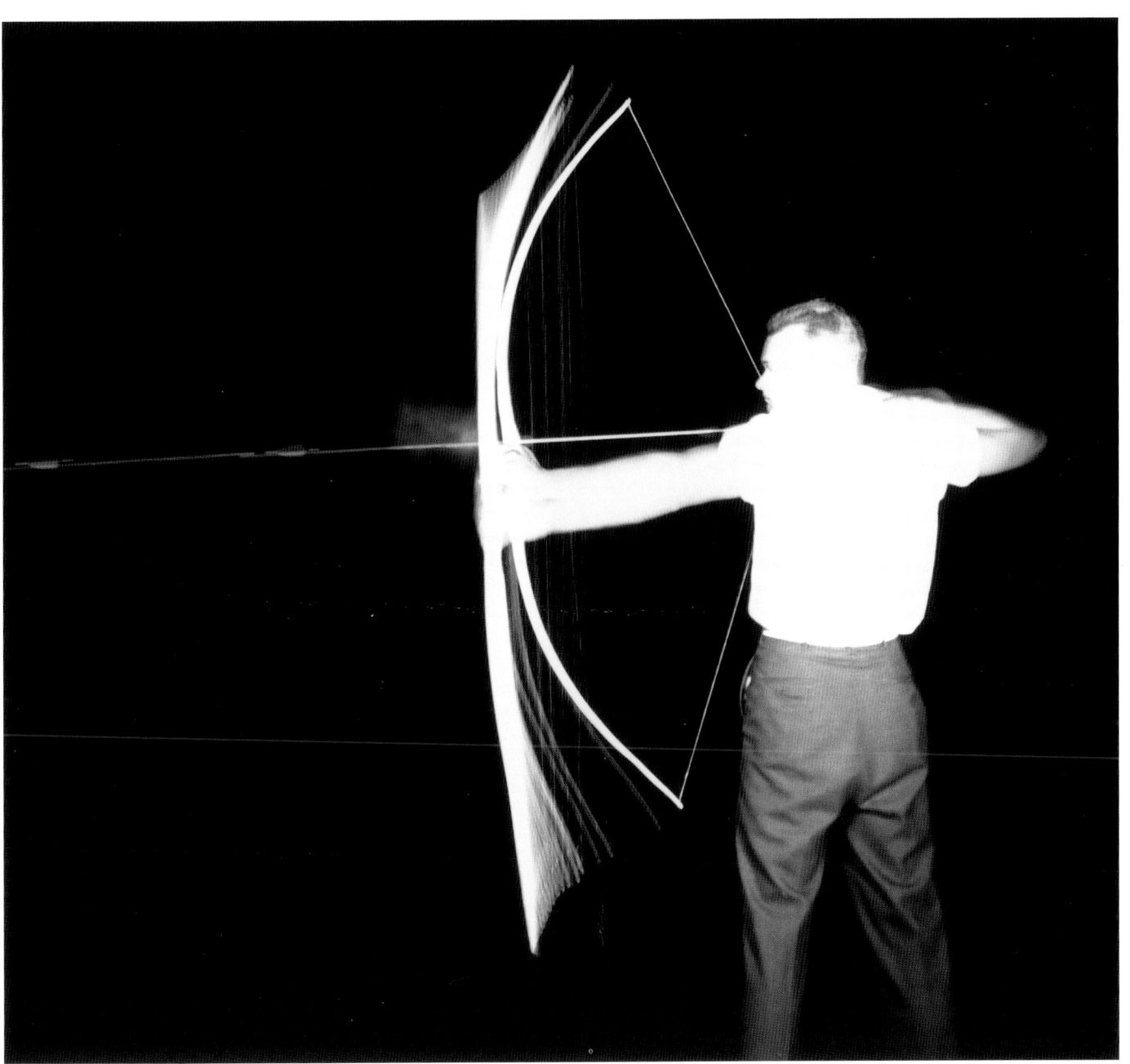

**Archer, 1939**

The multiflash image of the archer captures the bow and arrow at the moment of release.

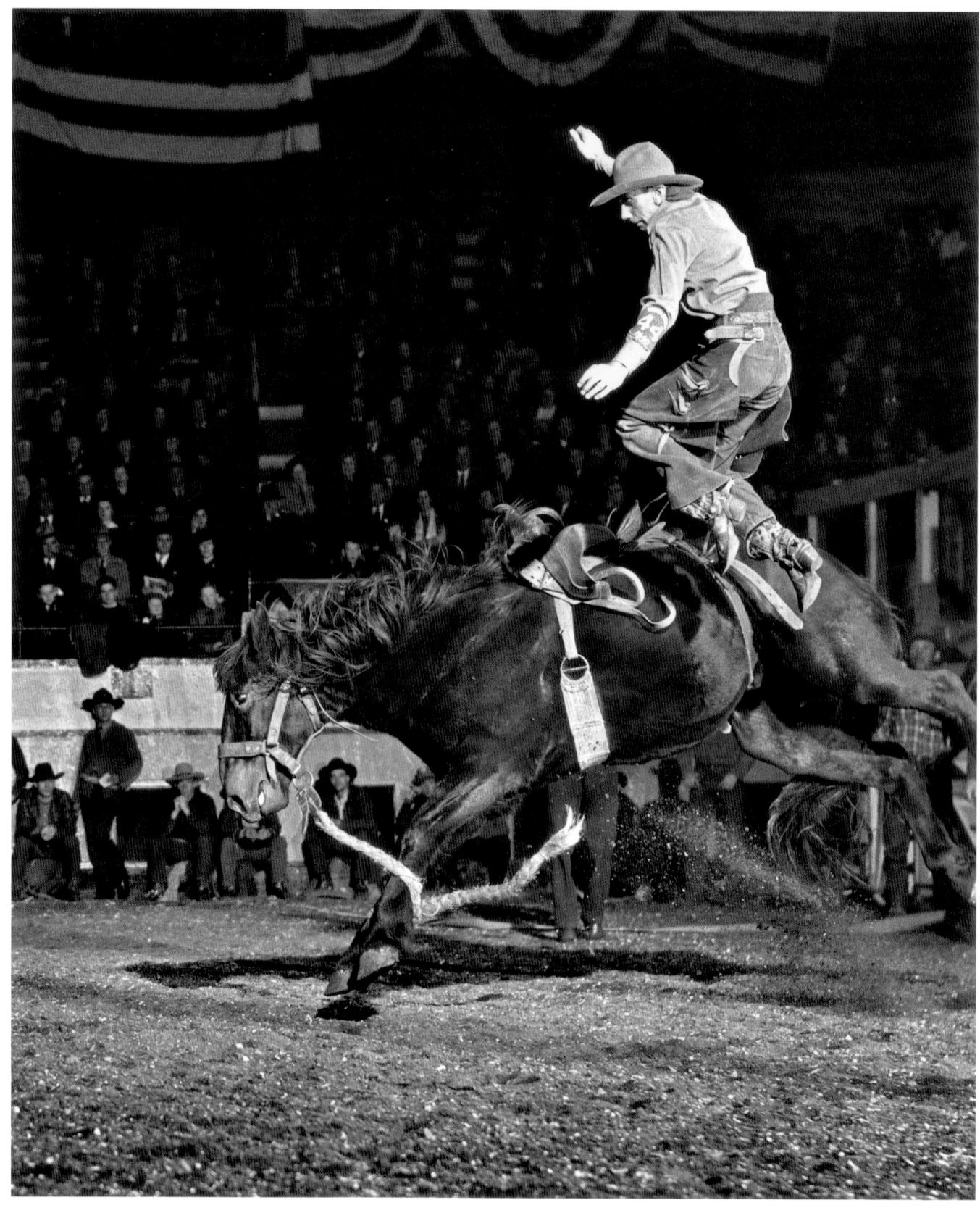

**Rodeo, 1940**

"Cecil Henley is leaving the horse, Home Brew, at a Boston Garden performance of the rodeo."
From *flash! Seeing the Unseen by Ultra High-Speed Photography* (2nd ed.).

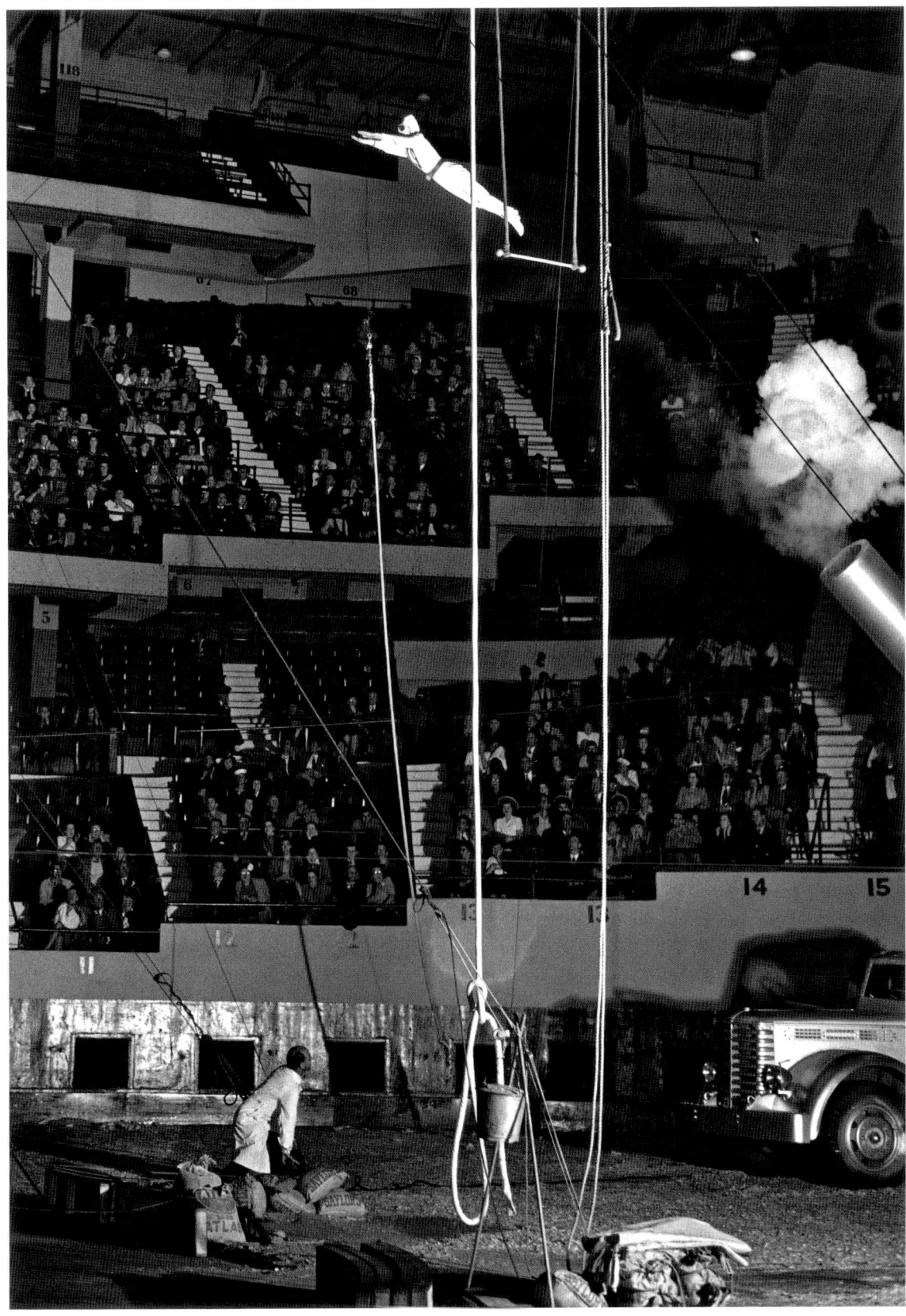

**Shot from a cannon, 1940**

The Zacchini family was famous for its cannonball acts featured in circuses around the world.
Edgerton captured Victoria on a dramatic 175-foot arc from cannon to safety net.

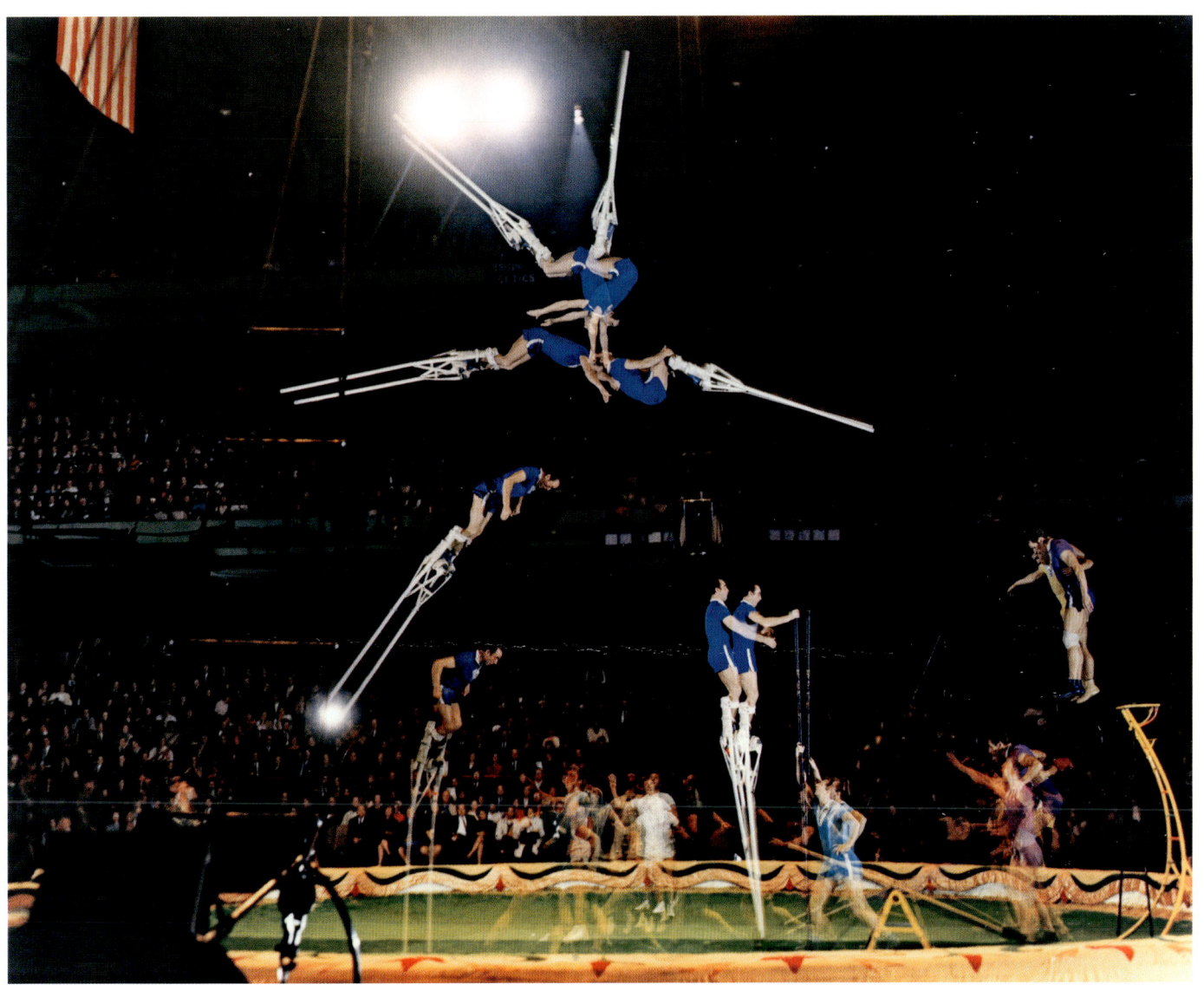

**Moscow Circus, 1963**

Multiflash photograph of Alexander Seleznev of the Moscow Circus on seven-foot stilts making
a spectacular backflip during a performance at Boston Garden in October 1963.

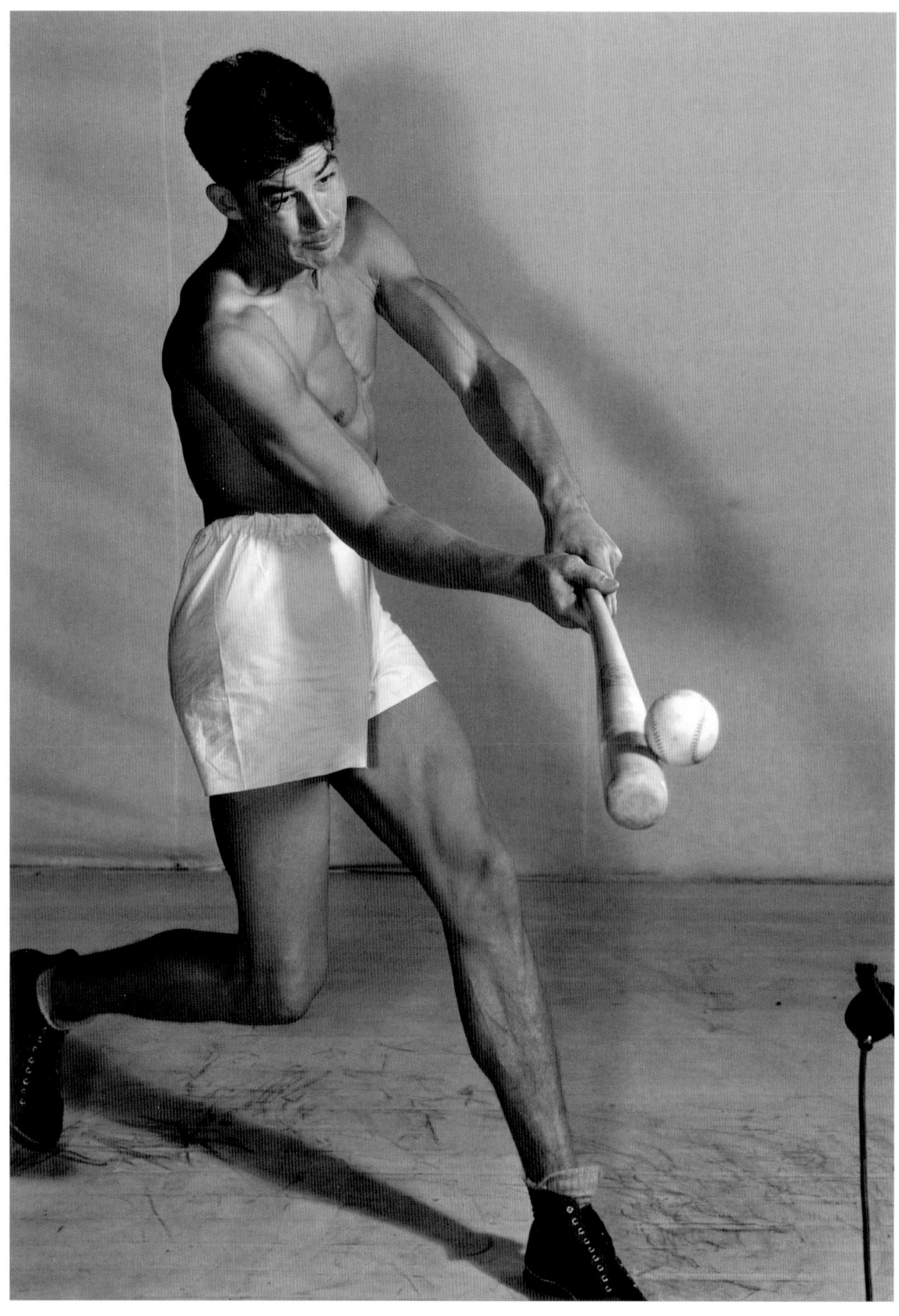

The bat bends, 1938

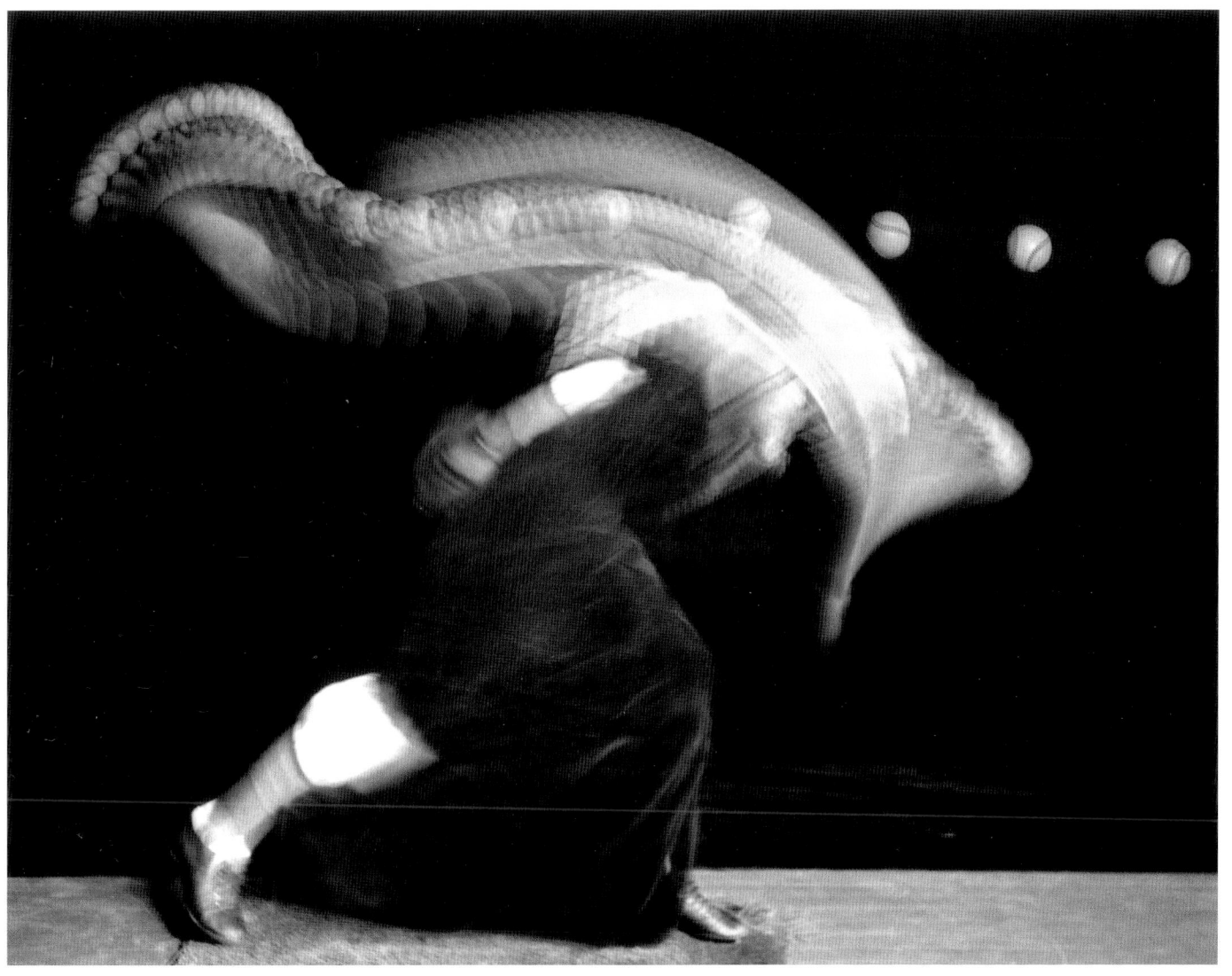

**Pitcher, 1938**

At 100 frames per second, you can clearly see the rotation of the curve ball thrown by Boston Bees pitcher Daniel MacFayden. He is wearing a black drape to help draw attention to the ball.

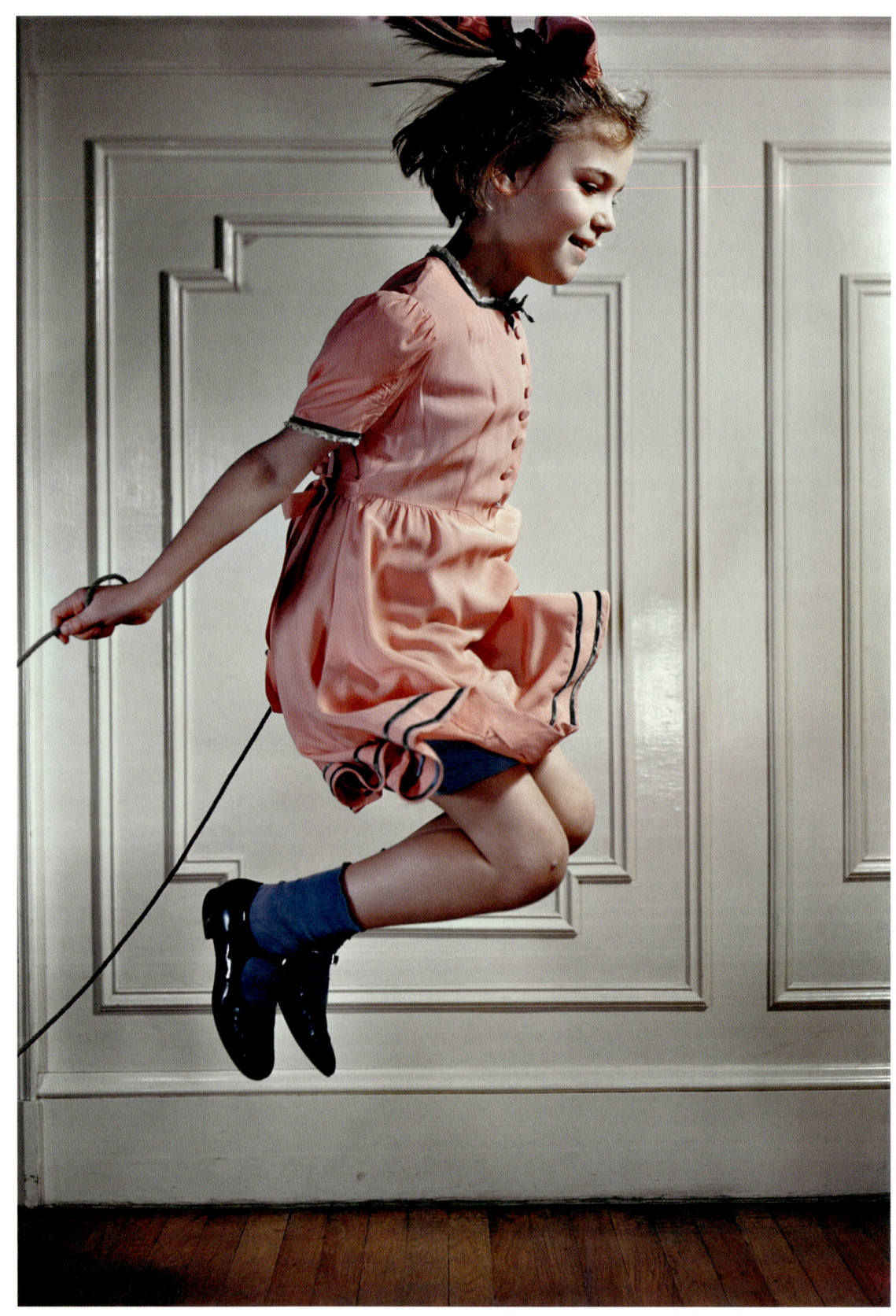

**Jumping girl, 1940**

Edgerton's picture of his daughter, Mary Louise, skipping rope in the family living room was taken using the new Kodachrome sheet film and his newly developed flash unit. It was one of the earliest indoor color snapshots.

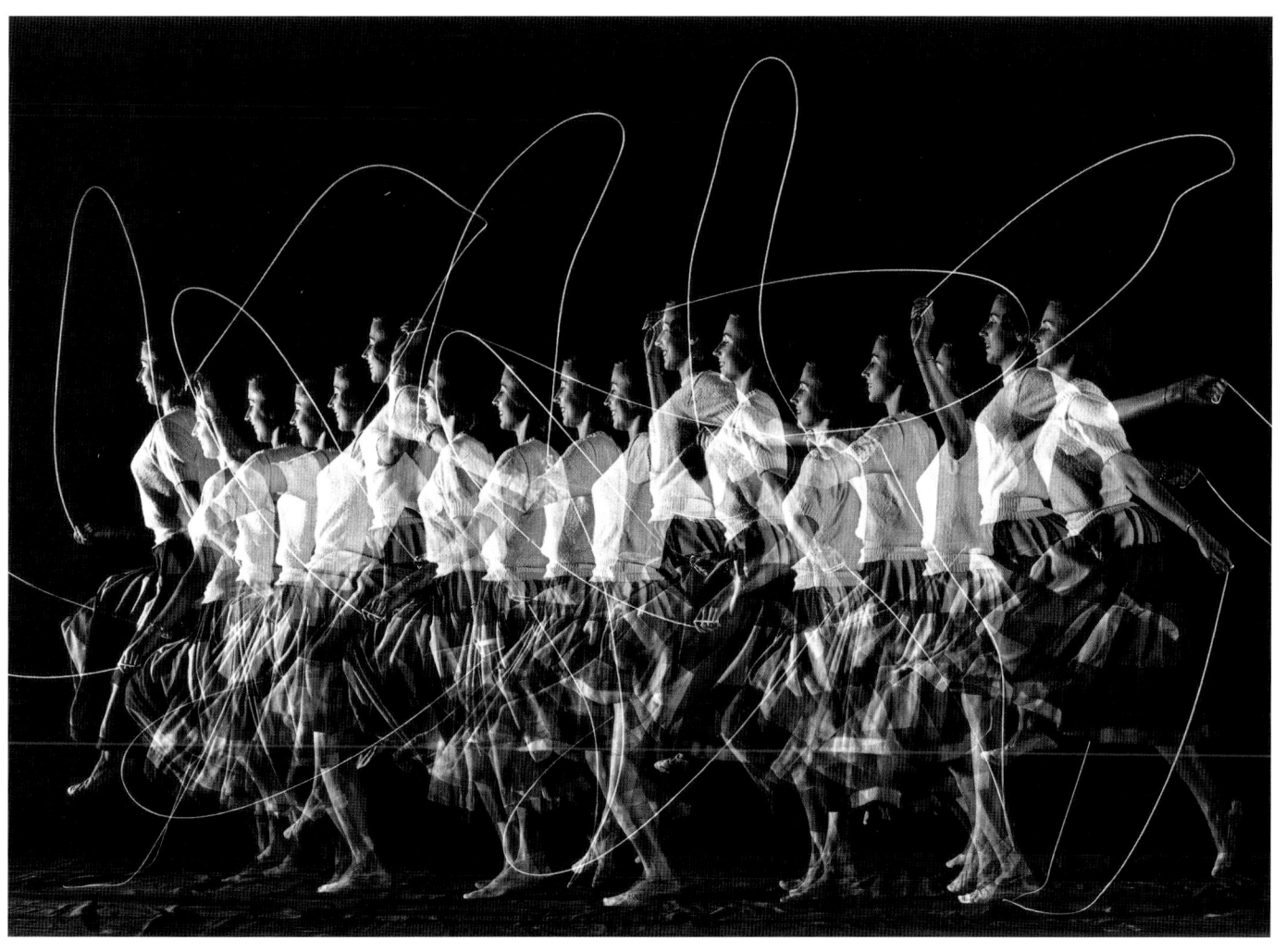

Skip rope, 1952

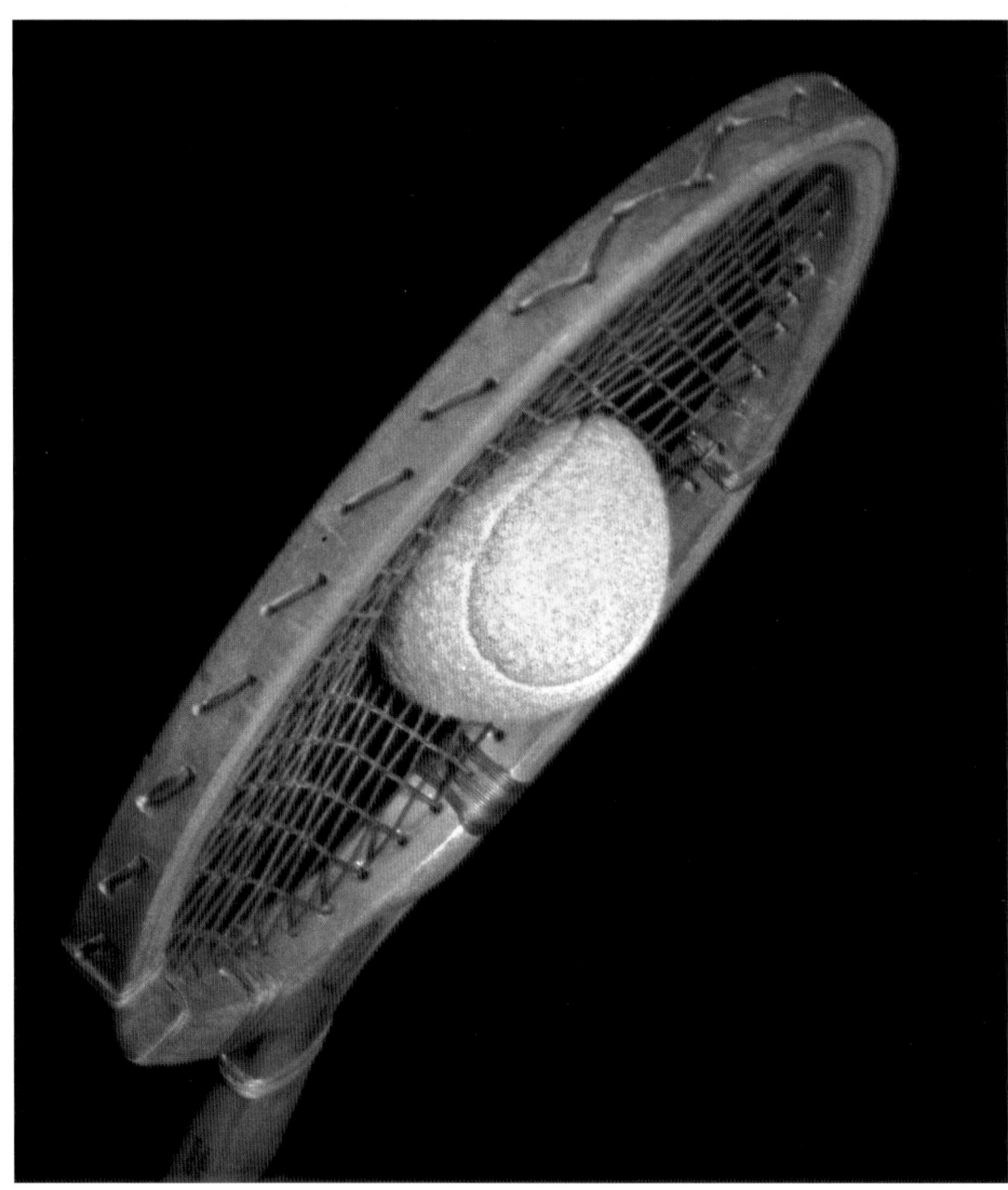

**Tennis ball impact, 1935**

Edgerton's single-flash and multiple-exposure photography opened up new opportunities to analyze all aspects of sports. This single-flash image shows the "squash of a tennis ball and the indenting of the strings as the ball is hit." From *flash! Seeing the Unseen by Ultra High-Speed Photography.*

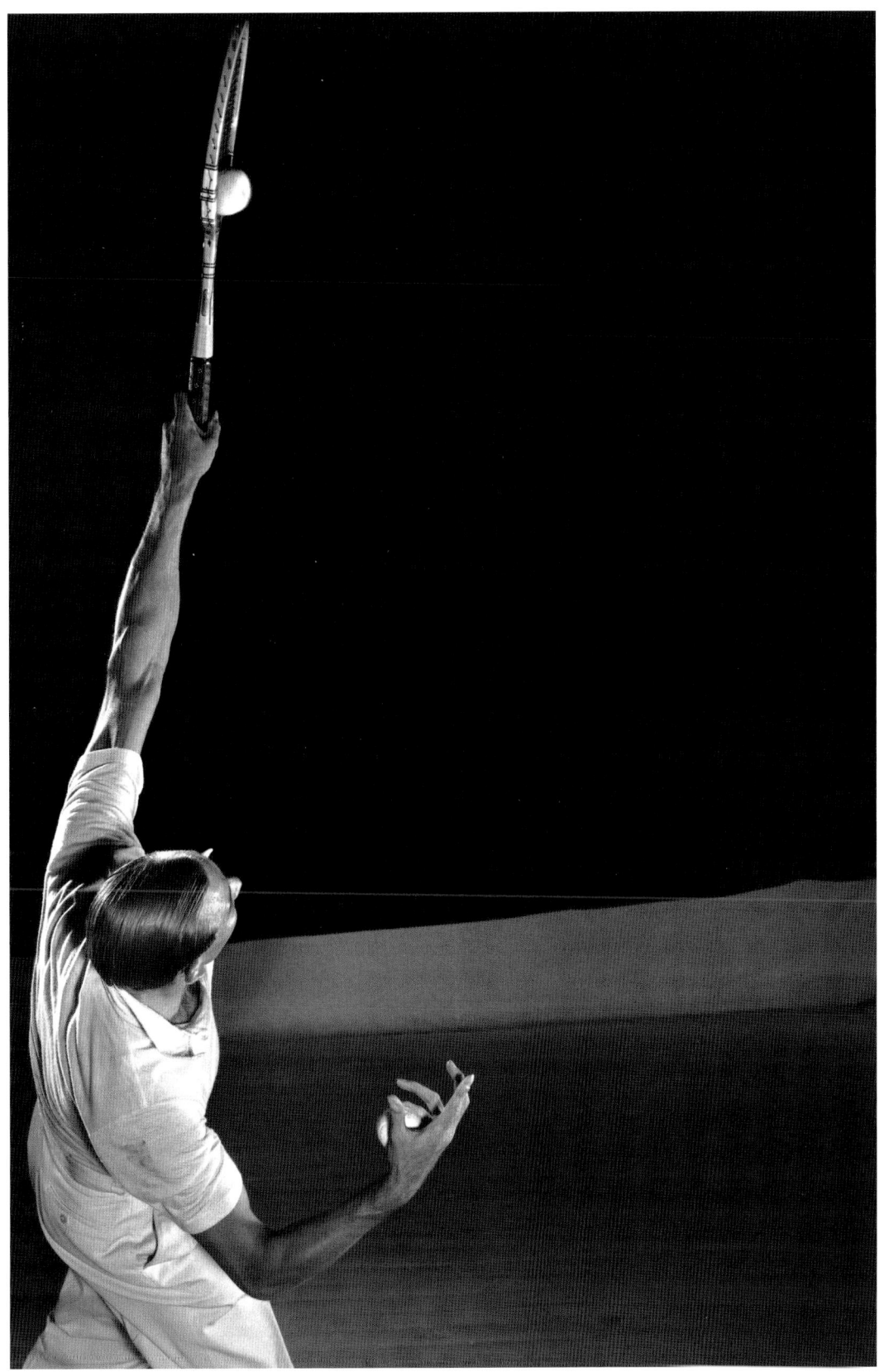

**Charles Hare serves, 1938**

The single-flash picture of English tennis player Charles Hare's serve shows
him hitting the ball too low as well as the bend of the racket.

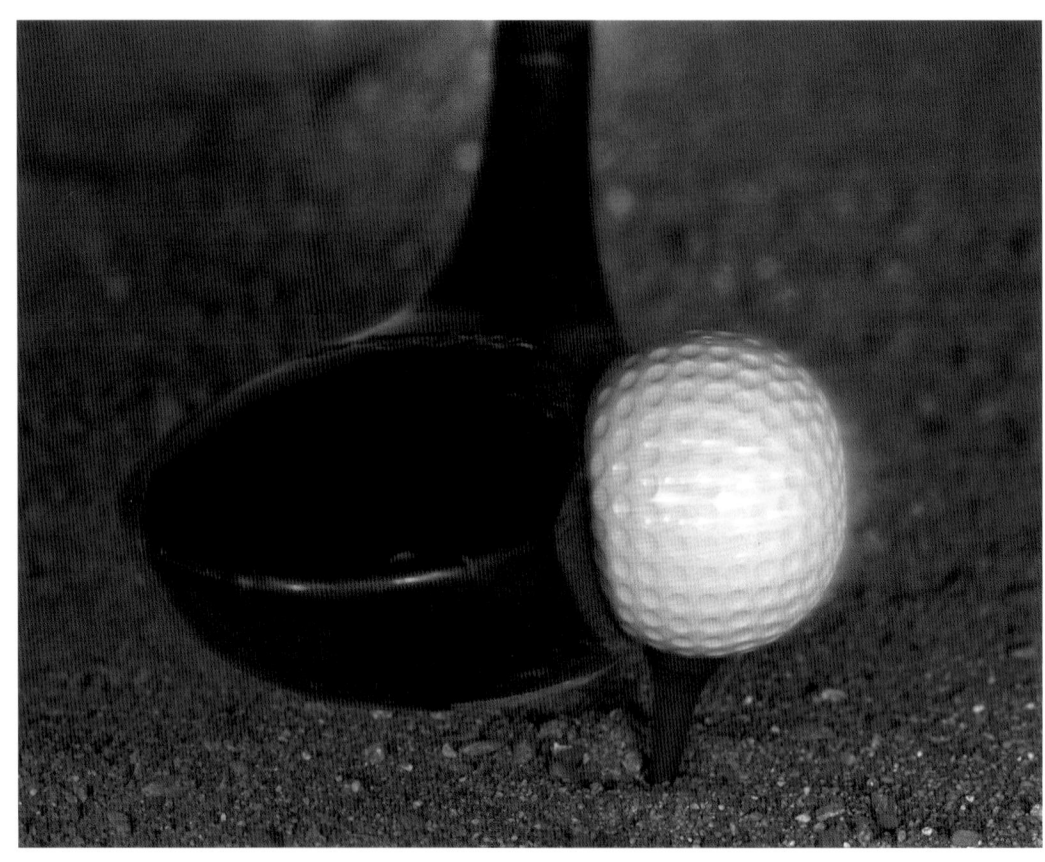

**When the ball is struck, 1935**

Of all the sports Edgerton studied, golf was the one he most thoroughly investigated.
This photograph reveals the compression of a golf ball after being struck by the club.

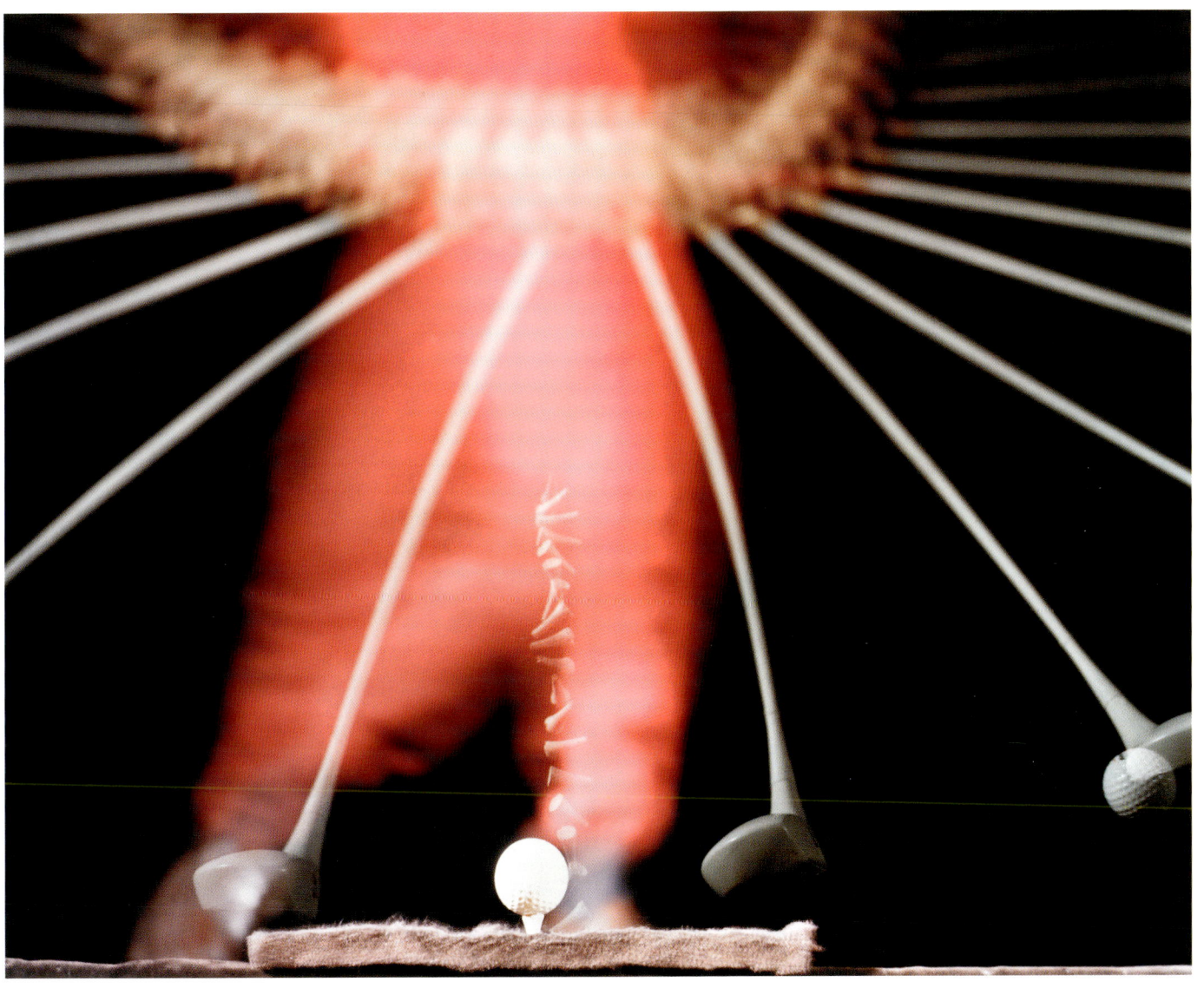

Golf tee-off, 1962

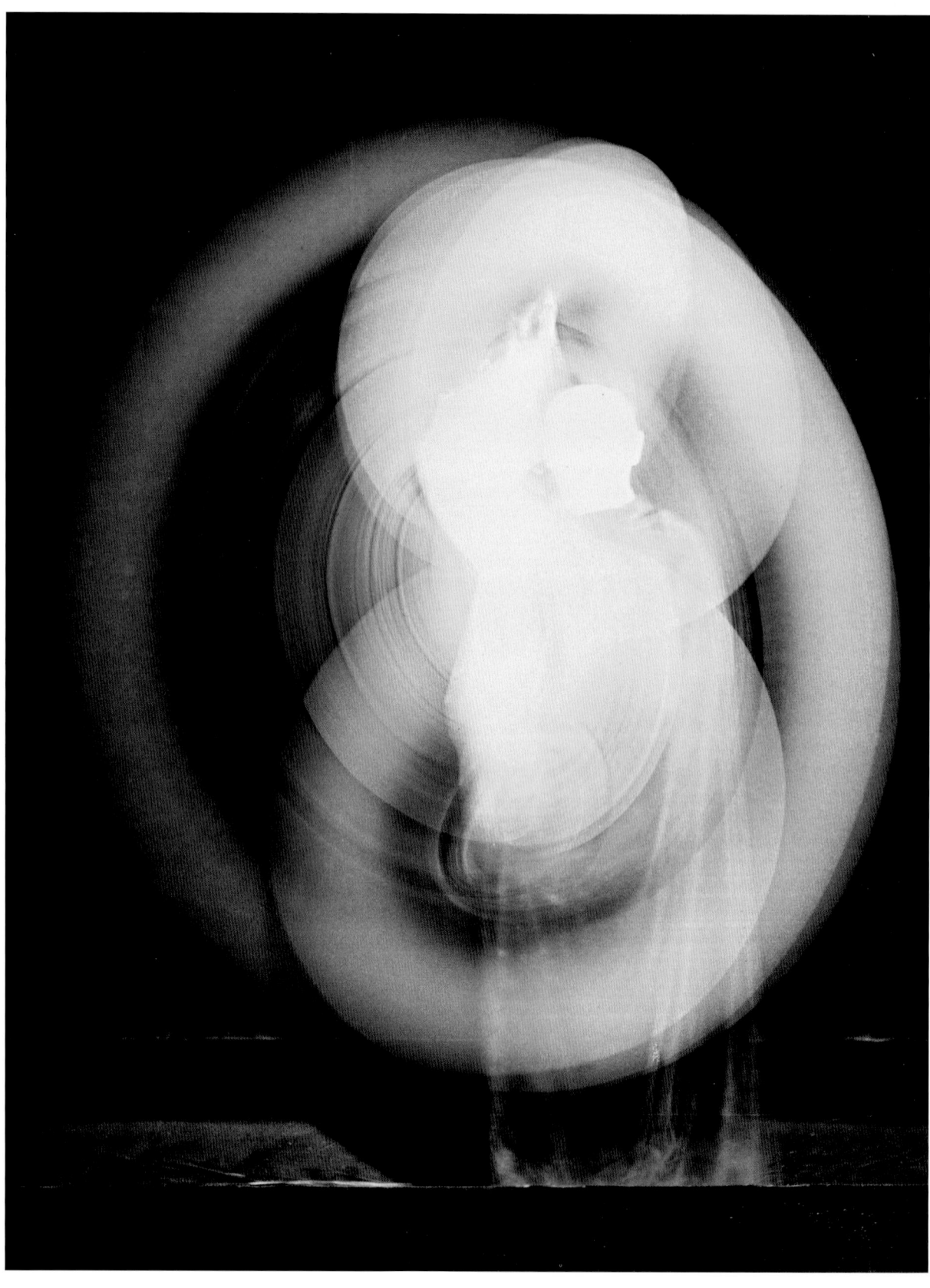

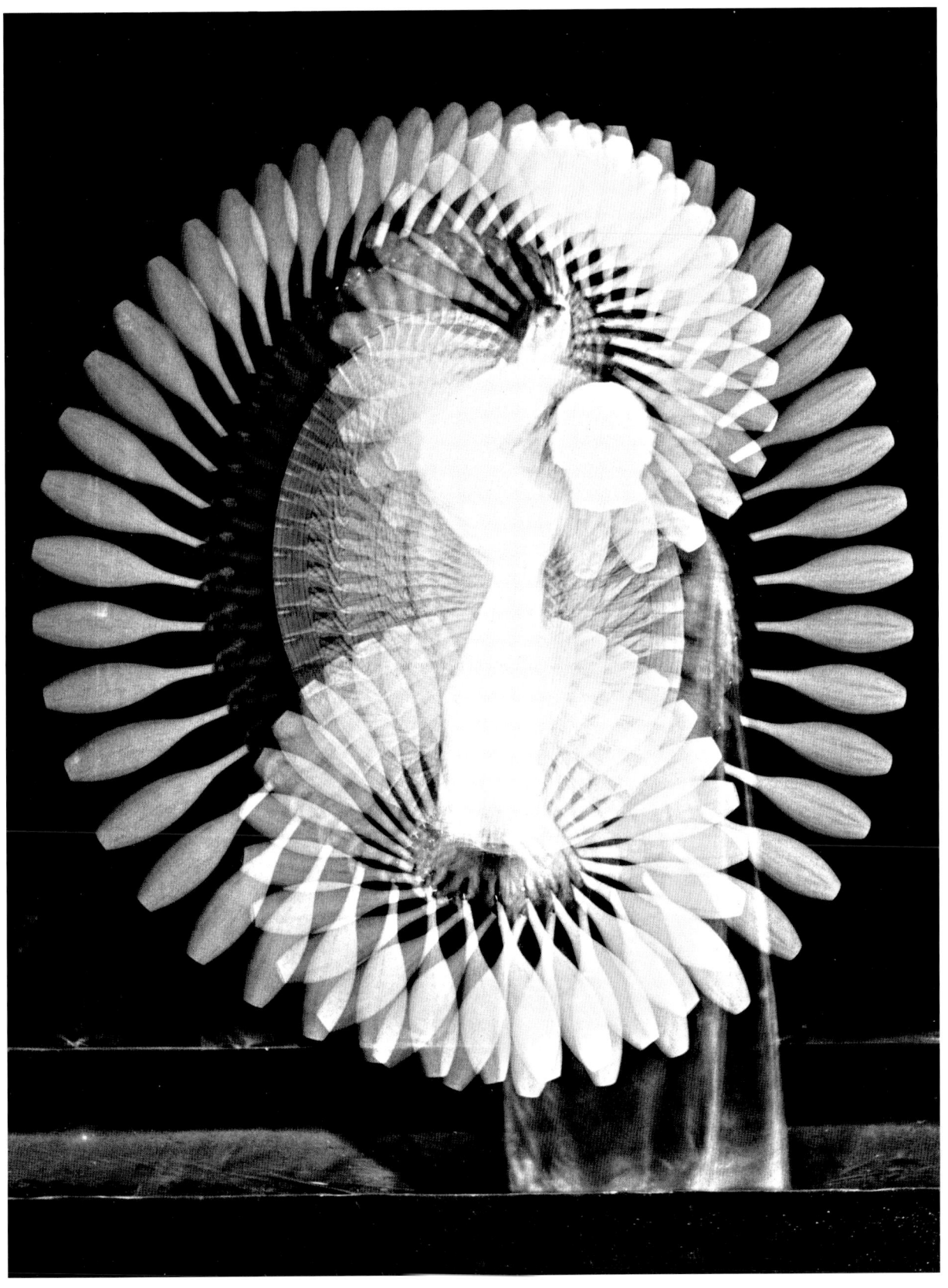

**"Indian" club demonstration, 1939**

Routines using weighted clubs were once popular for strength training. Edgerton described these two images as follows: "The first of these photographs is a result that can be obtained with a regular camera and is similar to the technique of recording abstract light patterns with which László Moholy-Nagy of the Bauhaus experimented. The second of these pictures shows the same routine recorded by stroboscopic light." From *flash! Seeing the Unseen by Ultra High-Speed Photography*.

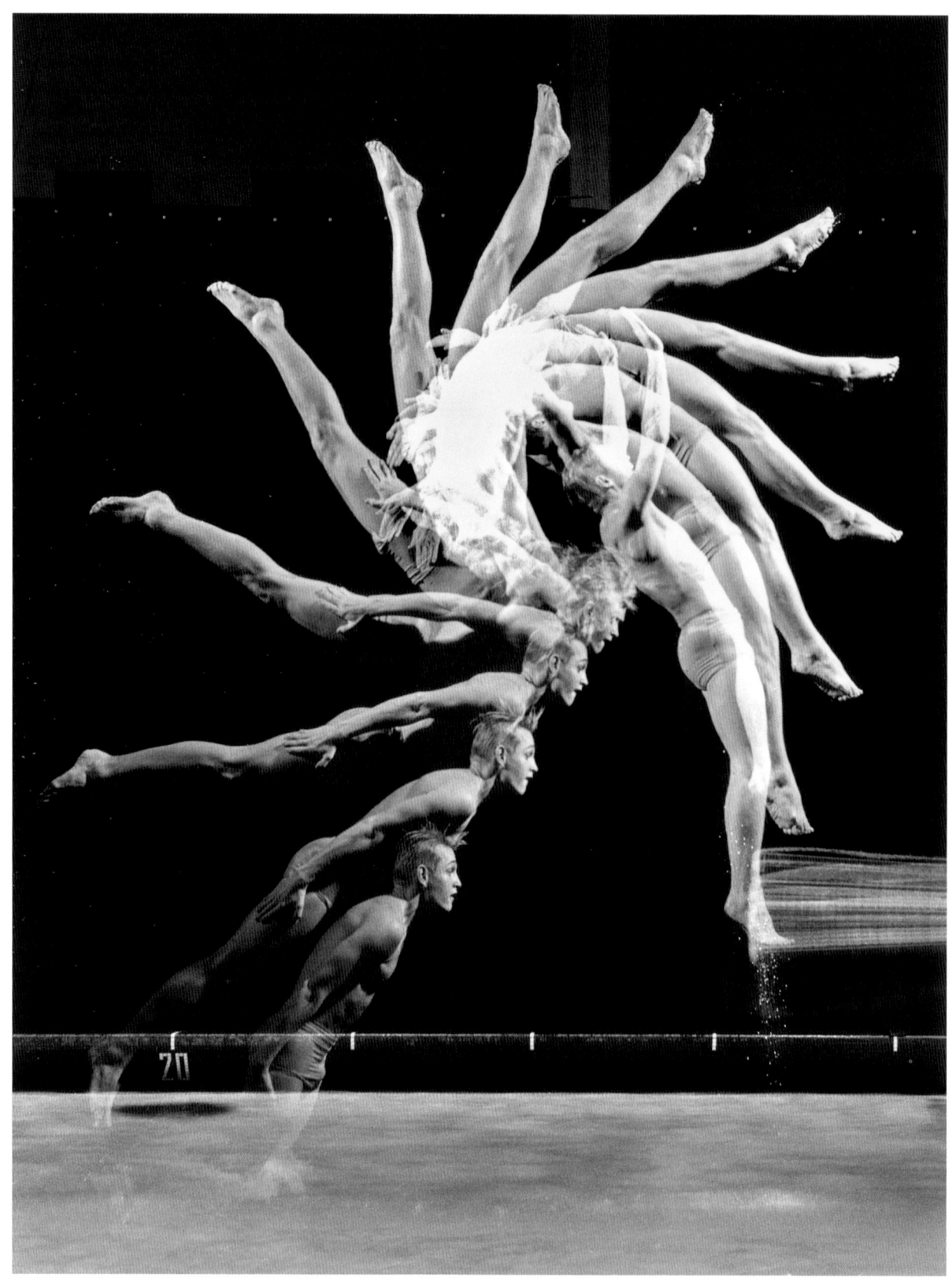

**Back dive, 1954**

Multiflash photograph of diver at MIT's Alumni Pool.

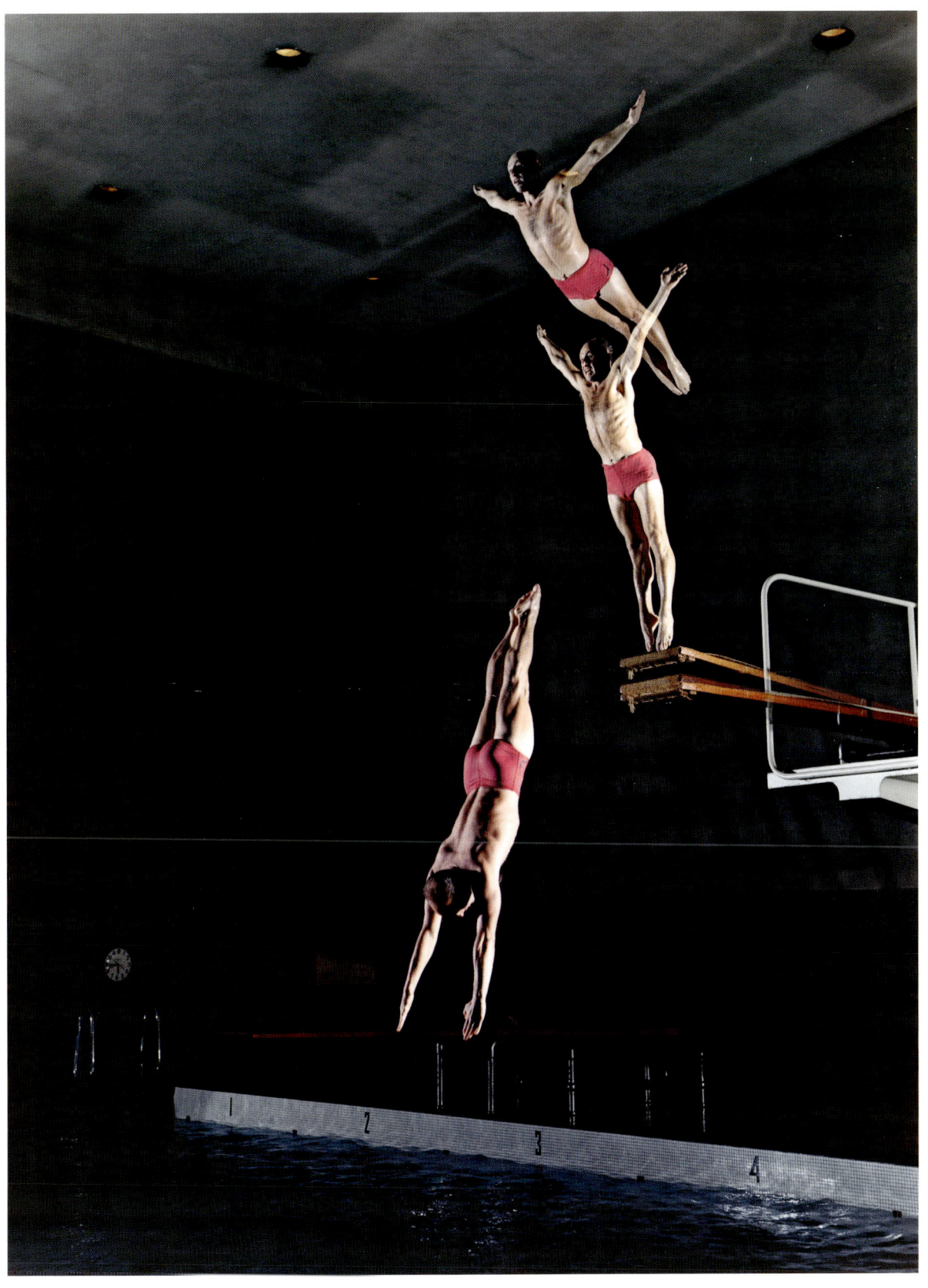

**Diver, 1955**

Multiflash exposure of Charles Batterman, former national diving champion and Harvard's diving coach (he later became MIT's diving coach), diving into the MIT Alumni Pool.

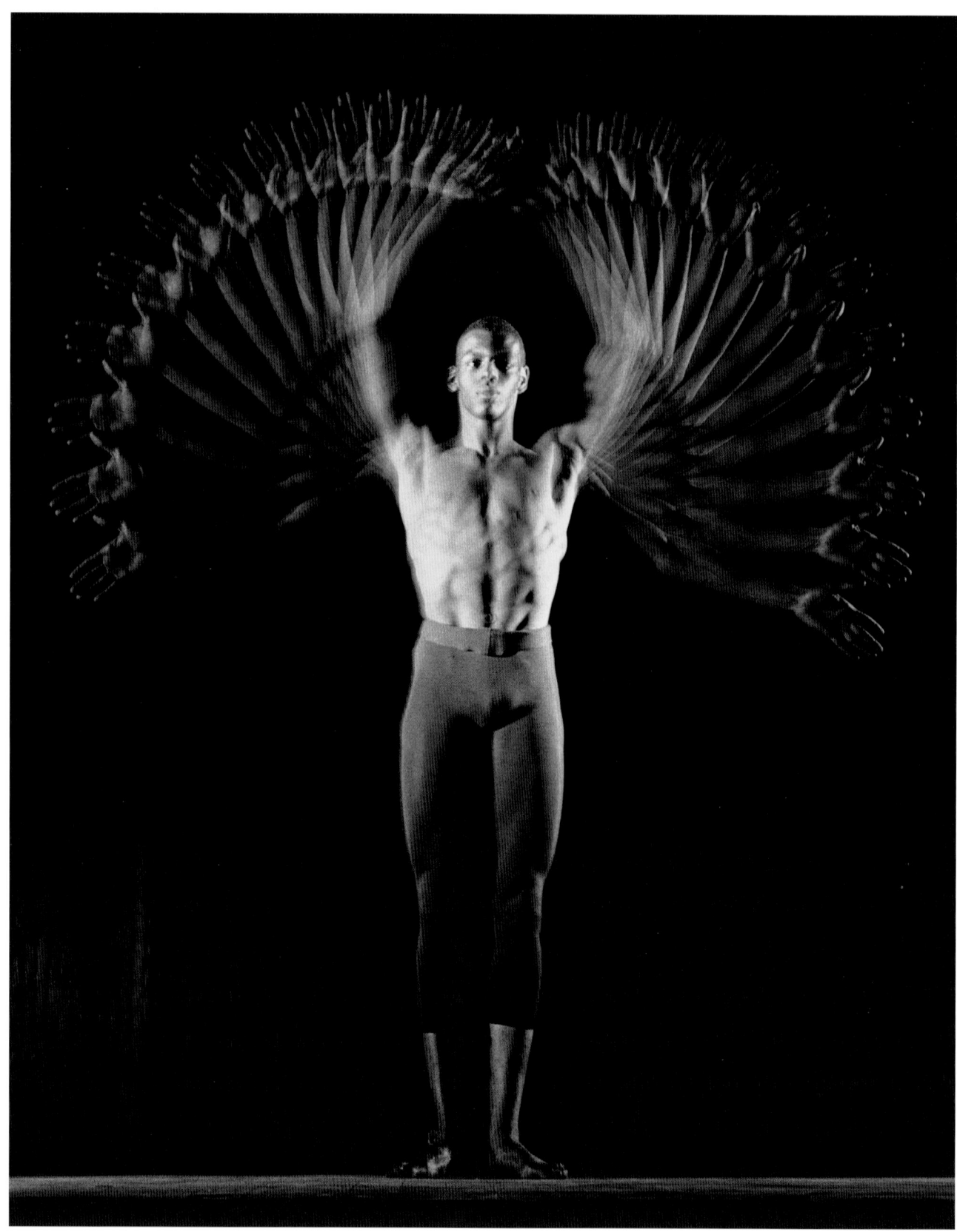

**Gus Solomons, Jr., 1960**

As an undergraduate at MIT, Solomons studied architecture; but even before graduating in 1961, he began
seriously training as a dancer. Edgerton made this multiflash portrait during Solomons' senior year.

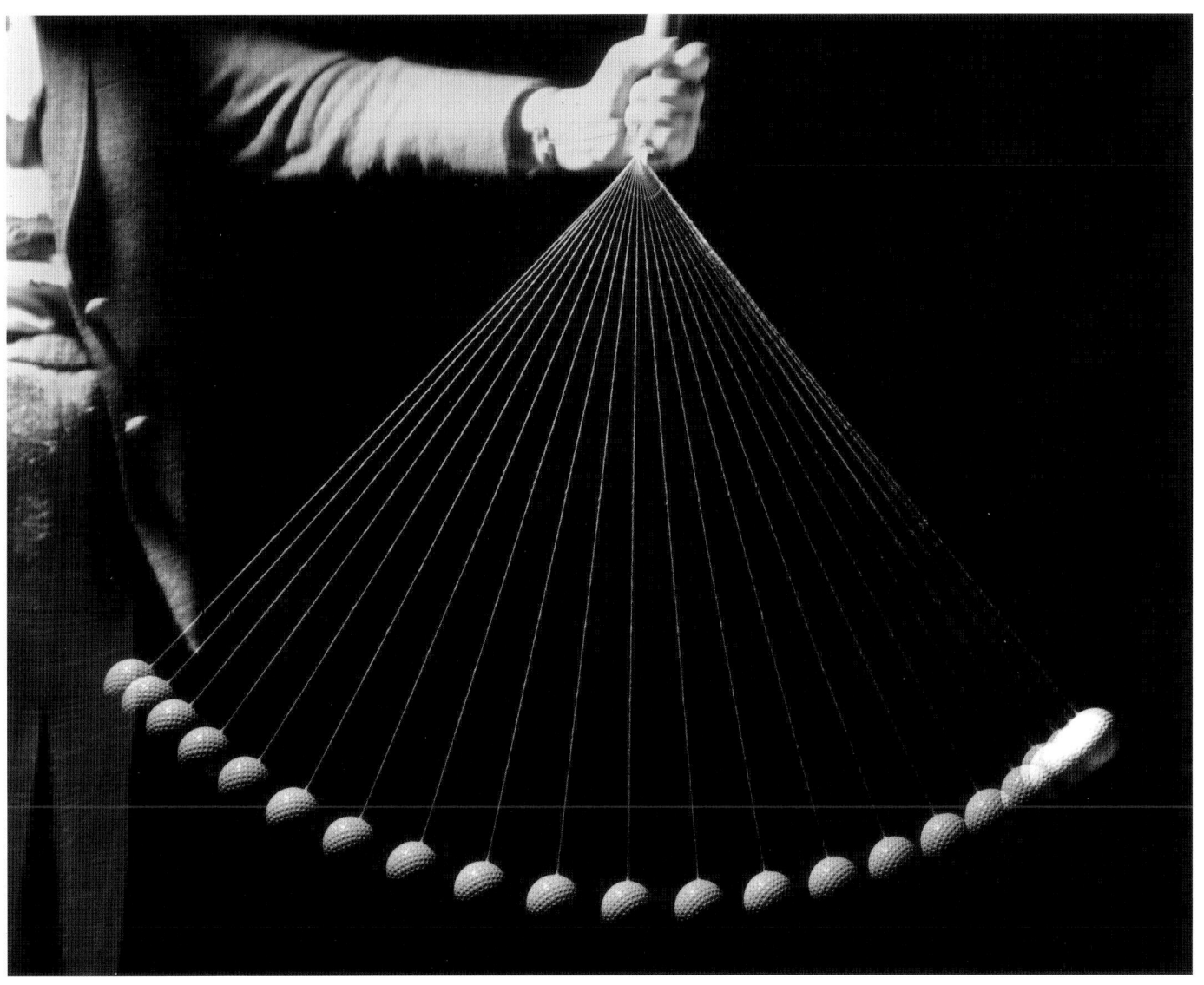

**Golf ball pendulum, 1982**

Esther Edgerton holds the pendulum at the pivot. The photograph harkens back to one that appeared in
*Life* magazine in 1941, when Edgerton provided a series of images to illustrate the basic laws of physics.

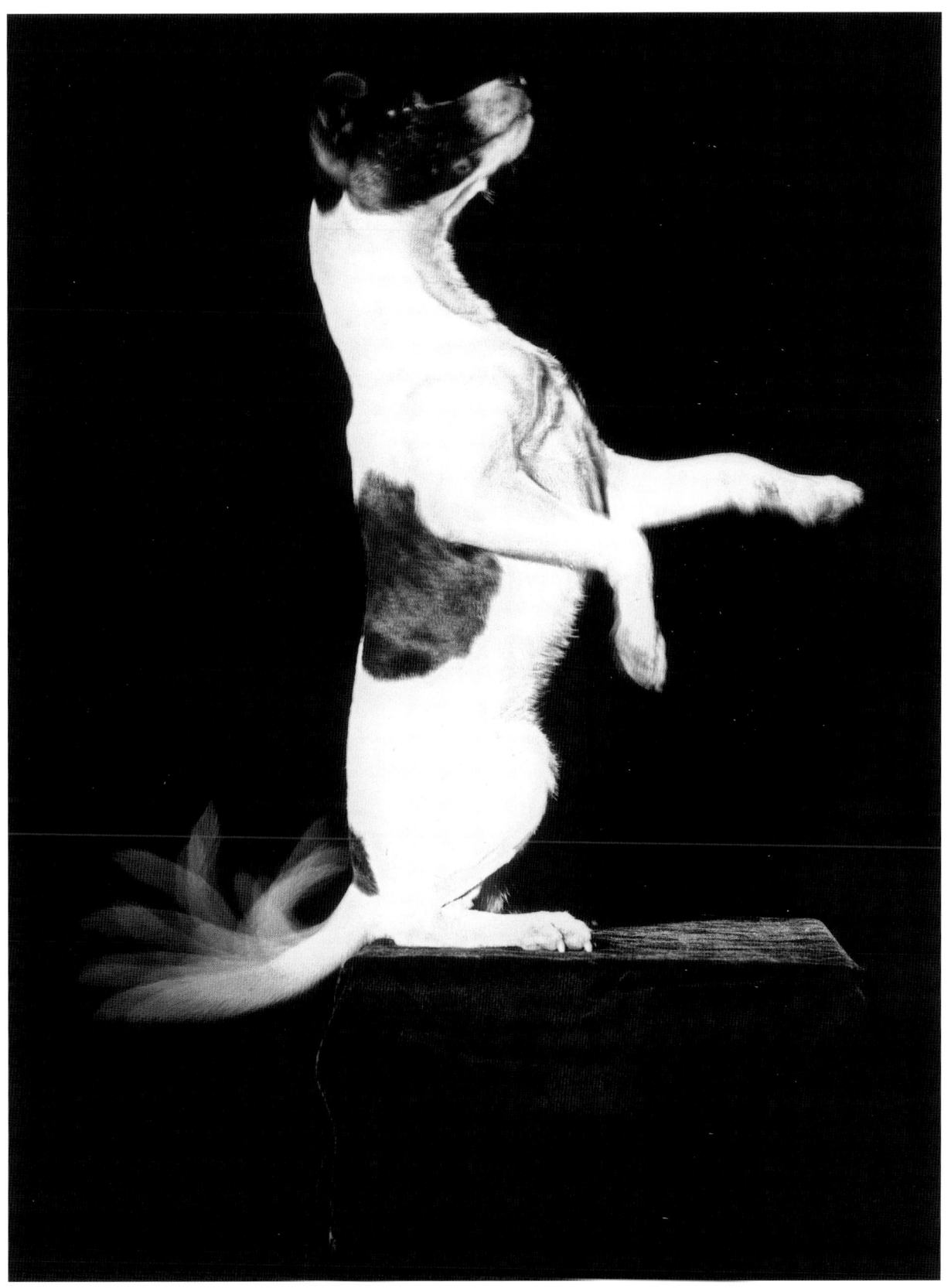

**Jackie wags his tail, 1948**

Many commentators have noted the similarities between Edgerton's image of the family pet and Italian futurist Giacomo Balla's famous painting "Dynamism of a Dog on a Leash." Edgerton shot several images of the family pet using his strobe.

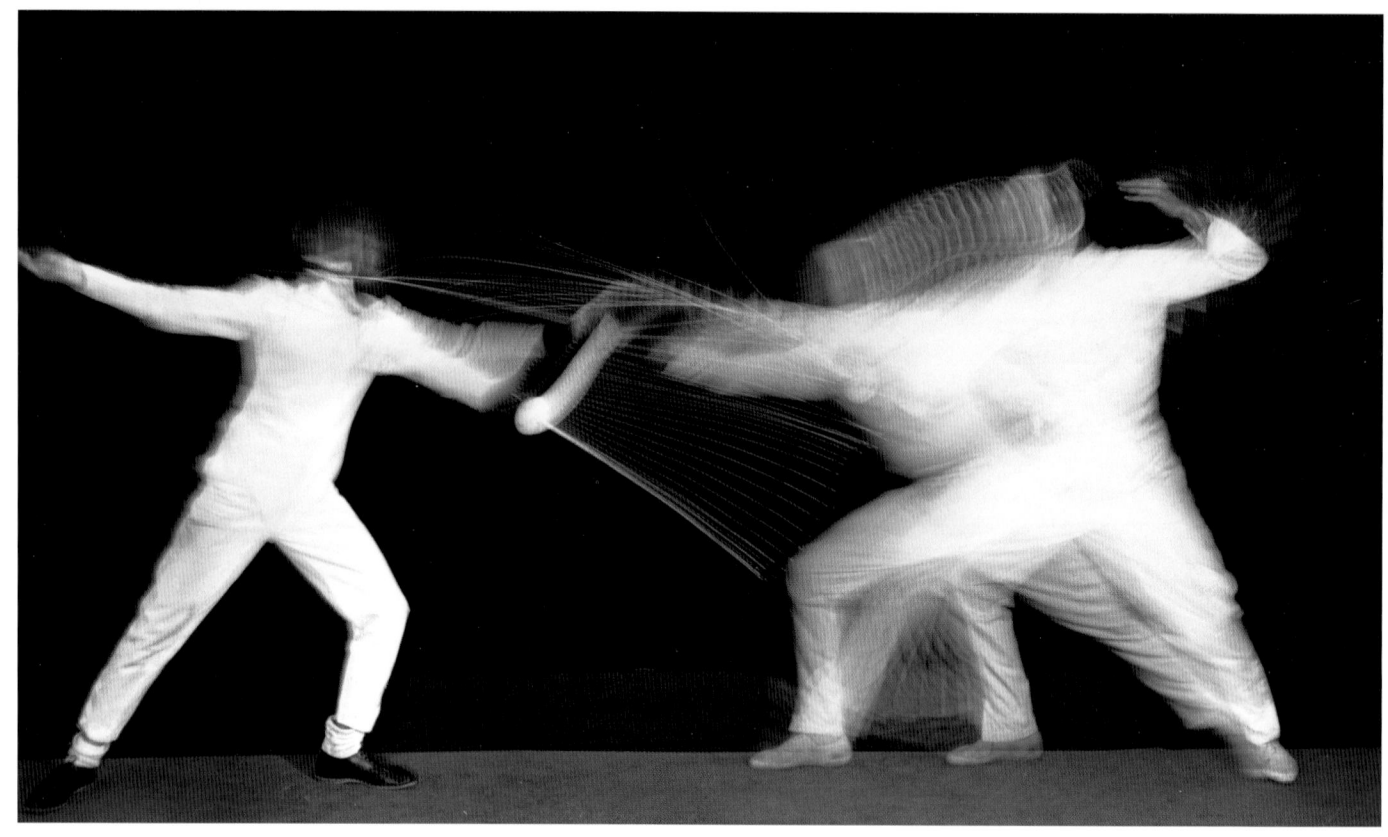

**Fencers, 1939**

Edgerton's multiflash captures national fencing champion, Joseph Levis (right),
as he parries his opponent's thrust, touching him on the collar.

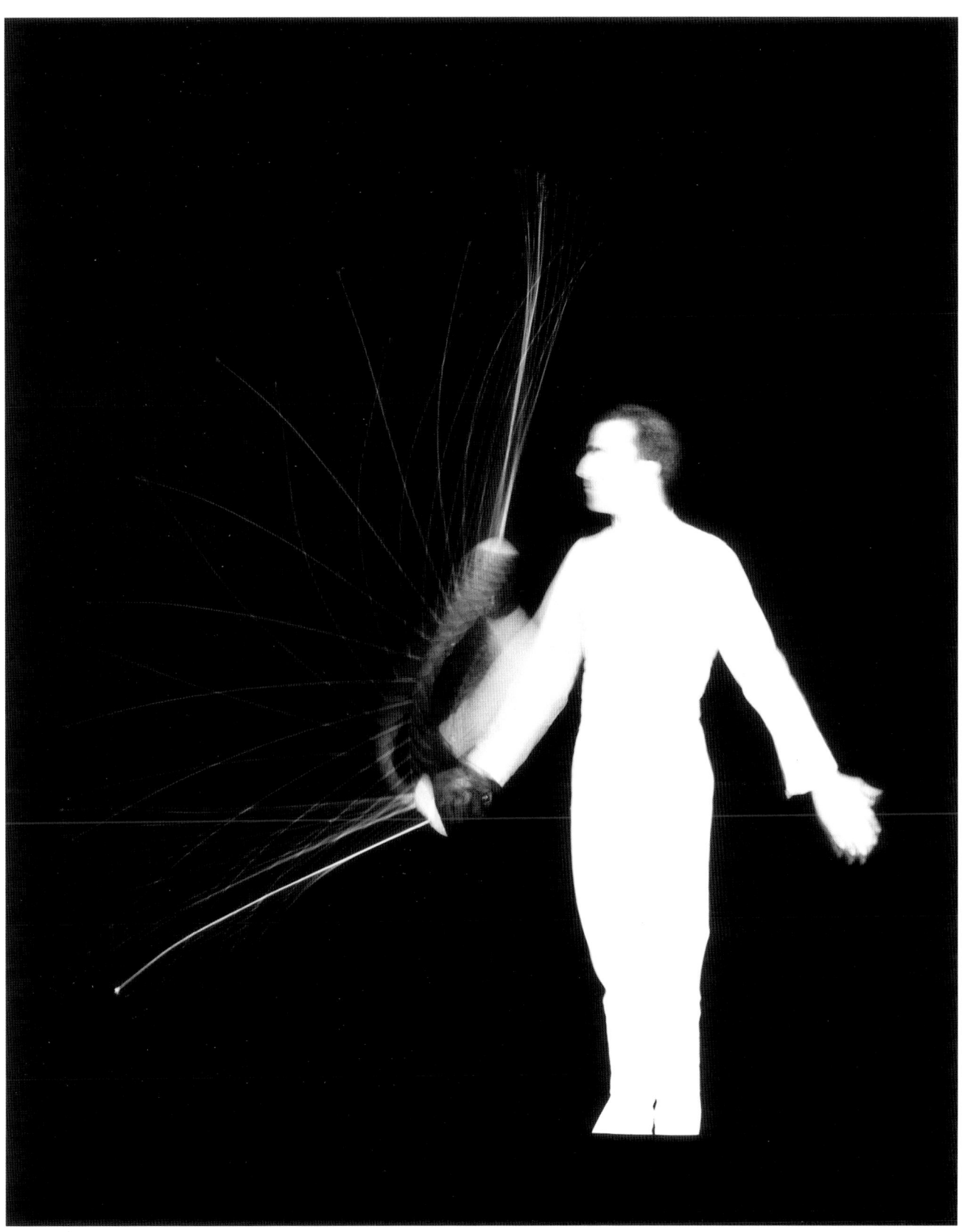

**A simple salute, 1939**

Joseph Levis executes the salute that all fencers give before engaging their opponents.

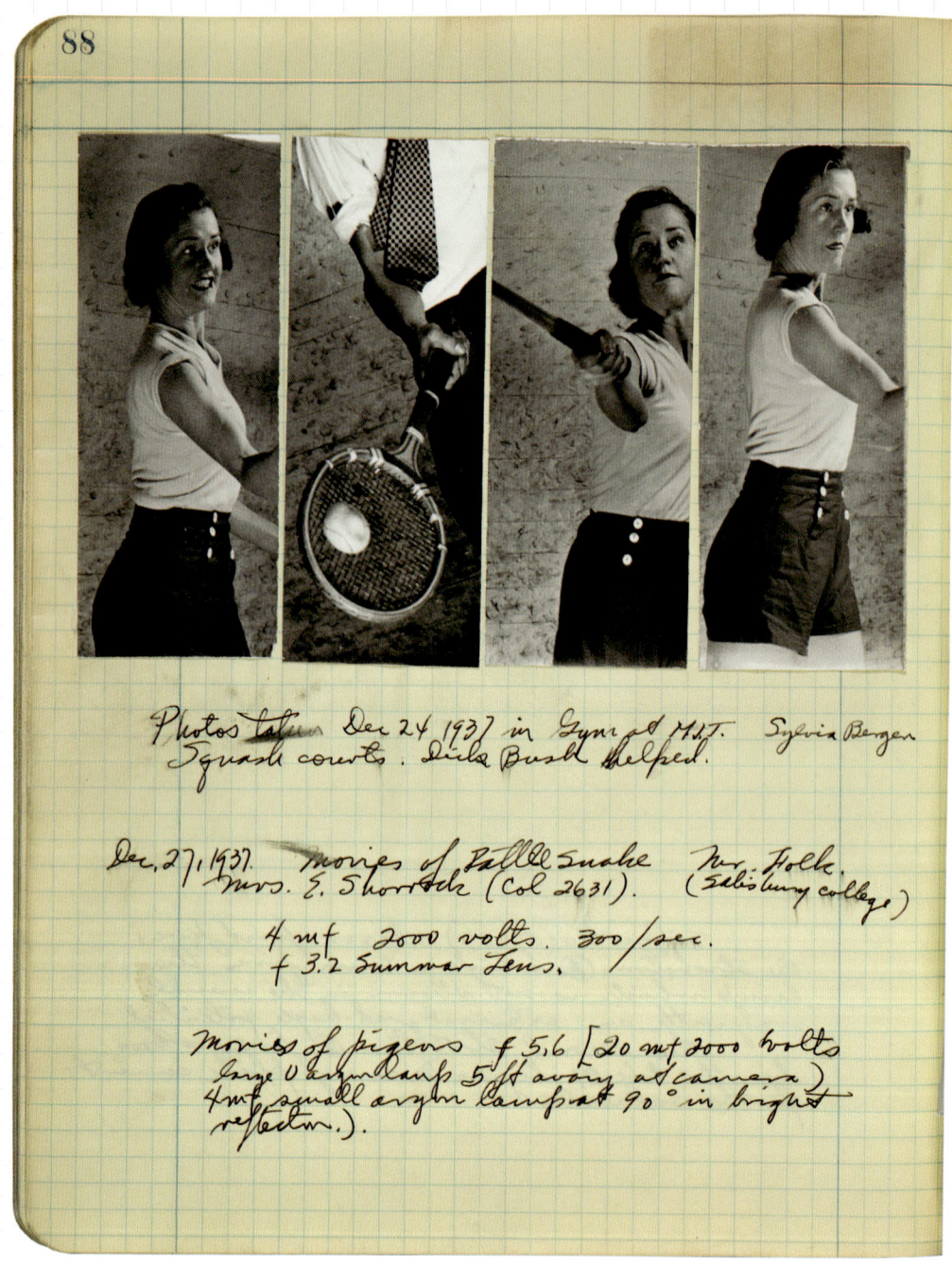

Edgerton's analysis of tennis strokes began early on. This notebook page includes copies of photographs made on Christmas Eve at the MIT gym. Notebook Number 8, December 24, 1937, p. 88.

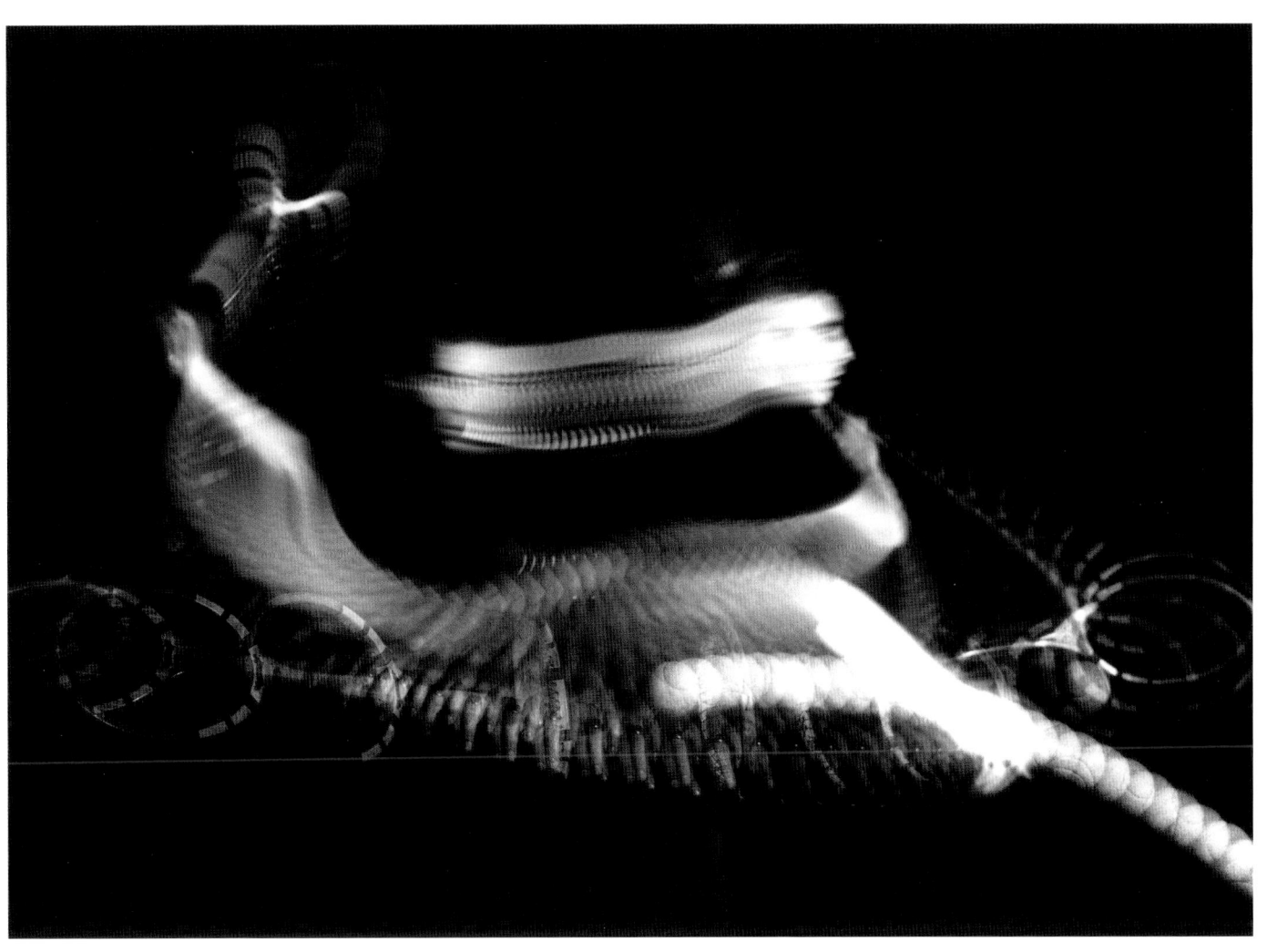

The swirls and eddies of a stroke, 1939

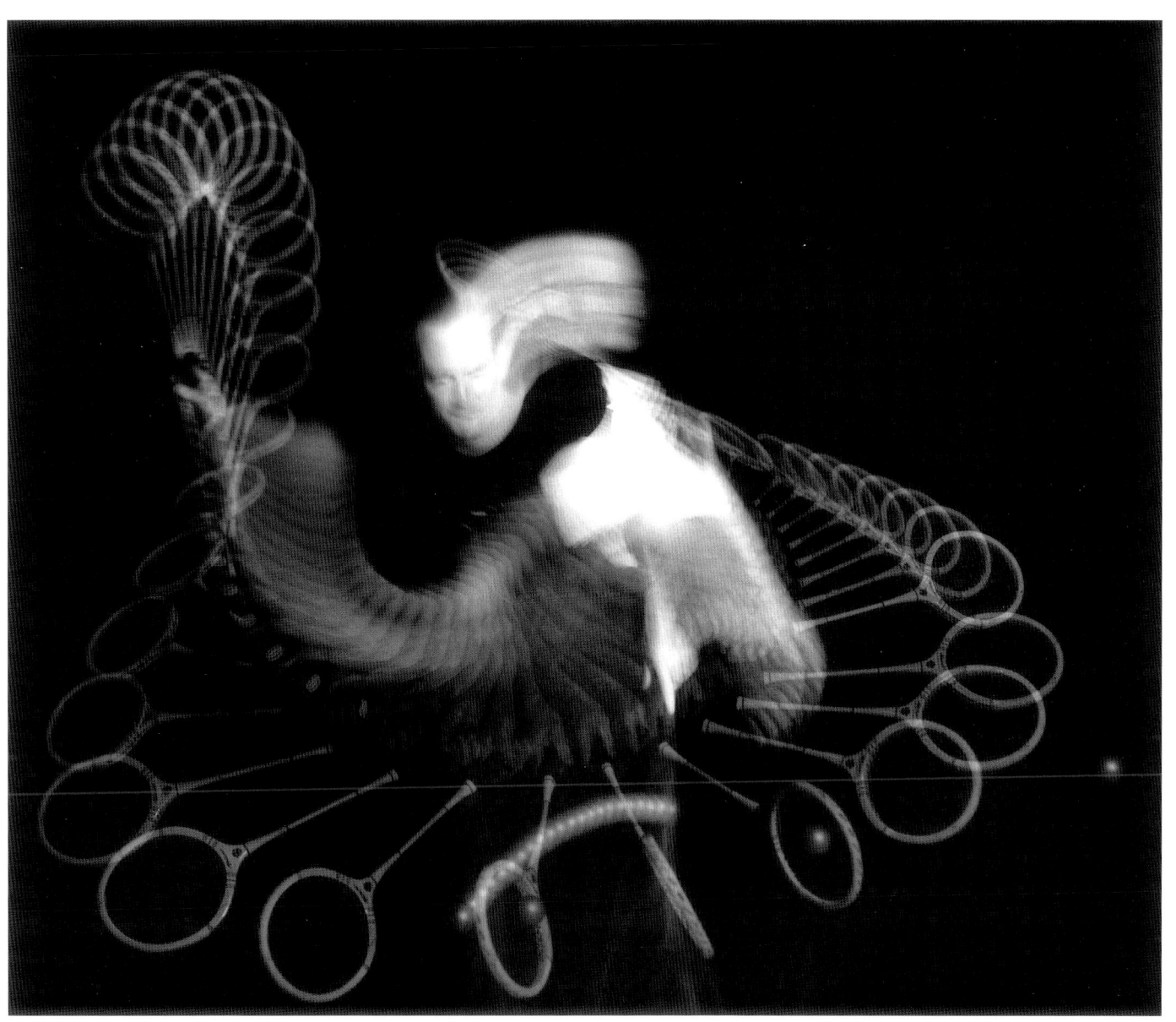

**Squash stroke, 1938**

Four-time US professional squash champion and longtime MIT squash coach John "Jack" L. Summers demonstrated a series of several squash strokes for Edgerton to capture using his multiflash technique.

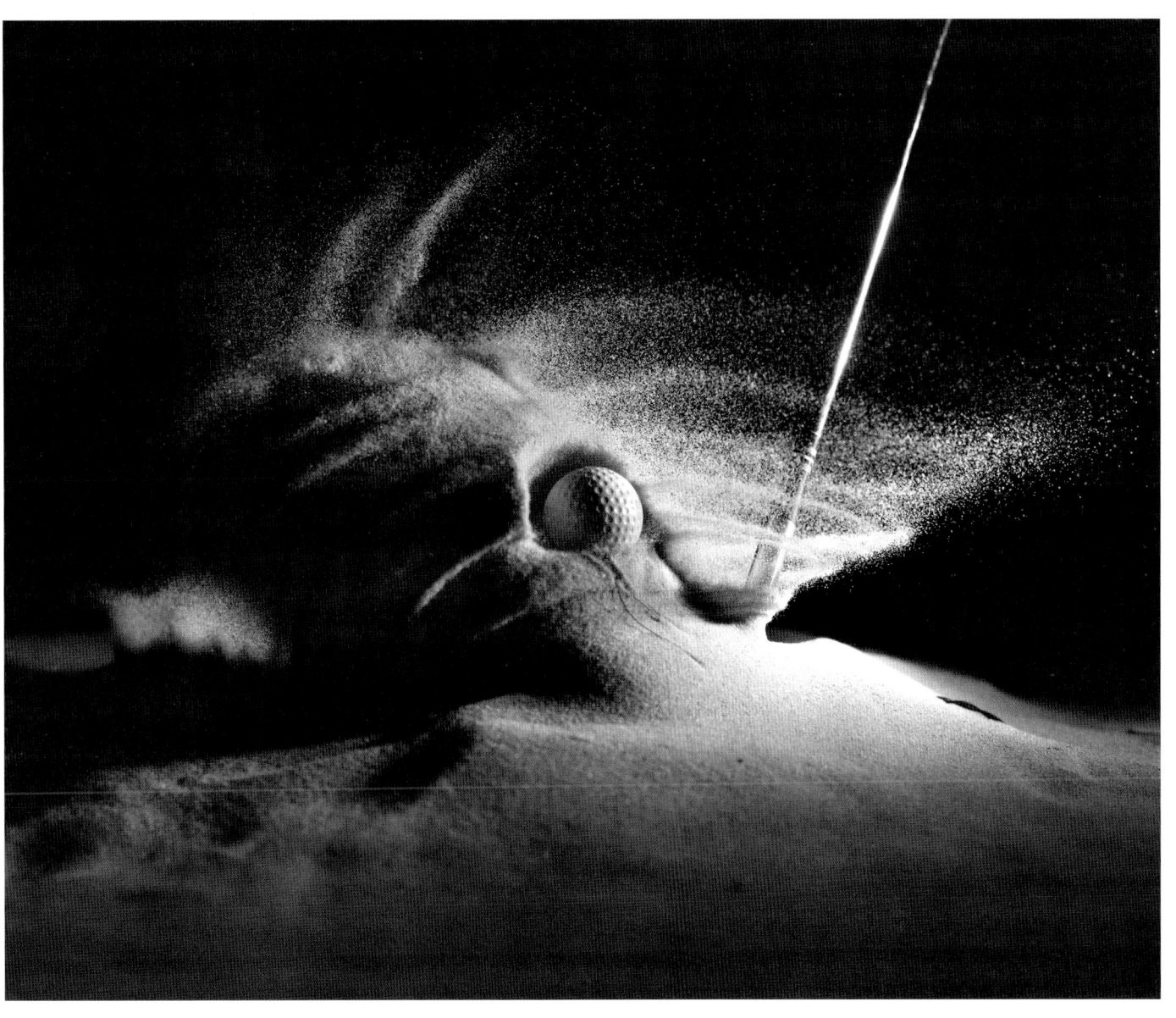

Golf sand trap, 1960

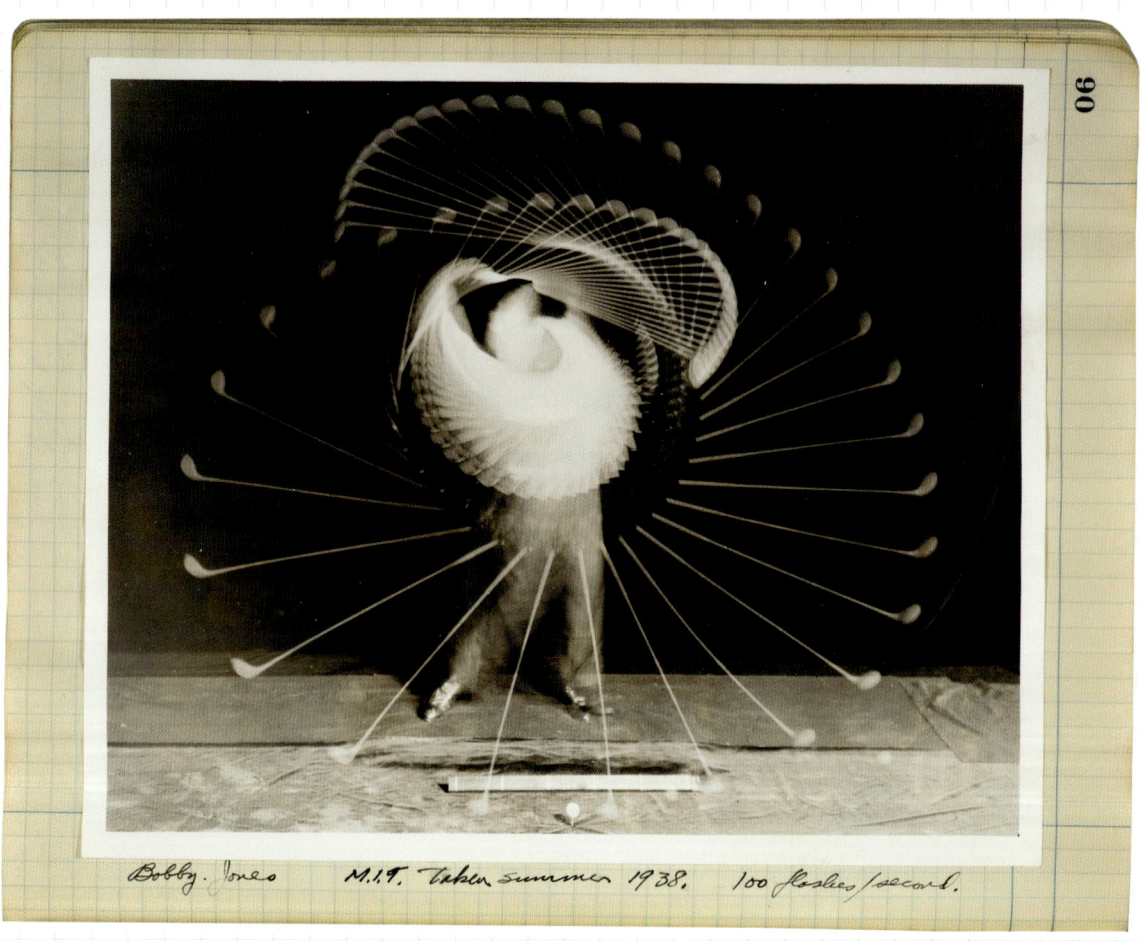

Edgerton conducted extensive studies of professional golfer Bobby Jones's swing to understand what happens when the club hits the ball. This 1938 side view was captured using the multiflash. Notebook Number 9, January 8, 1939, p. 90.

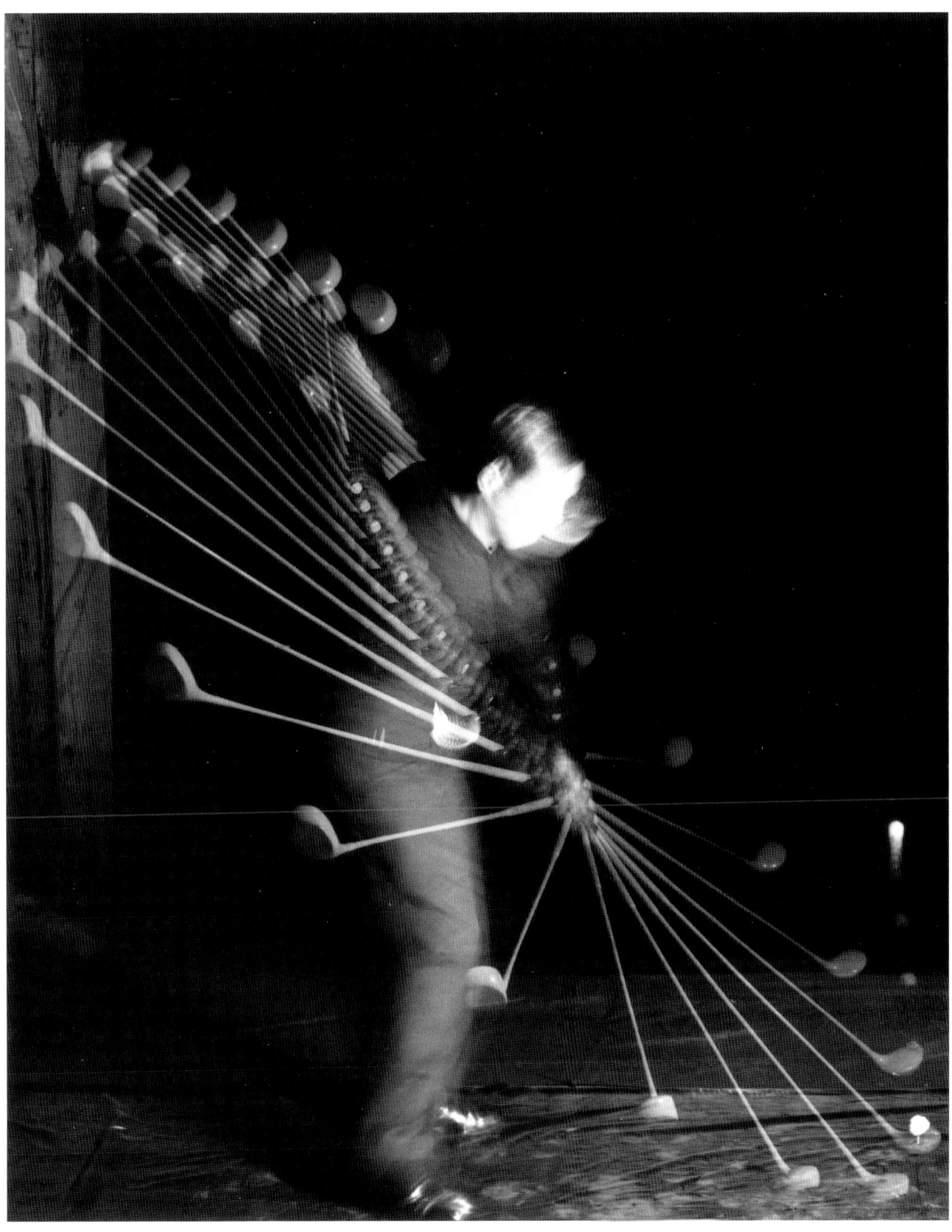

Bobby Jones swings a driver, 1938

July 7 1938
H. E. Edgerton.

Set up velvet curtain and white
curtain in Hanger last weekend. Single photography
also multiple shots arranged.

Denny Shute, wife, and Eleanor Reed
came over July 5 and we took photos of them
in evening.

Ralph Guldahl came over July 6 in
morning for a series of pictures.

Went out to Wonderland track Dgt. July 7 to
arrange for greyhound photos.

Revolver .38 with Fladding on July 8.
f 11 at 1 or 2 x $10^{-6}$ sec. SS pan press.

Discussed Spaulding studies with
Stevens of A D Little on Friday aft July 8.
We are to work for 6 months at $400 per
on studies of golf etc.

Took photos at Harvard swimming pool
SS pan Press film Agfa. f 16.
Lighting below

Pool.

48 mf Sprt.
300 v.

48 mf
300 v.

Edgerton makes note of his earlier photo shoot with Densmore Shute on July 5.
Notebook Number 9, July 7, 1938, p. 39.

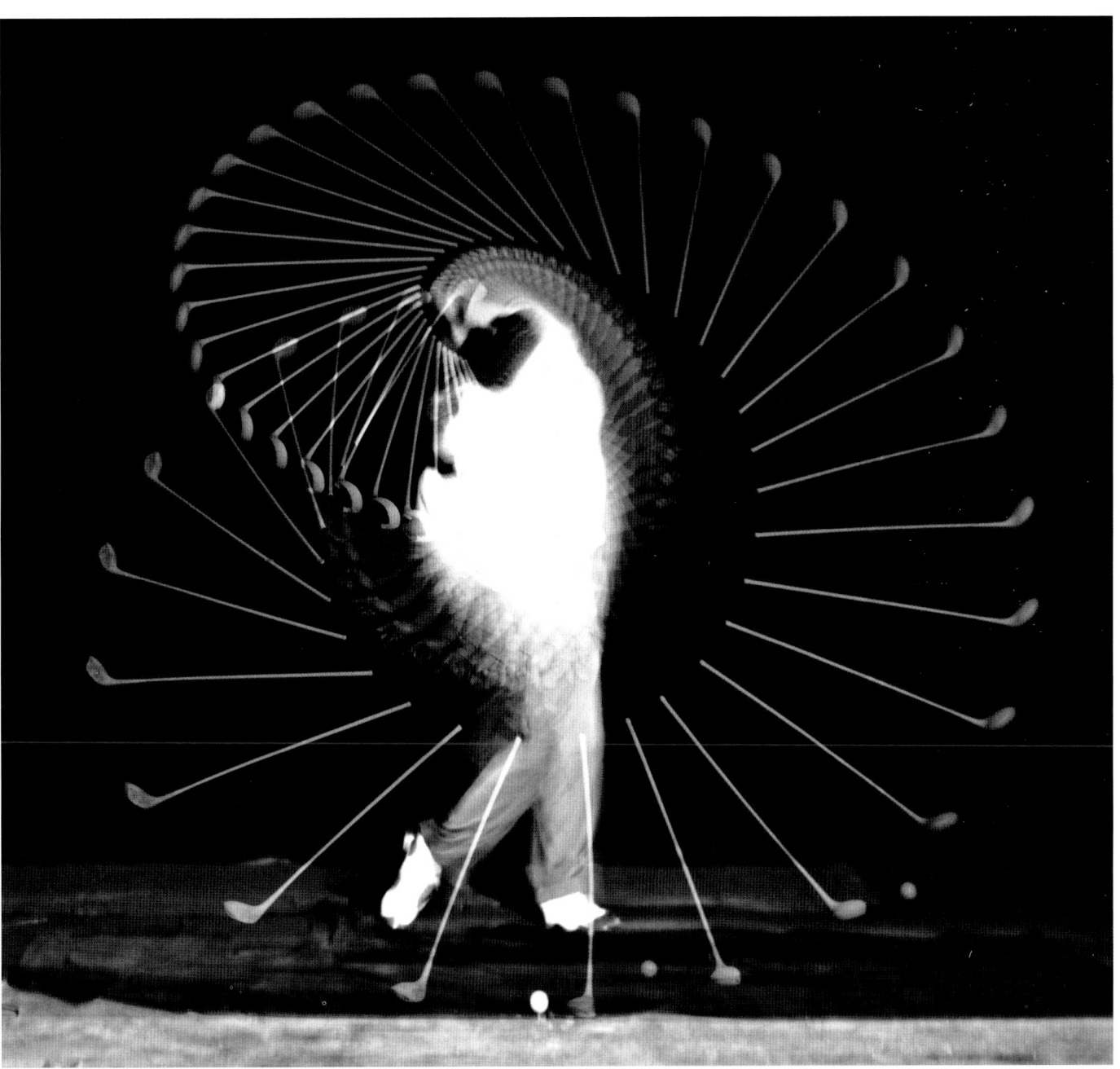

**Densmore Shute bending the shaft, 1938**

The flash fires 100 times per second for a half-second exposure that captured champion golfer
Densmore Shute's golf swing. The curve of the shaft after hitting the ball is clearly visible.

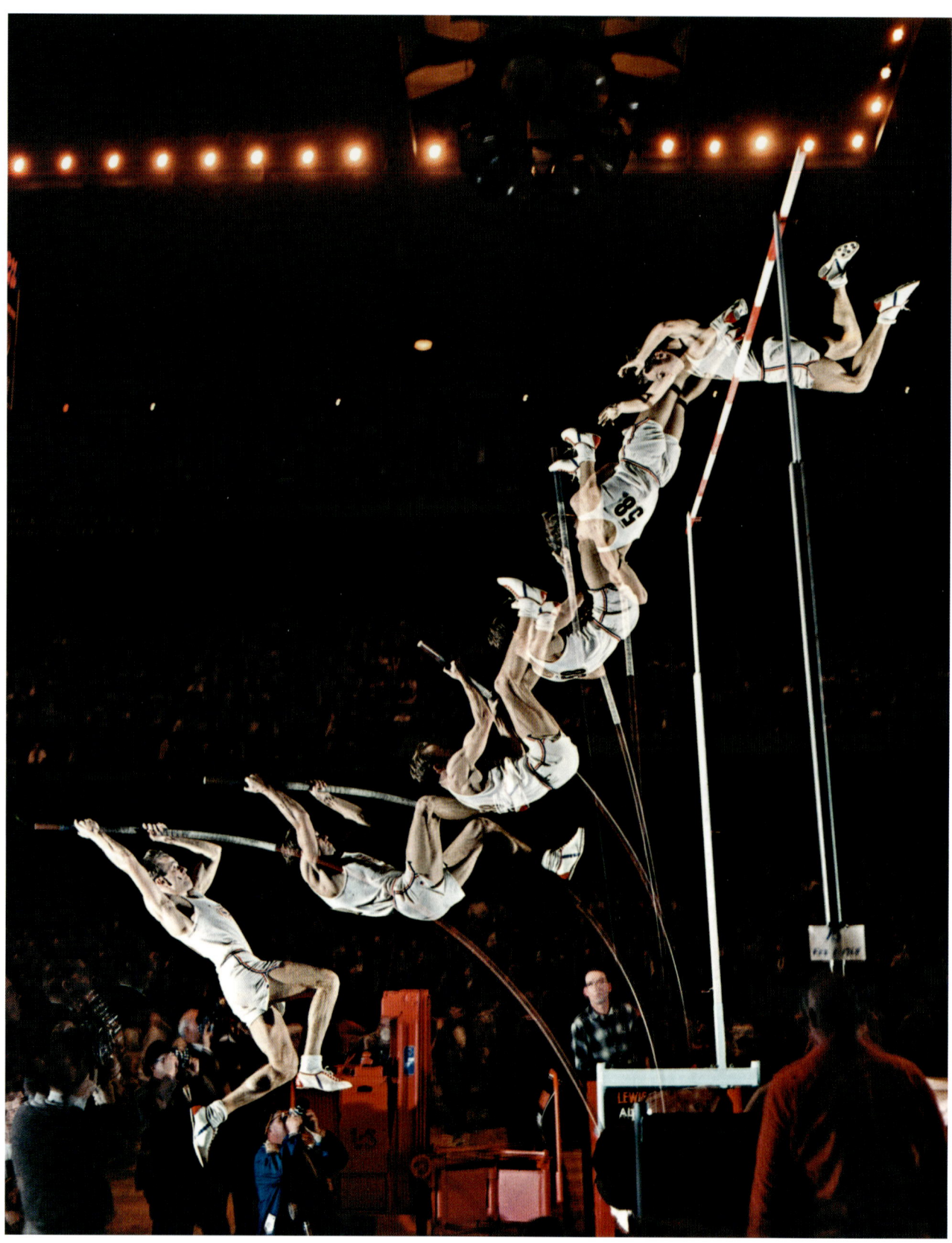

**Pole vault, 1964**

Edgerton captured West Virginia University pole-vaulter David Tork at the 1964 Boston Garden indoor track and field meet using a manually timed multiflash and synchronized shutter.

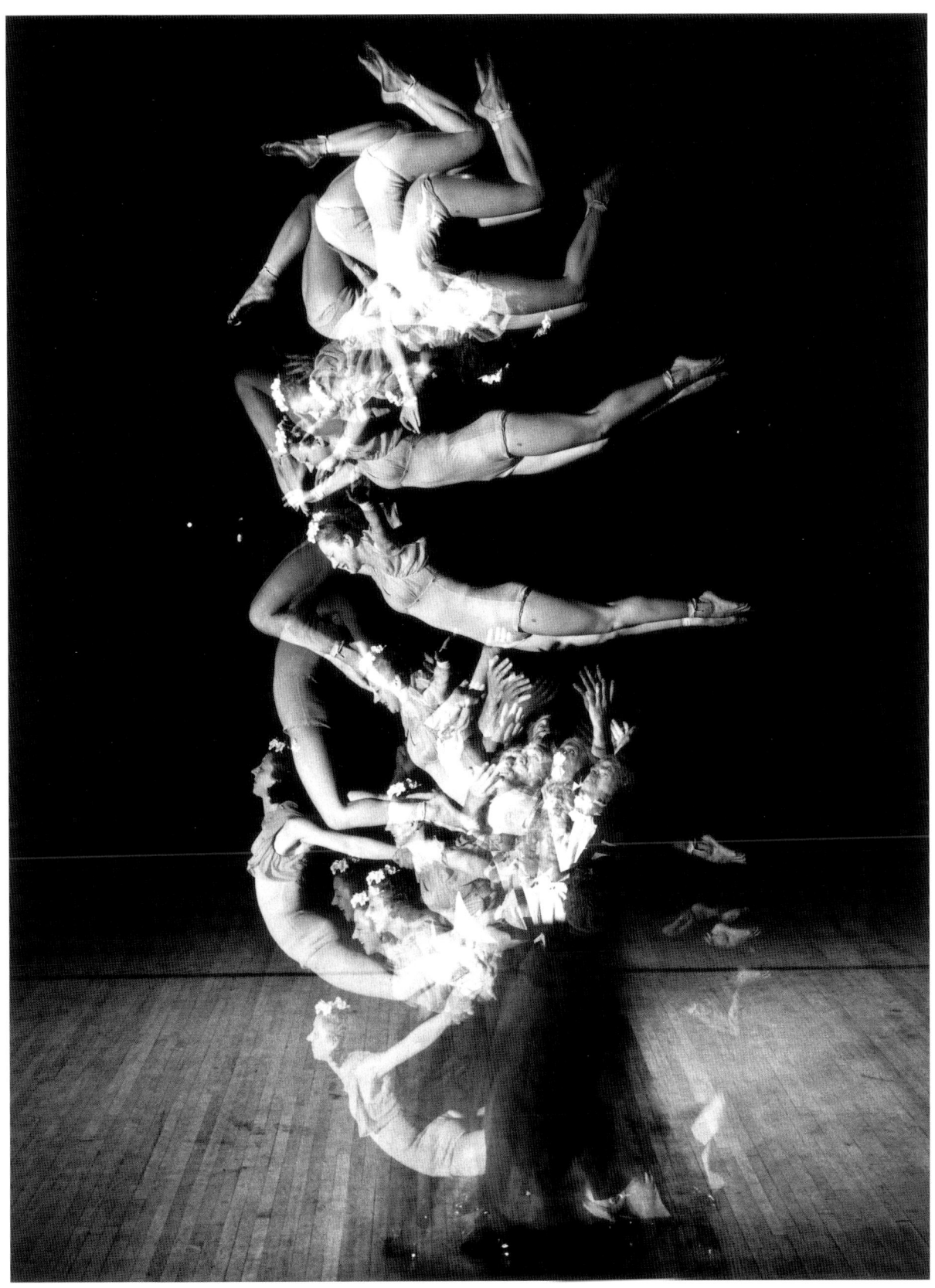

**Trick dancers, 1942**

Edgerton captured the Martells and Mignon dance team performing a half-flip maneuver for *Life* magazine.

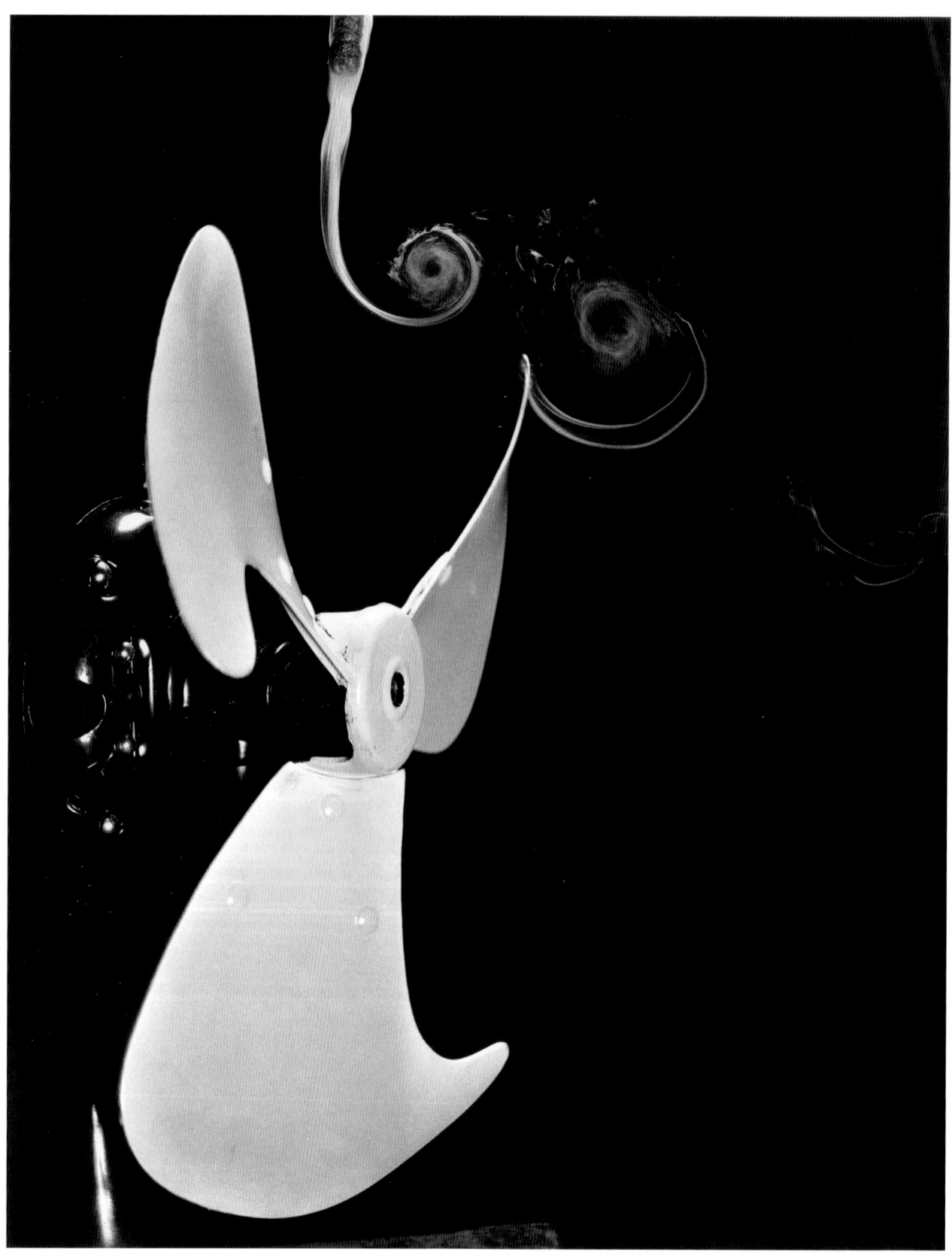

**Fan and smoke, 1934**

Edgerton exhibited this photograph at the Royal Photographic Society in London in 1934. Smoke from titanium tetrachloride and a stroboscope made it possible to see the vortices spiraling off the tips of the fan blades.

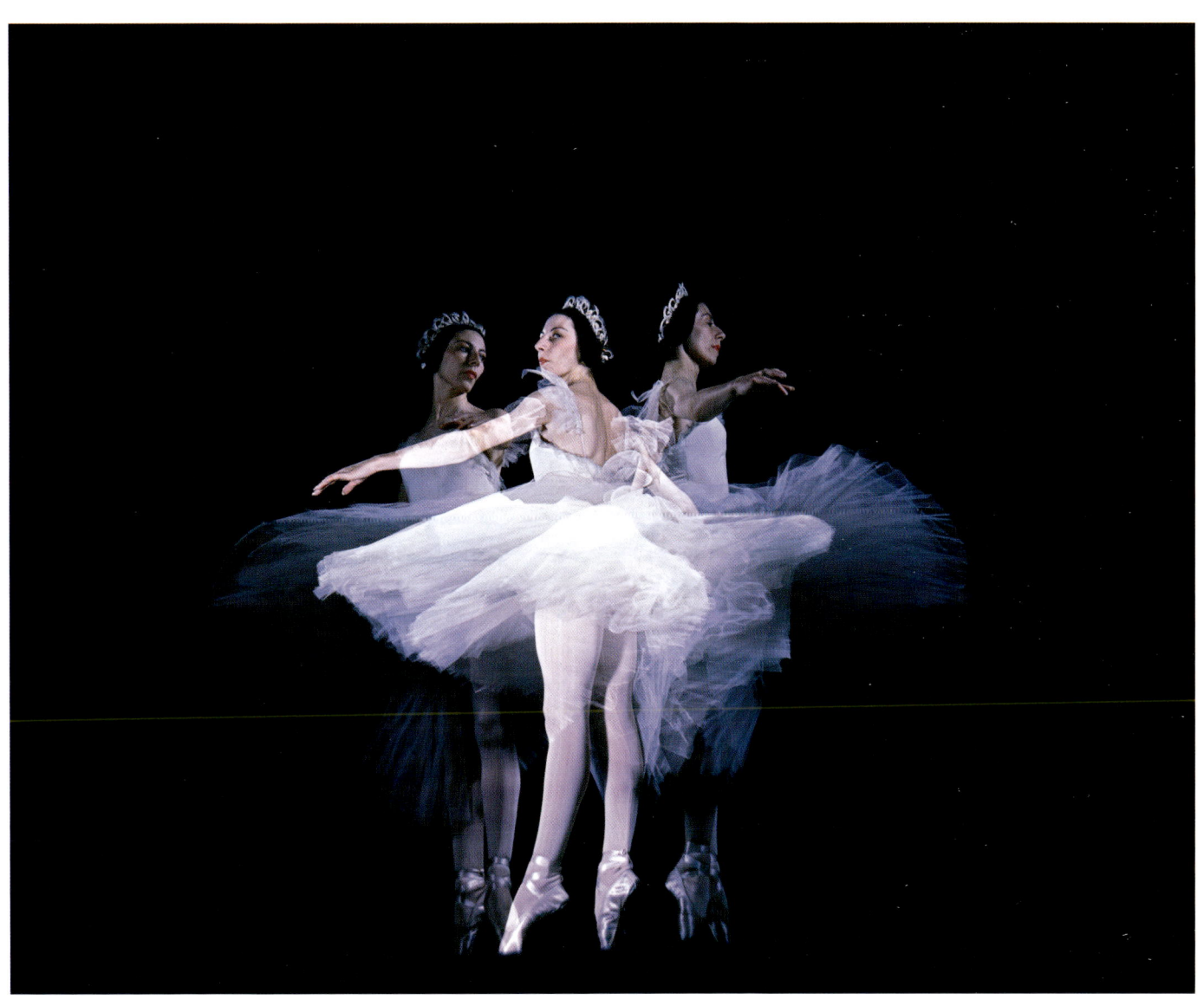

Ballerina (Margot Fonteyn), 1940

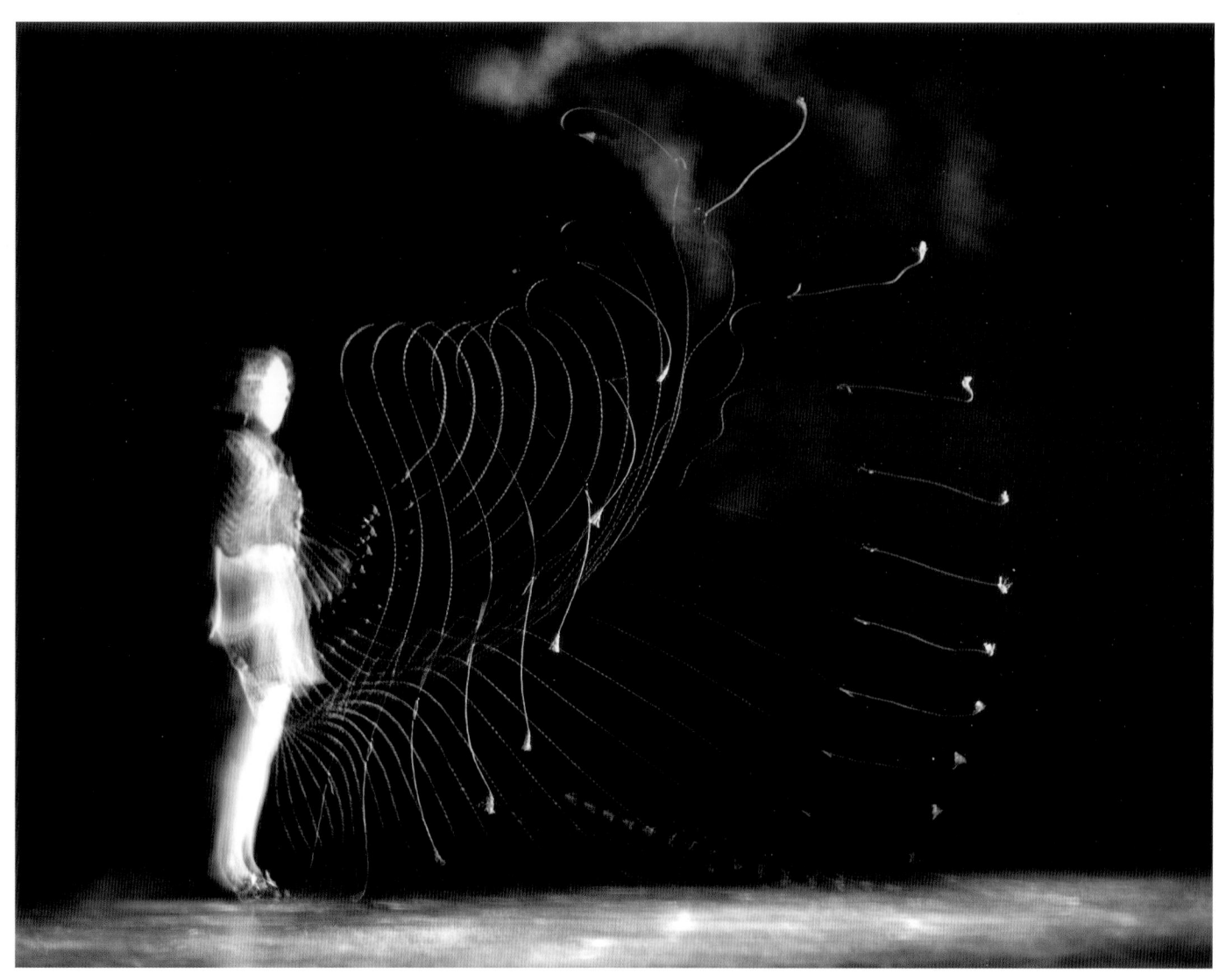

**Cracking the whip, 1972**

Lucy Sloan cracks a bullwhip. Edgerton put chalk at the tip to make it easier to trace its movement.

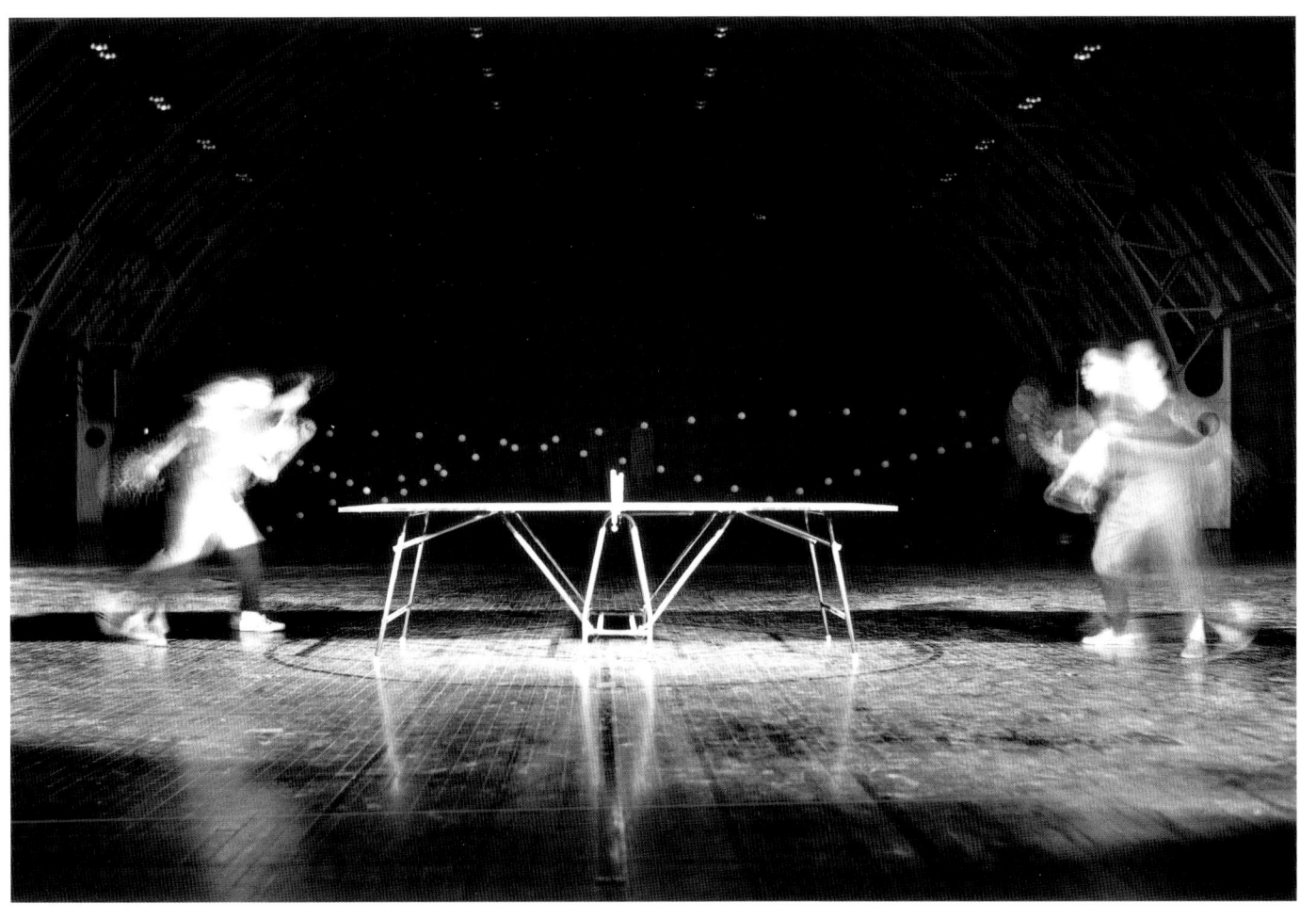

**Ping-pong, 1955**

Edgerton's multiflash fired 75 times (50 times per second) to capture this short 1.5-second rally.

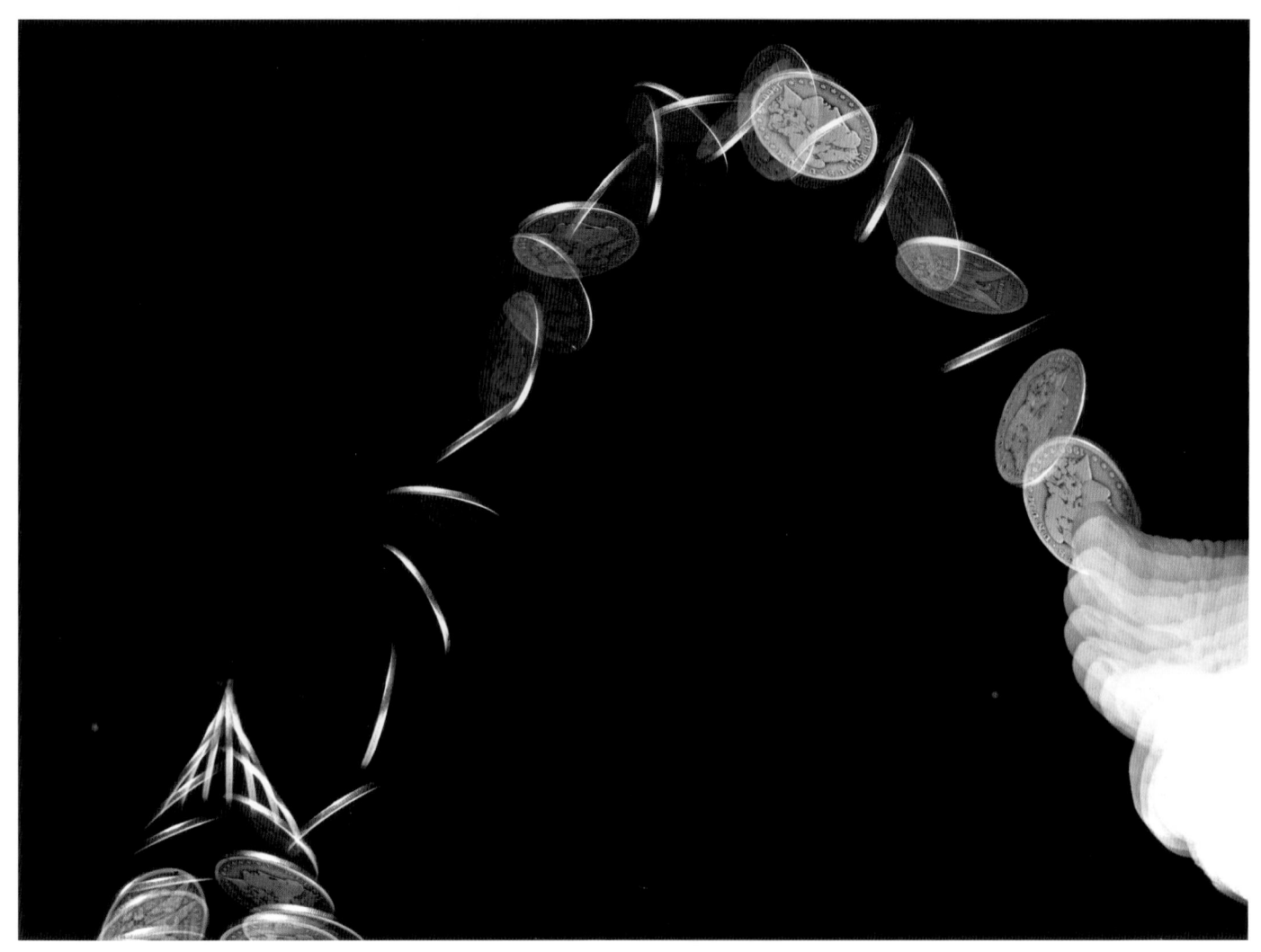

Coin Toss, 1965

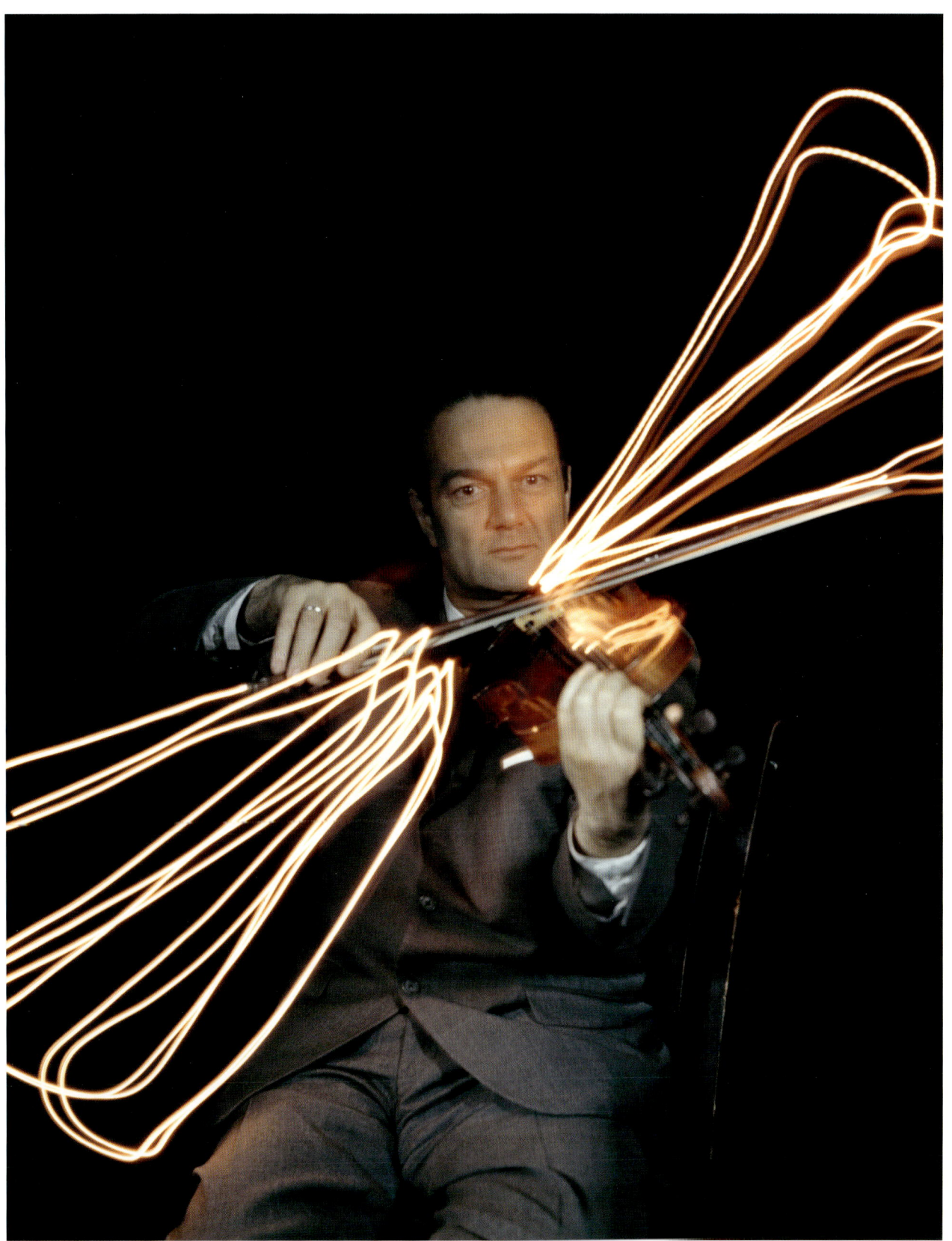

**Violinist, 1968**

Edgerton affixed small lights to each end of the bow, and the violinist played in
complete darkness except for a single strobe flash fired to make him visible.

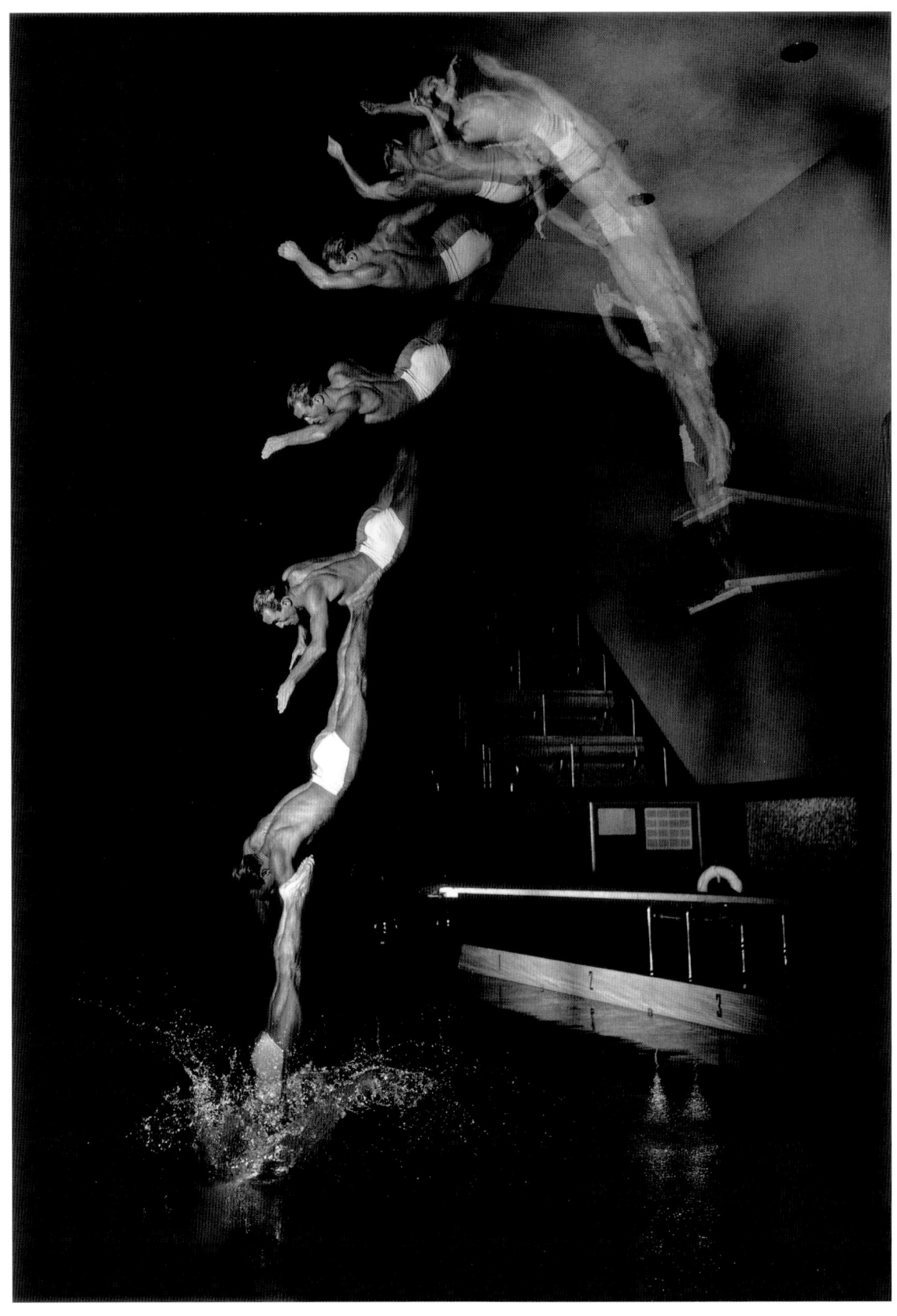

**Pete Desjardins diving, 1940**

Multiflash photograph of two-time Olympic gold medalist Pete Desjardins
diving off the high board at the MIT Alumni Pool.

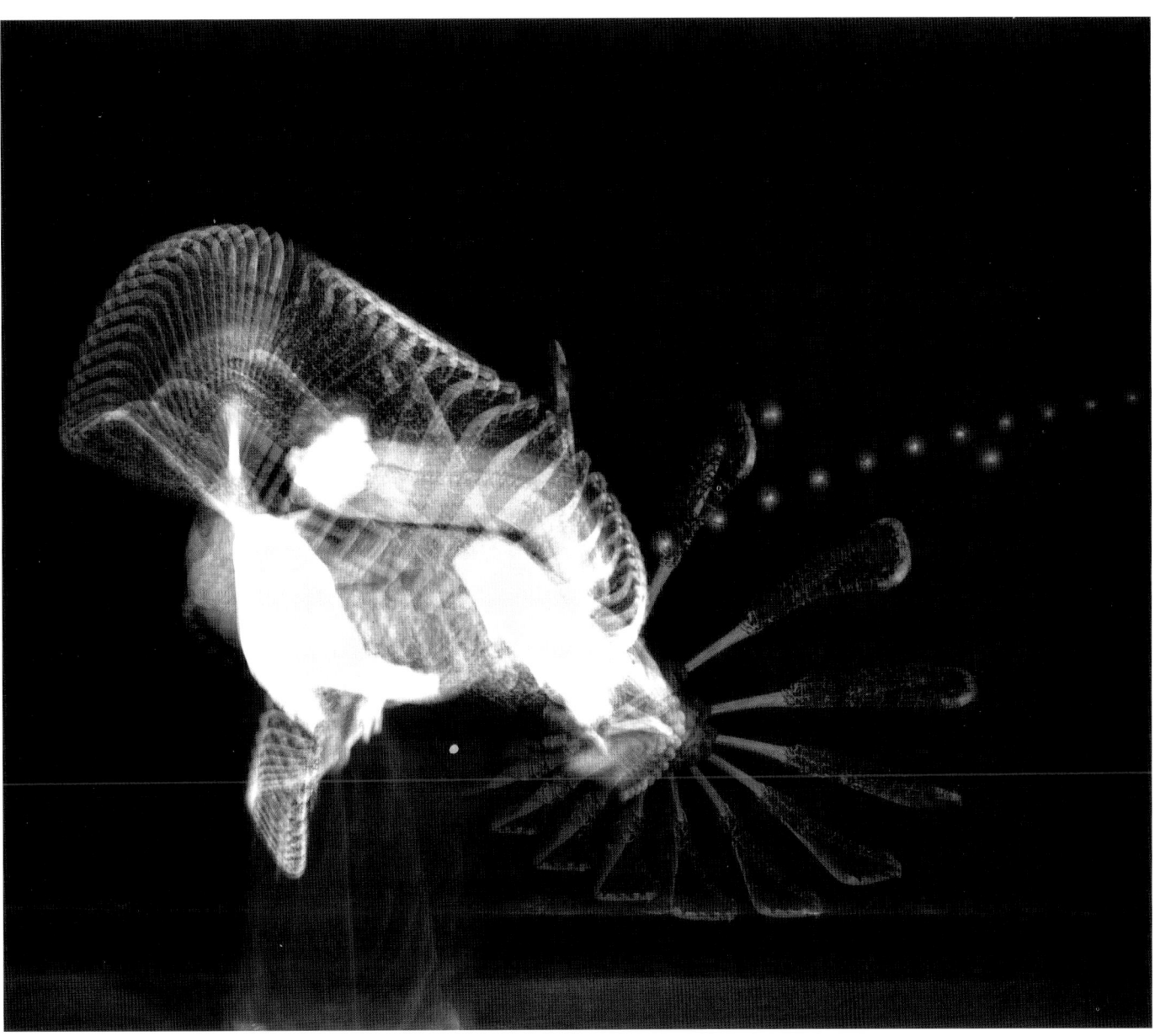

**Lacrosse, 1939**

"In the trajectory where the images of the ball are closely spaced, the ball is coming in toward
the player. He catches it by a twisting movement of the stick, and by a swinging action returns it."
From *flash! Seeing the Unseen by Ultra High-Speed Photography.*

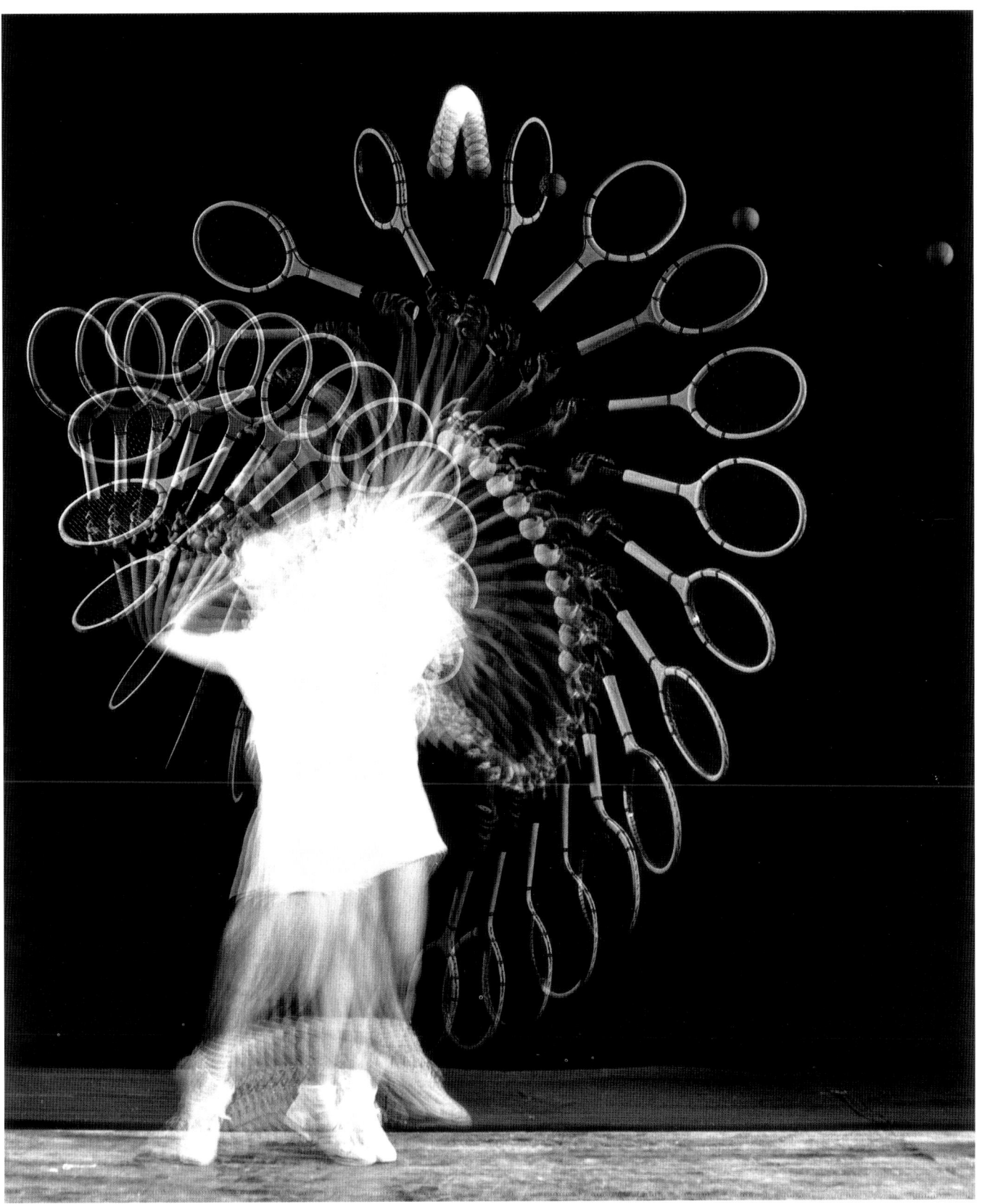

**Gussie Moran, 1949**

Edgerton photographed several tennis stars at a 1949 Longwood Cricket Club tournament. Tennis players
and photography fans alike appreciated Moran's perfect toss as she demonstrated a power serve.

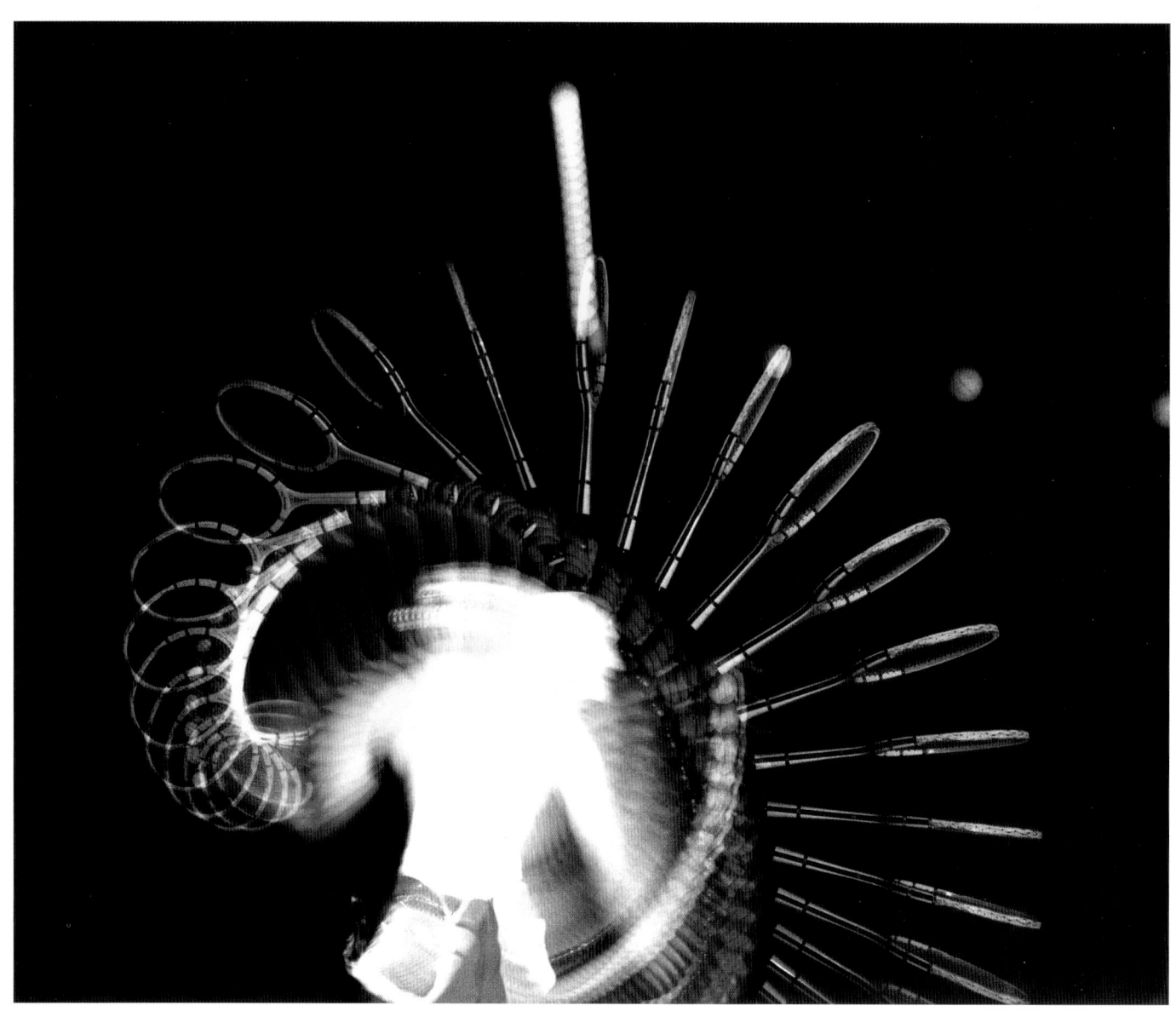

**Bromwich serves, 1938**

Edgerton describes John Bromwich's tennis serve: "Here the flashes were so timed in relation to the ball and racket that the moment of impact was caught exactly. Note that the ball is flattened on both back and front sides. Analysis shows that the tip of the racket vibrates back and forth after the impact." From *flash! Seeing the Unseen by Ultra High-Speed Photography*.

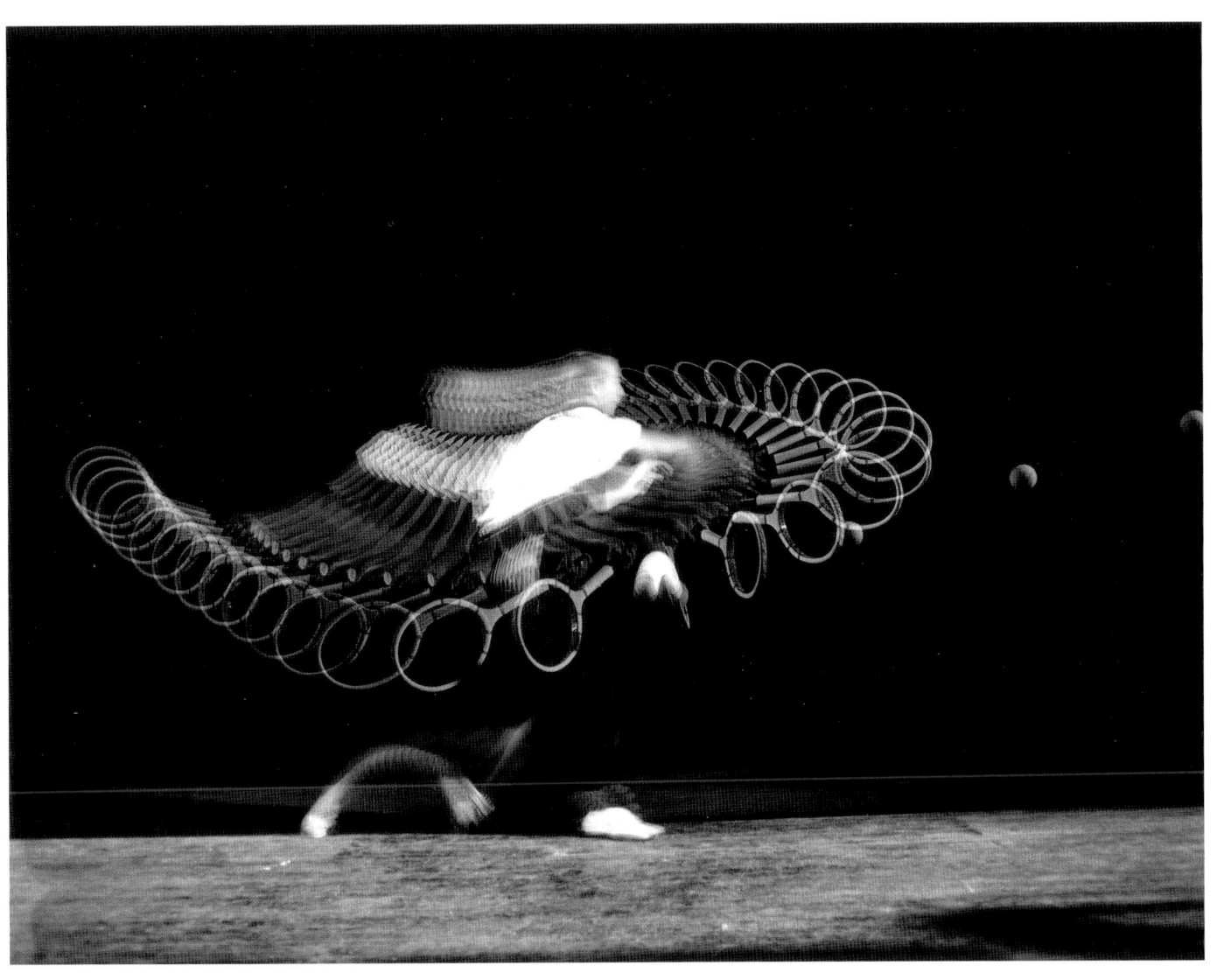

Kay Tuckey forehand, 1949

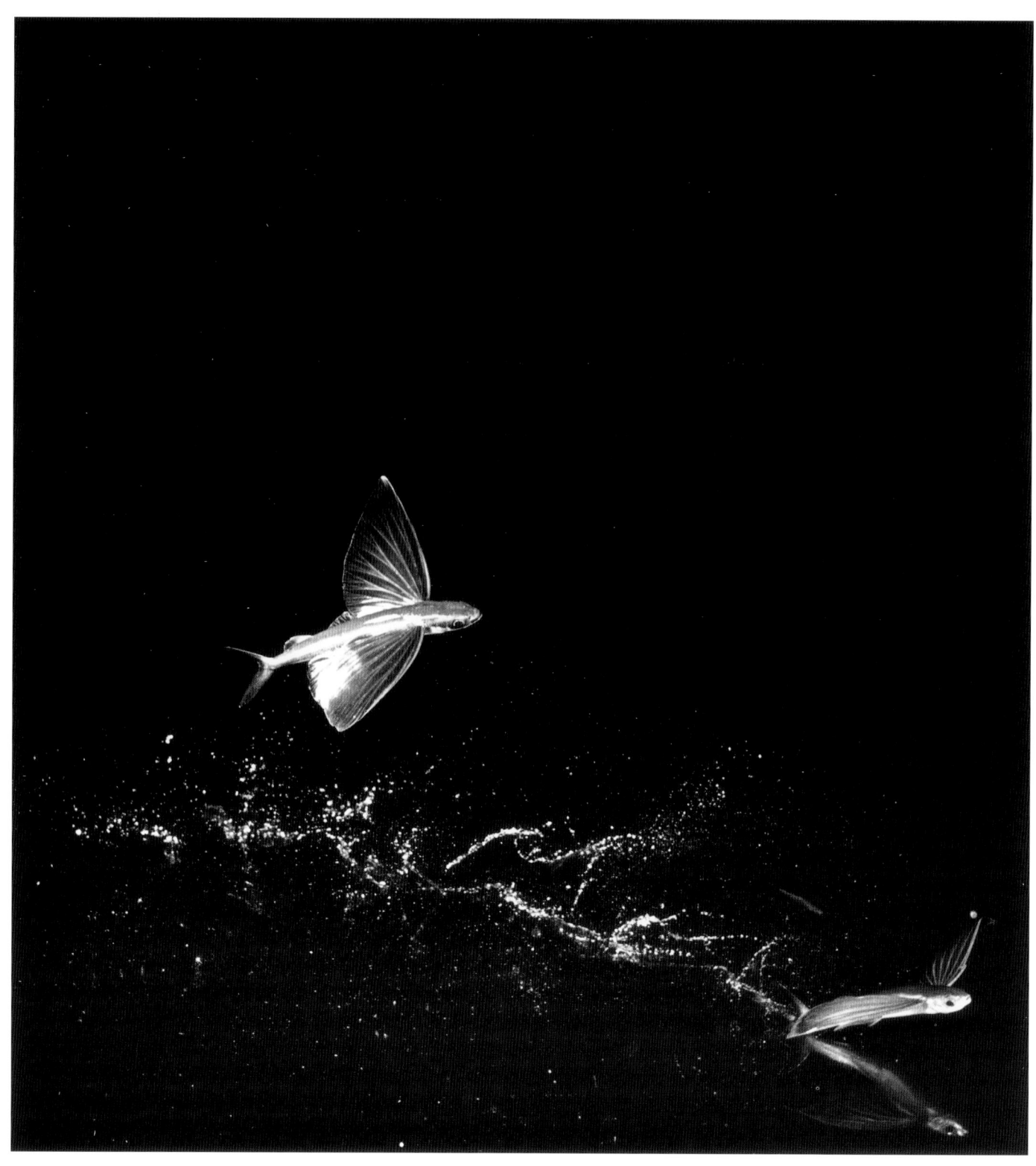

**Flying fish, 1940**

Composite photograph showing two "flying fish." The upper fish is in full flight while the lower fish is about to "take off." When this image was published for *Life* magazine in 1943, the image of the lower fish was reversed from how it was presented in a decade later in the second edition of *flash! Seeing the Unseen by Ultra High-Speed Photography*.

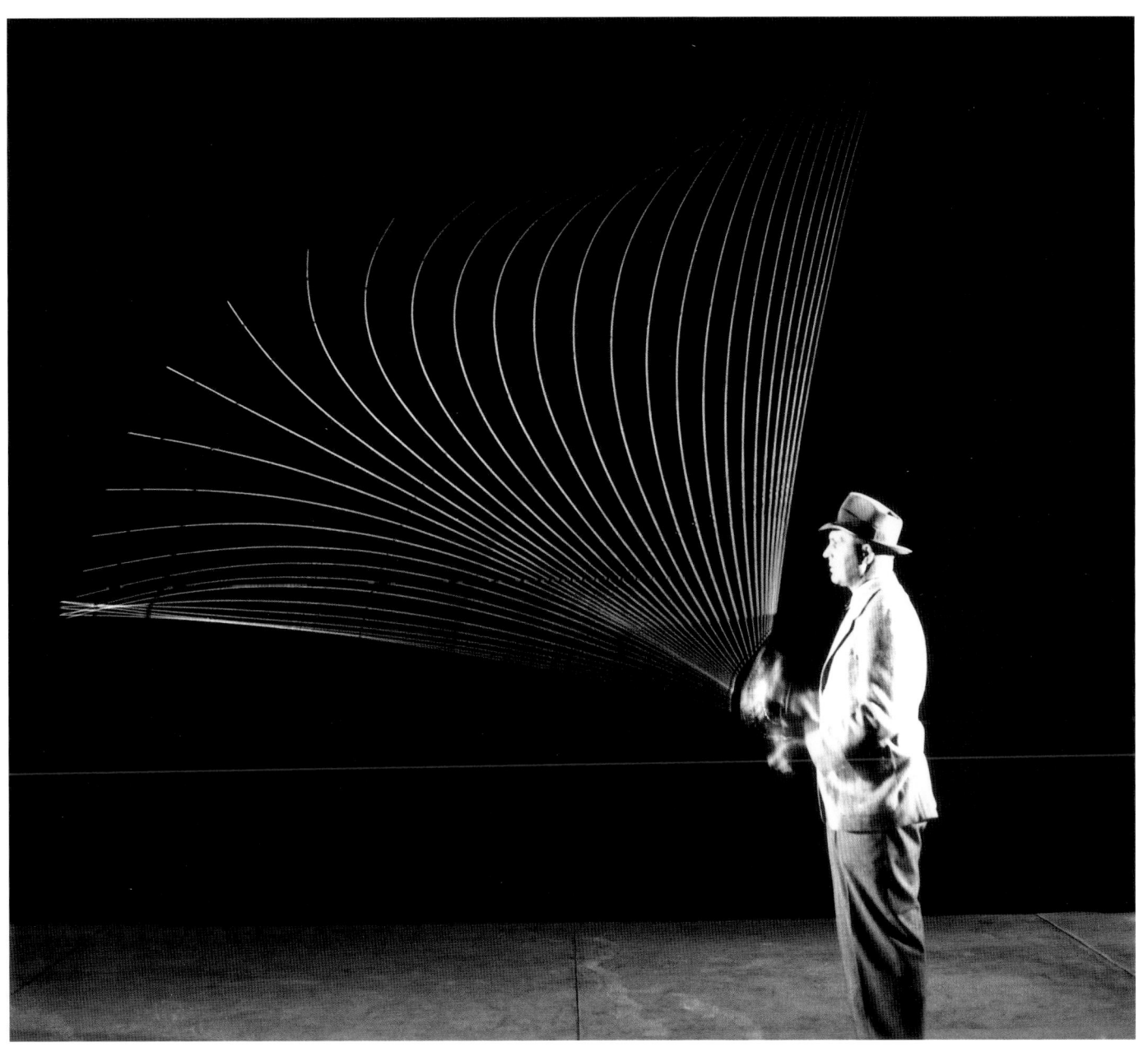

Fly fisherman, 1952

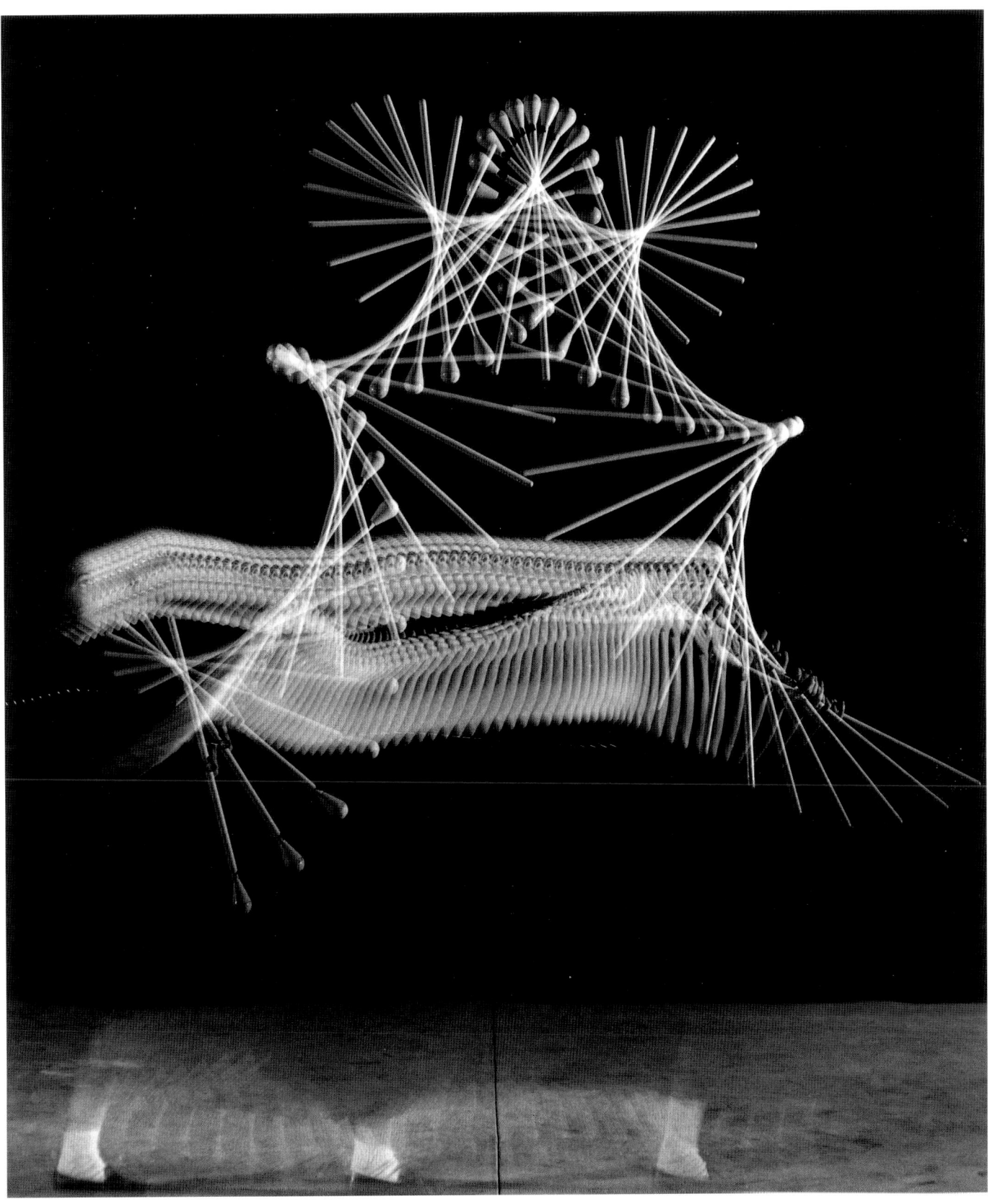

**Drum majorette, 1953**

Muriel Sutherland, a drum majorette from a local Boston-area high school, worked with Edgerton
to capture the complicated gyrations of her baton, tossing and catching, twisting and turning. The
multiflash fired 60 times per second to capture this photograph.

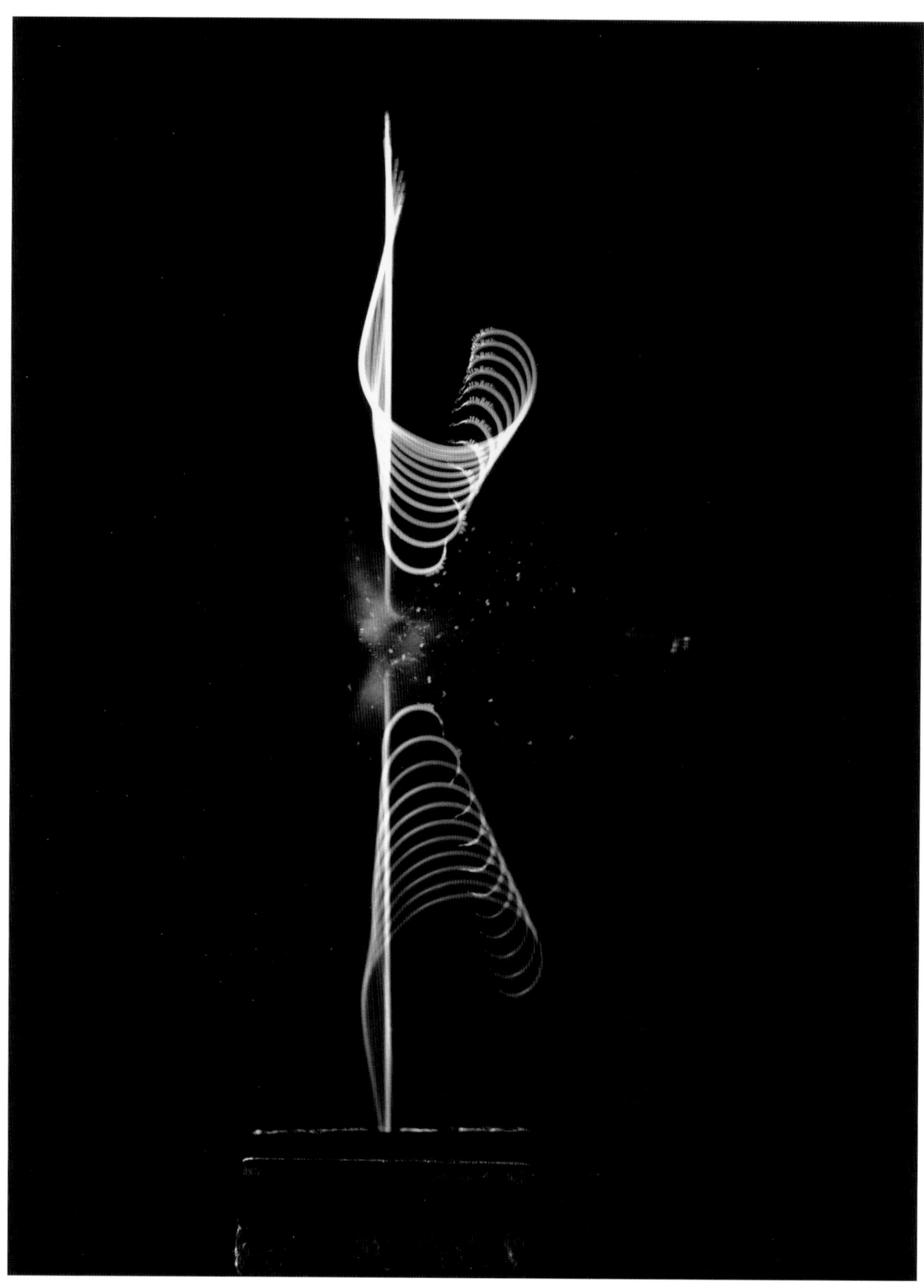

**Bullet plucks a copper wire, 1962**
Multiflash photograph of a .22 caliber bullet cutting a single copper wire.

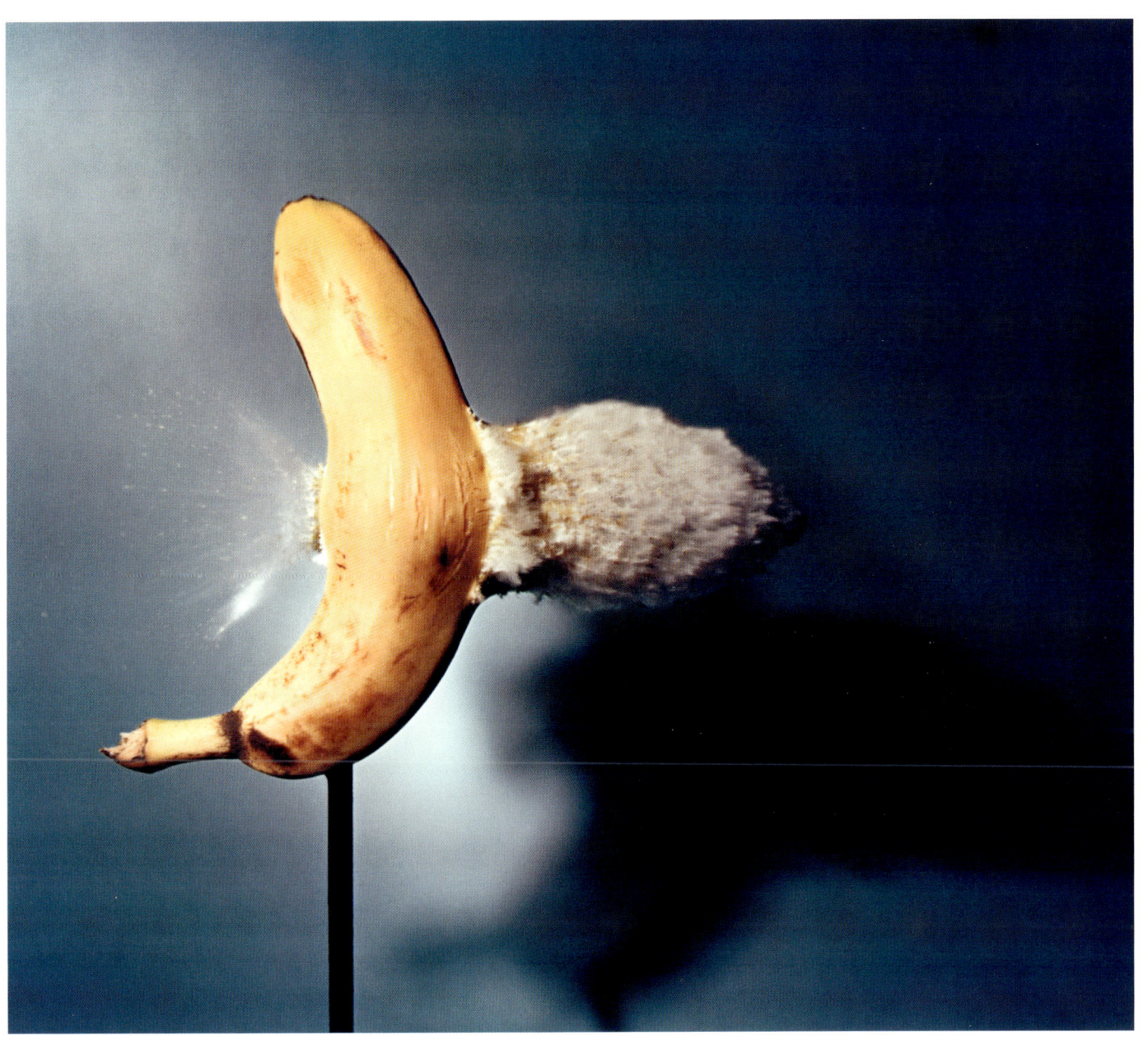

Bullet through banana, 1964

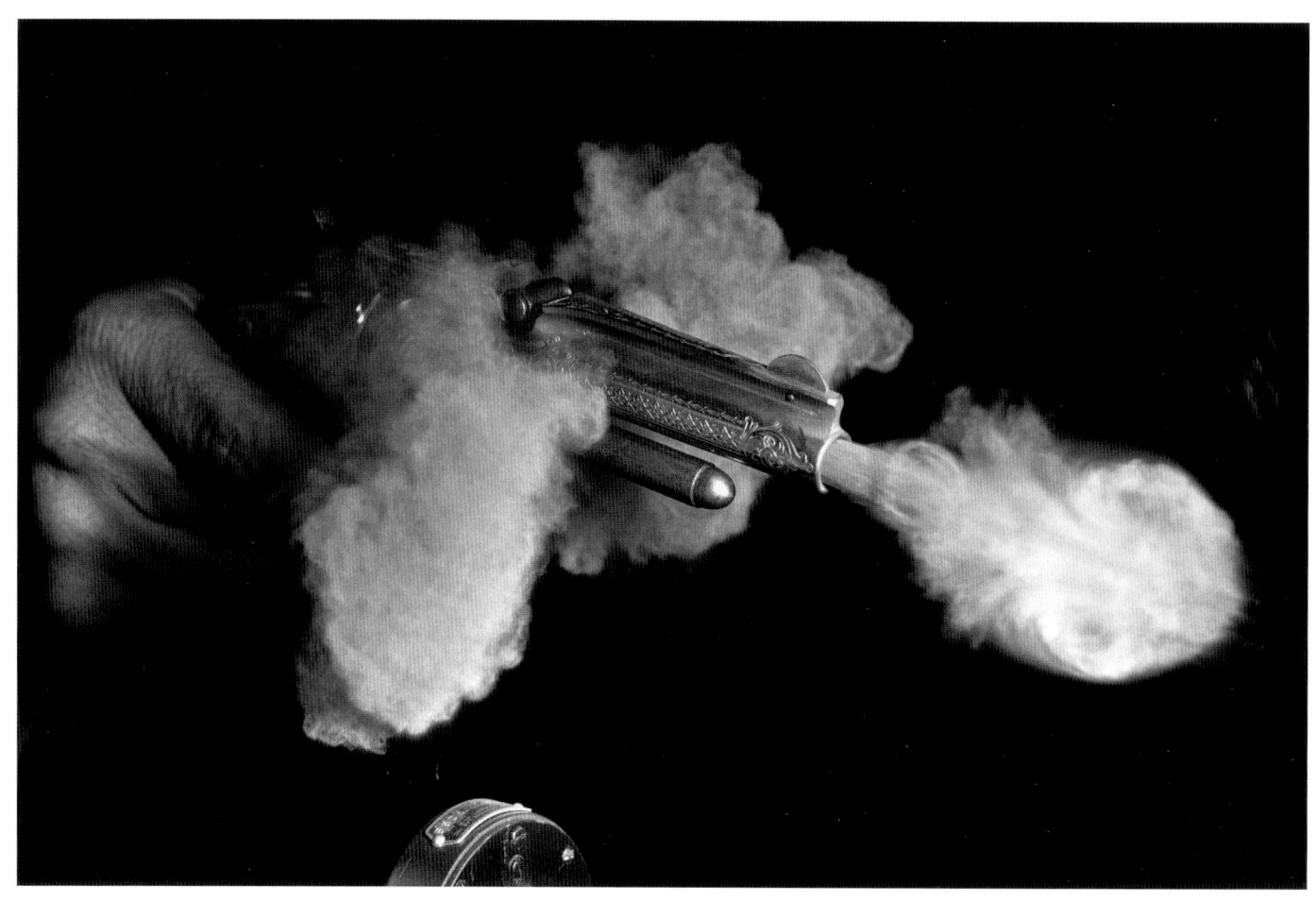

**Firing an old revolver, 1936**

Edgerton described this image as the second stage of firing: "The bullet is out but still surrounded by gas, the propelling charge rushes out of the muzzle, and powder particles from a previous shot are driven ahead of the gas." From *flash! Seeing the Unseen by Ultra High-Speed Photography*.

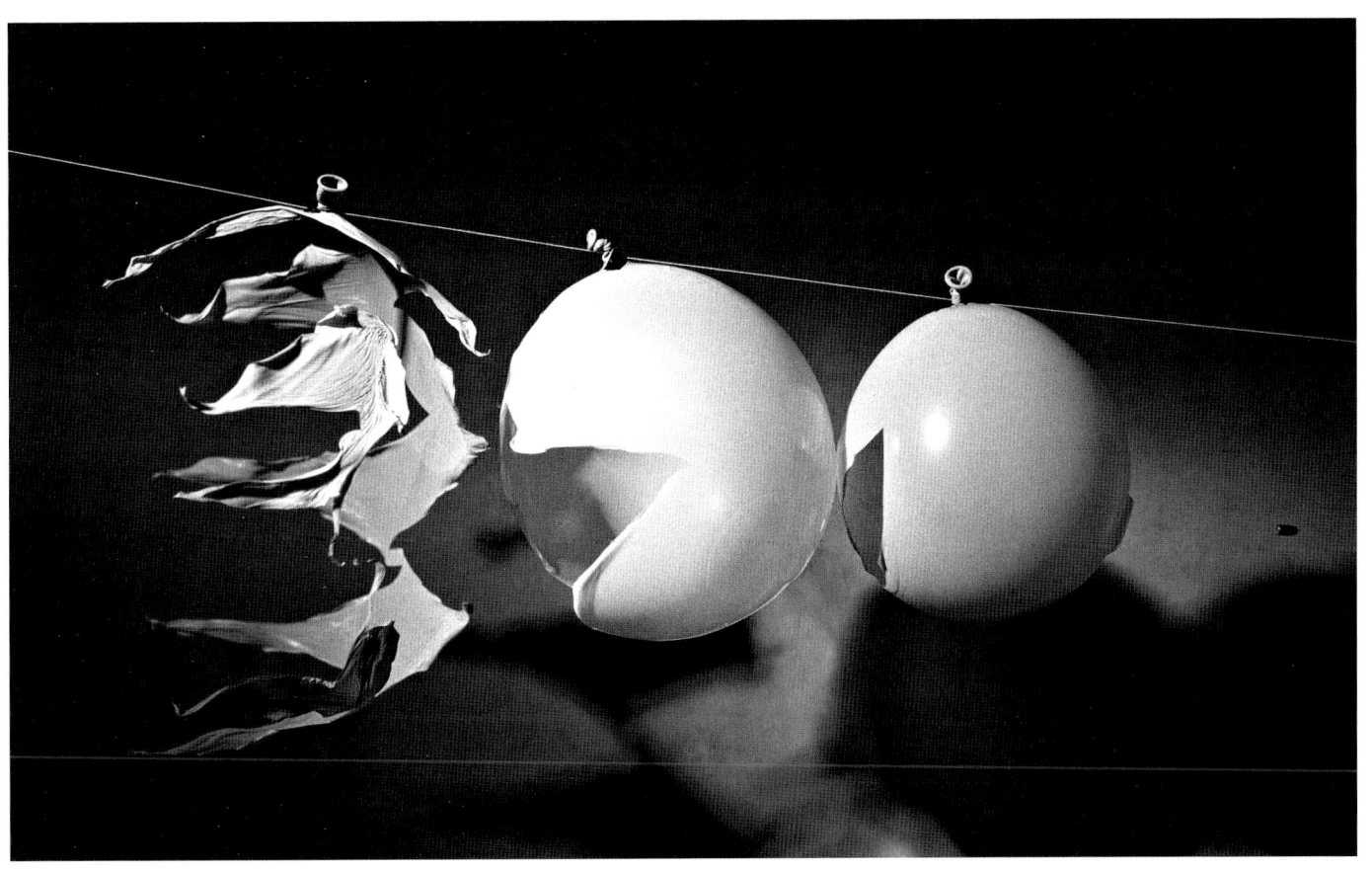

**Bullet through balloons, 1959**

Microflash picture of a .22 caliber bullet passing through three consecutive balloons.

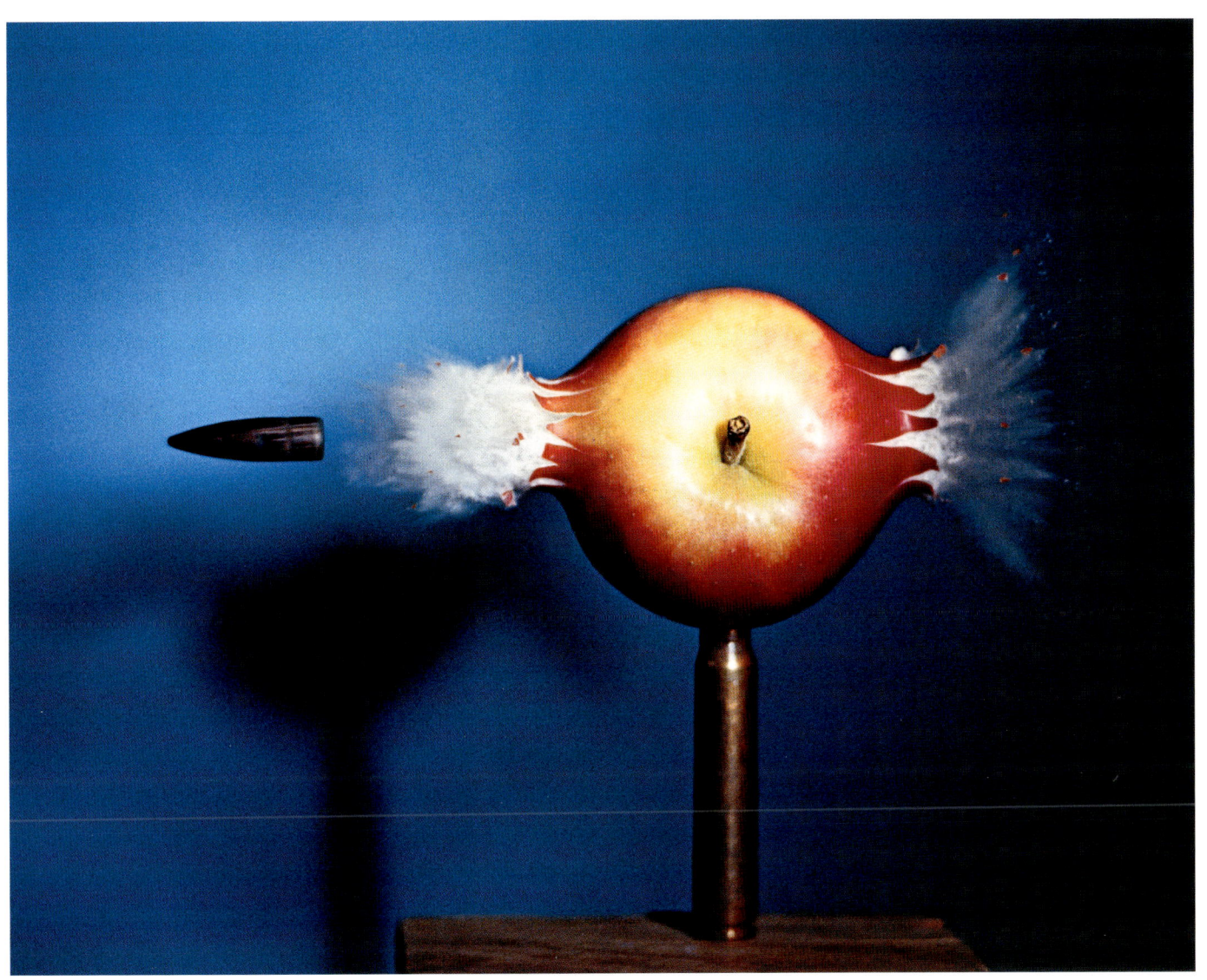

**Bullet through apple, 1964**

One of his most iconic images – the piercing of an apple by a .30 caliber bullet fired from a World War I-era army rifle – Edgerton used this photograph to illustrate his famous "How to Make Applesauce at MIT" lecture. Interestingly, Edgerton printed this photograph in both orientations. In the original, the bullet travels from left to right.

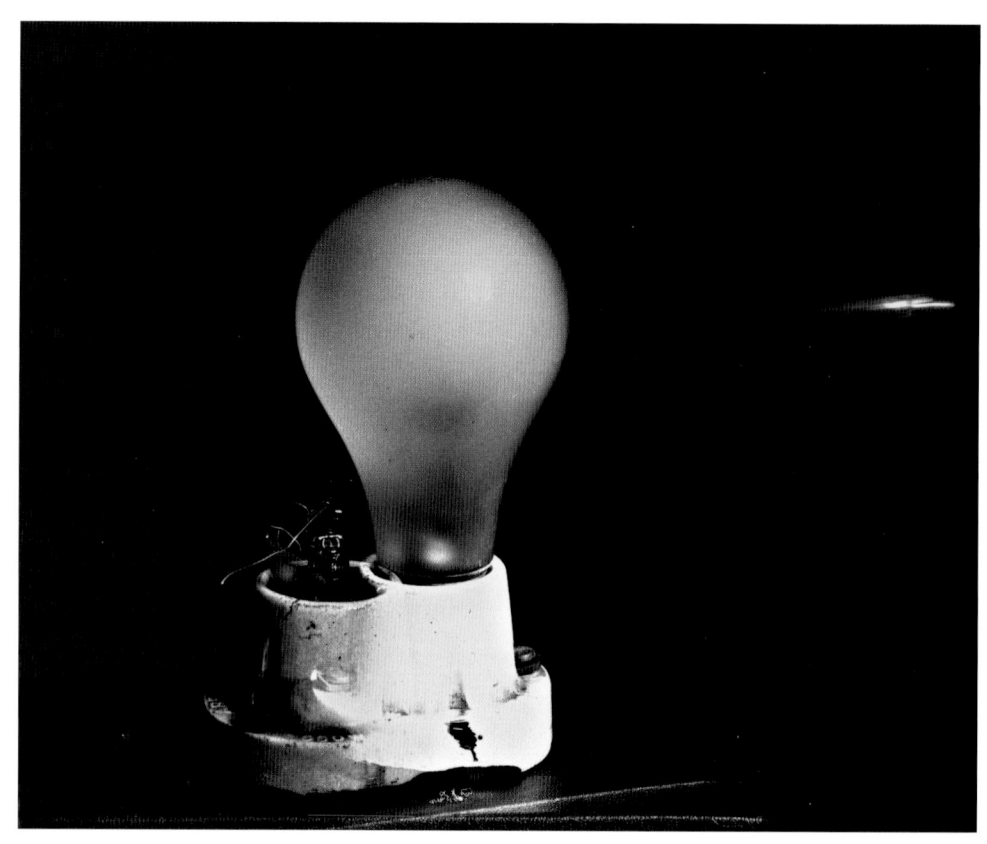

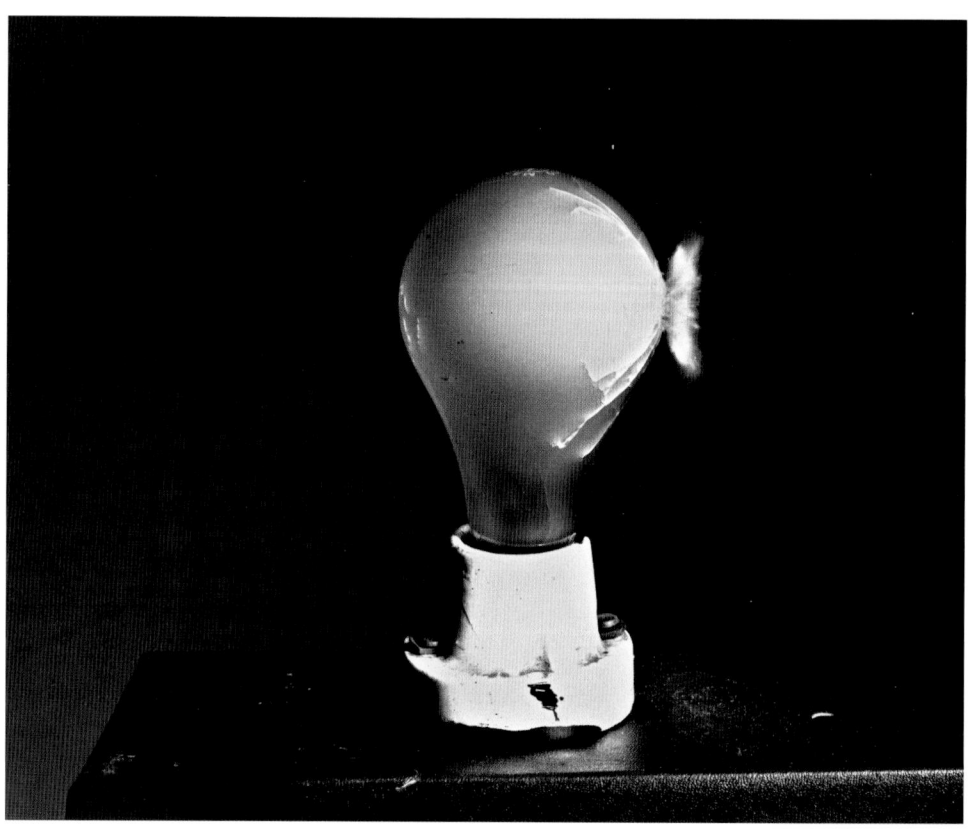

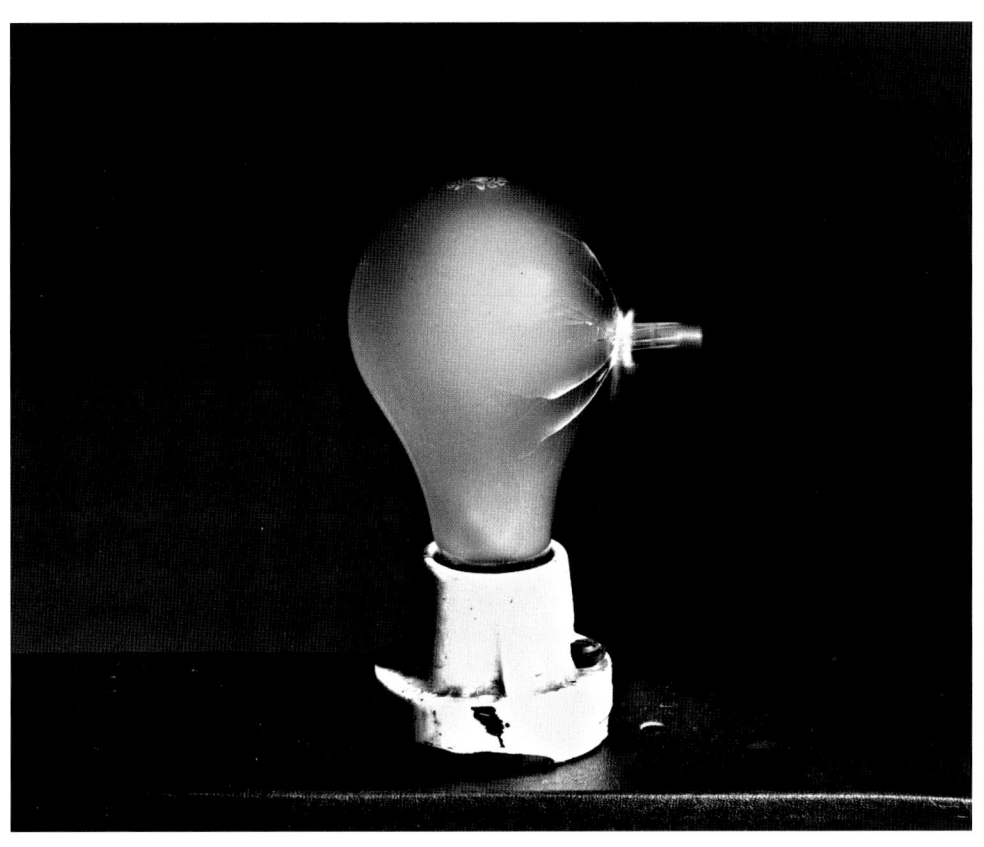

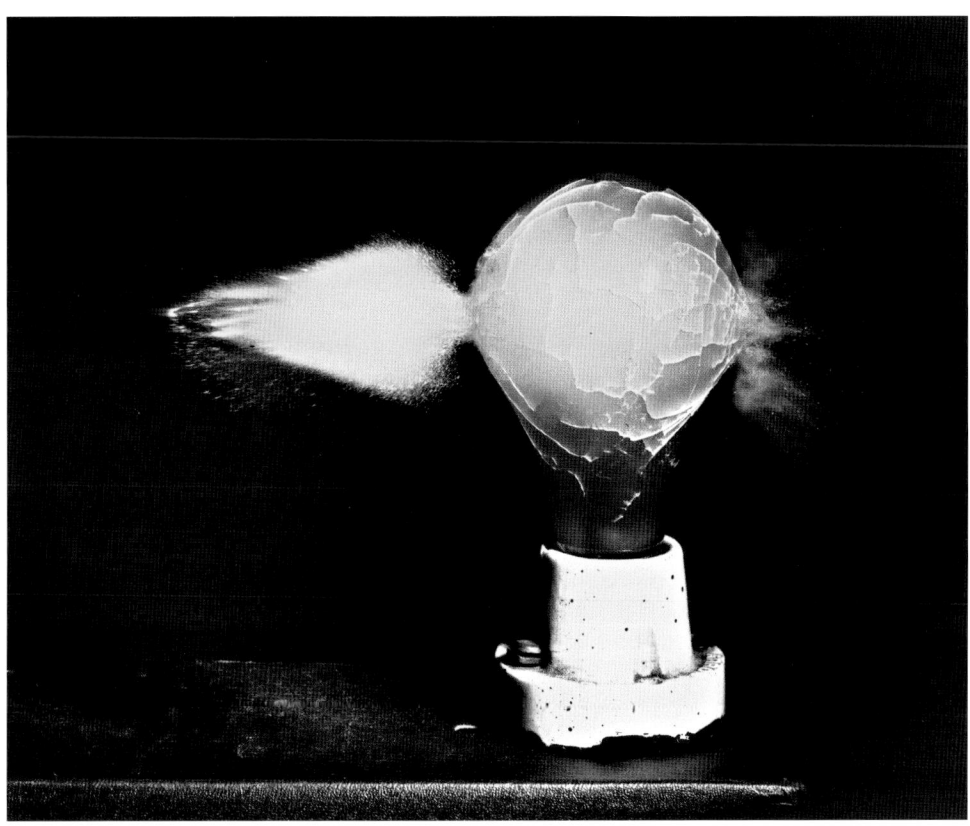

**Death of a light bulb, 1936**

These four unique images (different bullets, different bulbs) show different phases of what Edgerton called: "Collision at 1,800 miles per hour!" From *flash! Seeing the Unseen by Ultra High-Speed Photography.*

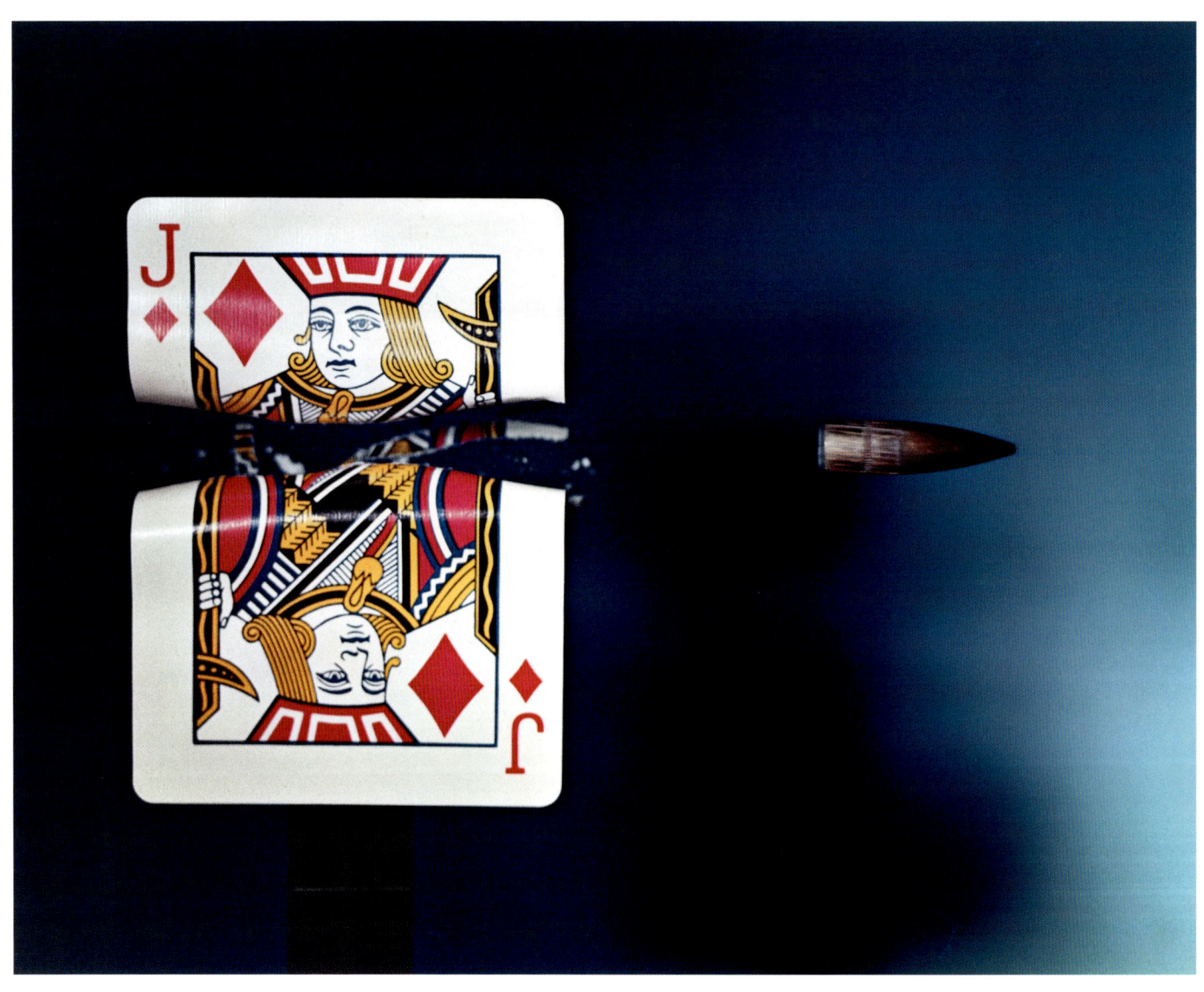

**Cutting the card quickly!, 1964**

Part of Edgerton's 1964 series of color images of bullets piercing various objects.
The sideways card created a strong sense of visual drama.

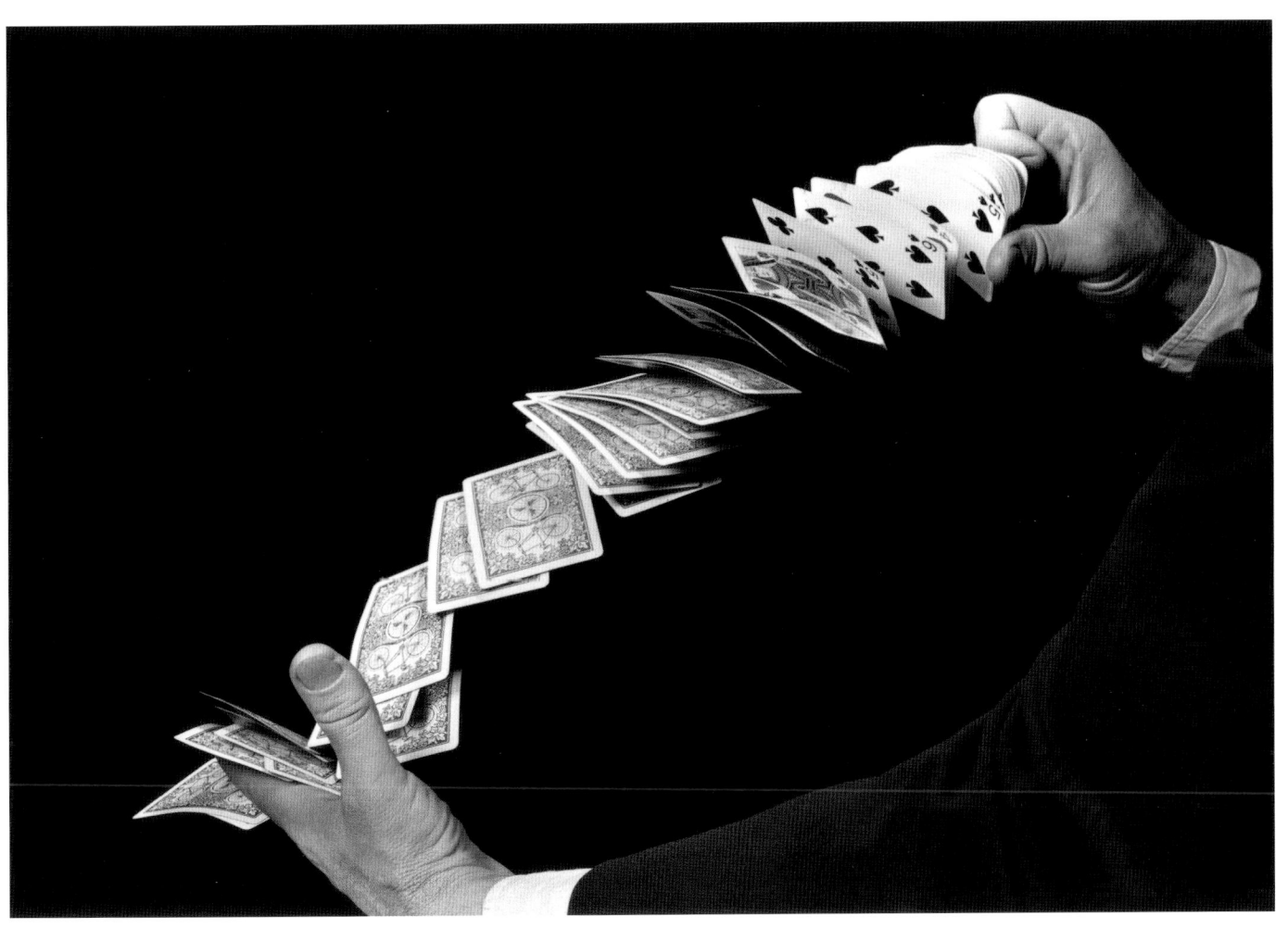

Fanning the cards, 1940

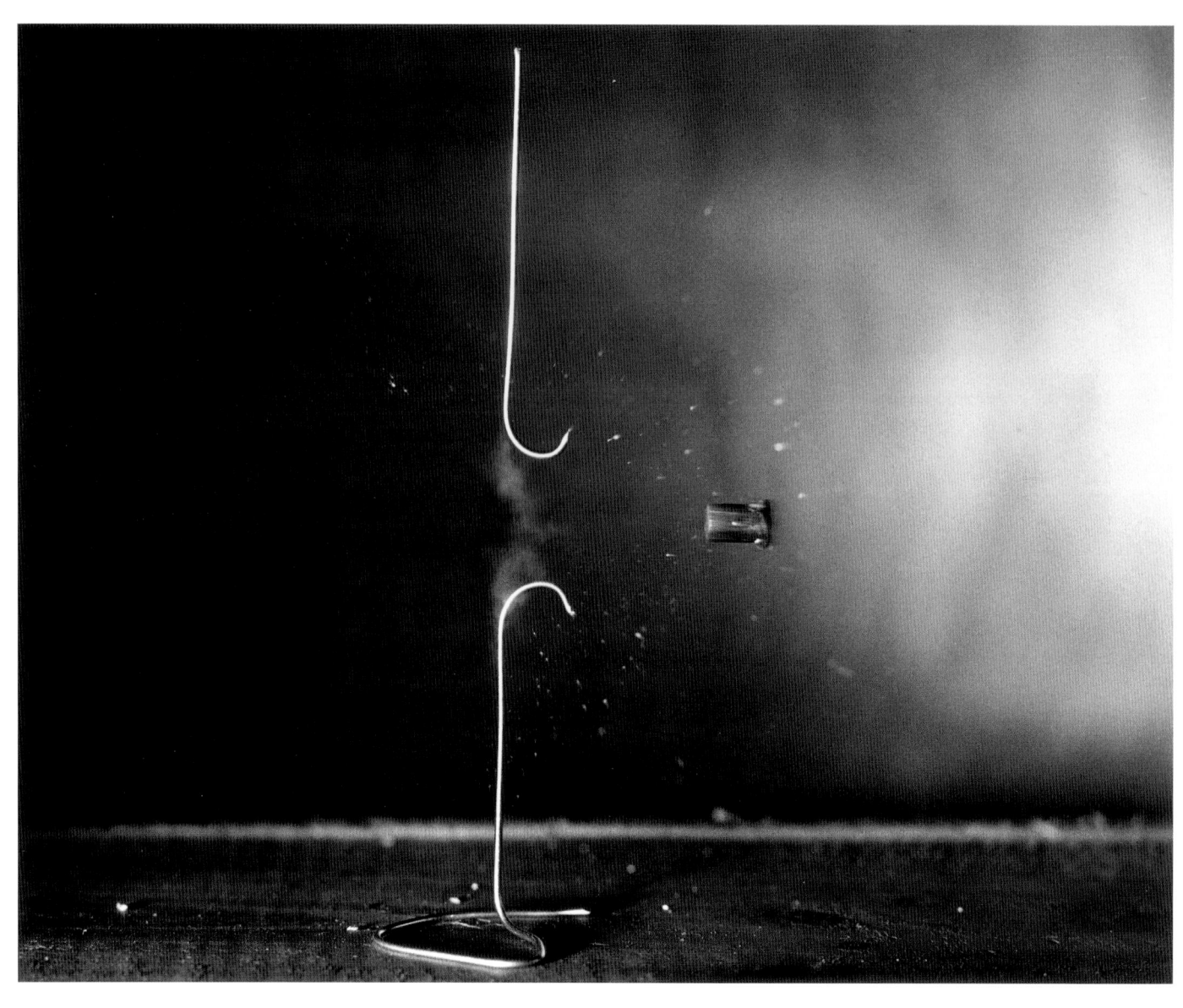

**Bullet plucks a copper wire, 1959**

Single-flash photograph of a bullet cutting a standing copper wire.

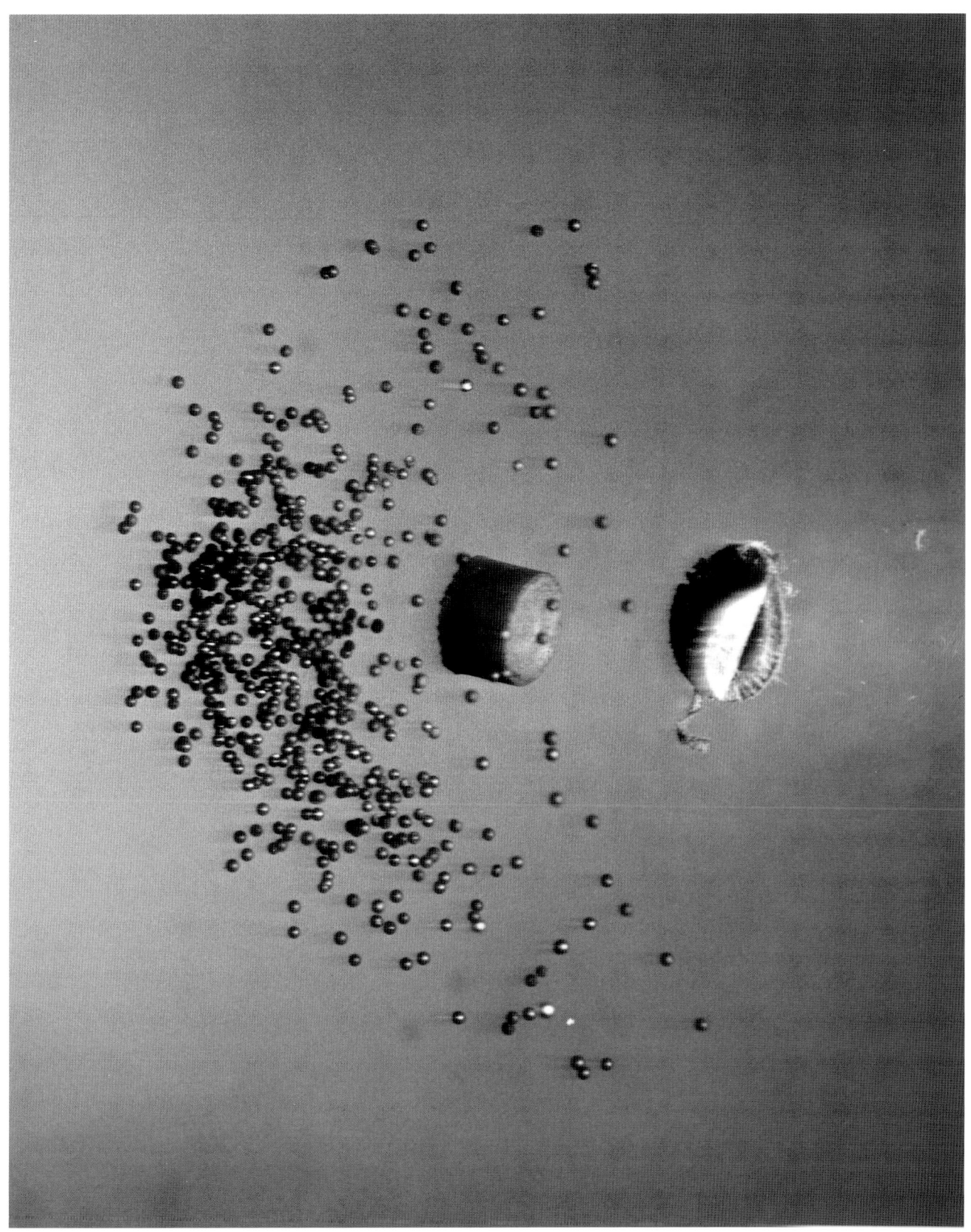

**Shotgun pallets, 1948**

Part of a series of photographs for a 1948 National Rifle Association study on shotgun compensators.

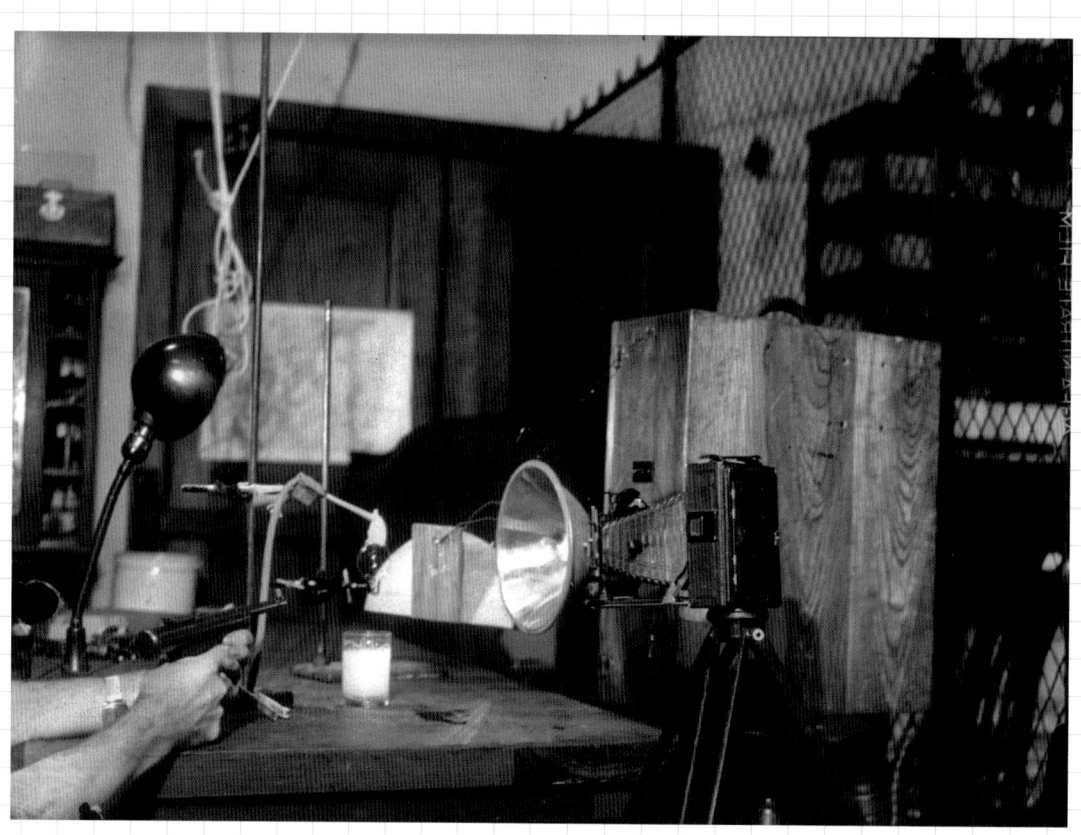

Laboratory setup for firing a pellet gun through a soap bubble.

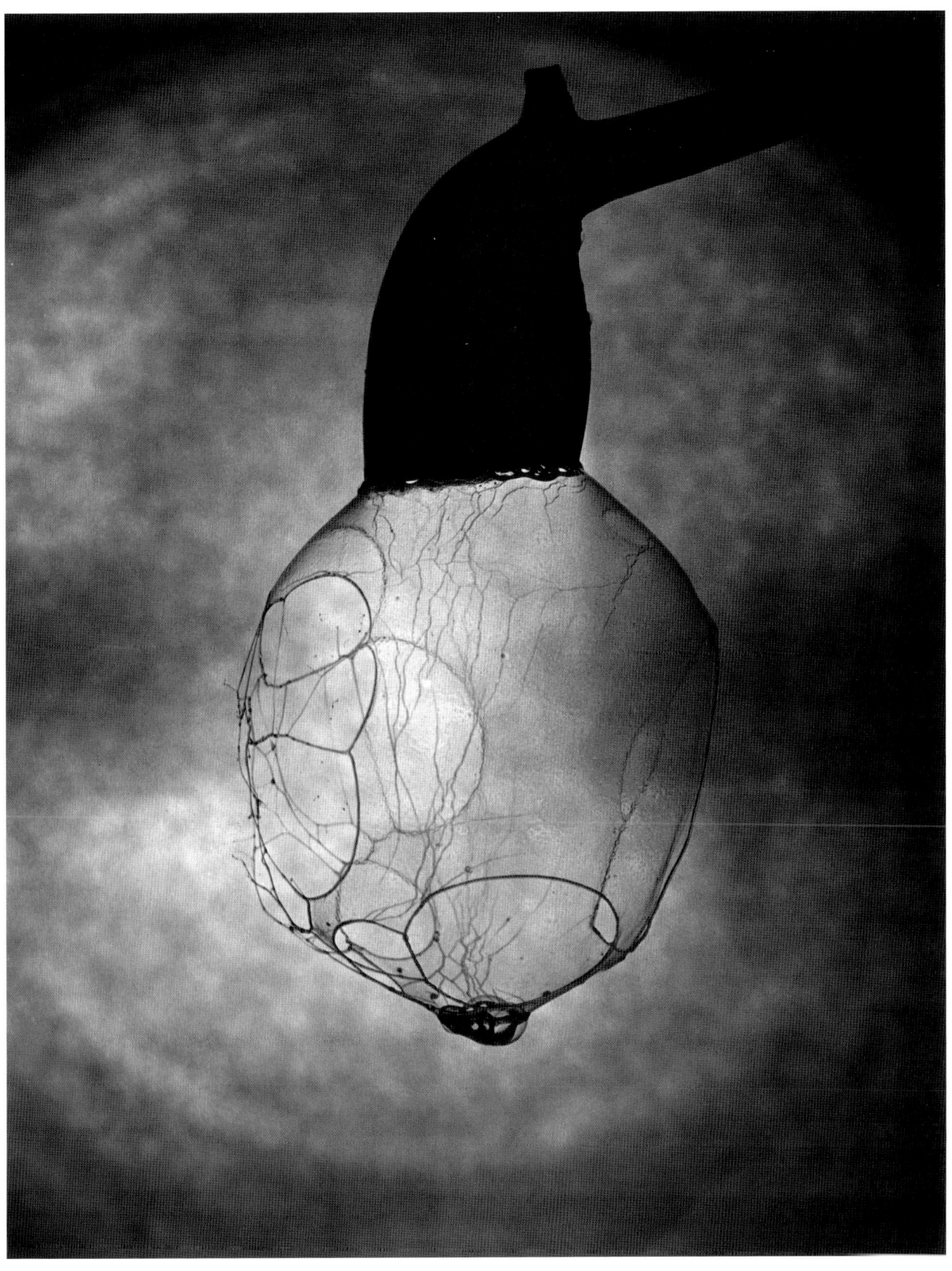

Soap bubble, 1933

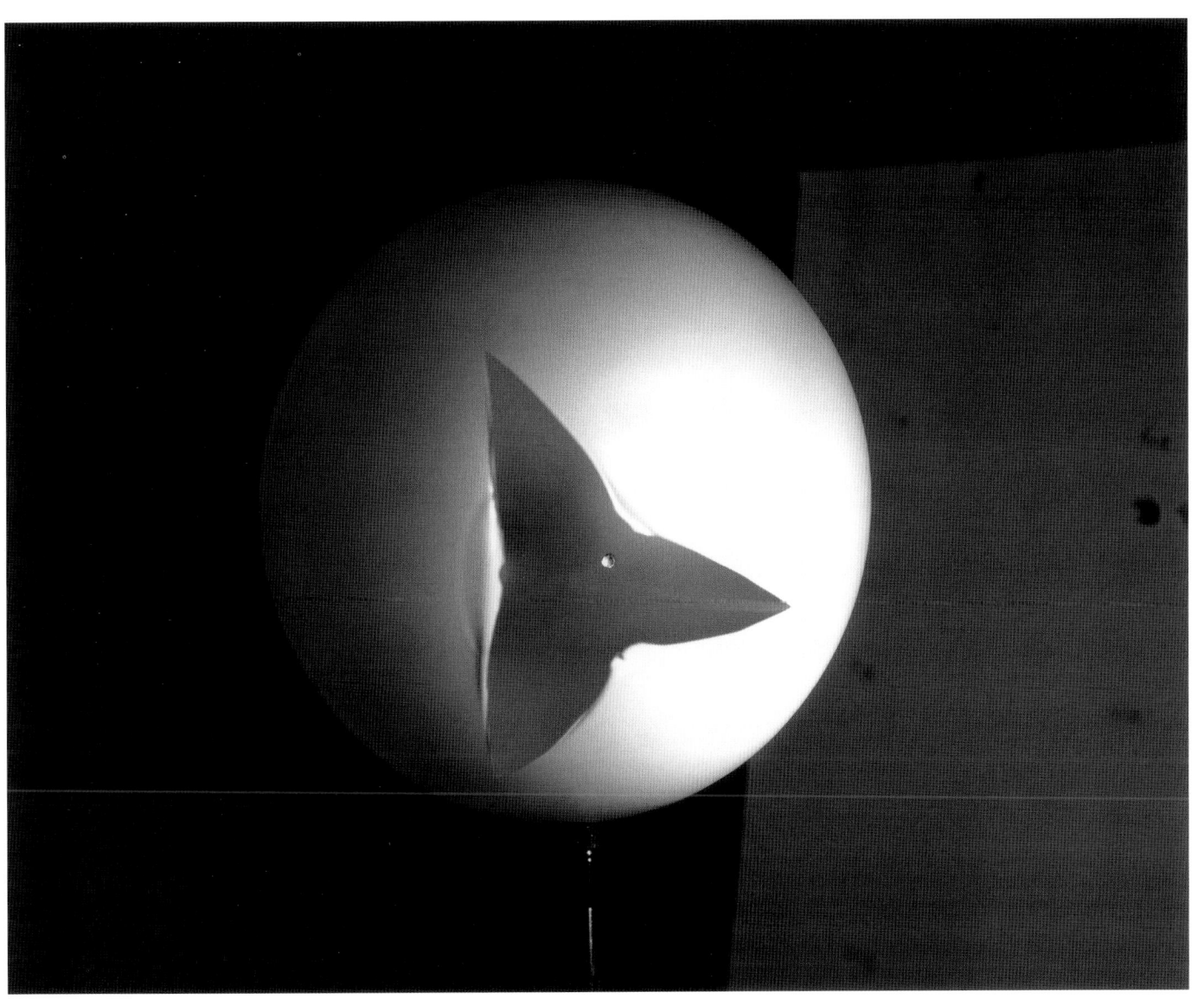

Bullet inside balloon, 1955

H.E. Edgerton.
Feb 19 1938

### Photographic Study of Johnson Automatic Rifle.

Mr. Howard and Mr. Johnson brought the gun in the morning. 30 caliber. The recoil of the barrel turns the lock and releases the bolt. A series of both still and movie pictures were taken to show what goes on in the mechanism of this gun.

Single photographs were taken with a 5×7 camera of the entire gun from the muzzle to the bolt. Timing of the flash was controlled by the bullet. Exposure due to ordinary light shows stationary position of the gun bolt.

A thyratron FG-17 800 volts on plate was used to fire an argon flash lamp.

Movies at 1200/sec. were taken by reflected light fd. 1 mf 1000 volts (2kw power supply).

1. Single shot.

2. two shots.

3. Extractor out single shot. This show shell cartridge goes out due to gas pressure in gun.

Edgerton conducted a detailed study of the Johnson automatic rifle (M1941) in February 1938, taking both still and motion picture images of the entire gun. This work was part of Melvin Johnson's campaign to get the U.S. Army to adopt his rifle over the much-favored M1 rifle. Notebook Number 8, February 19, 1938, p. 129.

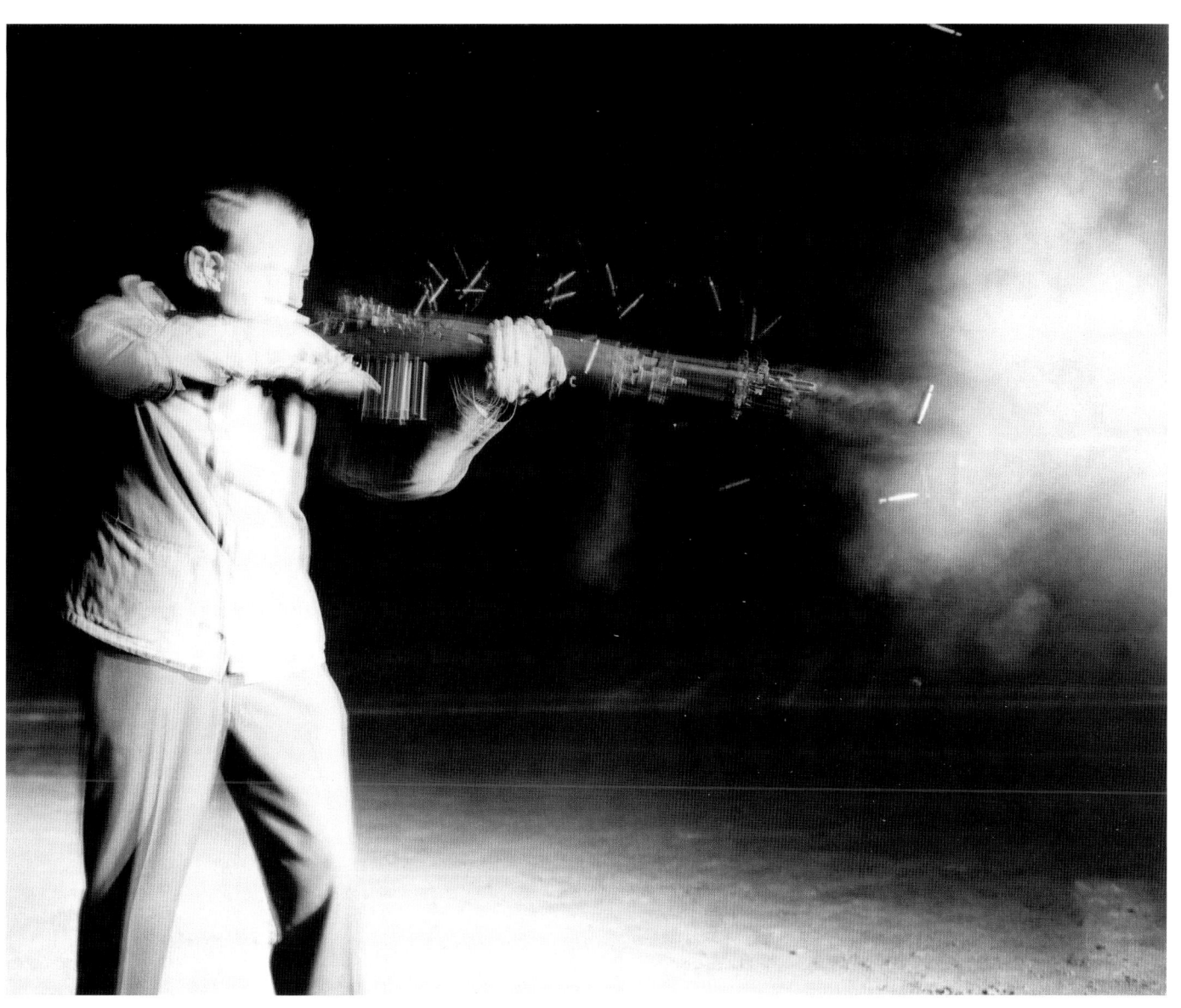

Johnson automatic rifle, 1938

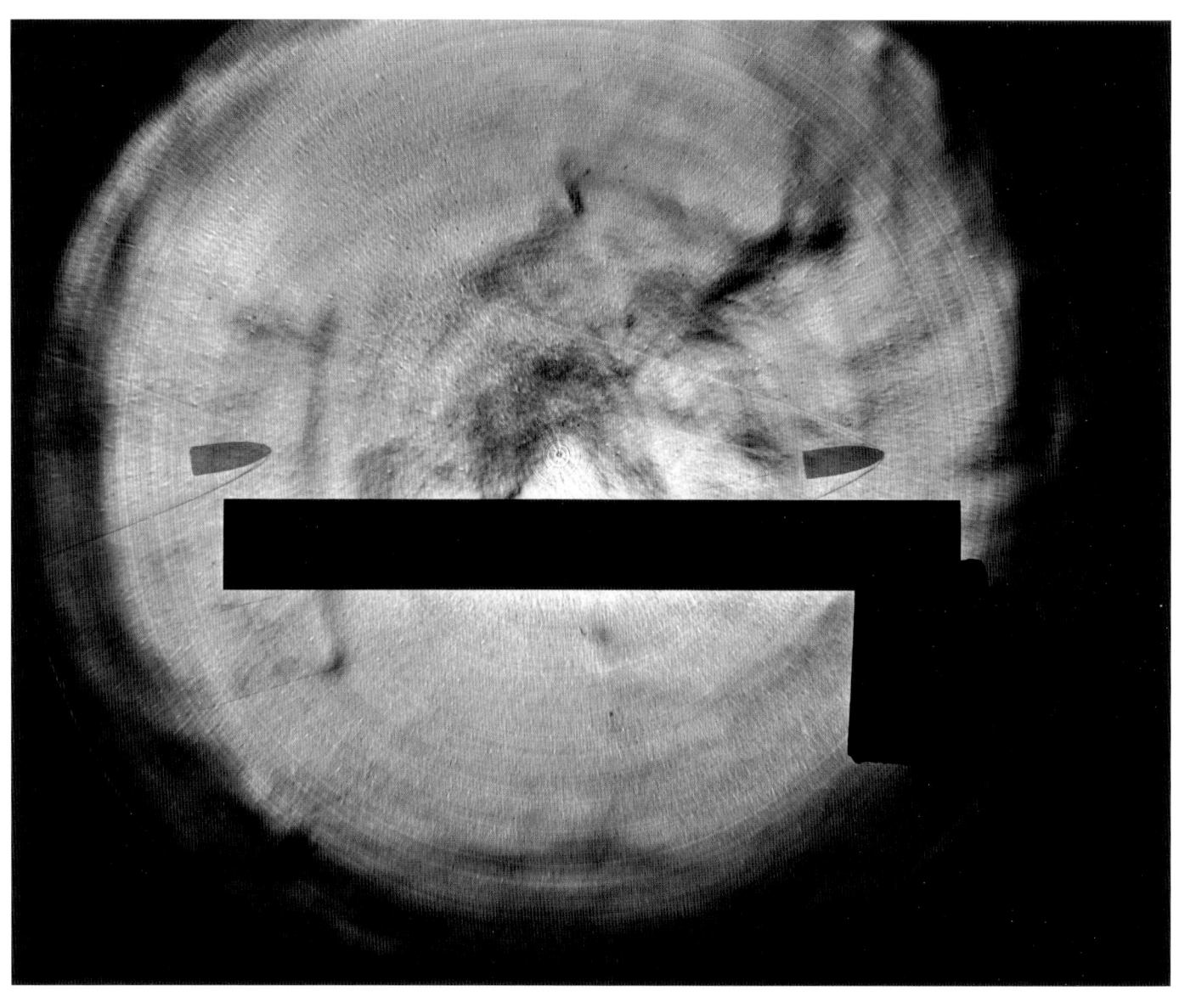

**.22 caliber bullet, 1957**

Silhouette photograph made using a double flash allows for the measurement
of the bullet and shockwave velocities produced by the .22 caliber bullet.

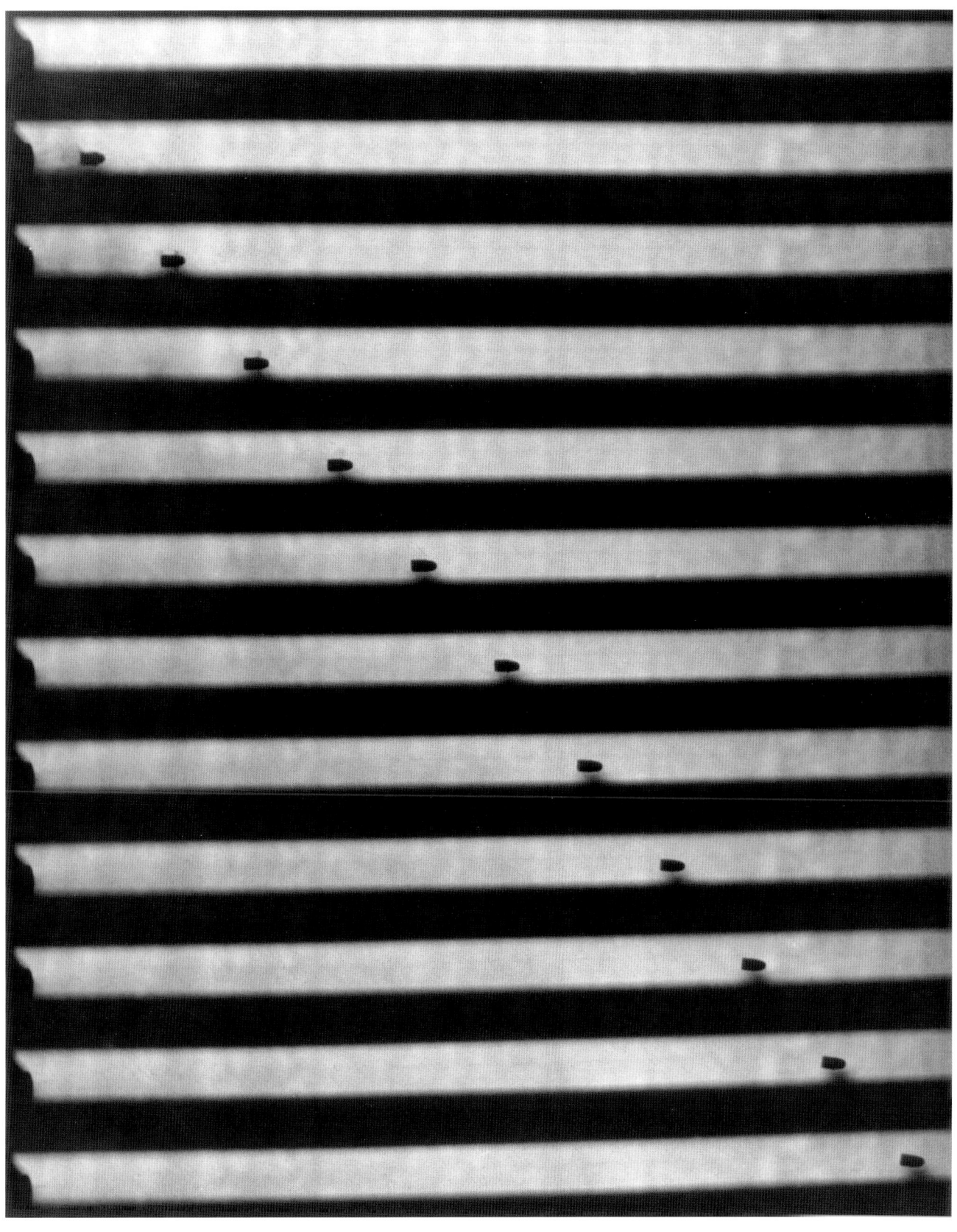

Streak camera sequence of a bullet at 50,000 frames per second, ca. 1963

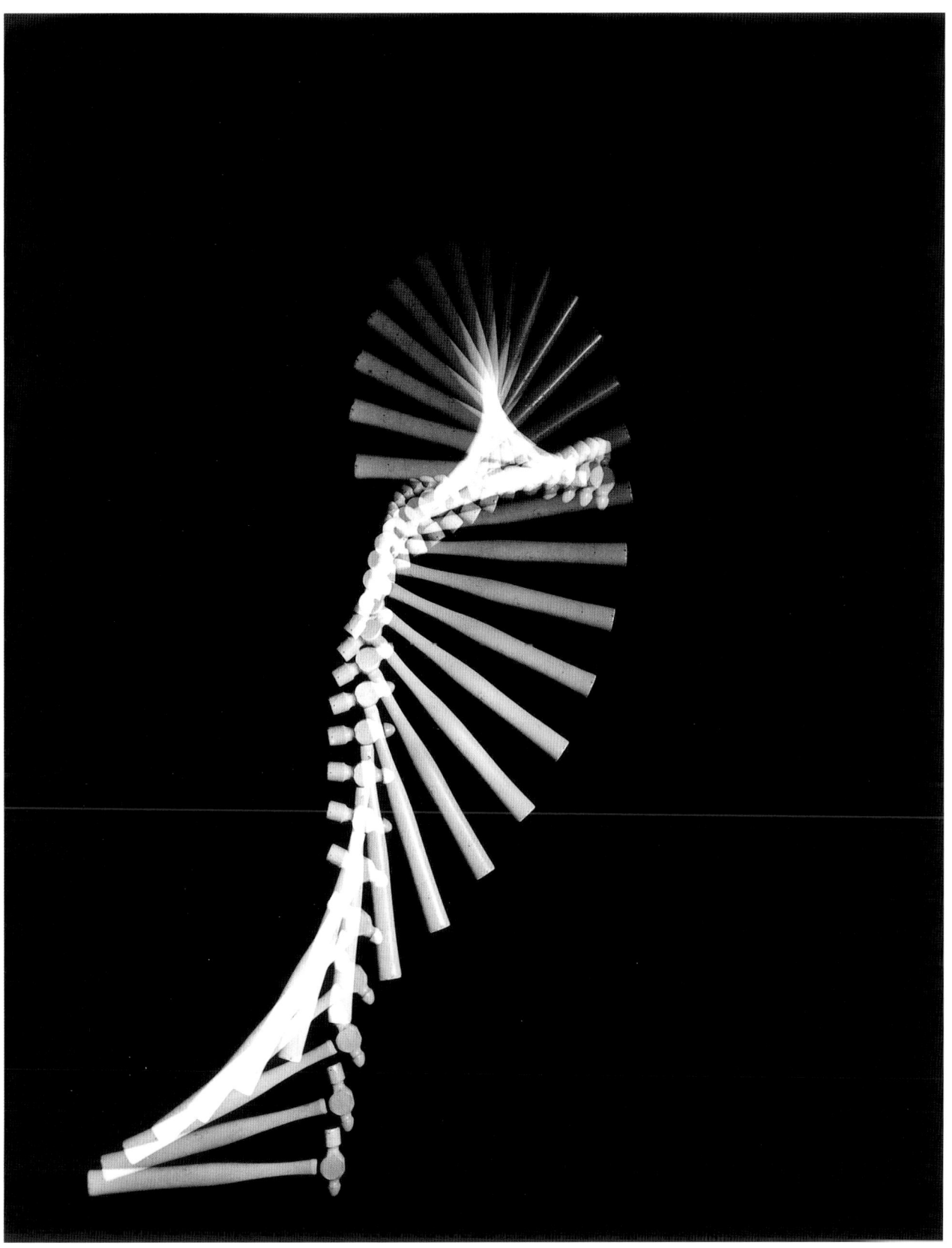

**Hammer toss, c. 1962**

Multiflash picture of ball-peen hammer being tossed.

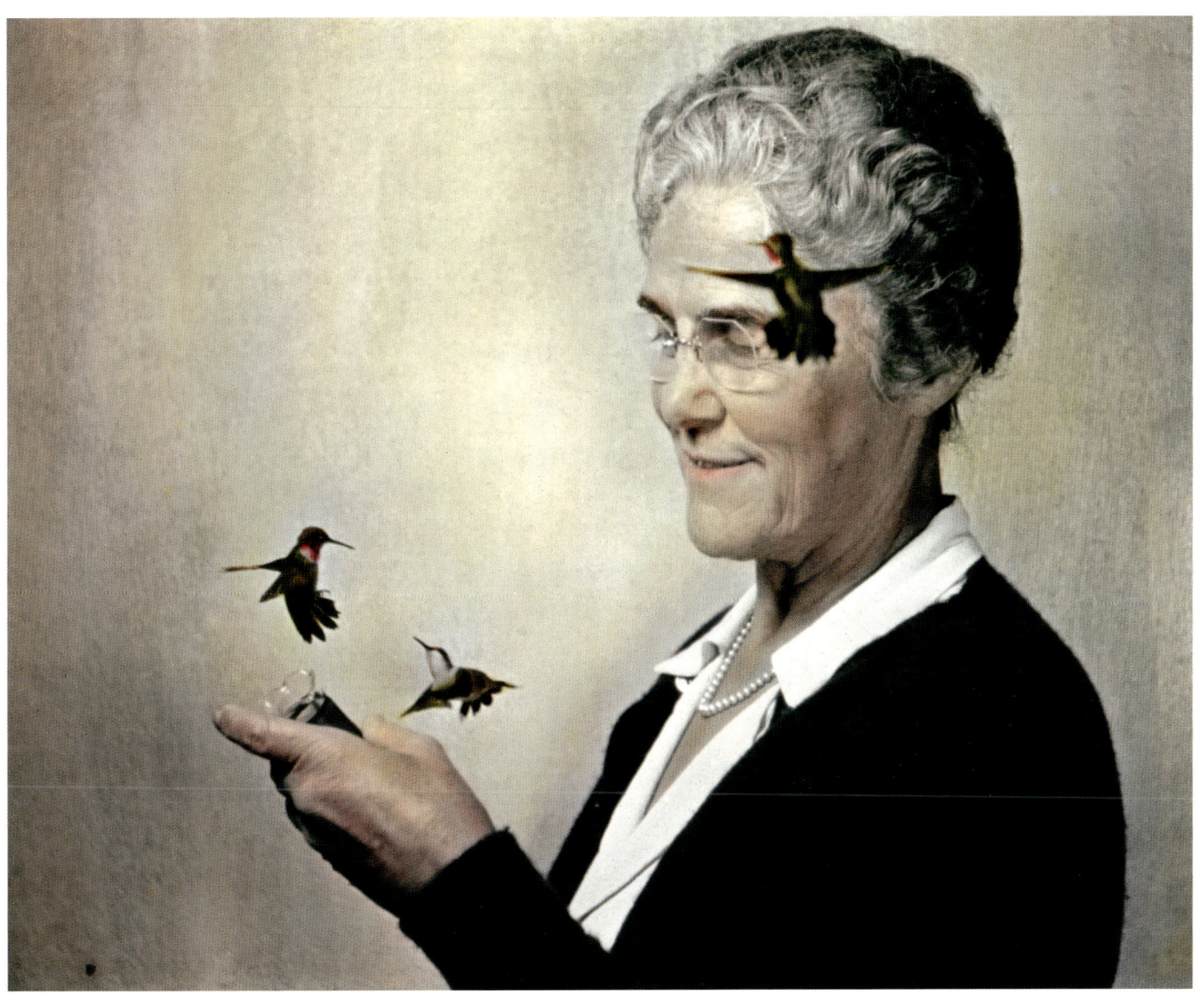

**Mrs. Webster with her hummingbirds, 1936**

May Webster (aka "The Hummingbird Lady") illustrating the success of the stroboscope in capturing the flight of these high-speed birds. This image is made from the hand-colored lantern slide, and was featured along with many other hummingbird shots in *National Geographic* and other nature publications.

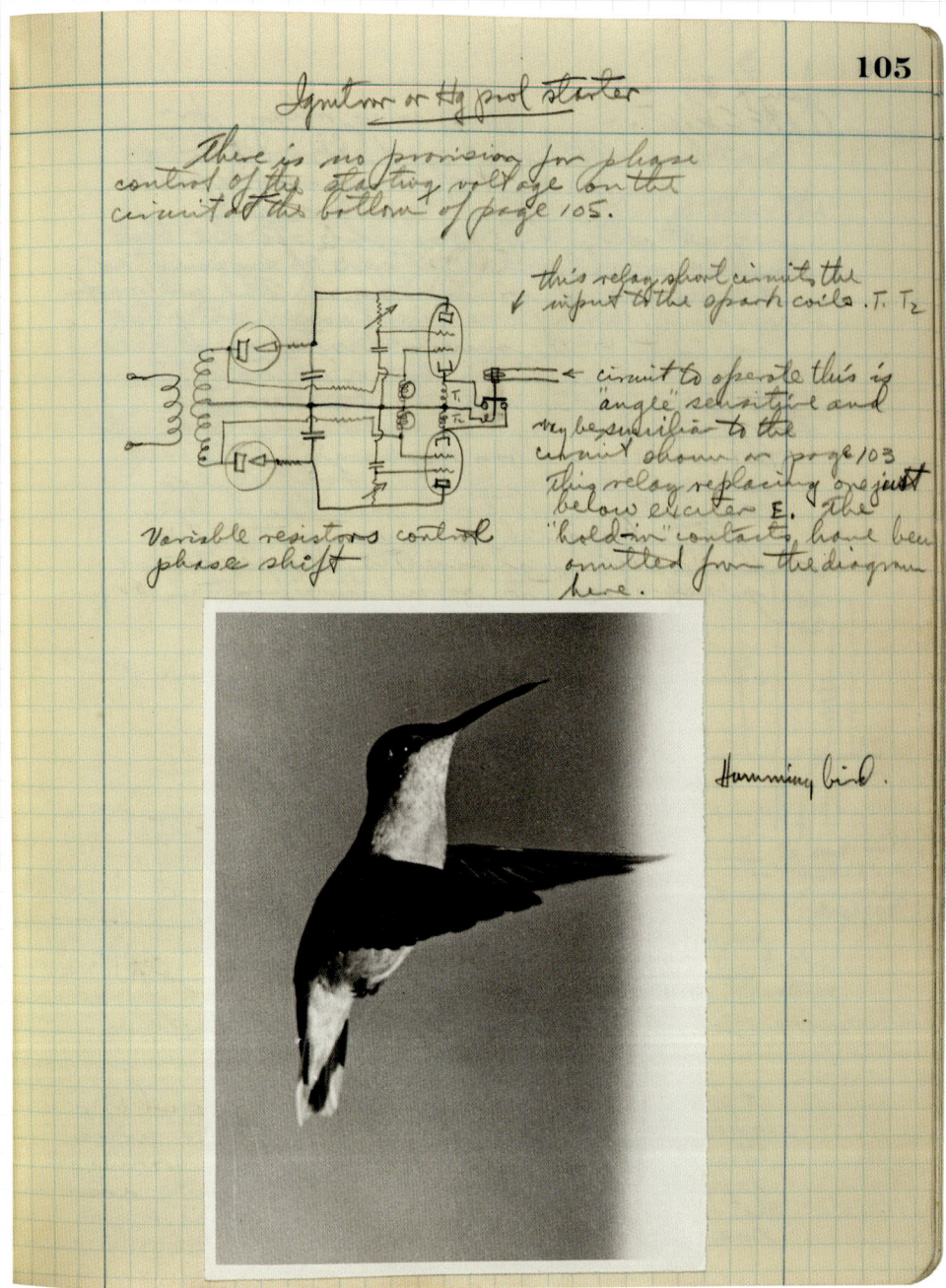

Edgerton took a two-day trip to Holderness, NH, in July 1936 to photograph hummingbirds. This image, taken in July, was pasted into his notebook about five months later in January 1937. Notebook Number 7, January 3, 1937, p. 105.

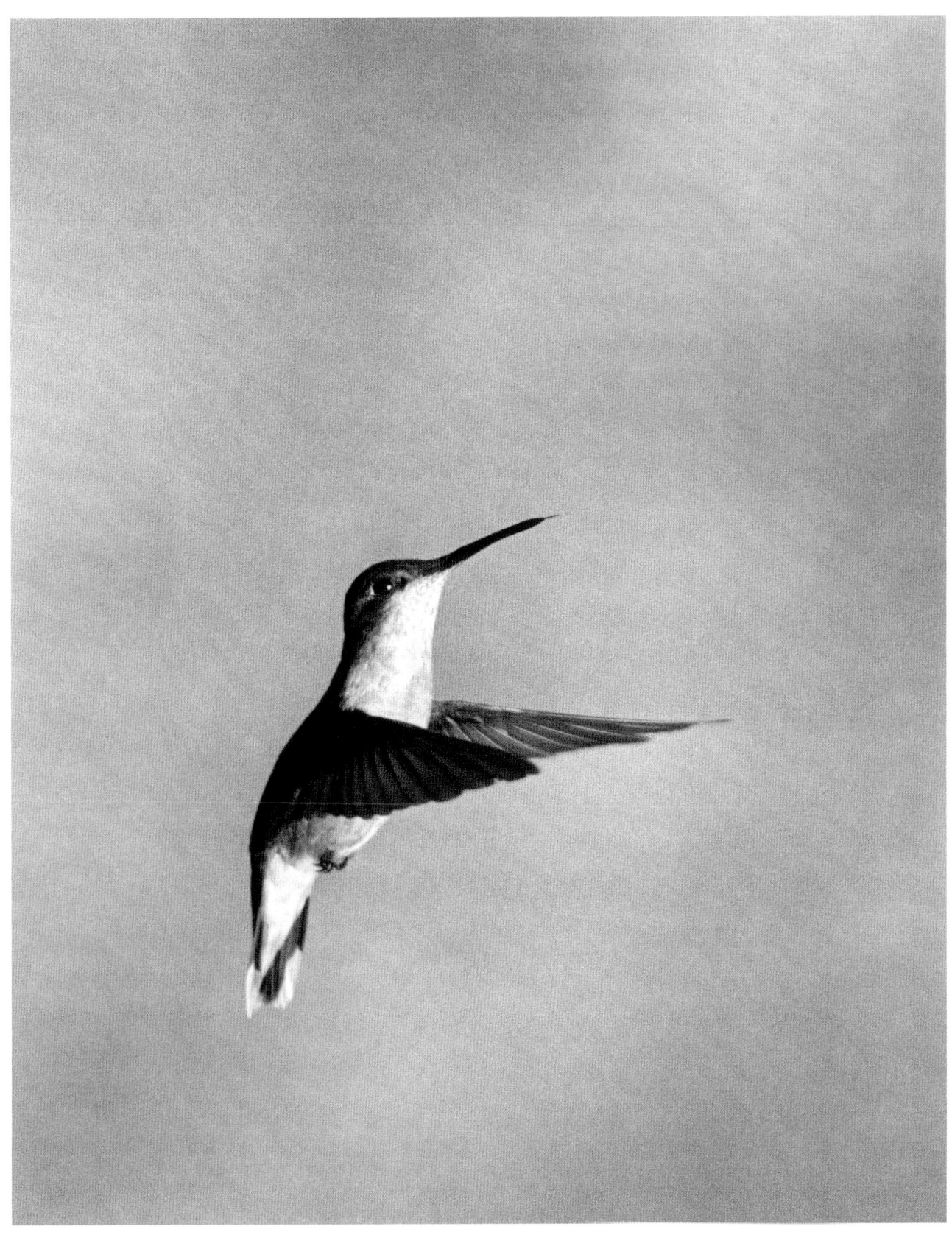

**The hummingbird's tongue, 1936**

"Here may be seen the tiny tubular tongue protruding from the bill after the bird has fed."
From *flash! Seeing the Unseen by Ultra High-Speed Photography.*

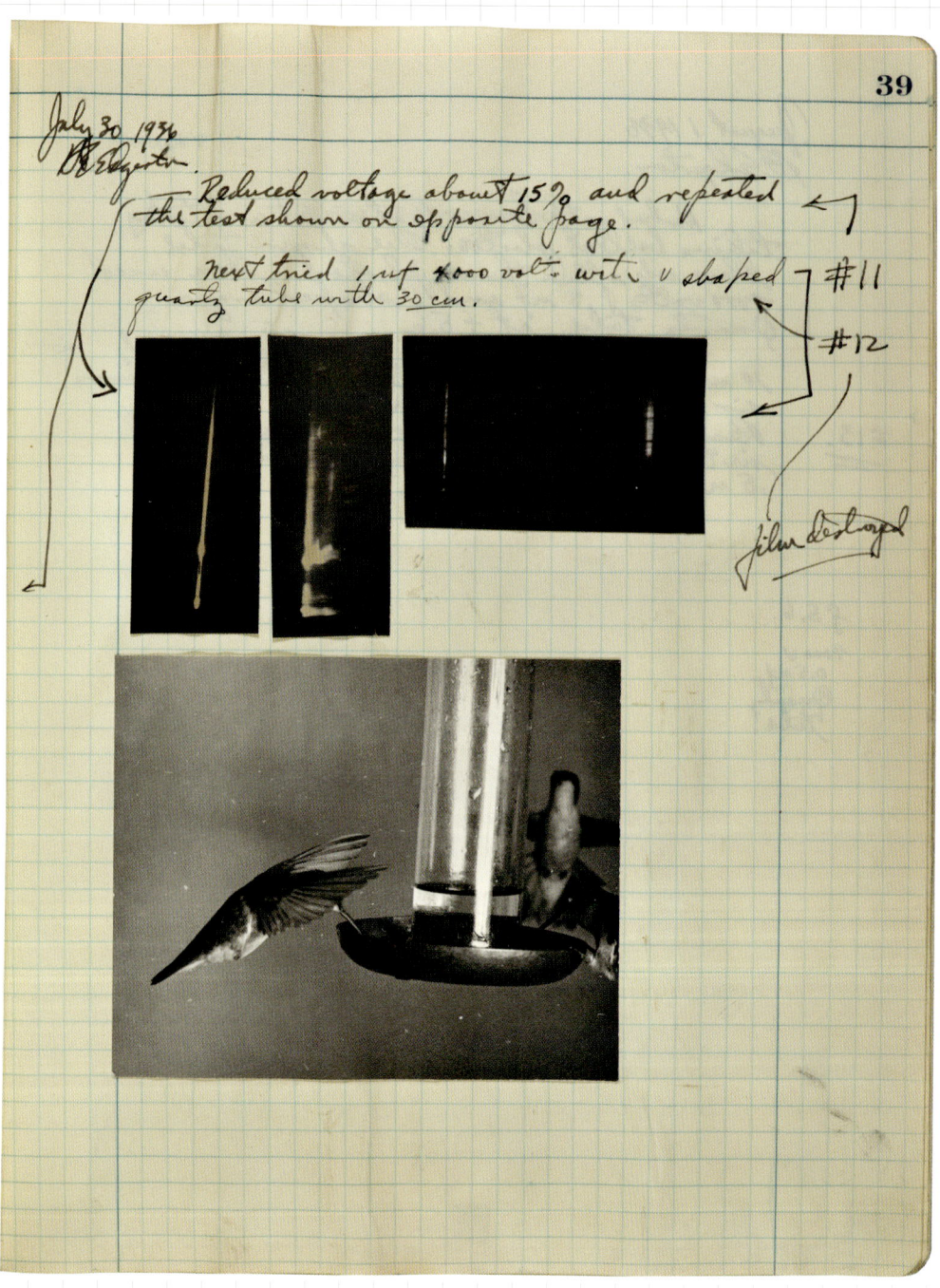

July 30 1936
Dr Edgerton

Reduced voltage about 15% and repeated the test shown on opposite page.

next tried 1 mf 4000 volt with v shaped quartz tube with 30 cm.

39

#11
#12

film destroyed

Another image from Edgerton's July 1936 trip to photograph hummingbirds. Notebook Number 7, July 30, 1936, p. 39.

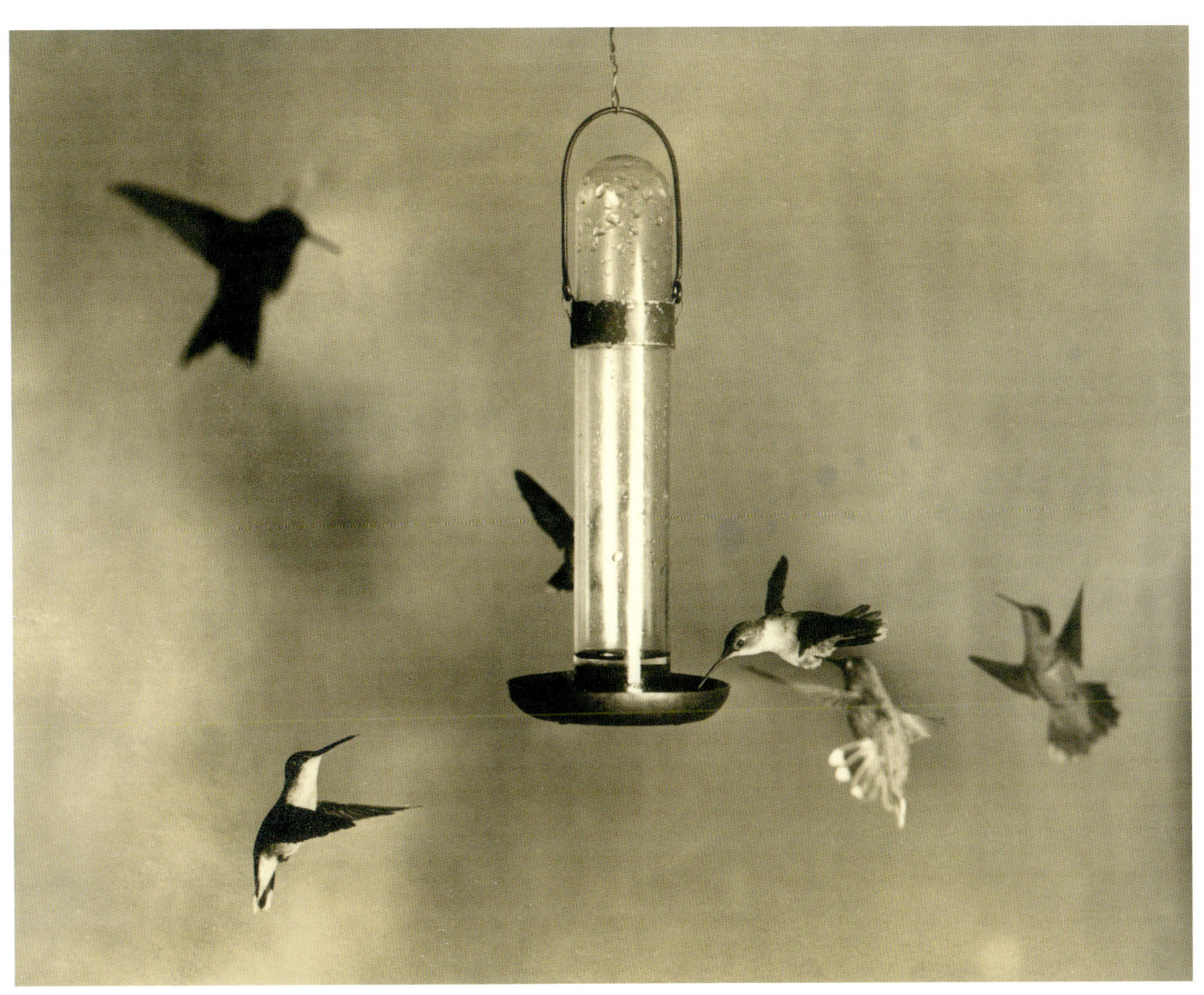

Hummingbirds at the feeder, 1936

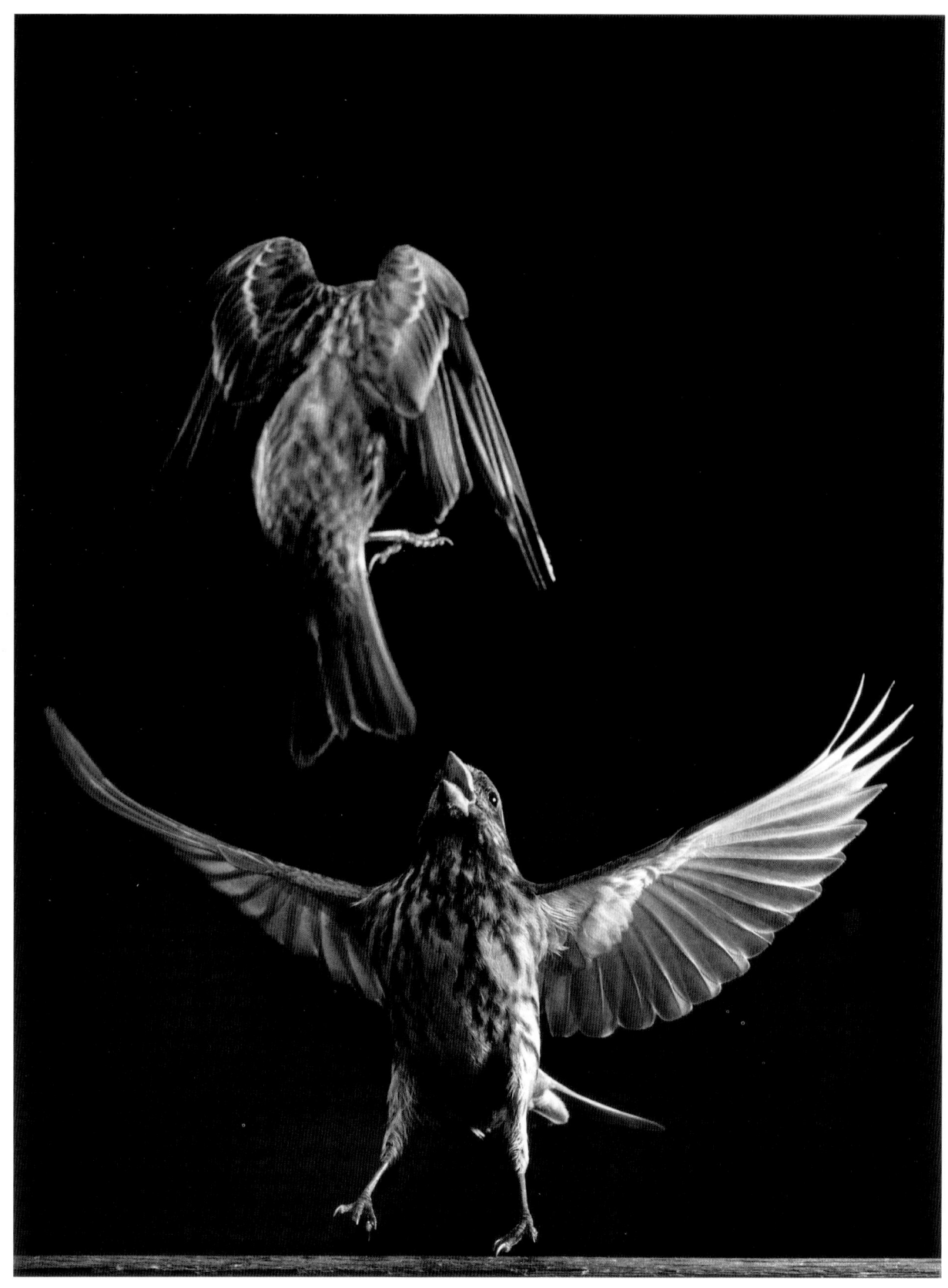

**Female fighting finches, 1936**

"The flight of birds has never been adequately studied and is veiled in controversy. Do birds propel themselves with the upward strokes of their wings as well as with the downward? The French investigator, Étienne Oehmichen, thinks that they do, that the upward stroke utilizes the moving air resulting from the down-stroke. Aeronautical engineers are doubtful."
From *flash! Seeing the Unseen by Ultra High-Speed Photography.*

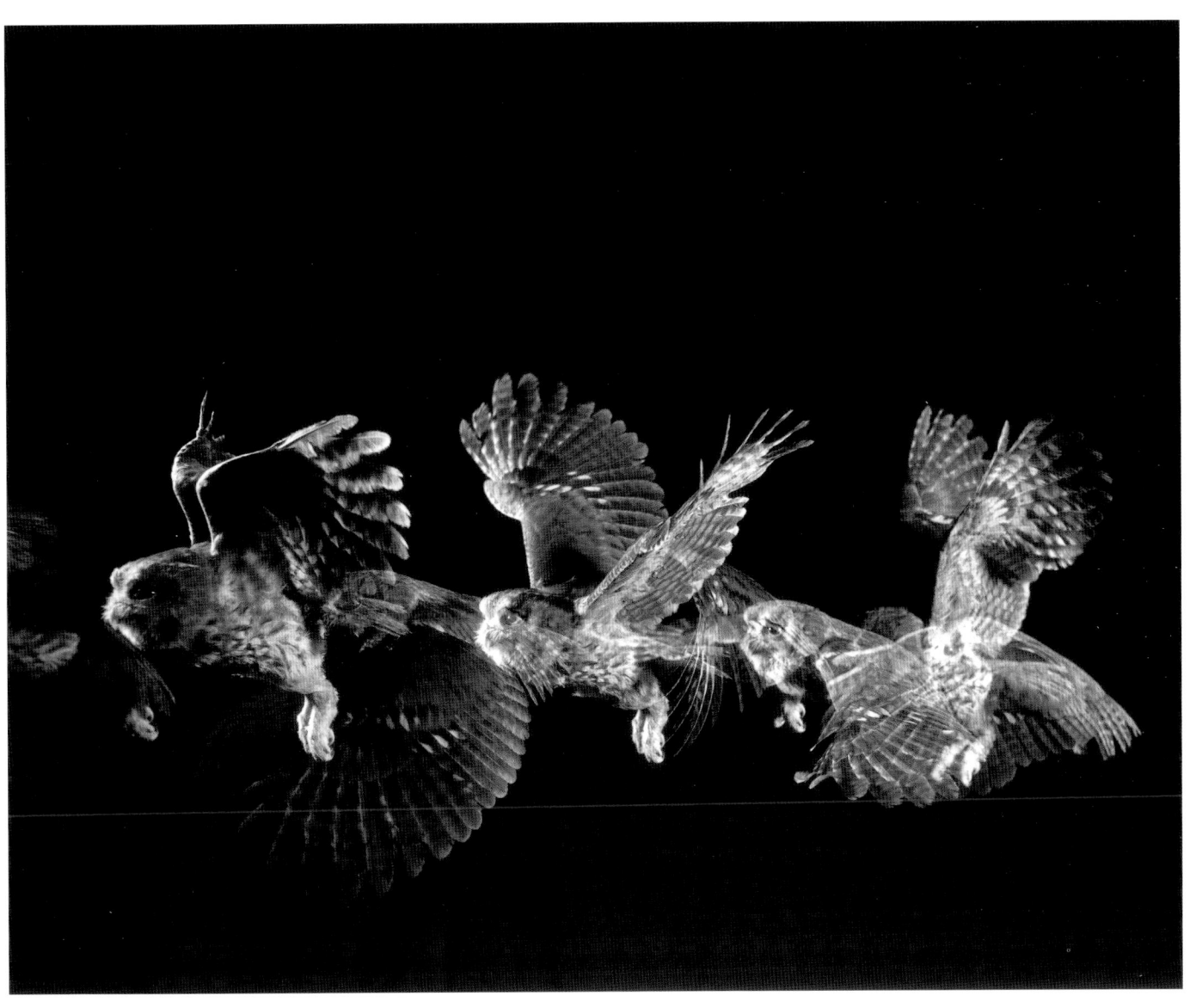

**Owl, 1965**

Spooky, the beloved "resident" of the Museum of Science, Boston from 1951 to 1989, was the subject of many Edgerton studies.

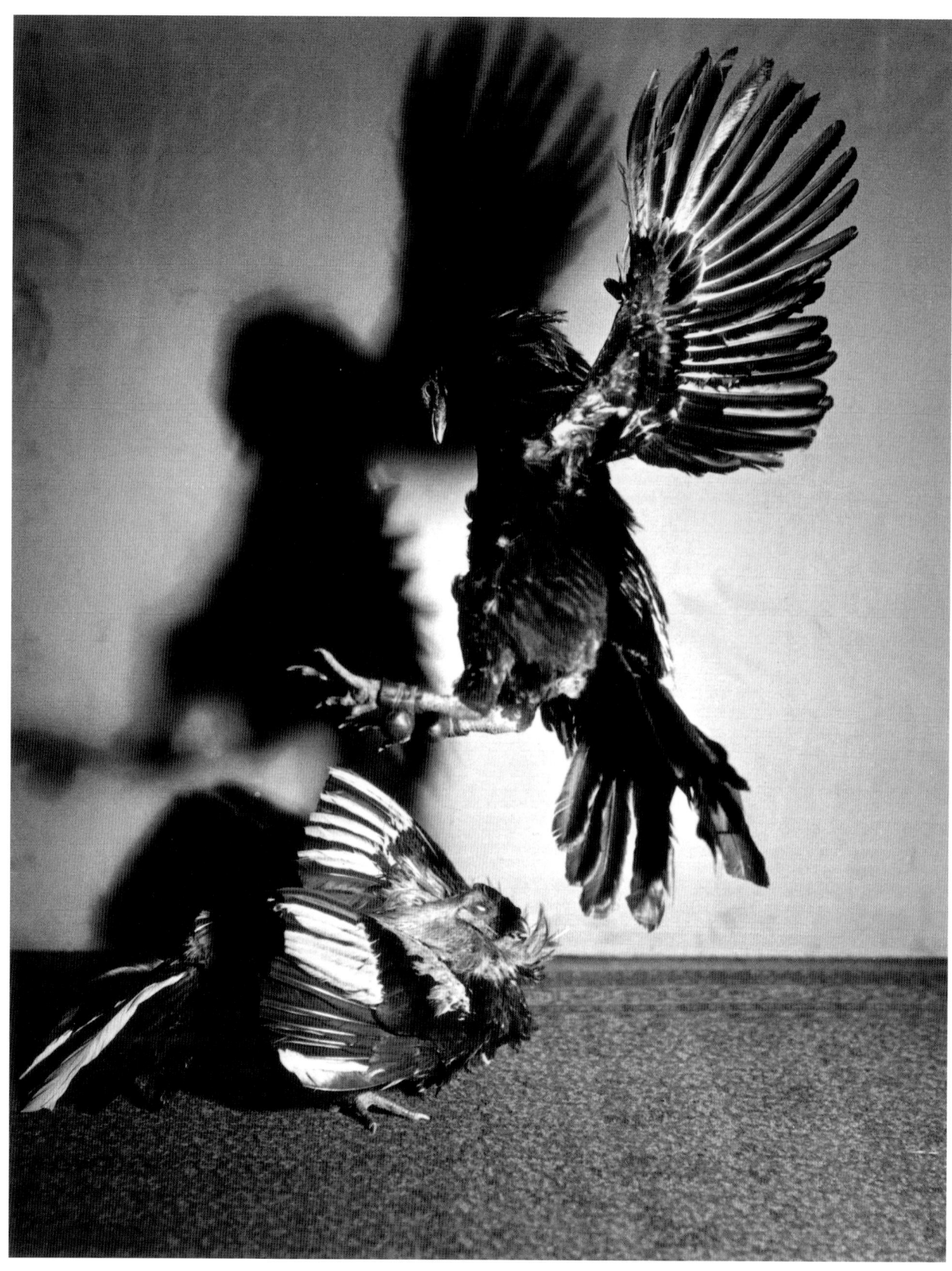

**Victory, 1934**

One of ten high-speed photographs by Edgerton included in the Royal Photographic Society of Great Britain's annual exhibition. Edgerton received the bronze medal, his first photography award. *Life* magazine would feature it in 1936.

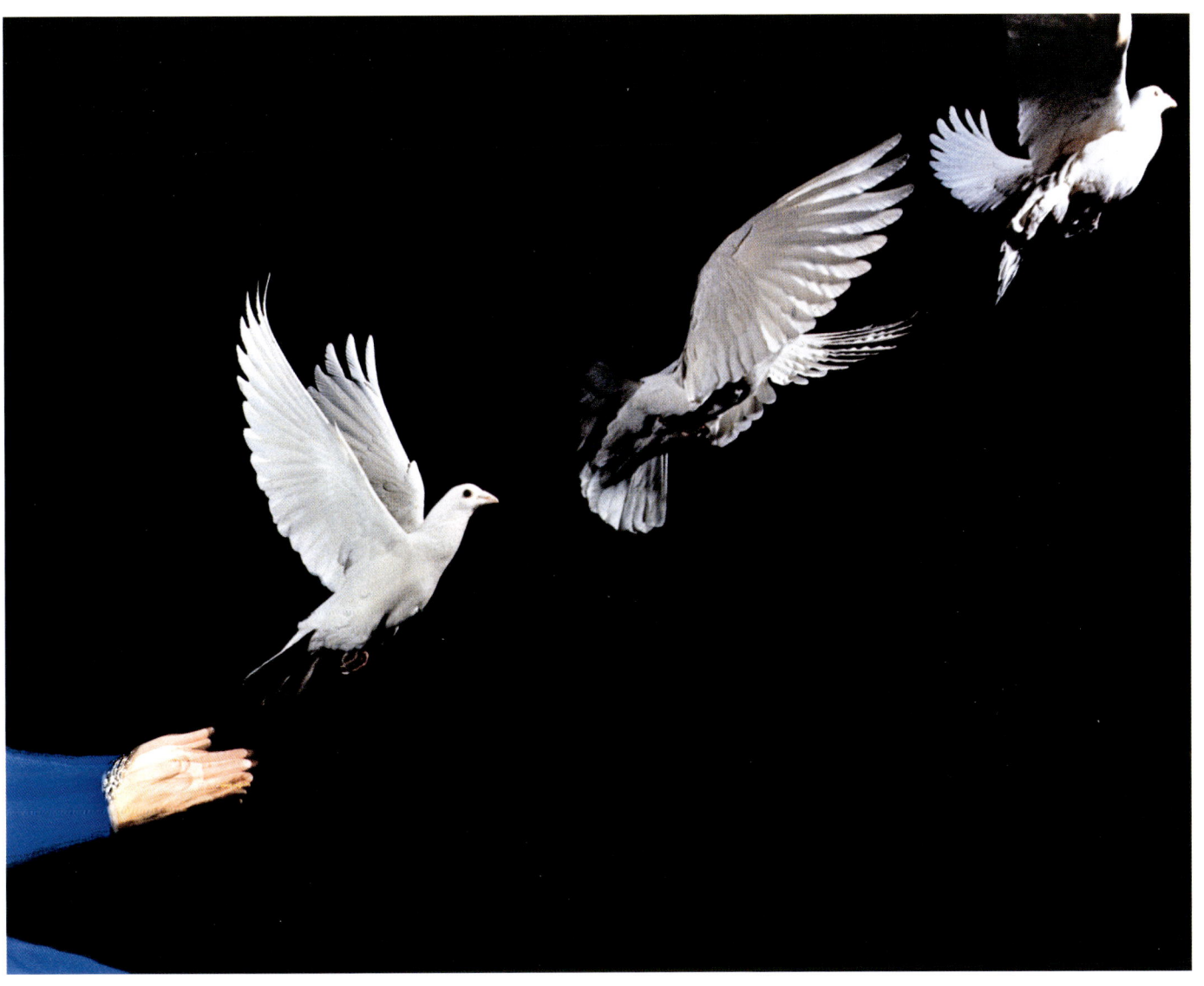

**Pigeon in flight, 1965**

Careful experimentation allowed Edgerton to set the sequence of exposures
that would showcase three moments in the flight cycle of a bird.

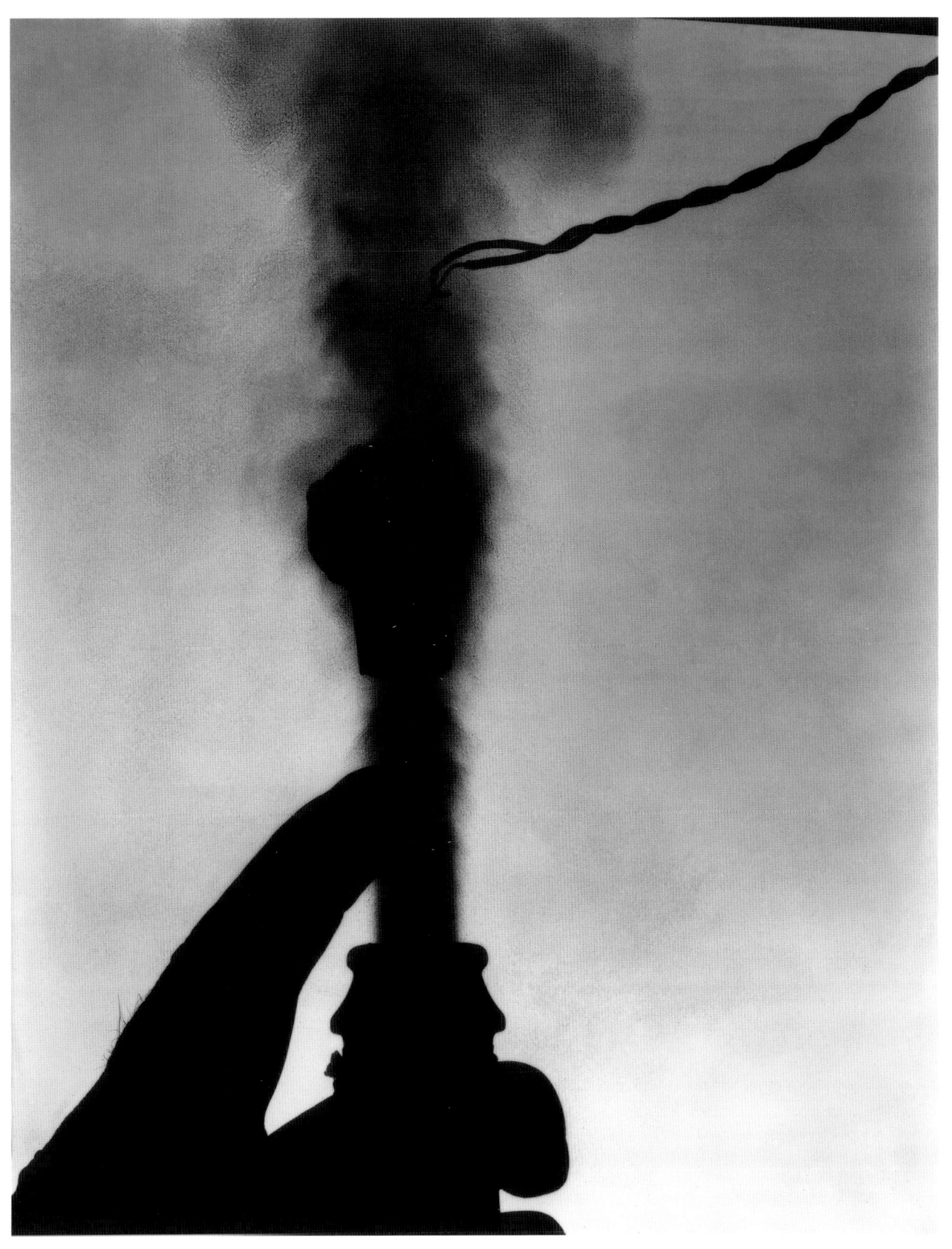

Champagne cork, 1982

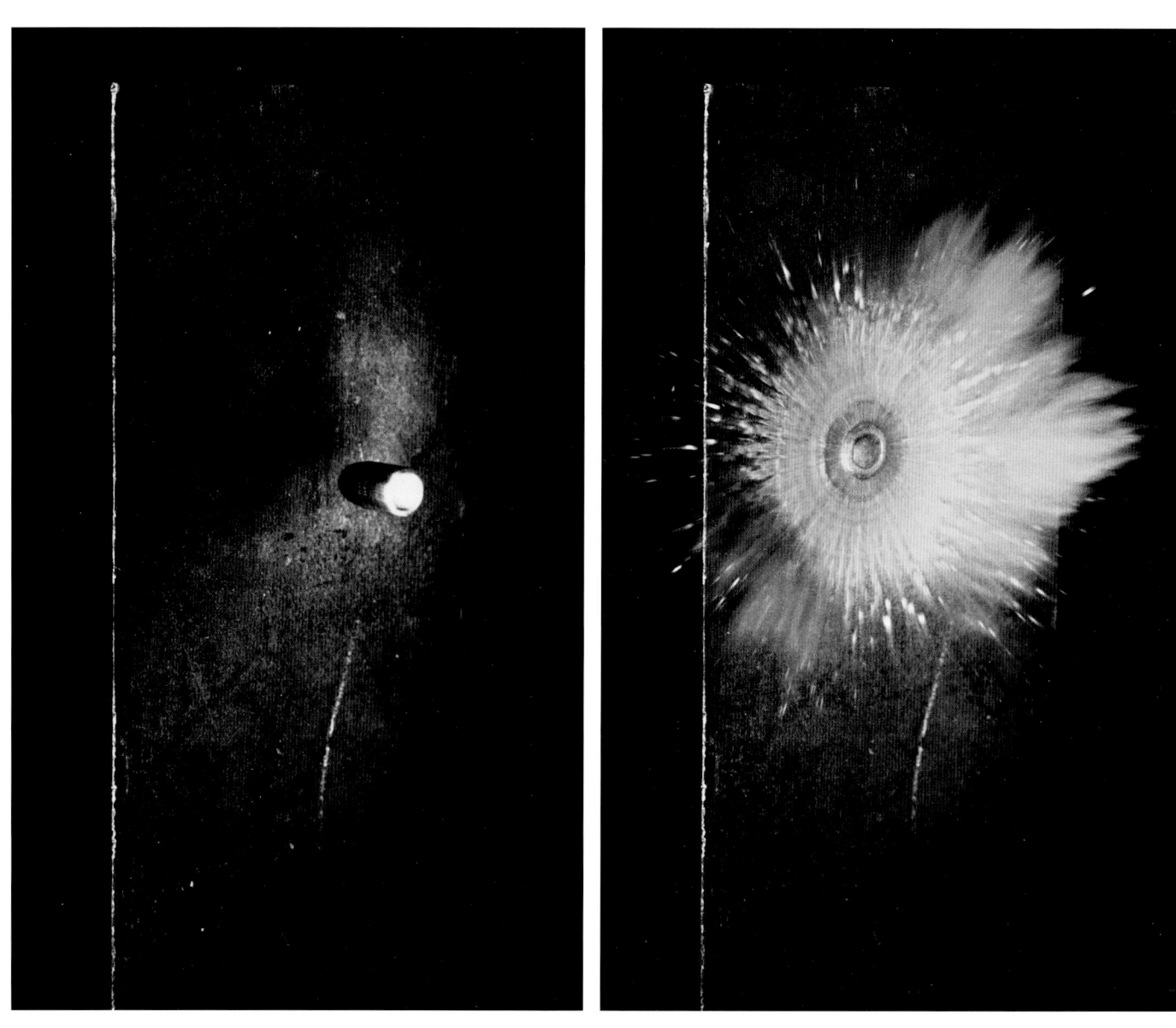

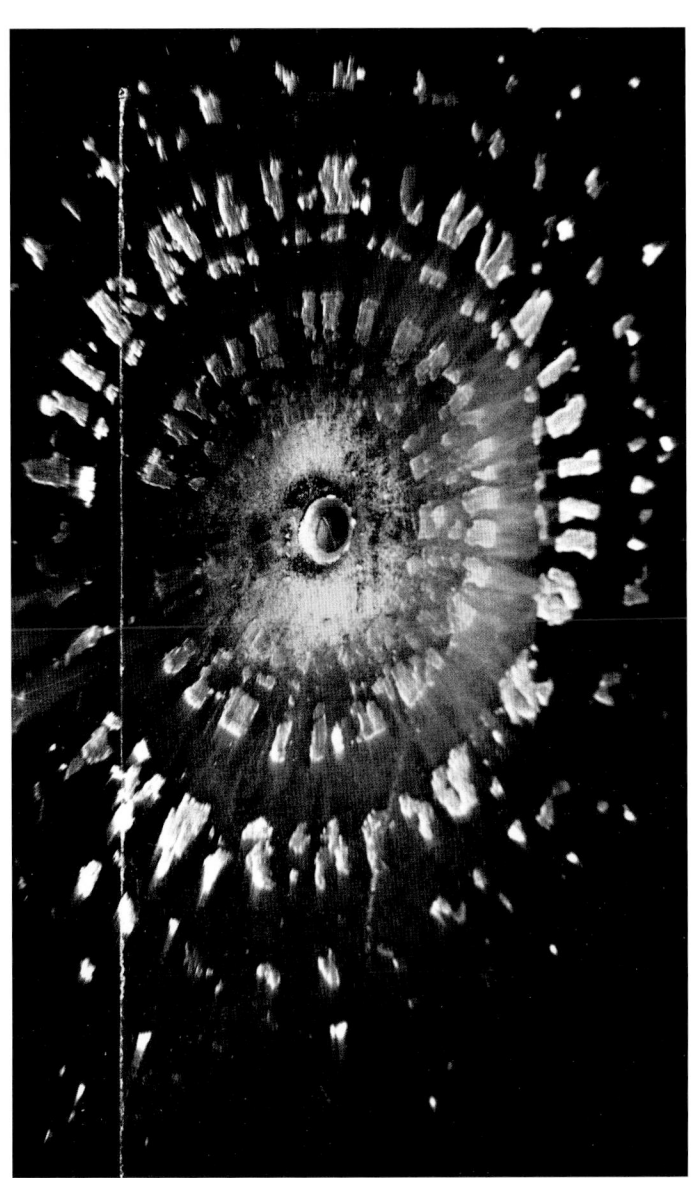

**This has never been seen before, 1938**

What happens when a bullet strikes a steel block?
Edgerton answers: "It apparently liquefies from
the force of the impact and splashes in a manner
not unlike the milk drop... ." From *flash! Seeing
the Unseen by Ultra High-Speed Photography*.

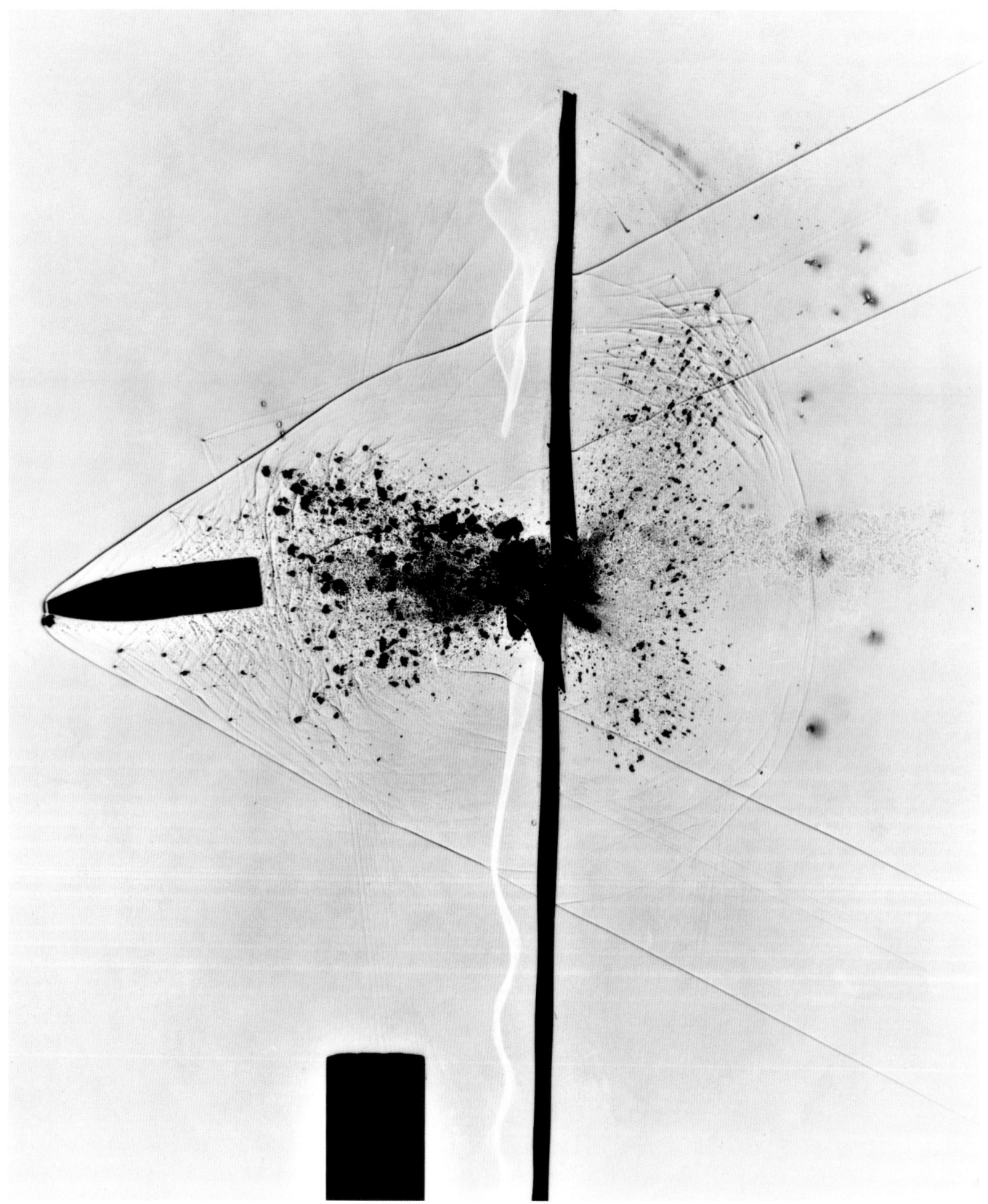

**Bullet through Plexiglas, 1962**

Silhouette photograph of a .30 caliber bullet after penetrating a thin acrylic strip. The faint waves that tripped the microphone (square at the bottom) caused by the bullet passing through the acrylic can be seen just ahead of the main wave.

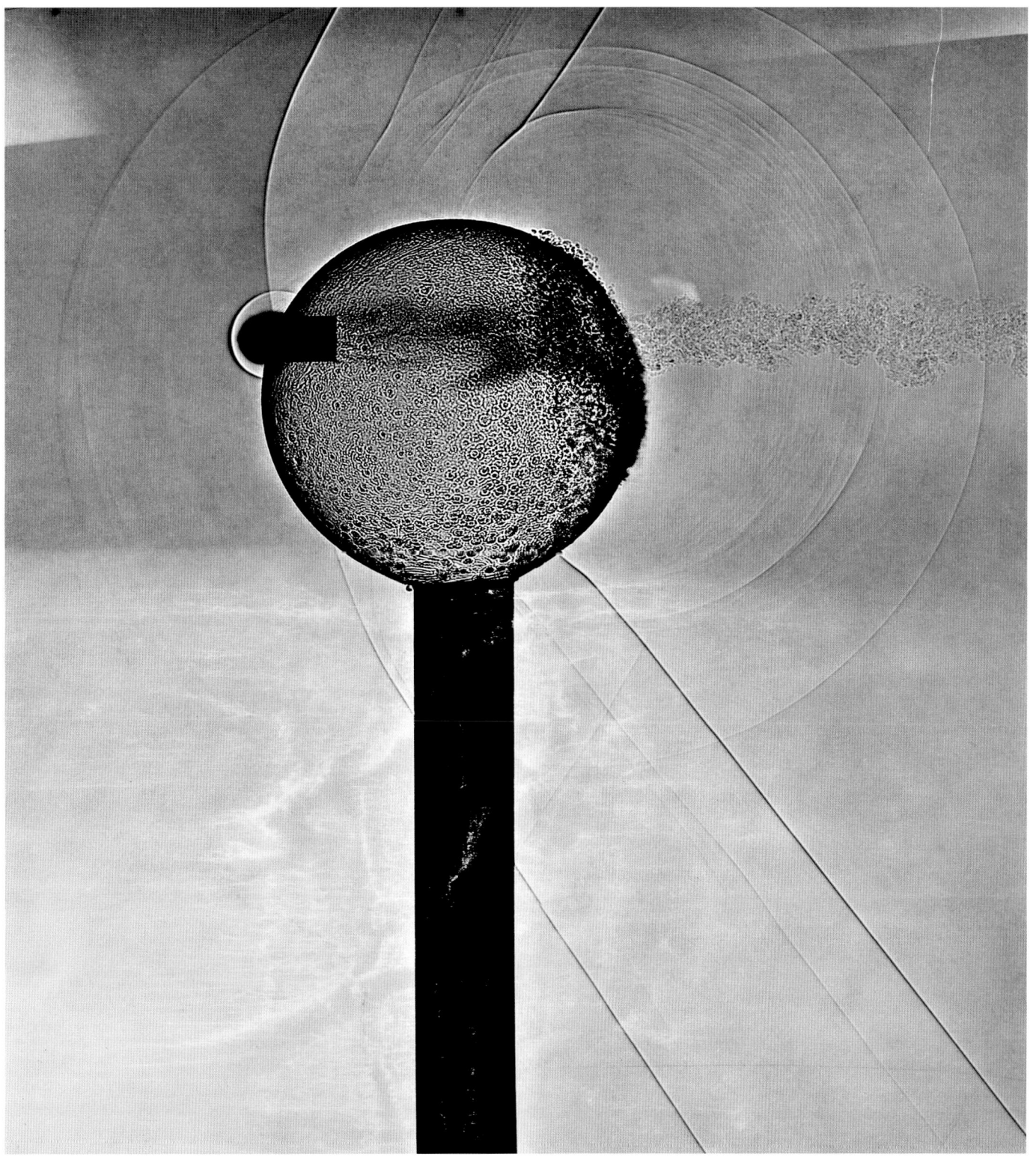

**Bullet pierces a bubble, 1970**

Silhouette photograph of a .22 caliber bullet piercing a soap bubble filled with helium gas.
The shock waves are clearly visible in this image.

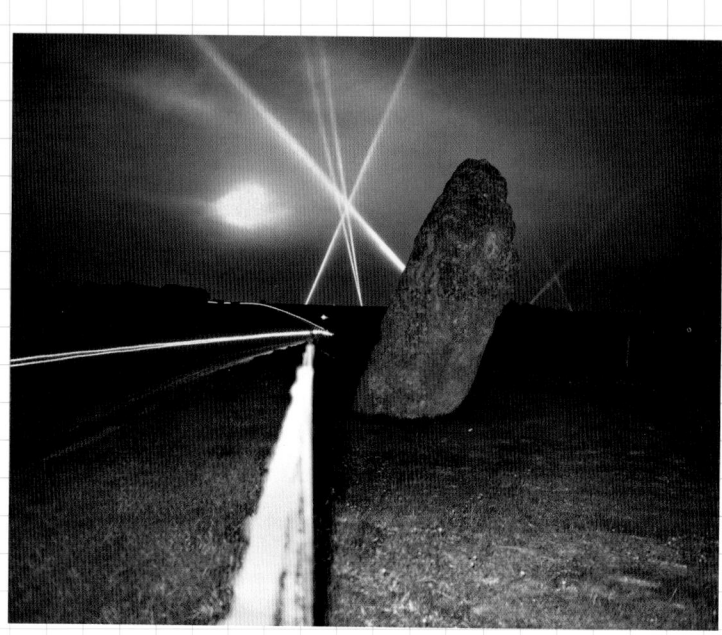

Search lights over Stonehenge, 1944

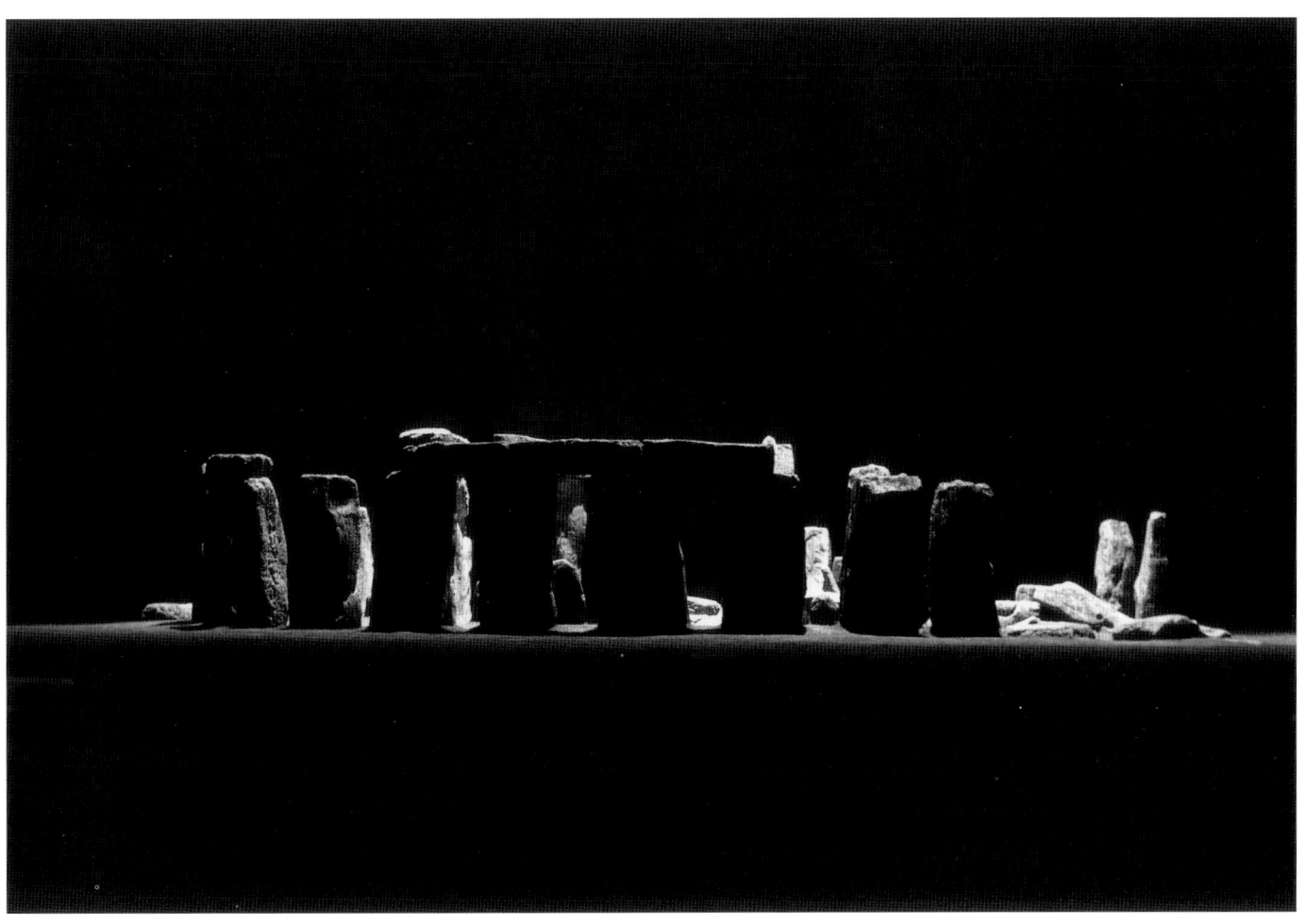

**Stonehenge at night, 1944**

During World War II, Edgerton consulted extensively with the Army Air Forces to develop aerial nighttime photography technology. For his contributions, Edgerton received the Medal of Freedom. For this photograph, Edgerton was on the ground and the airplane flew 1,500 feet overhead, triggering a single 50,000 watt-second flash.

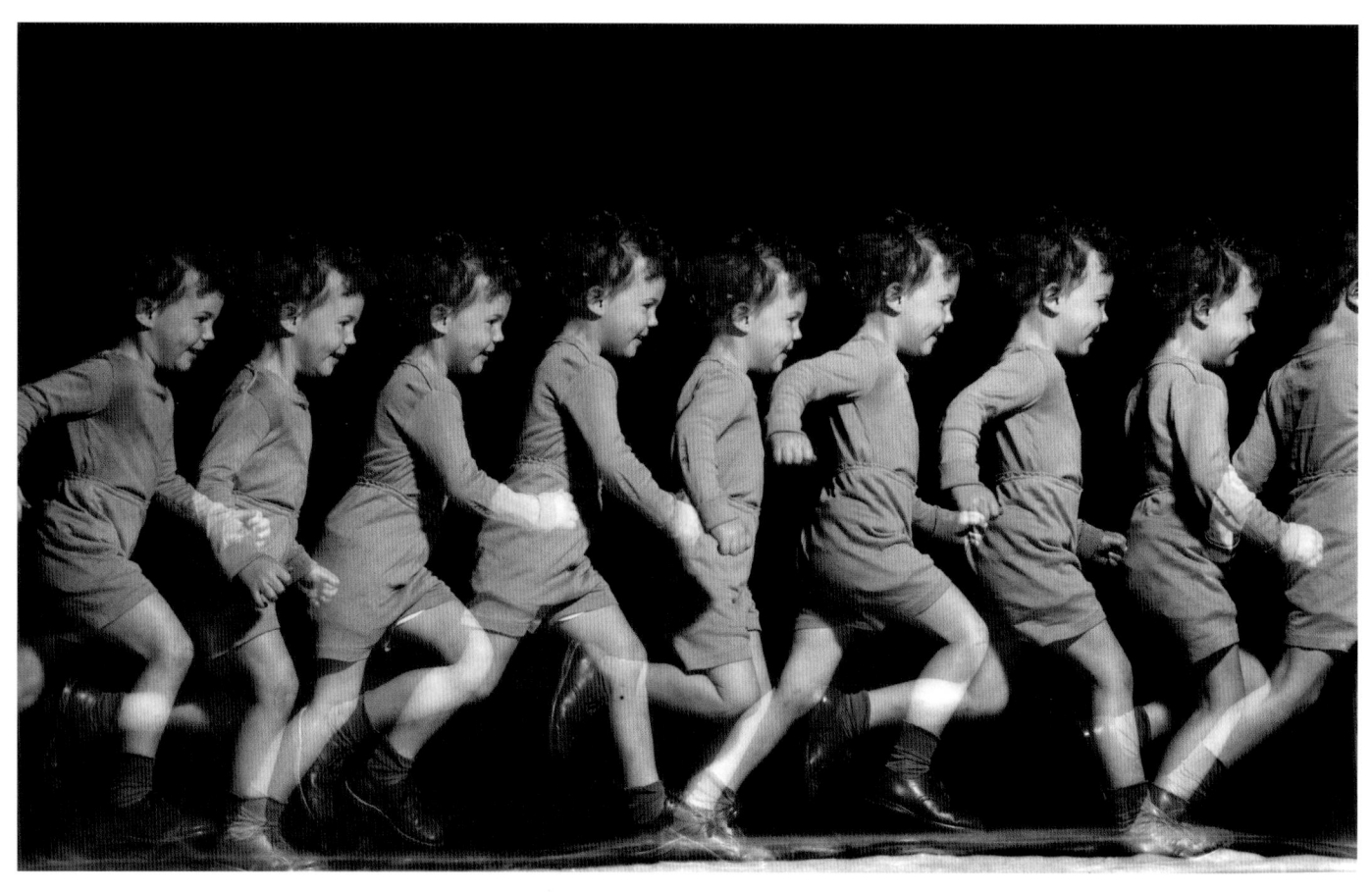

**Child running, 1939**
Edgerton caught the joy of his young son running.

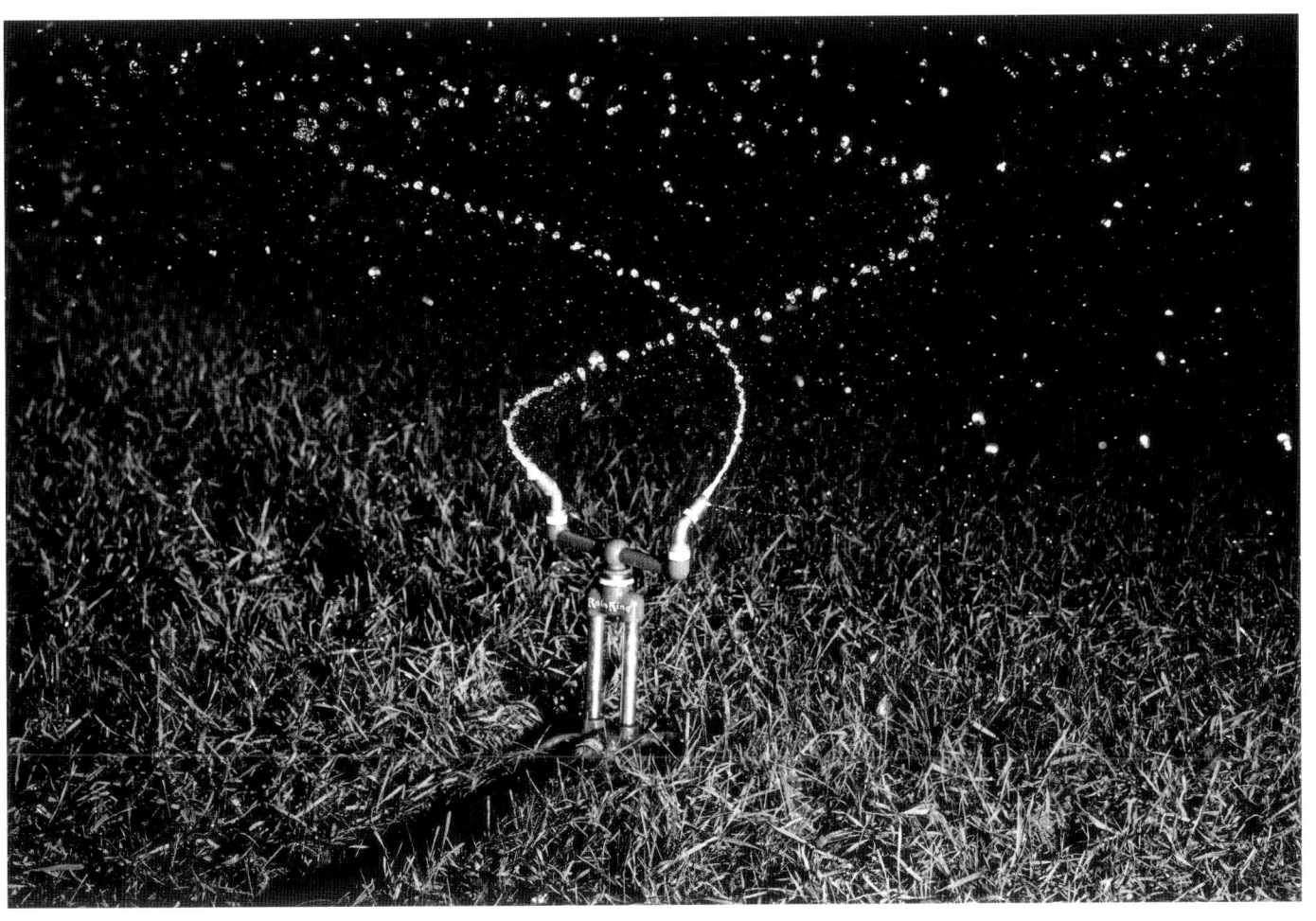

Lawn sprinkler at night, 1939

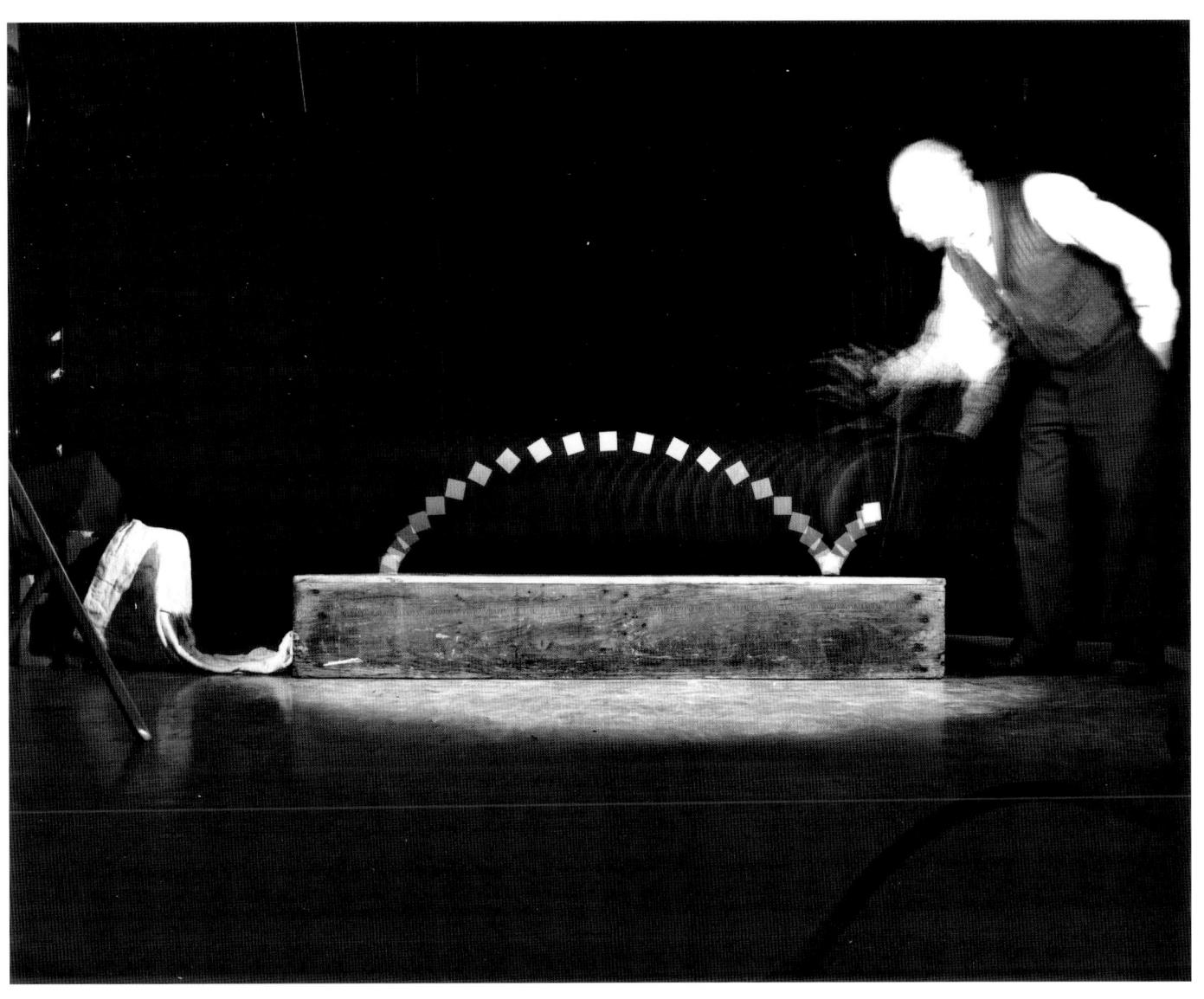

**Cycloid demonstration, 1987**

Edgerton's last important picture project involved a demonstration of a cycloid curve.

PAGES FROM EDGERTON'S NOTEBOOKS

May 16 - 1932

Pictures taken. 4 lamp in parallel
2 mfd at. 1000 v. per lamp. —

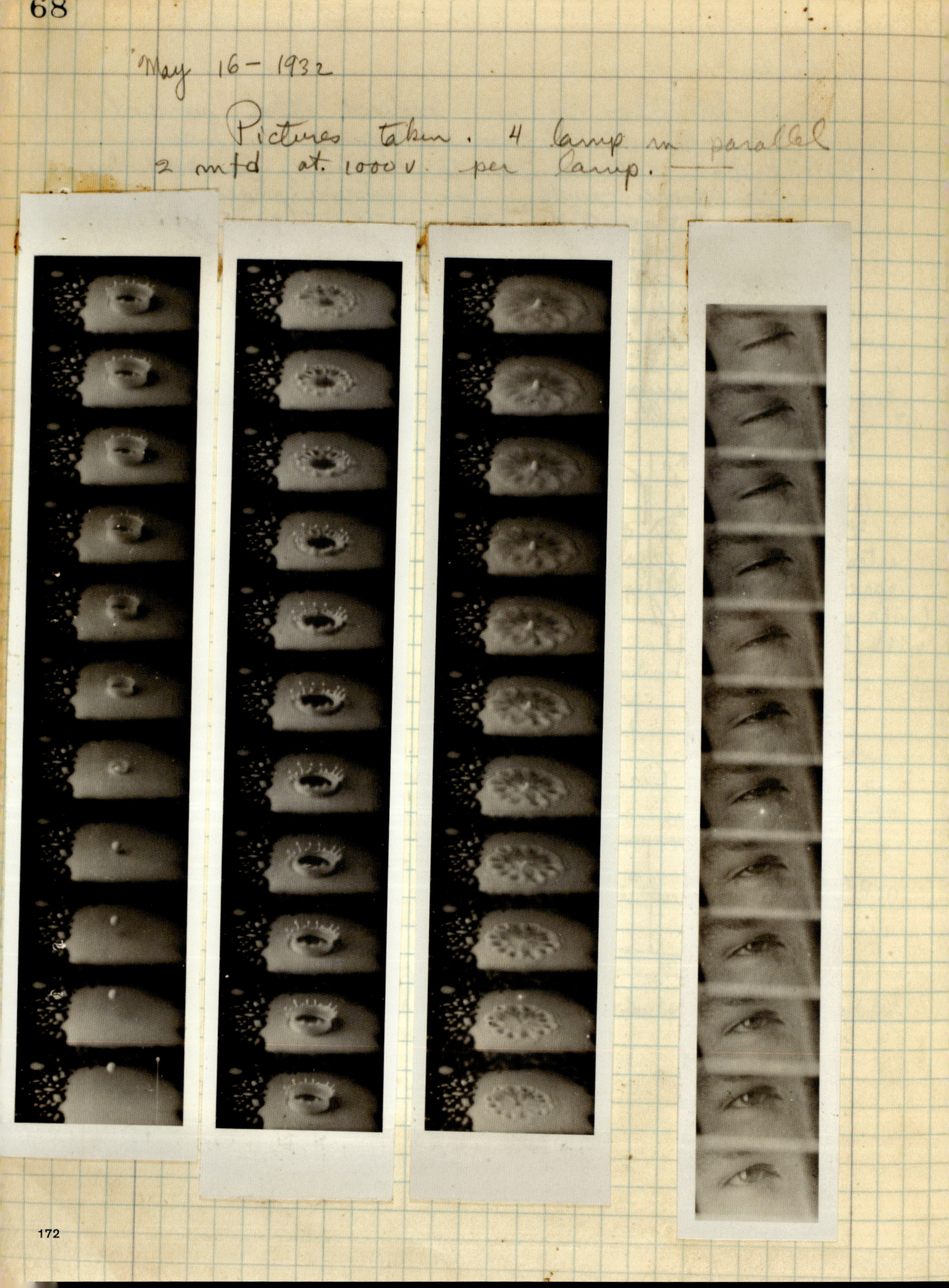

# STROBOSCOPE

This describes an idea for the utilizing of a-n ionized mercury vapor tube as a means of obtaining stroboscope action.

A current of sufficient magnitude to give enough light is sent through the mercury tube at definate periods of time. This is accomplished by having a variable speed motor drive a metalic disc. This disc has a small insulating segment on its rim. A narrow brush ⱷⱷⱷⱷ makes contact with the rim of the disc. When the insulated sector and the brush are together the current that normally passes from brush to disc is shunted into the mercury tube.

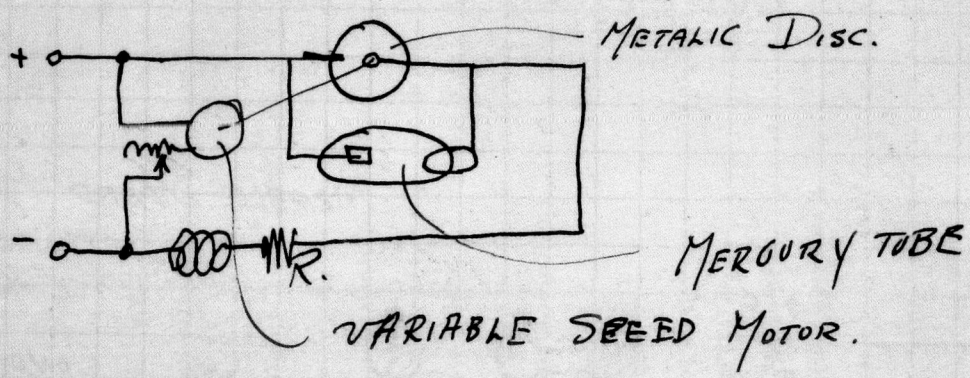

METALIC DISC.

MERCURY TUBE

VARIABLE SPEED MOTOR.

Witnessed in operation, May 16, 1929

Inman S. Gray
Cambridge, Mass

Jan 31 1932
H.E.Edgerton

Came down in the morning and set up the 60 cycle stroboscope (page 7) with a UX 280 in the spark circuit. Also changed tubes. Now using the one with broken glass on the surface of the mercury which Germ made some time ago.

I put some positive film in Day's camera and took some pictures of the 14 inch disc on the (1200 r.p.m.) 804 synchronous machine.

There seems to be plenty of light with even 2 mf at 1000 volts rectified. The tube gets quite hot.

Germ came about 11 and we set up a milk drop experiment. Took movies at 250 frames a second of the drops just as they struck the surface.

For these tests we used three tubes in parallel about 5 or 6 inches from the subject. Each tube was connected to the rectifier system and to 1 mf. Rectifier 1500 volts on each side. 18 mf filter cond.

36

Grid

contactor to
make grid pos.

+

Bias

keep alive

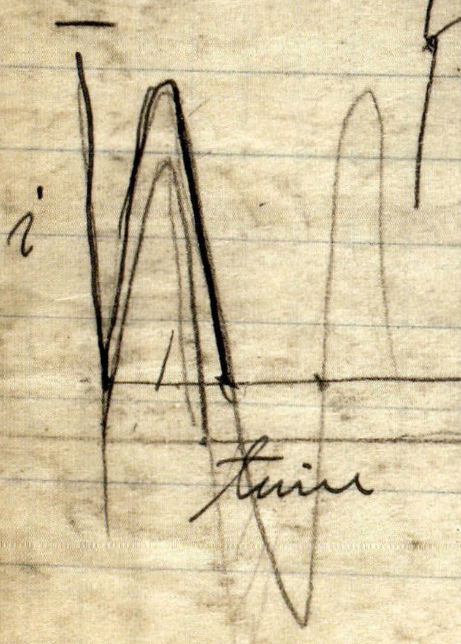

i

time

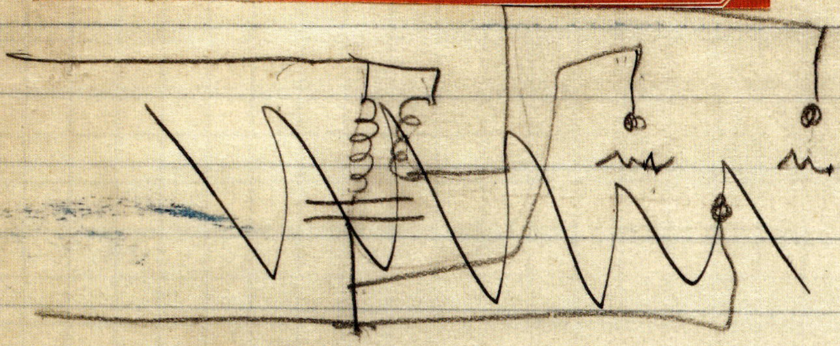

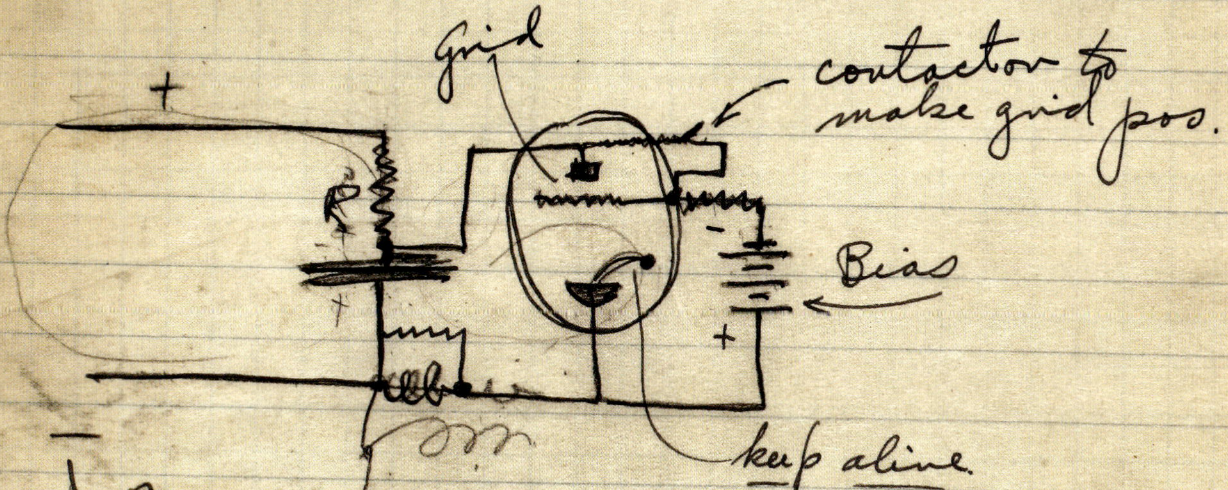

This circuit was shown
to me by H. E. Edgerton
on May 28, 1929
Charles Kingsley Jr.
Cambridge, Mass.

April 10 1933

Went to Bellows Falls with Hugh Spencer of the New England Power company to see about installing a stroboscope on the generators there. This strobo is to be automatic and is to trip when they have trouble with lightning.

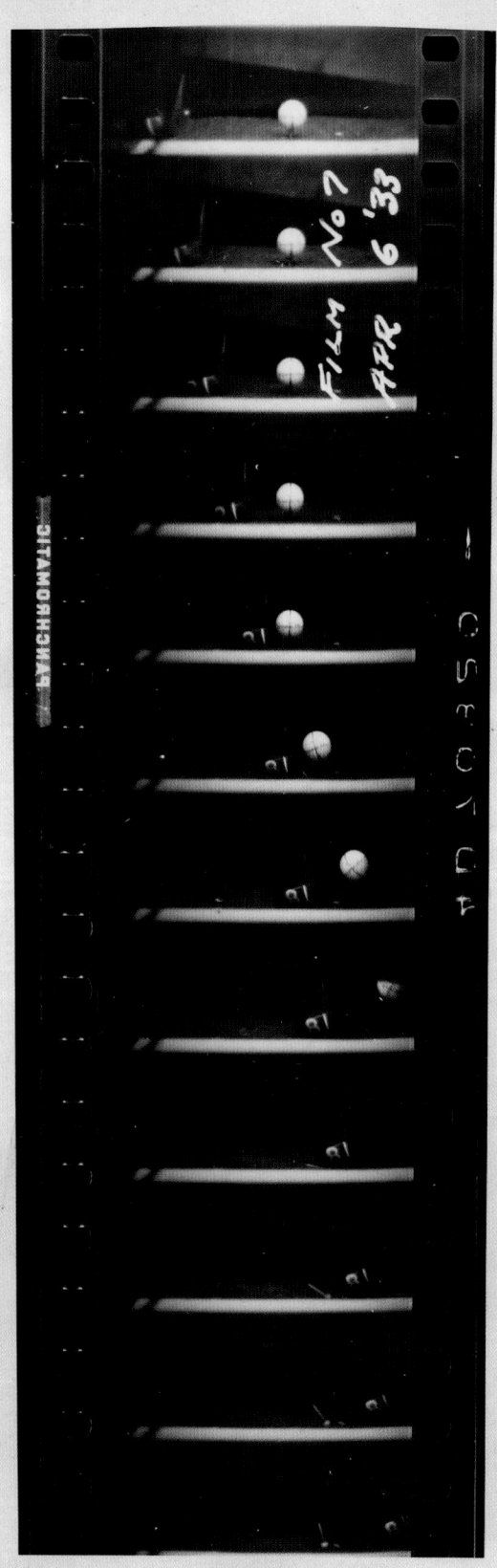

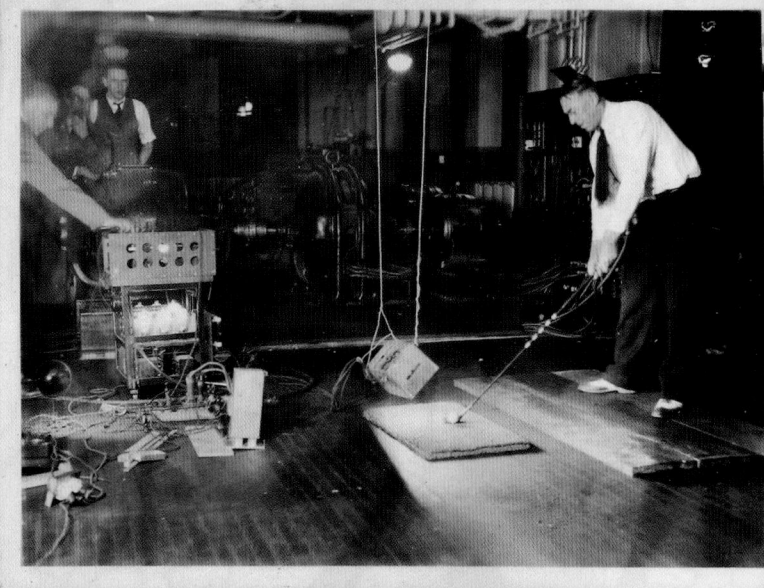

Francis Ouimet

↑
960 picture
per second
movie camera.

$$energy = \frac{1}{2}mv^2 = \frac{1}{2}\left(\frac{12}{16}\right)\frac{1}{32.2}(169)^2 = 335 \; lb \, ft.$$

The set up for the milk drop pictures and some of the results are shown below.

The power unit and lighting system used was that developed for the Int. Paper Co. and will be described on succeding pages.

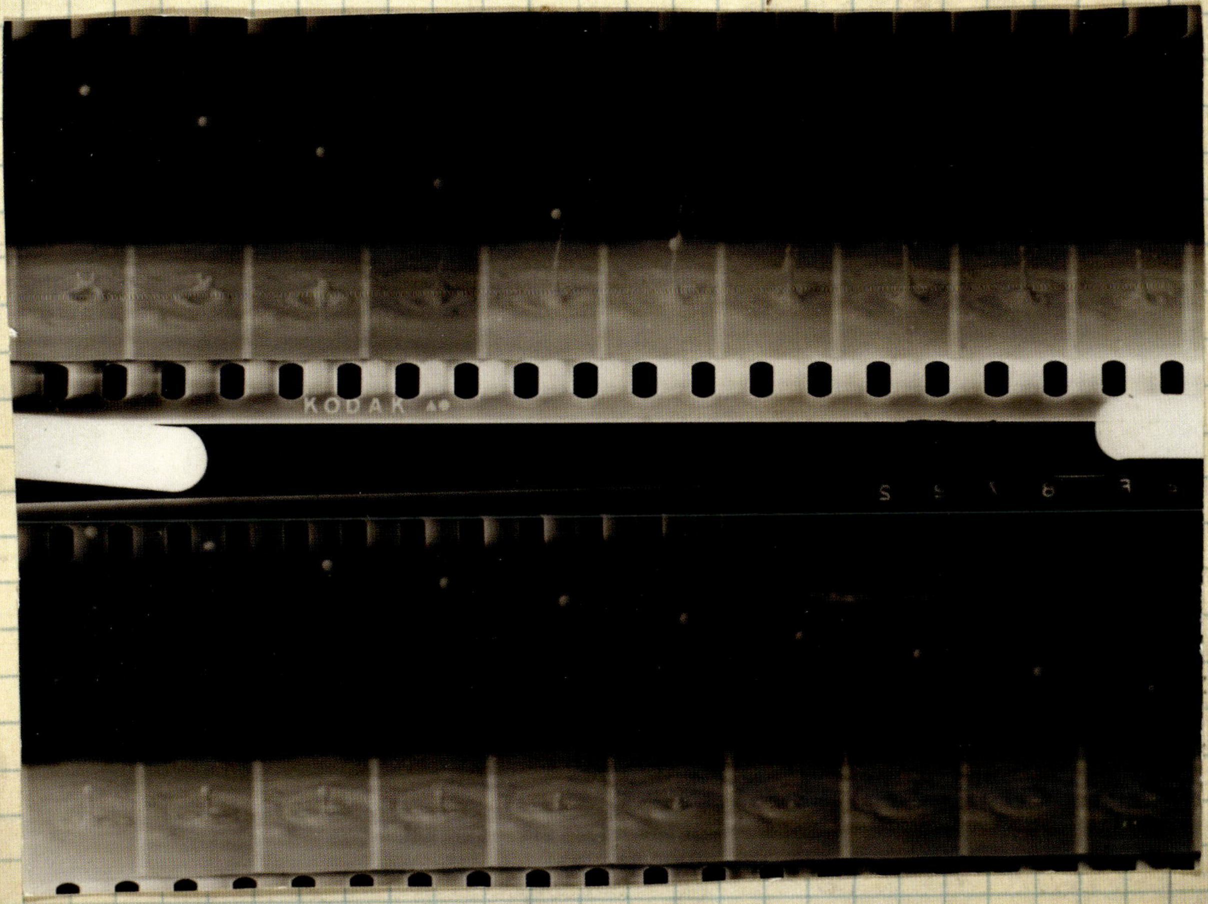

June. 16. 1931.          Photograph

H. E. Edgerton.          Movie Projection by means
                              of intermittant light.

Practically all present
projection schemes use a
concentrated light source
which approaches a point
source.

Such a point source appears
at the present to be impossible
with the mercury arc lamp.
It may be possible however
to use a line source of light
to advantage. I believe that an
intense capilliary can be
built which will be small in
diameter but very intense. A
parabolic mirror and parallel
light shields may make it
feasible to get a parallel beam
of light which may be directed
and focused by means of cylindrical
lenses.

light baffles to make the light
   parallel.

Parabolic reflector to make
   light directive.

Plane light source.

light grid to make beams
   parallel.

During the last week I worked at the Sprague
Specialties company at Quincy on the motor driving the
Visivox. These intermittant light schemes were discussed
at length with Bill Dunn. constant speed film seems to have a

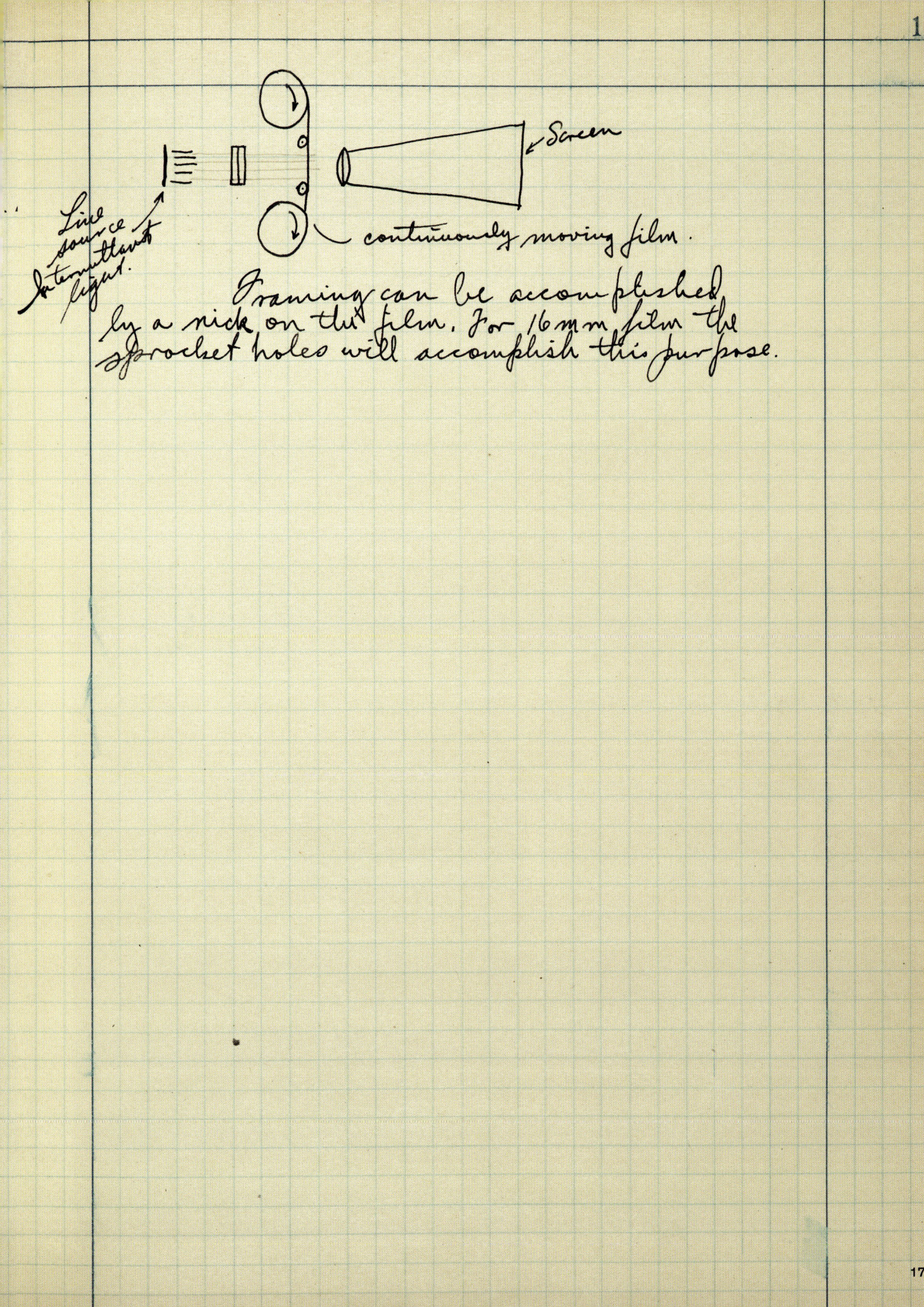

Line source of intermittent light.

continuously moving film.

Screen

Framing can be accomplished by a nick on the film. For 16 mm film the sprocket holes will accomplish this purpose.

Stroboscopic photograph taken by Conant,
of M.I.T. Photo Service.

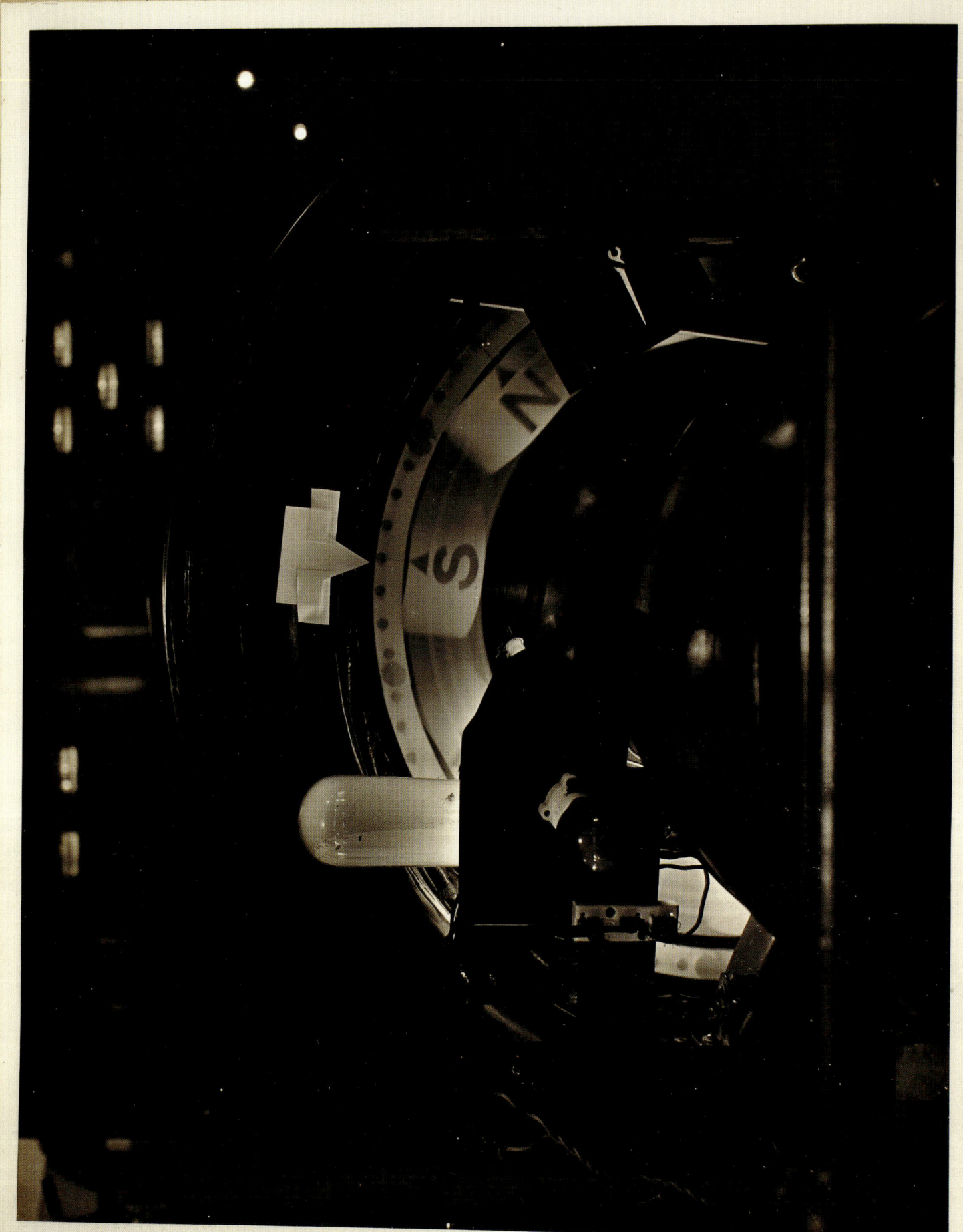

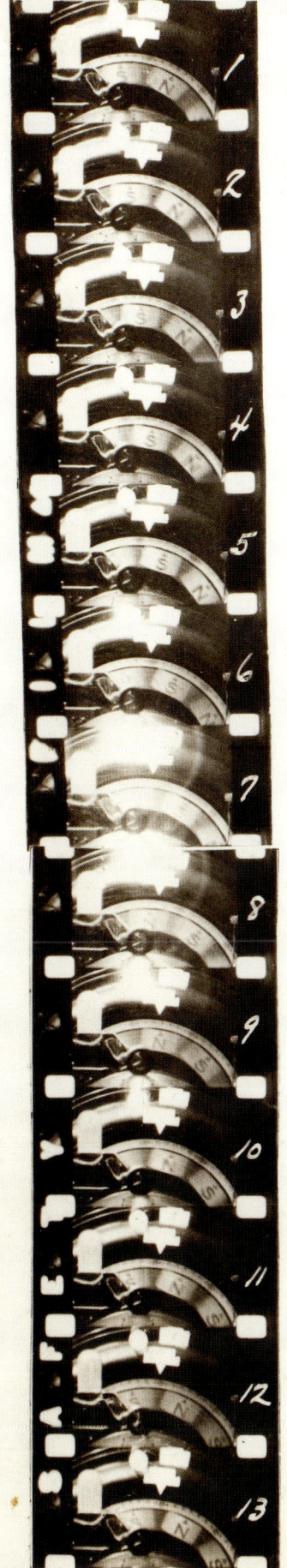

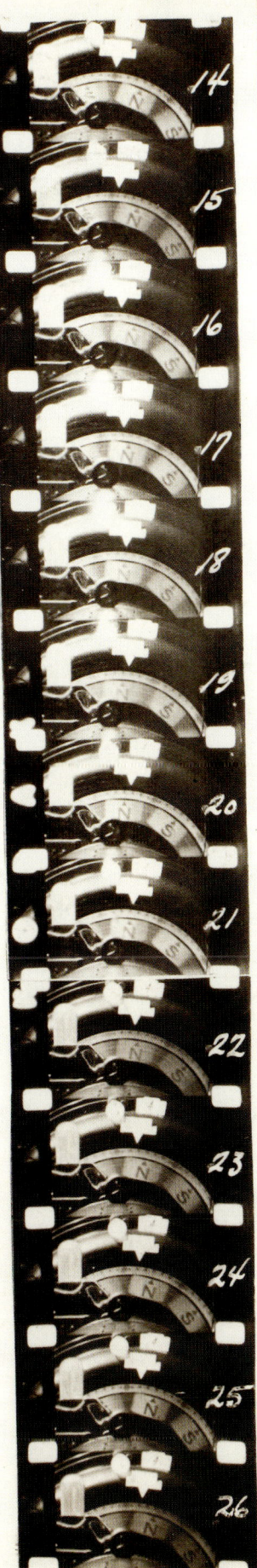

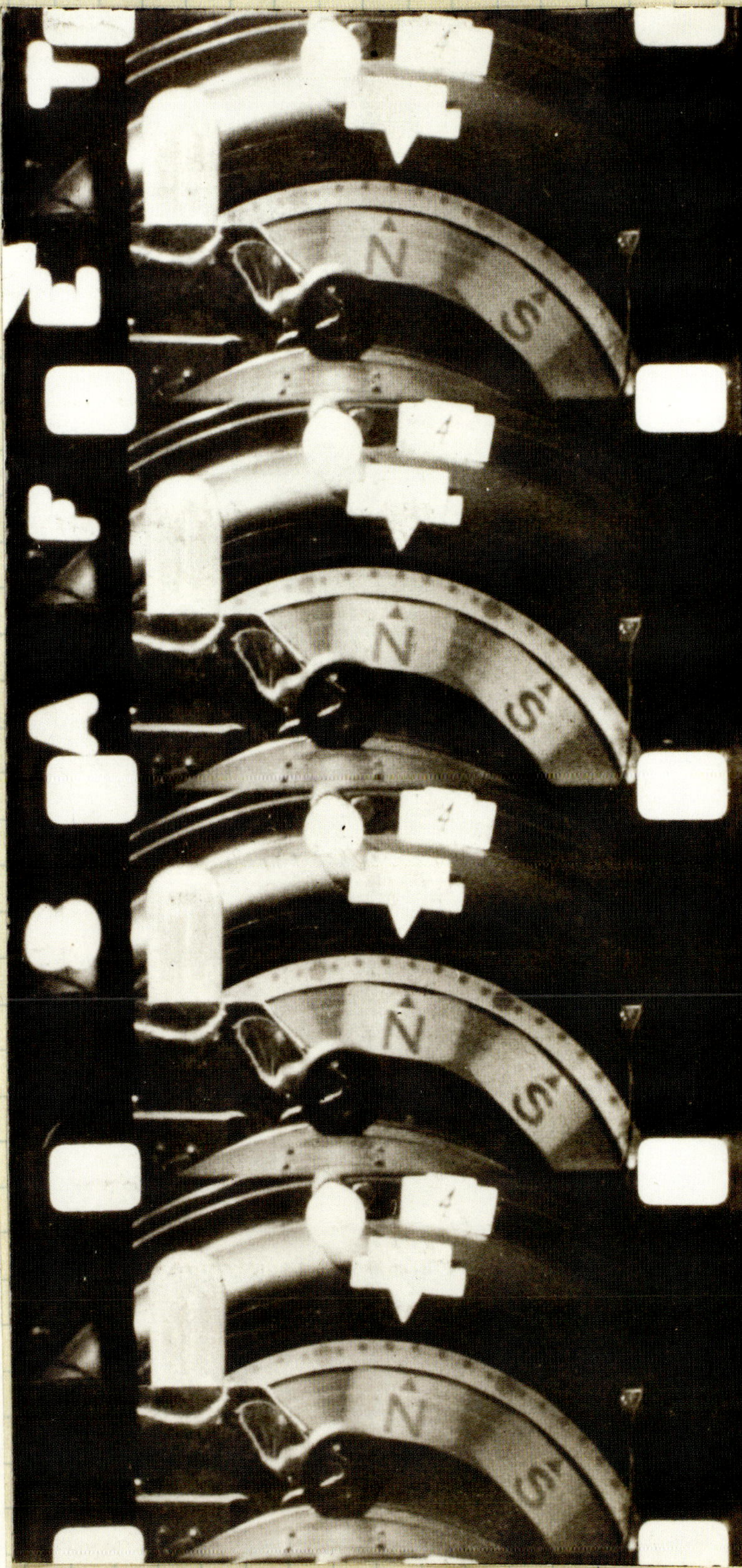

8× enlargement of 16 mm film that was showed in New York at the A.I.E.E. Convention on Jan 30 1931.

Jan. 20. 1932.
~~H. E. Edgerton~~

Last week, I went to see Mr. David Rines who is now working on a patent application for the stroboscope. I talked to him about an hour and a half and ~~sent~~ gave him my three note books to examine. He asked me to look up the prior ~~art.~~

On ~~Tuesday~~ Monday Jan. 18, Mr Hutchinson of the International Paper company was here and wanted a camera to take pictures at 200 a second with an exposure of 1/10,000 th of a second. This and more can be done. I told him we could make a camera go 400 frames a second with an exposure time of 1/10,000 th of a second. He is going to take it up with the New York office before going ahead on the job.

Today Germeshausen and I went over to the Russell Box company to see the strobo. We took out the strobo tube and replaced it with another which Germ made yesterday. At the same time we put in a new thyratron and a new UX280 rectifier. They seemed very pleased with the outfit out there and use it all the time.

At eleven we stopped in to ~~see~~ Mr. Horton of the G. R. Company to talk to him about the stroboscope, particularly about the Int. Paper company request. Mr. Sampson came in and is going to come over to get the circuit.

Sampson came over and we took some pictures with his new lens mount

Oct 5, 1932.

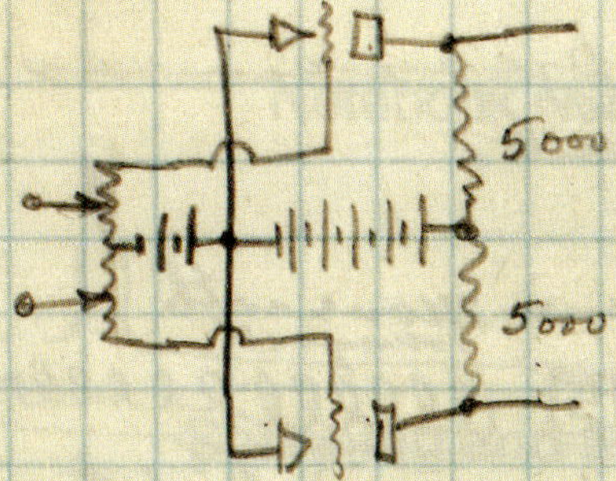

'10 type.   7.5v  1.25a

μ = 8.

425 volts.

−35  g

18 mils

1600 = mutual cond.

.018 × 5000 =      90,000 volts.

say use 10,000 Ω.

.018 × 10000 = 180 volts

180 + 425 =  $\dfrac{605}{35}$

+ 35 bias

          640 volts.

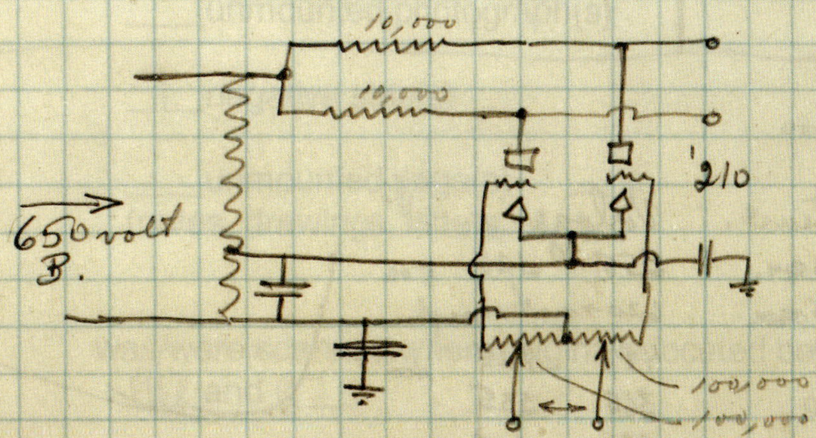

$\dfrac{2800}{42500}$ =

.018 m.s.

10,000

10,000

'210

650 volt
B.

100,000
100,000

10 steps or less.

35 × .6 × 8 = 144 volts.

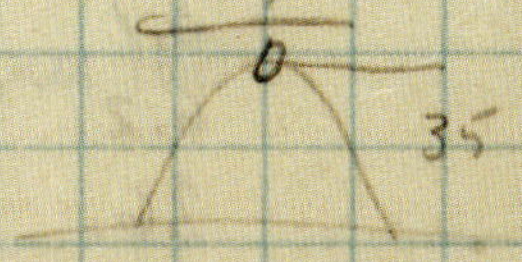

0          35

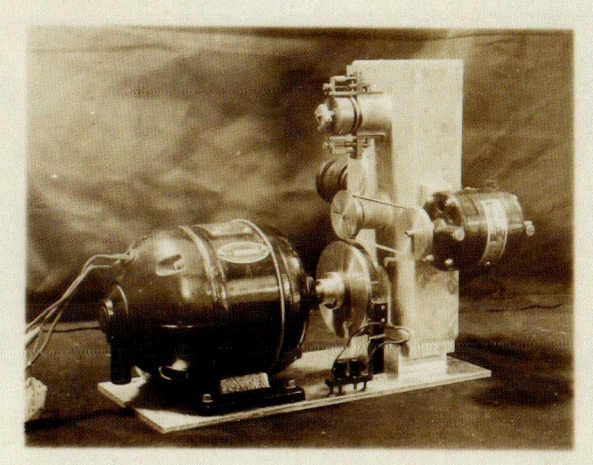

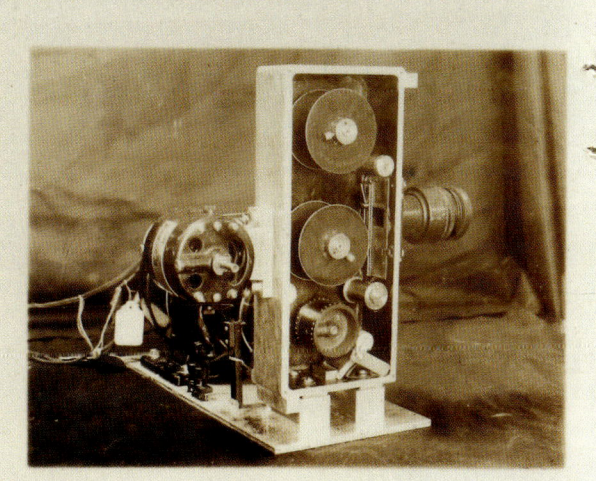

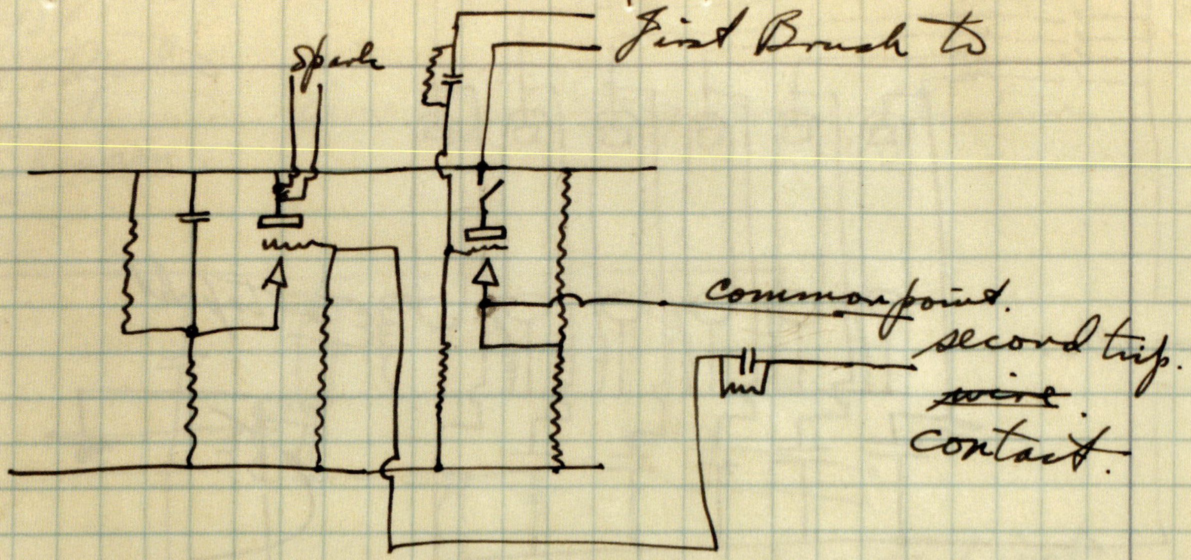

Spark

First Brush to

common point.

second trip.

~~wire~~.

contact.

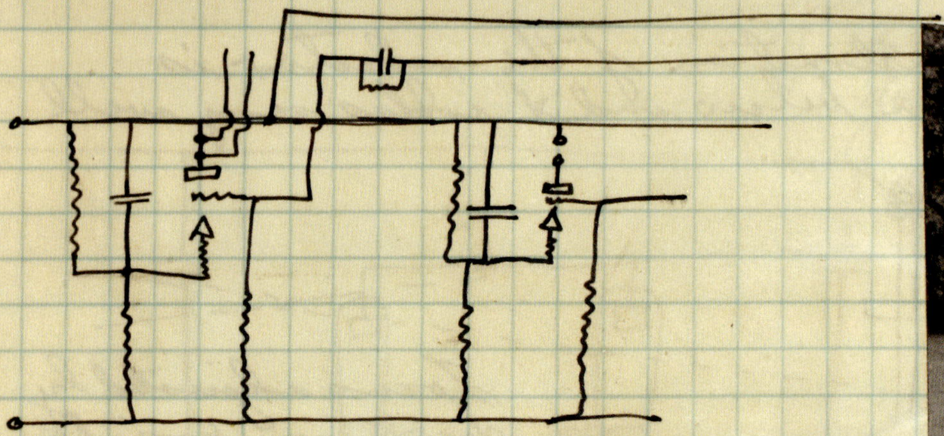

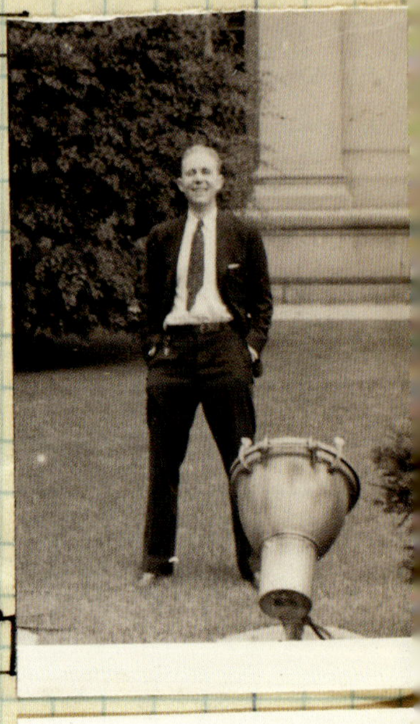

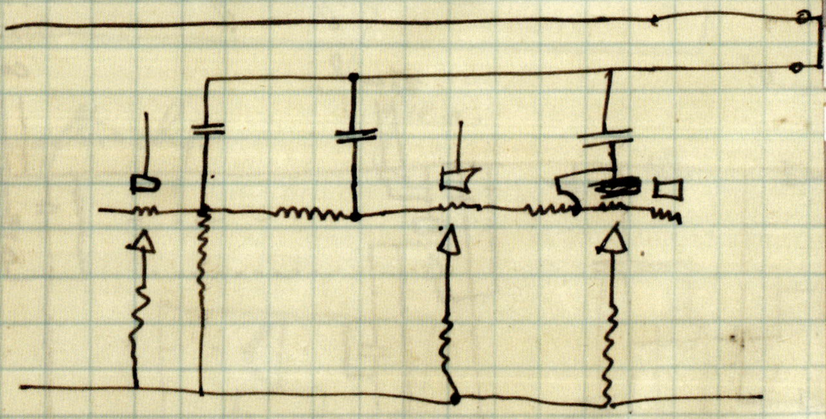

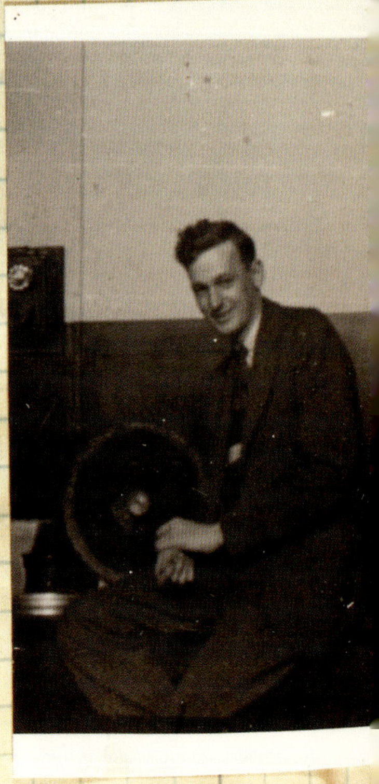

10-211 A: H.E. Brier with

tipe used for

time of flash

measurements.

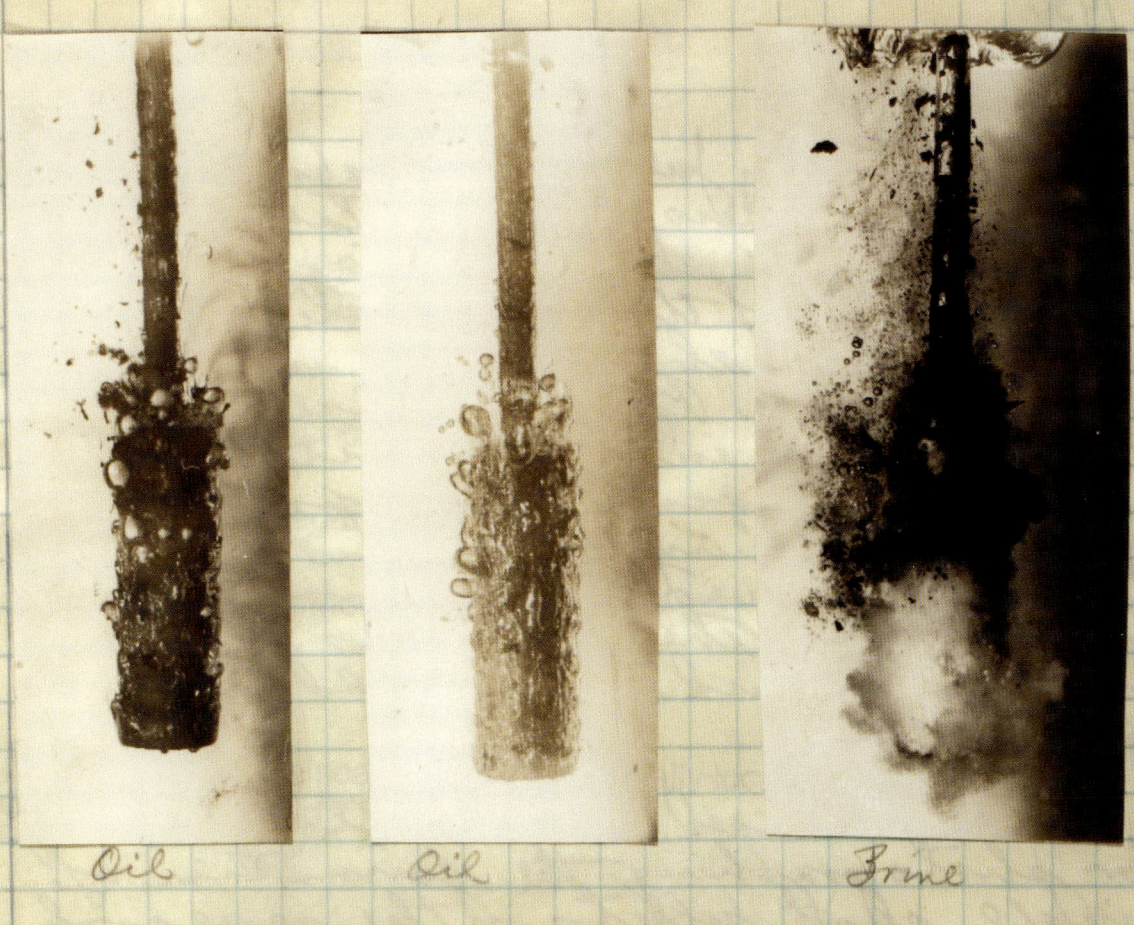

Oil          Oil          Brine

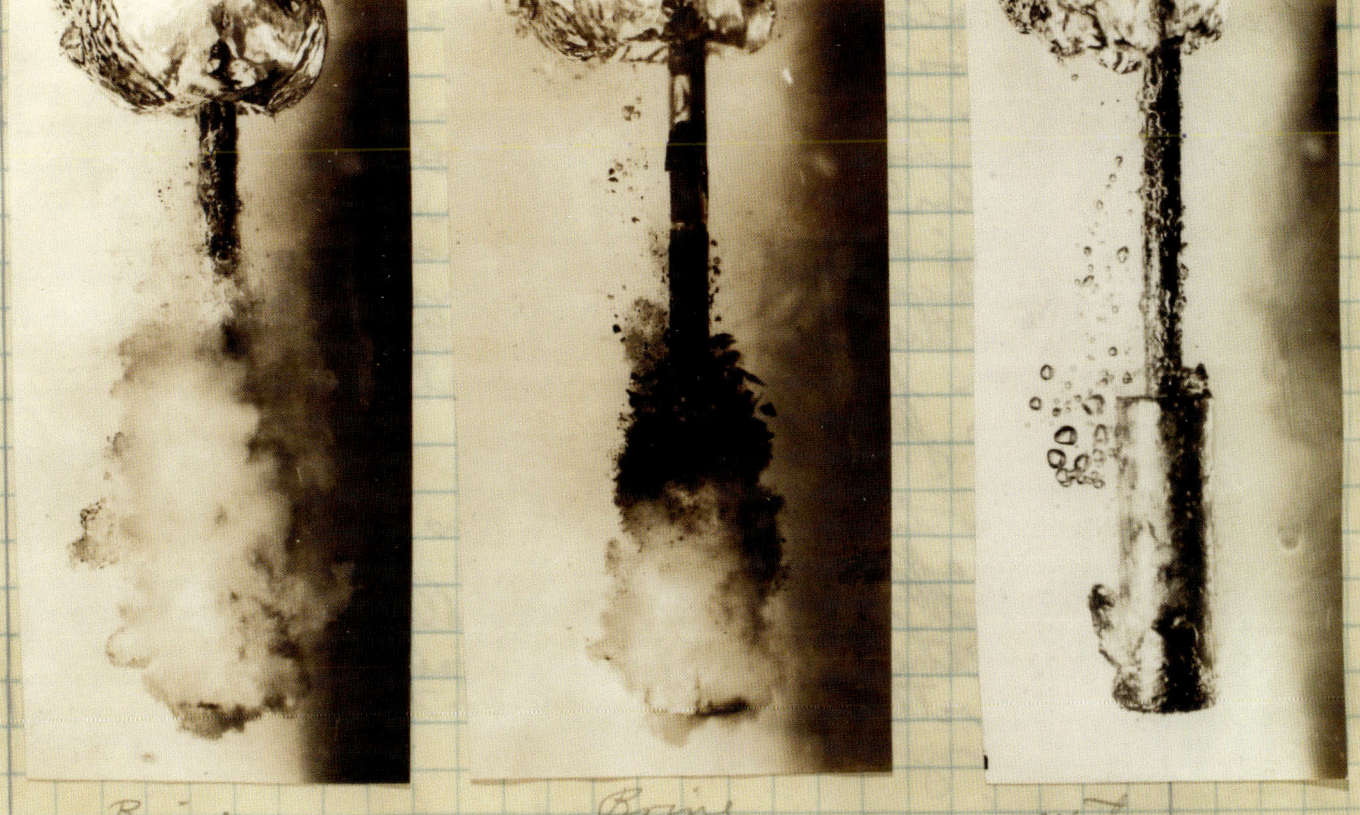

Brine          Brine          Water

Photographs showing Quenching.

July 13 1934
H. E. Edgerton

On Monday July 9 Germeshausen
and I went to New Haven to take spark
photographs of shot dropping in the
shot tower of the Winchester Co.
Left Cambridge about 7 am. and arrived
in Mr. Edwin Pugley's office at 11.
Met Mr. Foisy and Phil Smith with
whom we discussed the problem
of photographing lead as it dropped
from the tower in the process of
forming shot. There was no 110 volt
a.c. up there and so we could take no
pictures.

We discussed a laboratory set up
for photographing the formation of
single shot pellets in the research
laboratory where we could control
the variables better. As a result
of this conference we were to send
some pyrex tubing one ft long
with an inside diam. of 1½" from
Cambridge. Smith designed a
lead heater and a cup to fit on
top of the pyrex tube, the cup to
have a hole in the bottom for the
lead to flow from.

On Tues and Wednesday the
movie apparatus was put together
and tested in Cambridge for the
trip. The old 3 kw apparatus was
used with either one or two 12" Hg
mercury tubes.

Thursday we left my home in Watertown
at 5:30 with the apparatus which we
had packed in the car the night before. At
10 we were in New Haven and had started
our set up in the room just south of Mr.

Proposed design of
a camera with
film on the inside
of the wheel.

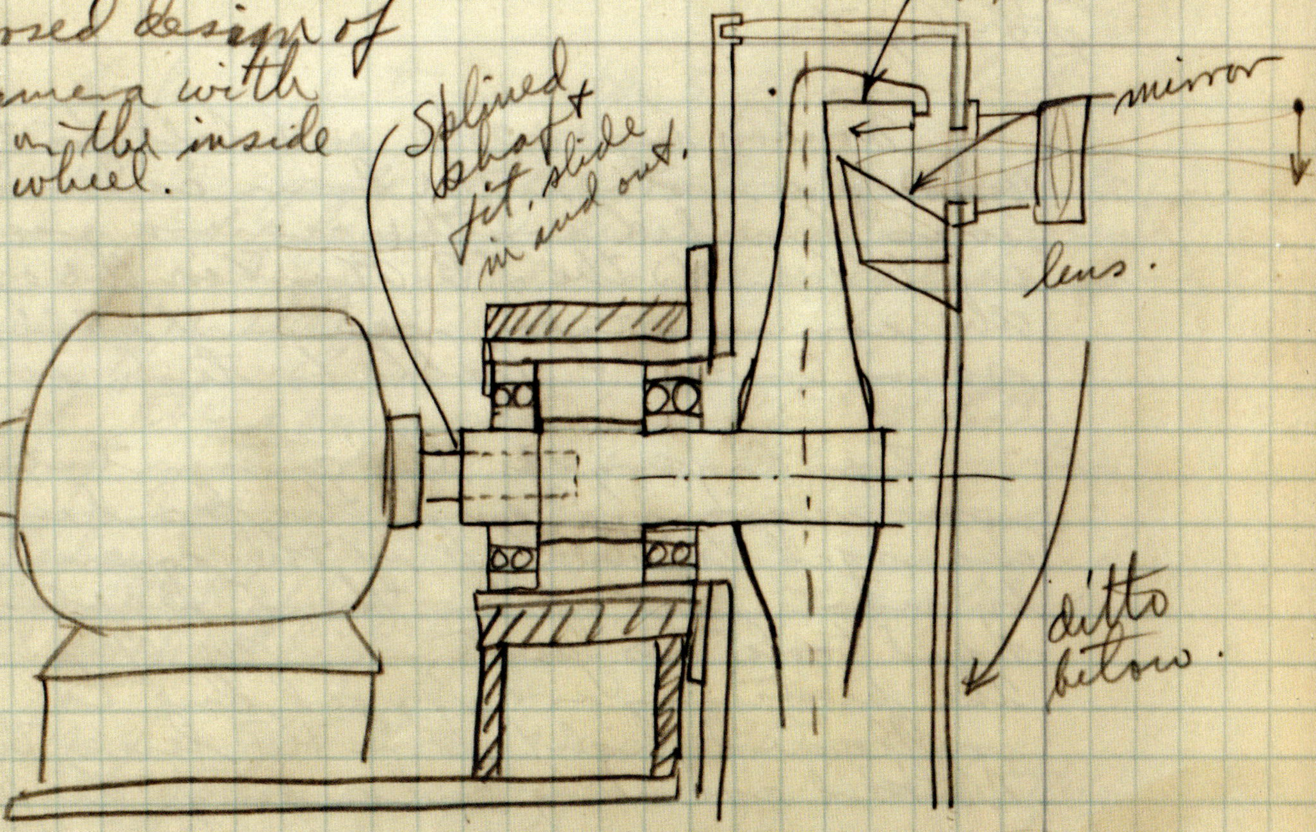

Splined shaft fit, slide in and out.

film bent

mirror

lens.

ditto below.

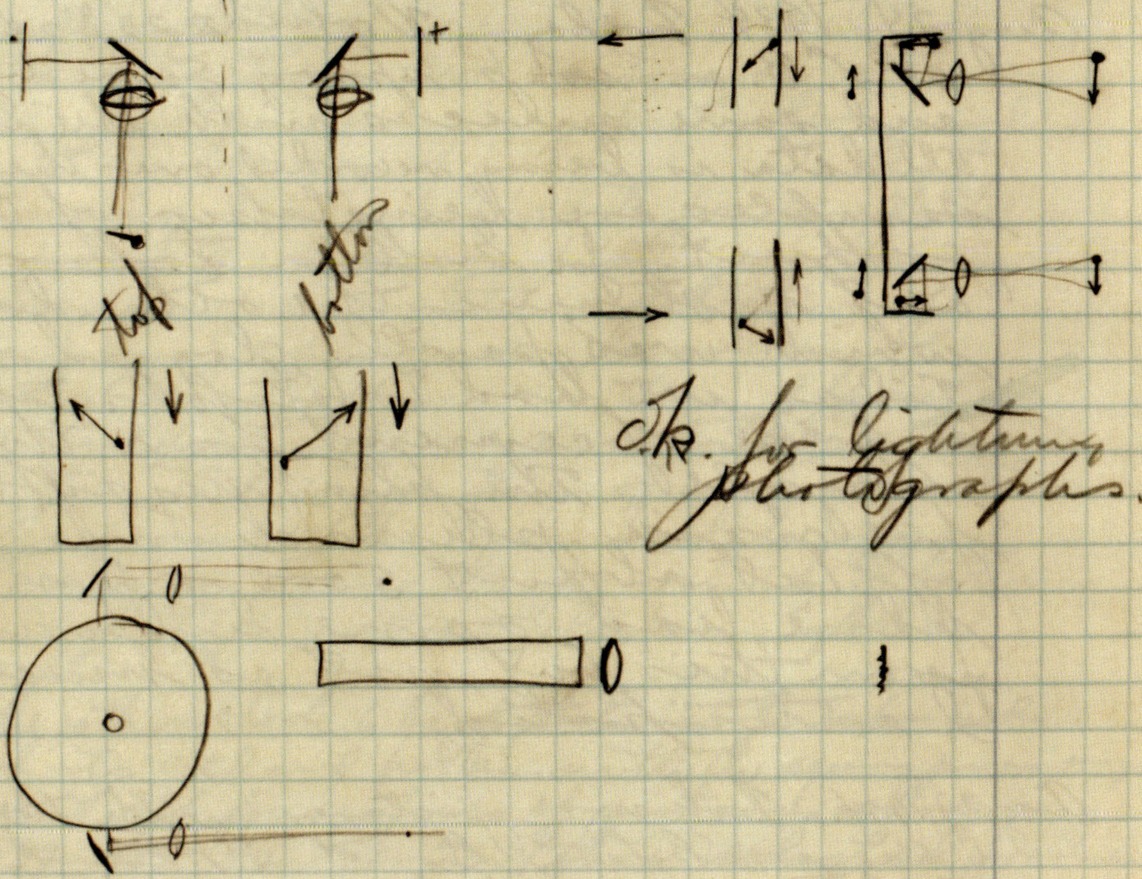

top

bottom

Ok. for lightning photographs.

Feb. 14, 1932.
H. E. Edgerton

The strobo lab. in 10-088 has been cleaned up for a demonstration tomorrow.

Mr. Hutchins of the Int. Paper Co. was here Friday and we showed him the pictures we had taken during the first of the week. We plan to go to his plant at Livermore falls Maine next weekend with the 480 cycle frame per second camera.

Germeshausen tried a max. energy developer which gave us fine pictures.

The super-sensitive panchromatic film gives no more denser picture than the standard negative film. We also tried positive but there was a 2:1 ratio between it and the negative.

Today Germ. and I took some 480 f.p.s. movies of milk drops splashing on a surface. We took a 20 ft film which we hope to project.

March 3 1932

H.E. Edgerton

A Photograph taken
by Germeshausen
in the Otis plant of
the Int Paper Co at
Livermore Falls, Maine,
during our trip there
a week or so ago.

The mercury tubes
are in the black box
just above the web.
The camera is above.
It is driven by a
synchronous motor.

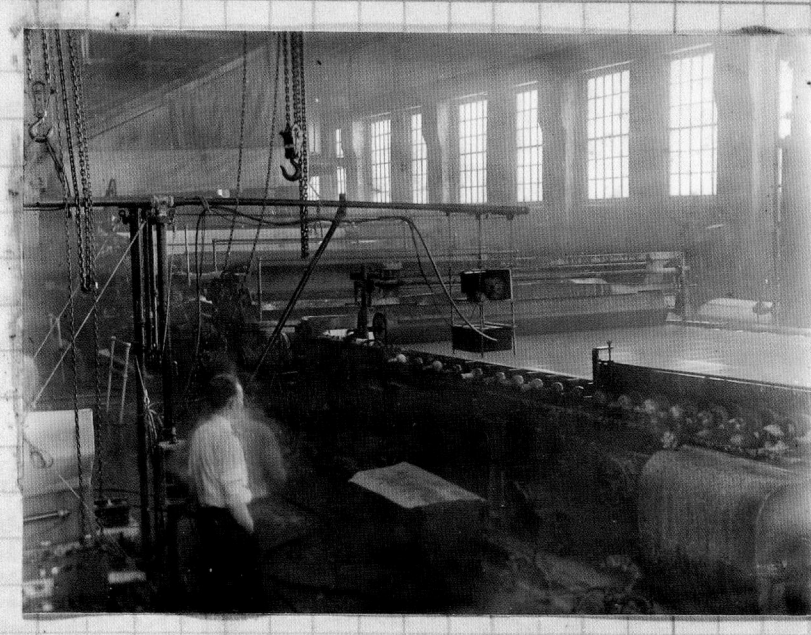

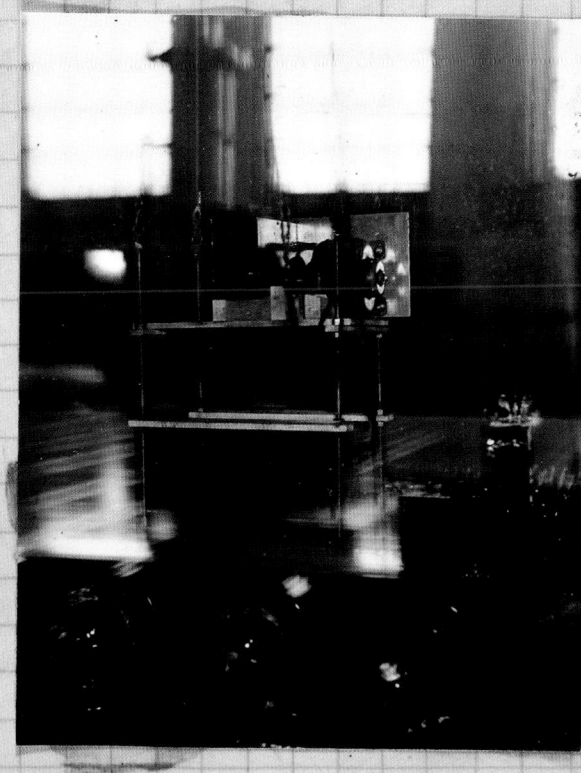

A close up of the camera,
motor and lamp house.
They are suspended
above the wire which
was travelling at a
rate of 826 ft a minute.

Germ and I saw
Lawson yesterday at G.R.
about the camera. It
is about finished.
He wants us to show
them the circuit that
we are using for
the final I.P. Co job.

which is to be used at the "2" street station of
the Boston Edison company.

Multiple unit stroboscope,
Spark may be obtained from one
spark coil or several.

The d.c. for the spark can be
obtained from the regular power
supply or from any other
source of d.c.

trip, osc, photocell commutator
or any d.c. voltage.

Spark apparatus for high frequency or
high intensity :

Spark gap.

air jet.

cylindrical mirror

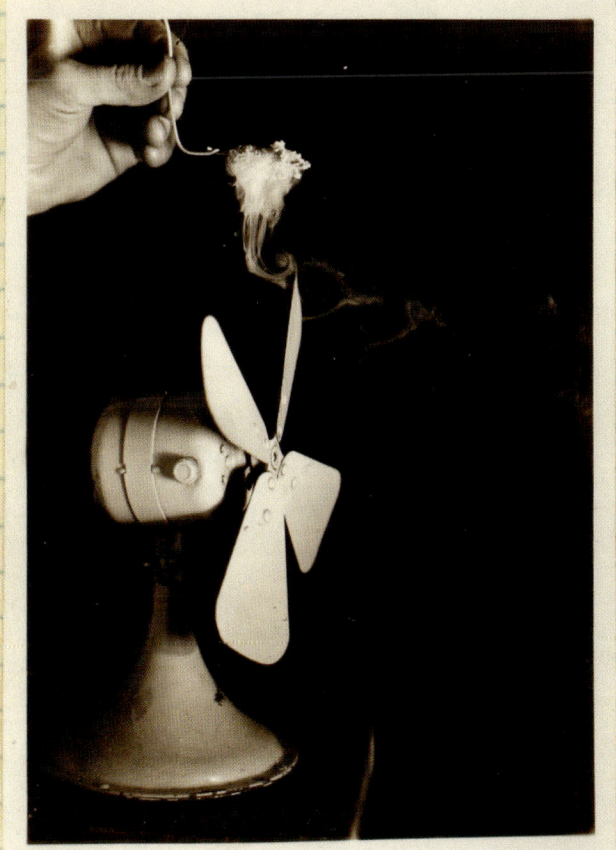
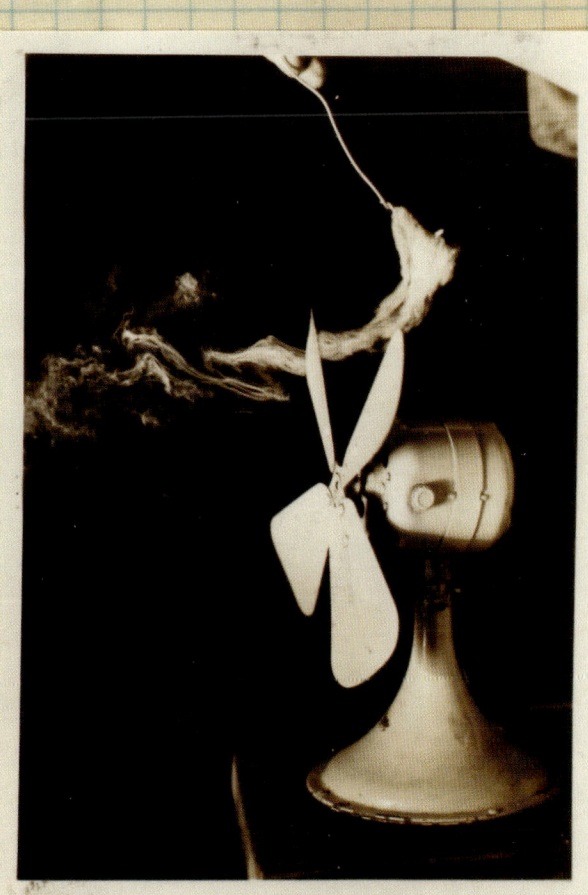

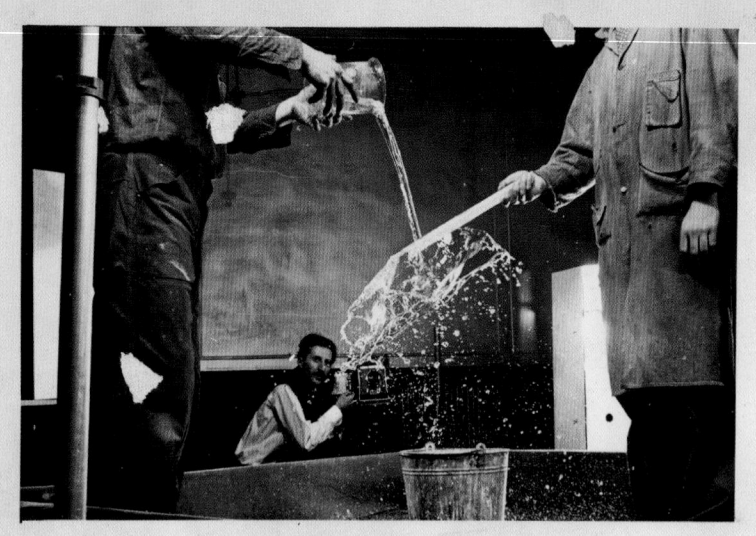

Gijon
Mili
Pete and Steve.
N.Y.

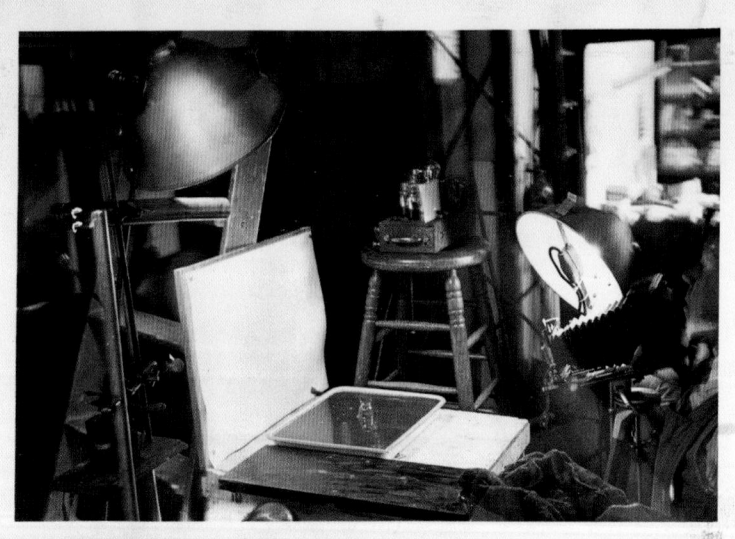

James
Laws

Soil
Cons.
dept.

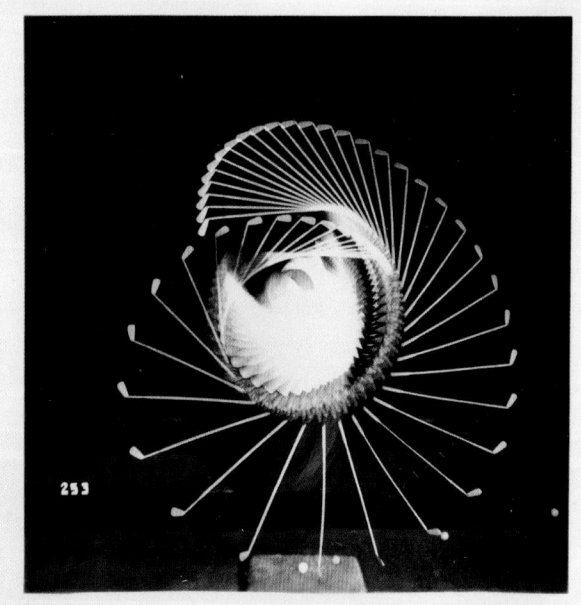

Jimmy Thomson
May 10 1939
100/sec.

Jimmy
Thomson
100/sec

Taken May 10 '39.

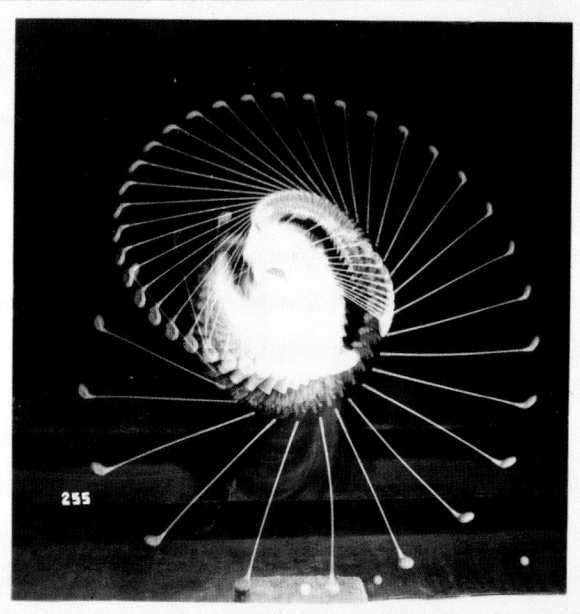

255

May 25? 1939

   Mr. Undersee of G.E. Co (textile dept)
was here today and took a new tube for
the flash lamp. He is going to use it today
at Taunton in a textile plant to
study the work of ~~a three~~ the threads.

| | Monday | Tuesday | Wednesday | Thursday | EDGERTON. Friday | Saturday | |
|---|---|---|---|---|---|---|---|
| 9-10 | | | | | 600 4-132 | | Subj. No. Room |
| 10-11 | 600 4-132 | | 600 4-132 | | ↓ | | Subj. No. Room |
| 11-12 | C Stanned | 6.632 4-290 | SILVEY C | 6.632 2-230 | | | Subj. No. Room |
| 12-1 | | | | | | | Subj. No. Room |
| 1-2 | 601 C | | | | | | Subj. No. Room |
| 2-3 | | | | | | | Subj. No. Room |
| 3-4 | Hopgood C | | | | | | Subj. No. Room |
| 4-5 | | | | | | | Subj. No. Room |

MASSACHUSETTS INSTITUTE OF TECHNOLOGY
SCHEDULE CARD—FOR STUDENT'S USE

4-37 55M AB     STUDENT KEEPS THIS CARD

May 27. 1939.

   Arrangement with
Eastman Kodak
complete today.

   Grier spent
yesterday in New York
with lamps for
Eastman in Worlds
Fair exhibit. A pane of
glass is broken for visitors.
Two lights flash.

Dec. 17, 1931.
H. E. Edgerton.

Saw C. S. Grover yesterday concerning search for stroboscope patents (using gaseous discharge lamps). and told him of my circuits and uses of the tube.

I called Lam#son of the General Radio Company yesterday and he plans to come over to tea today with his continuous speed film camera. We are going to try to get some photographs of the oscillations of a synchronous motor.

Sonneshausen is working on the circuit for the Engine Lab. This is the arrangement for obtaining indicator diagrams, using the thyratron.

Dec. 18, 1931. Lamson of G.R. Co came over yesterday aft and we took some movies on continuously moving film. Some of the pictures are attached to this sheet. The lens was rated f 2.9 and the picture was taken right on Bromide recording paper. The field of vision was rather small. The photograph was of a 12" disc on a 1200 r.p.m. synchronous motor. the lines are 5 electrical degrees apart and on the disc. the pointer is stationary. 6 to 8 muf were used in the discharge circuit (same as blue print pasted to page 45.) This was too much energy to put into the tube continuously as it would get too hot. The tube was one we made last tuesday.

Worked Friday evening with Germ, Stark Draper, and others to get Draper's camera to work Not enough amps. Finished Engine lab indicator and tested it in the aft. Looked at Spray from a diesel jet with Eddie Taylor.

Nov. 11, 1931.

H.E. Edgerton

"The Rotating Sectored Disc"   B.W. Bartlett.
Bowdoin College, Brunswick, Maine.
The Review of Scientific Instruments. Vol 2. new Series No 2.
page 96.
(Linckh and Vieweg Zt. f. Instrumentenkunde,
46, 30; 1926, Linckh and Vieweg; Archiv f.
Elektrotechnik, 15, 509; 1926.)

Bartlett expresses the reflecting power as a
function of the angle in a Fourier series. This is
multiplied by the intensity (expressed as a
Fourier series in time) to get the resulting
effect to the eye. A very interesting article.

For the determination of speed of a rotating
disc from a 60 cycle source I believe the
following method is useful. This is described
on page 35 and 36 to some extent.

60 cycle light.

A distinguishing mark can be put upon one
sector and this can be made to show
if the disc is at synchronous speed or
some fraction of multiple. Numbers also on the discs.

| $n=$ | 1 | 2 | 3 | 4 | 5 | 6 | 7 | 8 | 9 | 10 | 11 | 12 | 13 | 14 | 15 | 16 | 17 | 18 |
|---|---|---|---|---|---|---|---|---|---|---|---|---|---|---|---|---|---|---|
| first syn. speed | 3600 | 1800 | 1200 | 900 | 720 | 600 | 514.2 | 450 | 400 | 360 | 327.2 | 300 | 276.9 | 257.1 | 240. | | | |

Abstract in "The Review of Sci Instruments" Vol 2 new Series No 2. p143
A Stroboscopic Frequency Meter. L. B. Arguimbau
Gen. Rad. Exper. 5, 5-7, Nov. 1930.
Technical Practice in Light Production in the Light of modern atomic theory

Nov. 12, 1931.

The spark which starts the
mercury arc might be more effective
if connected as shown below.

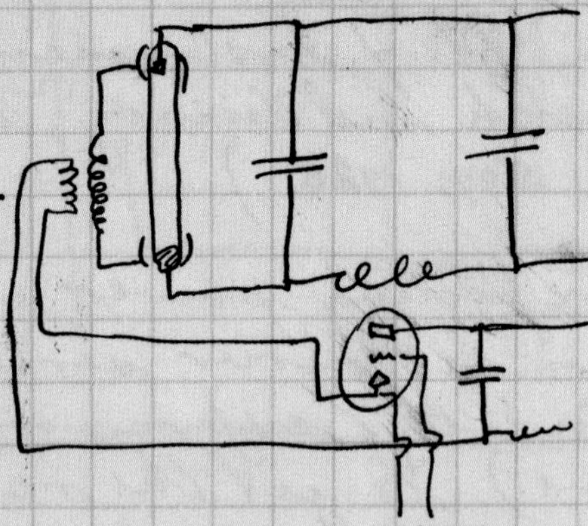

High
ratio
transformer

↑ trip.

"Der Strobograph" eine Vorrichtung zum Aufzeichnen
von Pendeldiagrammen.        G. Wagner (Wagner)
— Regierungsbaumeister in Wiesbaden. —
Zeitschrift des Vereines deutscher Ingenieure.
Vol 50  December 1906  page 1984.

Shows scheme with ~~an arc lamp for~~ a
method of obtaining pictures of the angular
displacement.

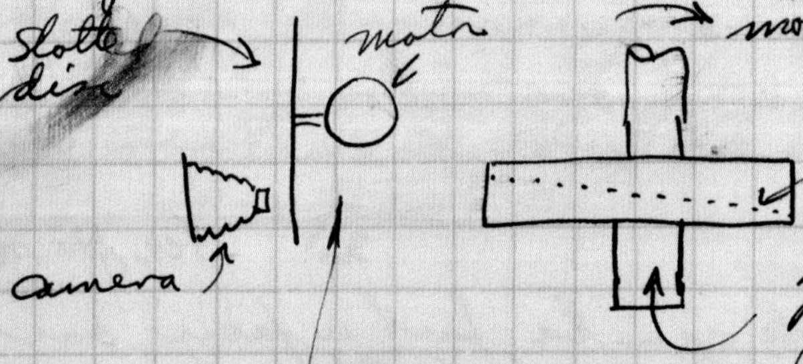

Slotted
disc

motor

motor, generator etc.

camera

holes to let out light from
the flash light powder.

Full of flash light
powder.

Run motor so that there is a slight
difference in speed between the drum
and the disc. Open camera and
touch off the powder.

J.B. McClure

Photographs taken
May 19, 1931.

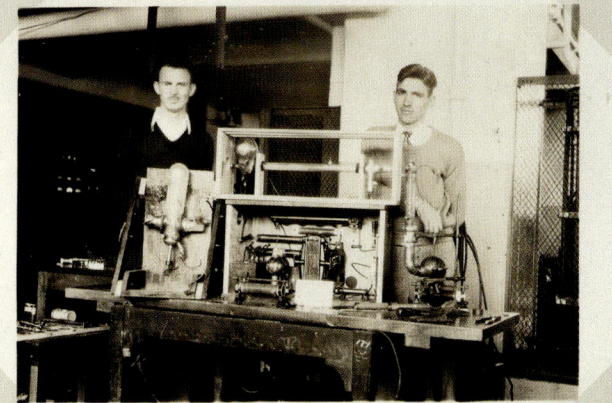

Lawrence
M. Stande

Stroboscope equipment

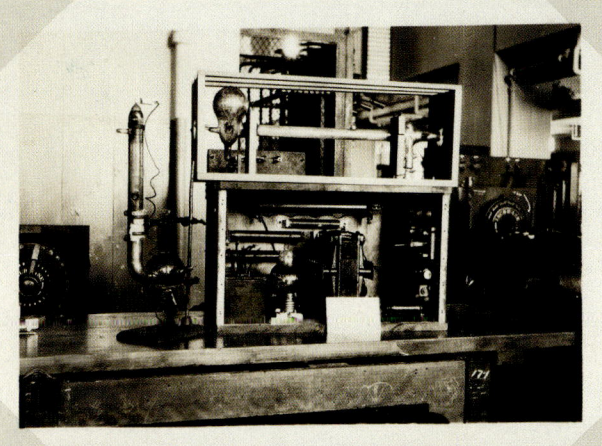

Machine transients
Laboratory.

Spring 1931.

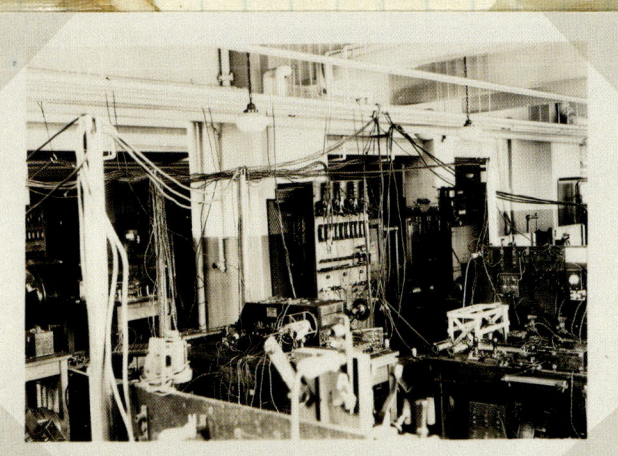

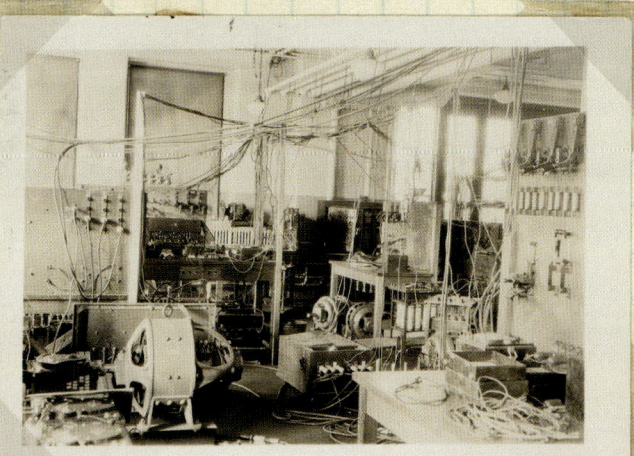

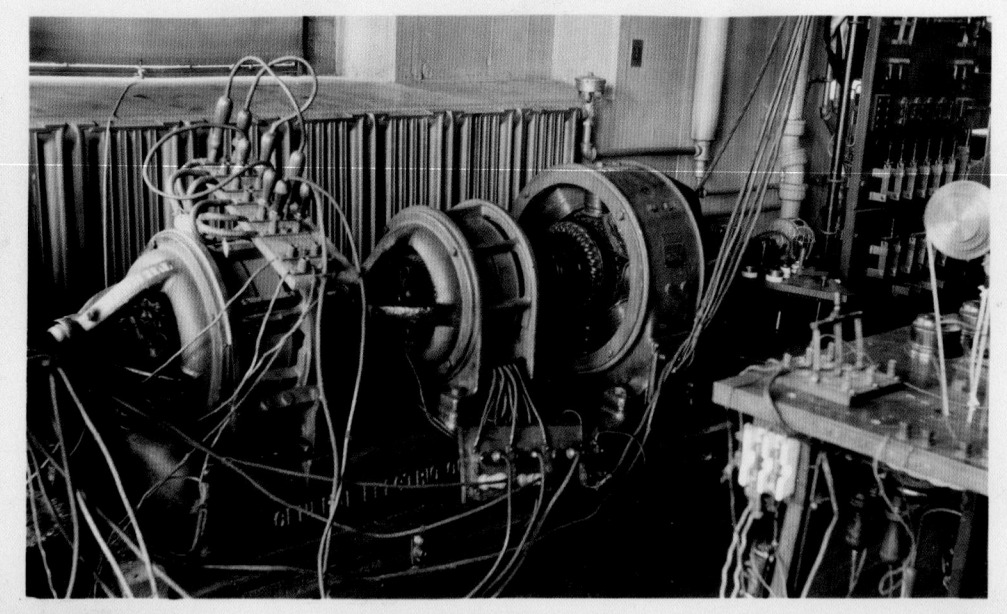

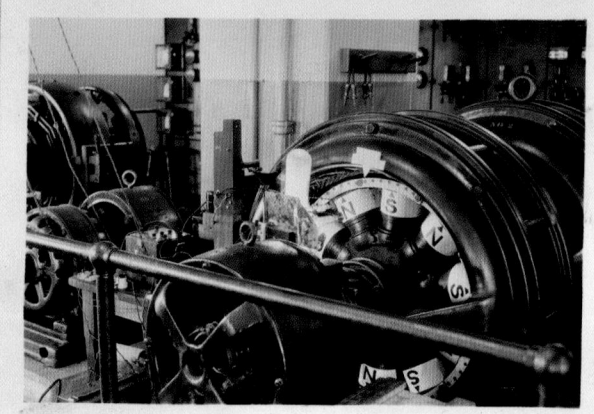

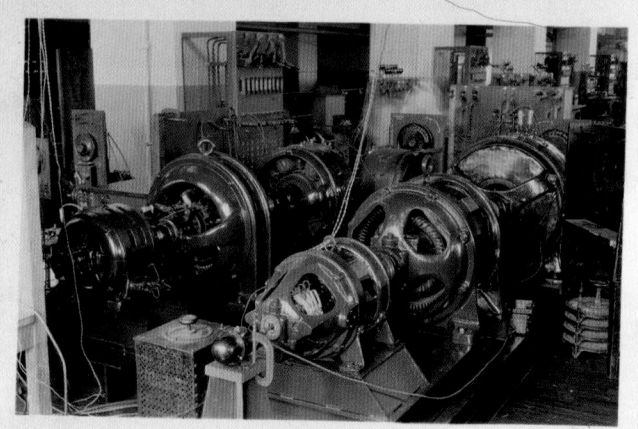

thyratron and motor.

AC & DC Machines at M.I.T.

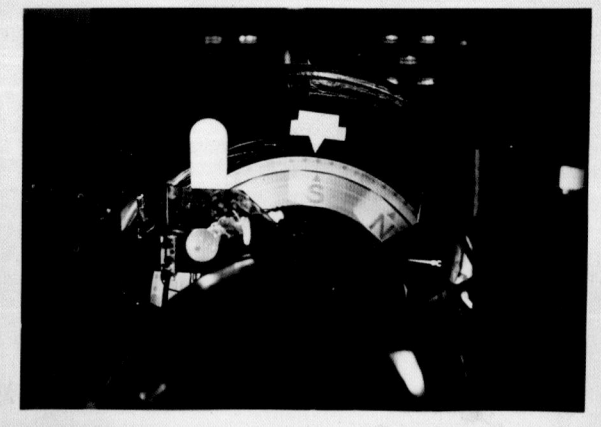

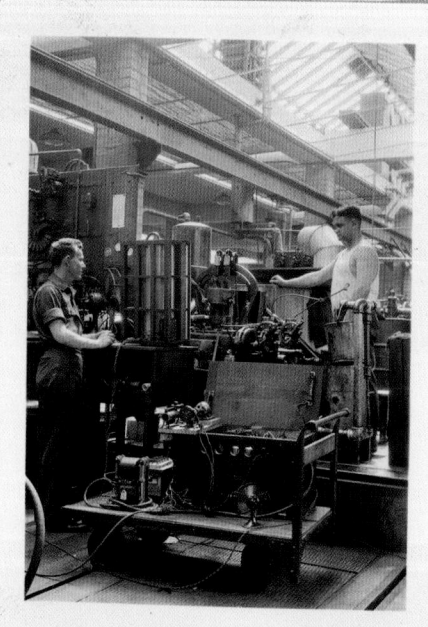

Stroboscope and
synchronous motor.
first setup.

Draper.

Stroboscope

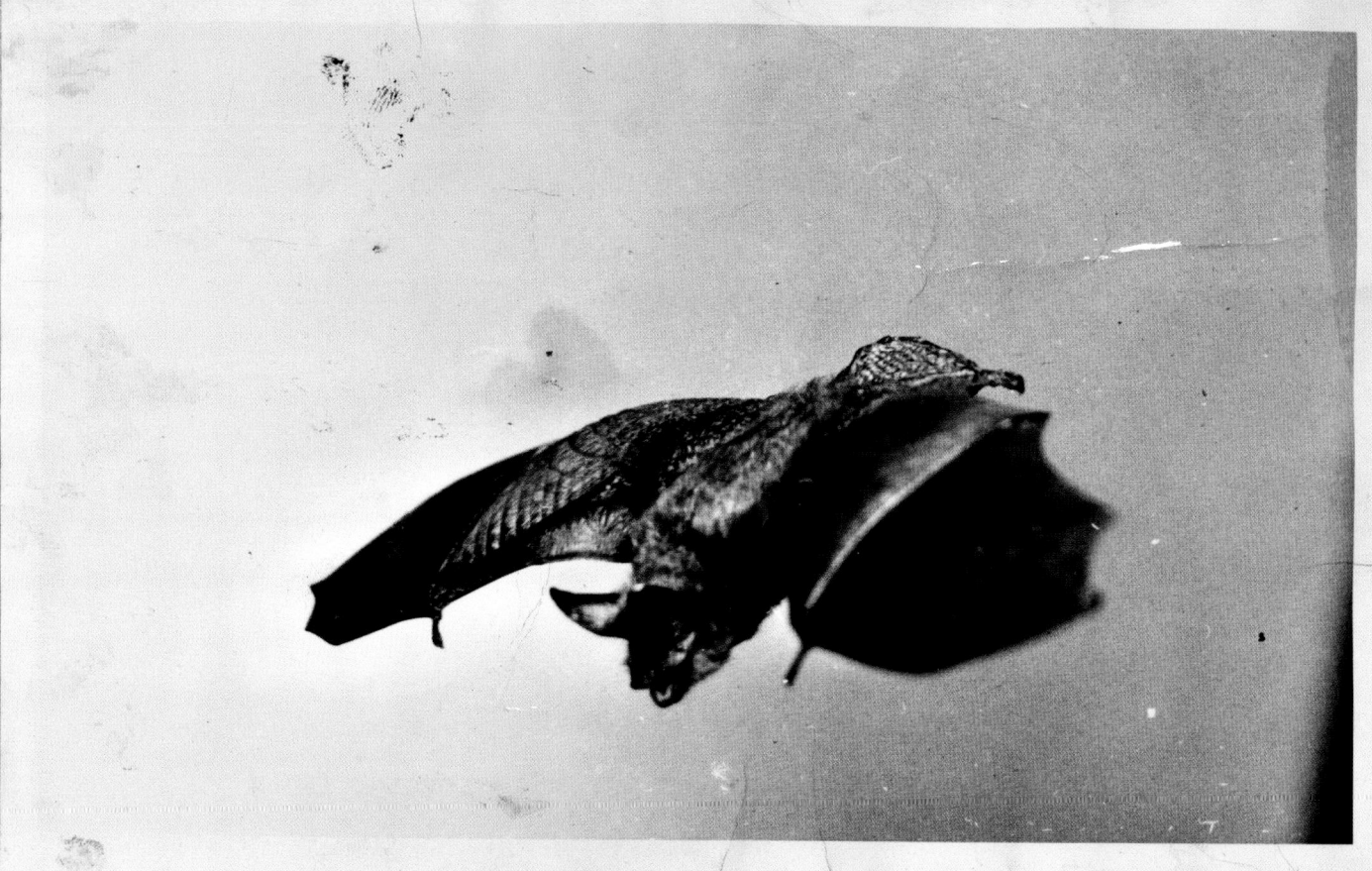

fast photo of a bat in flight.
Supplied by Griffin of Harvard.     f 8

Cont March 14. 1937.

On last Friday I put a mercury tube
on the excitation from a spark coil in the plate
circuit of one of the strobotrons and let it
run on life test since. the Hg tube was of
the following shape.

20 ohms.
R
110 volt ac.

6" ±      Hg

250 V ±   2mf.   Strobotron

Capable of 1/2 or 5/8" spark

$$\frac{200 \text{ volts}}{30} = 7 \text{ amps.}$$

On March 29 1938 Mili was here and we discussed
additional capacity for his speed light unit.

Suggested value 24 condensers 440 ac 28 mf.
2 additional outlets & plugs.
Unit to fit under cabinet.

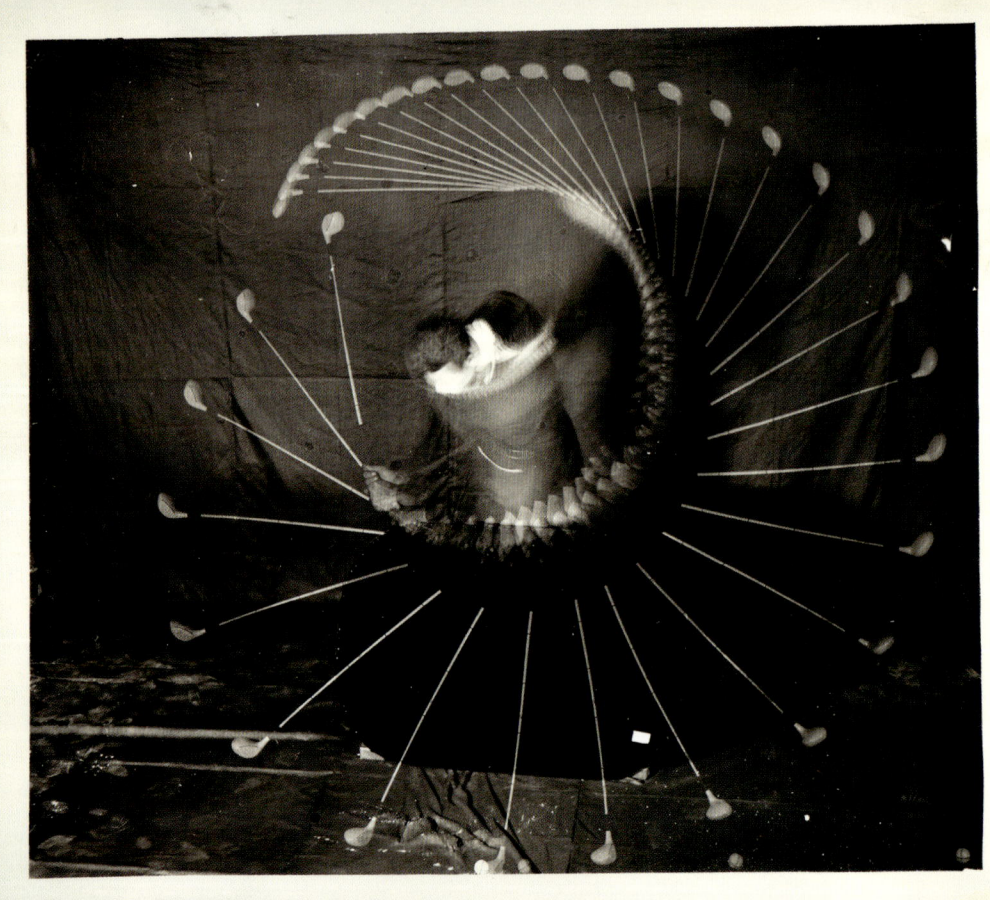

H. E. Edgerton.
March 29, 1938.

Pictures taken last night with Brotzman
of A.F.& Hoe Co. Elmer Reed hit the ball for us.
5×7 camera f 6.3    Agfa Pan Press.
            5 min dev. in std. devel recommended.
two lights were used.
        4 mf  2200 volts.    large U tube  12" long. total.
            800 ohms.                    5/8" diam.

    100 cycles. a second.

    lights about 6 to 8 ft. from subject.

    about 20 pictures were taken last night.

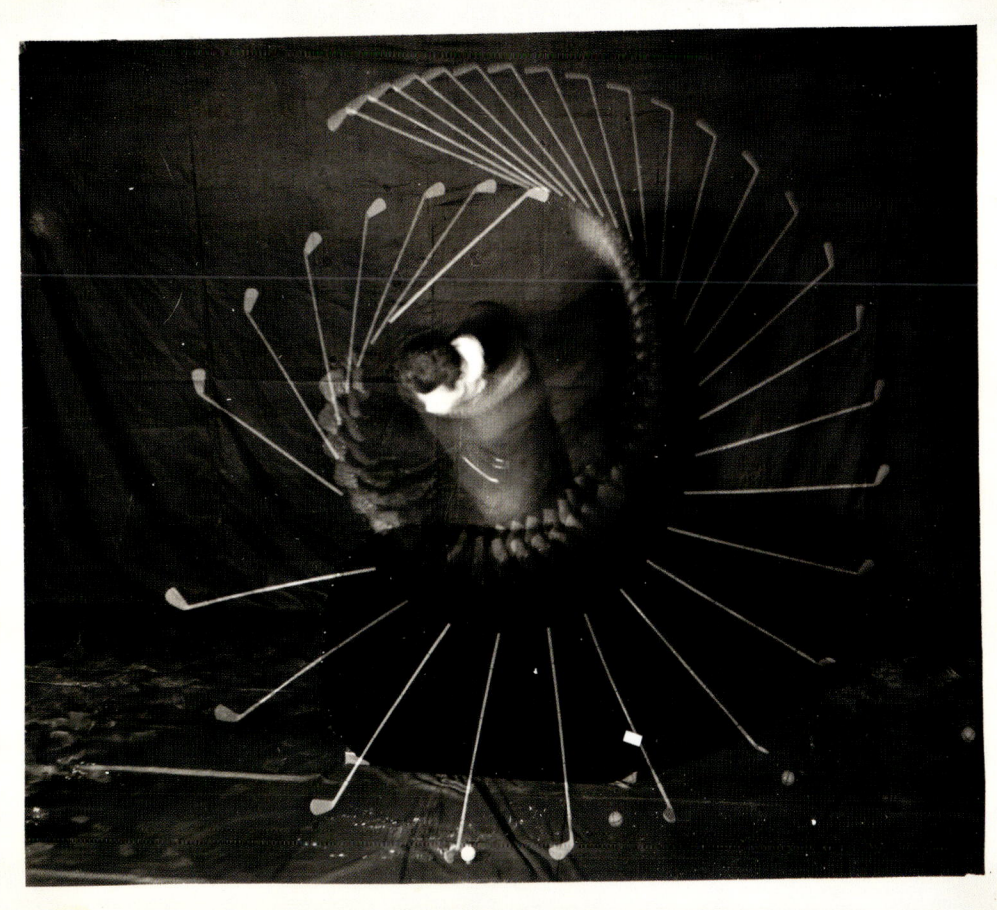

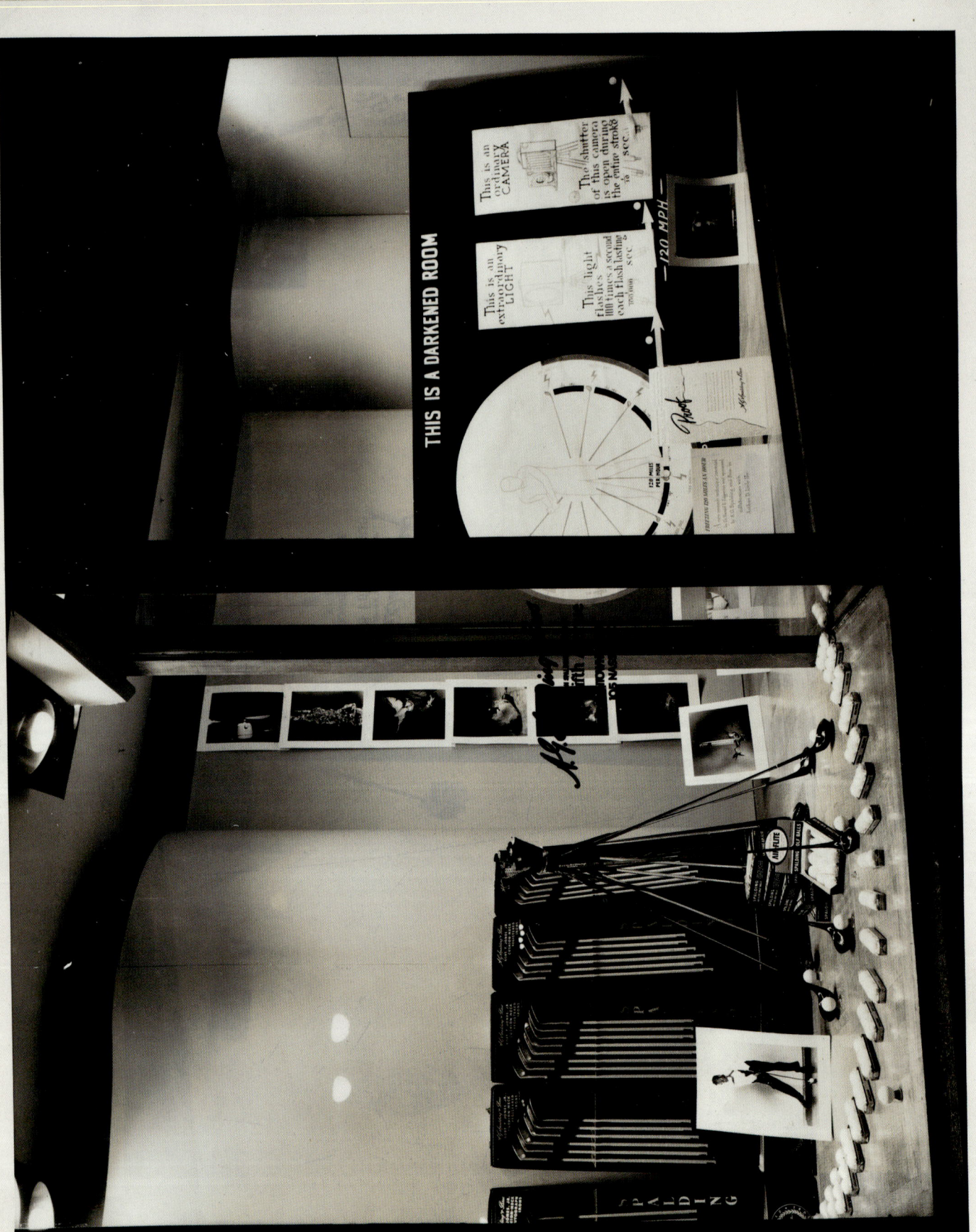

South window of A. G. Spalding & Bros. Fifth Avenue Store, designed and executed under the direction of Miss Eleanor Treacy and Mr. W. B. Okie, using the Spalding Research Department as the theme, placed January 5, 1939.

found that the coupling condenser between
the first and second stage was open
circuited. This is $C_1$ on page 7. on first
tube. The back coupling capacity was
removed as I do not believe it to be
needed.

June 20 36. Continued experiments with
Reflected light photos of 22 long rifle bullets.

1. One shot taken with Sept. camera f 3.5.
0.05 uf capacity 8000 volts ?±

   Focus bad. about 3:1 reduction on film.

2. Repeat. above but with better lineups.

3. Changed capacity to 1.5 uf. 8000 volts.
   Changed to 16 x 9 cm 9 x 12 cm camera.
   Photos at f 5.6 on
   Wood penetrated by bullet

4. Same with less magnification
   Rubber strip to be penetrated by bullet.

Mary Lou

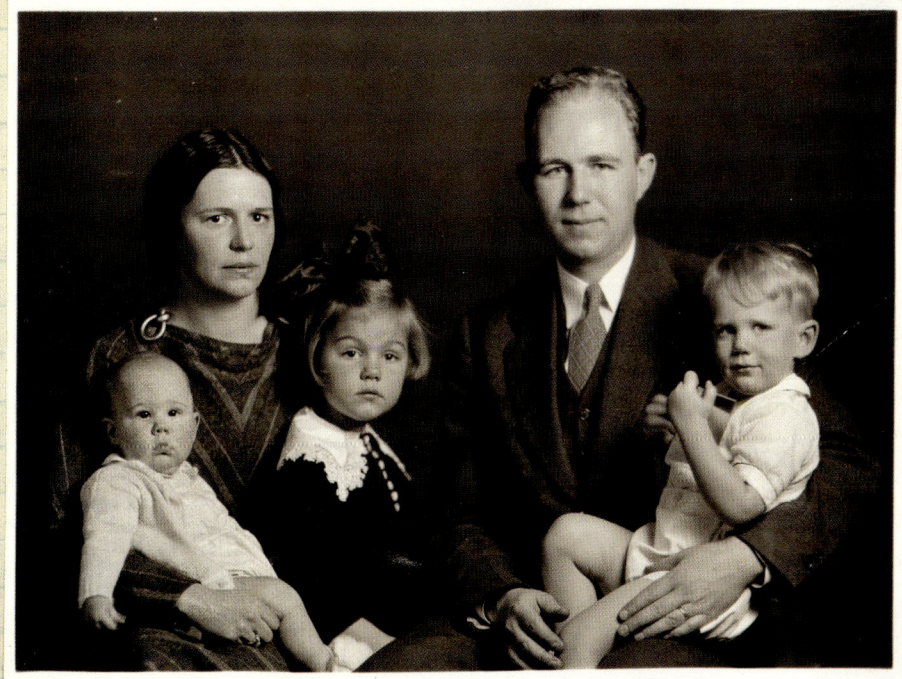

Robert                    Bill

# PAGES FROM EDGERTON'S NOTEBOOKS

Edgerton's Laboratory notebooks are a fascinating record of his professional life, documenting experiments, inventions and projects, but so much more. A careful search revealed many pages that provide details related to the images included in this volume. The editors gratefully acknowledge the Institute Archives and Special Collections of the MIT Libraries for permission to reprint these pages. The originals may be found in the Harold E. Edgerton Papers, MC-0025, Box 50. The captions below identify the specific notebook, pages and entry dates.

**p. 172**   Contact prints from high-speed film that captured the first sequence of a milk drop and the blink of an eye. Notebook Number 2, May 16, 1932, p. 68.

**p. 173**   Patent statement documenting the operation of Edgerton's first mercury vapor stroboscope. Notebook Number T-I, May 16, 1929, p. 34.

**p. 174**   Piece of original film from a milk drop experiment. Edgerton and Kenneth Germeshausen used a high-speed motion picture camera that could shoot 250 frames per second to capture the drops as they struck the surface. Notebook Number T-3, January 31, 1932, p. 14.

**p. 175**   Design for electronic circuit witnessed by Charles Kingsley on May 28, 1929 for patent purposes. Notebook Number T-I, May 1929, p. 36.

**p. 176**   The images show Edgerton's lab setup for capturing golf swings. Notebook Number T-3, April 10, 1933, p. 123.

**p. 177**   Contact print from the 20 feet of high-speed film that Edgerton took at 480 frames per second of a milk drop. Edgerton noted: "very good results." Notebook Number G-2, February 14, 1932, p. 21.

**pp. 178–79**   Description of some of Edgerton's earliest high-speed movie setups. Notebook Number S-3, June 16, 1931, pp. 112–13.

**p. 180**   In the winter of 1931, Edgerton was conducting many experiments using stroboscopes to capture synchronous motors in motion. This documentary photograph was taken by the MIT News Service. Notebook Number T-I, February 5–6, 1931, p. 82.

**p. 181**   Contact print and enlargement of a film Edgerton showed at the winter meeting of the American Institute of Electrical Engineers in January 1931. Notebook Number T-I, February 7, 1931, p. 85.

**p. 182**   Edgerton discusses his patent application for the stroboscope. Notebook Number T-3, January 20, 1932, p. 2.

**p. 183**   The photographs show two views of Edgerton's early high-speed movie camera. Notebook Number T-3, October 5, 1932, p. 95.

**p. 184**   Two portraits. Upper portrait is of Edgerton in front of MIT and below is Herbert Grier, Edgerton's student and subsequent business partner. Notebook Number T-4, June 15, 1934, p. 120.

**p. 185**   Photographs showing quenching in different solutions. Notebook Number T-4, July 2, 1934, p. 129.

**p. 186**   Describes the challenges of photographing molten shot. Notebook Number T-4, July 13, 1934, p. 130.

**p. 187**   Sketch of a proposed high-speed camera modification. Notebook Number T-4, August 19, 1934, p. 139.

**p. 188**   Discusses plans to visit the International Paper Company's plant as well as making high-speed movies at 480 frames per second of milk drop splashes. Notebook Number T-3, February 14, 1932, p. 20.

**p. 189**   Description of trip to Otis Plant of International Paper Company. Notebook Number T-3, March 3, 1932, p. 27.

**p. 190**   Description and sketch of multiple unit stroboscope. Notebook Number T-3, January 20, 1932, p. 3.

**p. 191**   Spark photographs of smoke going through a fan. Notebook Number T-4, May 27, 1934, p. 109.

**pp. 192–93**   Three pictures on the left were taken in May 1939. At top is Edgerton's portrait of his student and photographic collaborator Gjon Mili. Notebook Number 9, May 22, 1939, pp. 150–51.

**p. 194**   Details and clip of high-speed motion picture film taken of a synchronous motor. Notebook Number T-2, December 17, 1931, p. 100.

**p. 195**   Summary of an article by B.W. Bartlett on rotating sectored discs published in *The Review of Scientific Instruments.* Notebook Number T-2, November 11, 1931, p. 81.

**p. 196**   Notes from a 1906 German article on stroboscopes suggesting new techniques. Notebook Number T-2, November 12, 1931, p. 82.

**p. 197**   Photographs of equipment and laboratory. Notebook Number 3, May 19, 1931, p. 105.

**p. 198**   On Saturday, January 14, 1939, Edgerton cleaned up his laboratory. In his notebook he wrote: "I salvaged the prints on the following pages from the outcasts and pasted them here for record purposes." Notebook Number 9, January 14, 1939, p. 91.

**p. 199**   Picture of a bat in flight and sketch of a new type of stroboscope. Notebook Number 7, March 14, 1937, p. 135.

**p. 200–01**   Picture of Elmer Reed hitting the golf ball. Also mention of a meeting with Gjon Mili. Notebook Number 8, March 28, 1938, pp. 140–41.

**p. 202**   Shop window of A. G. Spaulding & Brothers in New York City, featuring Edgerton golf images. Notebook Number 9, January 5, 1939, p. 124.

**p. 203**   Portrait of young Edgerton family, from left: Robert, Esther, Mary Louise, Edgerton, and William. Notebook Number 7, January 20, 1936, p. 23.

# RECOMMENDED READING

There are dozens of articles, books, and films about Harold Edgerton and his work, ranging from popular articles in newspapers to complex technical papers. The most important online resource is the MIT Museum's Edgerton Digital Collections website: http://edgerton-digital-collections.org, which provides access to images, films, original archival records, as well as biographical information. This website incorporates information previously available on the CD-ROM, *Exploring the Art and Science of Stopping Time*.

For a good introduction:

Stratton, Julius A. "Harold Eugene Edgerton (April 6, 1903–January 4, 1990)." *Proceedings of the American Philosophical Society* 135 (1991), pp. 443–50.

Vandiver, J. Kim and Kennedy, Pagan. "Harold E. Edgerton (1903–1990)." *Biographical Memoirs* 86 (Washington: National Academies Press, 2005), pp. 1–23.

Two publications associated with the previous MIT Museum exhibition, *Flashes of Inspiration: The Work of Harold "Doc" Edgerton*, are also recommended:

Bedi, Joyce E. "The Man Who Stopped Time." *American Heritage of Invention and Technology* 13 (Summer 1997), pp. 34–41.

Bruce, Roger R. ed., *et al., Seeing the Unseen: Dr. Harold E. Edgerton and the Wonders of Strobe Alley* (Rochester, NY: The Publishing Trust of George Eastman House, distributed by the MIT Press, 1994).

Three works co-authored by Edgerton are essential references:

Edgerton, Harold E. and Killian, James R., Jr. *flash! Seeing the Unseen by Ultra High-Speed Photography* (Boston: Hale, Cushman & Flint, 1939), as well as the revised edition published by Charles T. Branford Co. in 1954.

Edgerton, Harold E. and Killian, James R., Jr. *Moments of Vision: The Stroboscopic Revolution in Photography* (Cambridge: The MIT Press, 1979).

Edgerton, Harold E., Jussim, Estelle, and Kayafas, Gus. *Stopping Time: The Photographs of Harold Edgerton* (New York: Harry N. Abrams, 1987).

For those interested in acquiring a more in-depth technical understanding of Edgerton's research, and perhaps seeking inspiration to replicate some of his techniques, a serious yet very accessible book is Edgerton's textbook:

Edgerton, Harold E. *Electronic Flash, Strobe.* 3rd ed. (Cambridge: MIT Press, 1992). The original edition was published in 1970. New material was added in 1979 and 1987. The 1992 version is the second printing of the 3rd edition.

Edgerton has been featured as author and scientist in several *National Geographic Magazine* articles since his initial collaboration with the NGS began in the 1940s. Many of his projects are celebrated in the following article:

Swingle, Erla. "Doc Edgerton: The Man Who Made Time Stand Still." *National Geographic* 172 (October 1987), pp. 464–83.

Finally, serious researchers will want to explore the more than 50 cubic feet of archival records—including Edgerton's original notebooks—at the Institute Archives and Special Collections of the MIT Libraries. The collection finding aid is available online at: https://libraries.mit.edu/archives/research/collections/collections-mc/mc25.html.

# ACKNOWLEDGEMENTS

I have been in awe of the work of Edgerton for decades. An email from Peter Kayafas, admiring the recent Steidl publication of Berenice Abbott's *Paris Portraits,* started me thinking of a Steidl rendition of Edgerton. (Peter's father, Gus Kayafas, was a student of Doc's, as well as his printer, friend, and the primary curator of Edgerton's photos for many, many years.)

Knowing that Gerhard Steidl and his team could produce an exceptional tribute to Edgerton and his photography, I asked Gerhard, and was delighted when he gave his enthusiastic go ahead. I then contacted John Durant, Director of the MIT Museum, who confirmed that the Edgerton copyrights were now held by MIT. John gave his endorsement of the project and introduced me to Debbie Douglas, Director of Collections and Curator of Science and Technology, who oversees the Museum's Edgerton Collection.

There are no words in my vocabulary to describe the enthusiastic and energetic person that is Debbie—the main force in producing this book. Her willingness to take on all the tasks of coordinating all the material necessary for the book (in addition to contributing an essay and biography of Edgerton) deserves more than mere recognition.

Special thanks to Gus Kayafas who generously permitted the MIT Museum to use original prints from the Arlette and Gus Kayafas Collection for this project. Gus reviewed his personal collection as well as the MIT Museum's negatives and together with Debbie identified the final set you see in this volume. Knowing the stories behind Doc Edgerton's photos, Gus also provided valuable insight for the titles and captions. I also want to thank him for his essay, "Doc in the Darkroom." Joan Whitlow, Registrar and Collections Manager at the MIT Museum, organized and packed the prints for scanning at Steidl in Germany.

It is a pleasure to also acknowledge the Institute Archives and Special Collections of the MIT Libraries. Kari Smith, Institute Archivist, Tom Rosko, Head of the Institute Archives, and Nora Murphy, provided the high-resolution scans of pages from Doc's notebooks. I am grateful for permission to publish them here. Likewise, thank you to the family of Arnold Newman for permission to publish Arnold's wonderful portrait of Doc.

I would also like to express my gratitude to Professor J. Kim Vandiver and Gary Van Zante for their essays. Kim, as his essay reveals, was also a student and colleague of Doc's. Since the 1992 founding of the Edgerton Center, Kim has been the Director of this remarkable facility that has perpetuated Doc's legacy of hands-on learning at MIT. Gary, Curator of Architecture and Design at the Museum, is a specialist in the history of photography and a longtime colleague who has helped make the MIT Museum an important new center for photography exhibitions and research.

I have the deepest respect and unbounded gratitude for Gerhard Steidl and his staff, particularly Holger Feroudj, who produce books with vision, love, and a passion for excellence. It is difficult to imagine a more dedicated publisher.

And of course, my wife Carol, who has shared my life for 60 years, has accompanied me to Göttingen to work with Gerhard Steidl to make many wonderful books, and has always provided love and support.

Finally, it gives me much joy to dedicate this book to Doc and to present it to MIT, a tribute to one of my heroes, as well as to thousands of others whose paths also crossed with Doc's at this special place.

Ron Kurtz

First edition published in 2018


All Edgerton images (courtesy MIT Museum) and notebook pages
(courtesy Institute Archives and Special Collections) are copyrighted by
the Massachusetts Institute of Technology and used with permission.

© 2018 the authors for their texts
© 2018 Steidl Publishers for this edition

Book design: Holger Feroudj, Gerhard Steidl
Scans and separations by Steidl image department


Production and printing: Steidl, Göttingen


Steidl
Düstere Str. 4 / 37073 Göttingen, Germany
Phone +49 551 49 60 60 / Fax +49 551 49 60 649
mail@steidl.de
steidl.de


ISBN 978-3-95829-308-3
Printed in Germany by Steidl